8/21

Hayner PLD/Large Print
Overdues .10/day. Max fine cost of
item. Lost or damaged item: additional
$5 service charge.

THE LAST AMERICAN ARISTOCRAT

THE LAST AMERICAN ARISTOCRAT

THE BRILLIANT LIFE AND IMPROBABLE EDUCATION OF HENRY ADAMS

DAVID S. BROWN

THORNDIKE PRESS
A part of Gale, a Cengage Company

**LIBRARY OF CONGRESS CIP DATA ON FILE.
CATALOGUING IN PUBLICATION FOR THIS BOOK
IS AVAILABLE FROM THE LIBRARY OF CONGRESS.**

ISBN-13: 978-1-4328-8769-8 (hardcover alk. paper)

Published in 2021 by arrangement with Scribner, a division of Simon &
Schuster, Inc.

Printed in Mexico
Print Number: 01   Print Year: 2021

For my teachers, gratefully

I've outlived at least three quite distinct worlds since 1838.

Henry Adams, 1915

CONTENTS

ILLUSIONS

BOSTON

WASHINGTON

PART II: PERFORMING HENRY ADAMS

FLIGHT

FURY

DYNAMO

RESONANCE

INTRODUCTION

For some years now a remarkable interest in the John Adams family has nourished a thick forest of books and biographies, surveying the public and private lives of its resident presidents. Recognized as the nation's most prominent political dynasty, the family appears over and again as emblems of a vital if irretrievable past. Theirs, however, is a cottage industry incomplete, for looking a little further down the line of descent it is evident that not one among them matched the marvelously improbable portfolio of Henry Adams. He seemed to know everybody, travel everywhere, and do everything. Historian, political reformer, journalist, novelist, world traveler, Washington wise man, and member (by investiture) of a venerable Tahitian island dynasty — these are just a few of the several identities he so casually adopted. Such occupations and attitudes he used to elude a pressure-packed political family familiar with depression, alcoholism, and suicide. His uncommonly wide horizons allowed, rather, for a respectable detour from the comparatively narrow paths pioneered by grandfather (John Quincy Adams) and great-grandfather (John Adams) heads of state. One might argue that given the eclectic range of his resolutions, he led a rarer life than either.

Born in a Boston still cleaving, as he once put it, upon "a nest of associations so colonial," Adams observed from various angles America's Industrial Revolution, its Civil War, and its entry into the Great War. He met Lincoln and befriended Edith Wharton, bowed before Queen Victoria and shared a spartan meal in the unkempt Samoan home of *Treasure Island*'s author Robert Louis Stevenson; he married into a family with strong ties to the Transcendentalism of Emerson and Thoreau, visited Jefferson's Monticello with Jefferson's granddaughter Sarah Randolph, and suffered, so he said, an "indifferent, very badly served" White House dinner with Theodore Roosevelt; from an anxious Paris he witnessed the German invasion of 1914 and enjoyed in his final years the occasional company of a young, attractive political couple — Franklin and Eleanor Roosevelt.[1]

Drawn to the unusually broad scale of Adams's relationships and experiences, I emphasize in this biography his importance as a transitional figure, one bridging the chasm between "colonial" and "modern." To put this another way, I believe that to understand much of America's history, and more specifically its movement in the late nineteenth century toward an imperial, industrial identity, one both increasingly beholden to technology and concerned with the fate of the white race, is to understand Henry Adams.

More than merely living a long and colorful life, Adams actively engaged and commented on his times, endeavoring to interpret their structure, pace, and meaning. In 1838, the year of Adams's birth, Sam Houston served as president of the Republic of Texas; the removal of the Cherokee Nation west of the Mississippi gave rise to the anguished expression "Trail of Tears"; Frederick Douglass, carrying the identification papers of a free black seaman, escaped from bondage; and a twenty-eight-year-old Abraham Lincoln spoke on "the perpetuation of our political institutions" before the Springfield, Illinois, Young Men's Lyceum. Many older American citizens at that time had been subjects of the British Empire; eighty years later, in 1918, the year of Adams's death, few relics of the early American republic remained. The Ford Motor Company was coming off its biggest year to date, selling an astounding 735,000 automobiles; Babe Ruth smacked eleven home runs for the Boston Red Sox in what proved to be the final season of the dead-ball era; James Joyce's controversial novel *Ulysses* began serialization in the American modernist literary magazine *Little Review;* and Woodrow Wilson, attending the Versailles Peace Conference, became the first U.S. president to travel outside of the Western Hemisphere while in office. Kellogg's and Coca-Cola, Budweiser and Buick were on the rise.

Adams, the child of an impossibly distinguished New England family, assumed something of a divided perspective, for the residue of regional custom in America quite emphatically gave way, as he grew older, to stronger and more eclectic currents. The Dutch-speaking Martin Van Buren, the first New Yorker and first candidate of non–British Isle ancestry to become president (the year prior to Henry's birth), might conveniently be identified as a harbinger of change. He reigned, if only for a single term, over a rising republic; expansion across the frontier coupled with a lessening of suffrage restrictions for white men resulted in a dramatic increase of voters — from roughly 400,000 in 1824 to some 2.4 million by 1840. Henry grew up with an increasingly restless, ethnically complex, and democratic nation that had moved beyond the purview of its former first families. But far from defending his own class, he wondered at the mystery of its virtual extinction in a land of plenty. "How few of our college mates, with all their immense advantages," he wrote his brother Charles late in life, "seem to have got or kept their proportional share in the astounding creation of power since 1850."[2]

To leave the impression, however, that Adams languished in the past, alienated from his times, would be an error. He embraced the fruits of invention traveling in the latest Mercedes, the fastest Union Pacific luxury train cars, and the smoothest steamships (purchasing a never used ticket for the *Titanic*'s return voyage). A connoisseur of spiritual expressions, he dropped his boyhood Boston Unitarianism to sample Buddhist, Catholic, and South Seas ceremonies and aesthetics; when writing selectively of his life in his most well-known work, *The Education of Henry Adams* (1918), he famously rejected the parameters of classic memoir for an irony-laced narrative that challenged long-ingrained notions of material progress in America. Though a product of colonial trappings, he clearly traced with real interest the various tributaries of contemporary social, cultural, and industrial development.

This enthusiasm, attuned to the surface and sweep of civilizational change, is illustrated well in Henry's vicarious if telling connection to America's emerging naval prowess. Its rather brisk evolution implied other far-reaching innovations. In early March 1862, while Adams served in London as secretary to his father, the U.S. minister to the Court of St. James's, a brief battle raged between Union and Confederate ironclad warships — the *Monitor* and the *Virginia* — in Hampton Roads, a deep-water channel leading to the Chesapeake Bay. Though inconclusive, the four-hour duel offered an unsettling lesson that reverberated across the Atlantic. "Only a fortnight ago," Henry wrote shortly after the skirmish, the British shockingly "discovered that their whole wooden navy was useless."[3] Just how useless became undeniably evident some years later when, in 1907, Adams's Washington neighbor Theodore Roosevelt sent an American armada — nicknamed the "Great White Fleet" — on a fourteen-month world cruise, making twenty port calls and touching six continents. Eighteen vessels in all participated, with the battleship USS *Connecticut* leading the flotilla out of Hampton Roads. Henry may have felt a particular satisfaction, even a sense of possession, in the squadron's launch. For back in 1775 an insistent John Adams had prodded a plodding Continental Congress into building ships to defend the colonies. This poetic blue-water phase of maritime development suggested certain modest standards of size and scale, mission and mandate rendered obsolete by the shining steel fleet unleashed by Roosevelt. As a more general way of reading the world, such transitions as that from sail to steam captivated completely Henry's historical imagination.

Accordingly, he worried as Wall Street financiers and Chicago factory owners gained power in the republic; he watched as distances shrank before the sovereignty of trains, telegraphs, and (beginning in 1883) time zones; and he wondered about Darwinism's bid to become "the very best substitute for religion." Determined to experience this change directly, he hunted down the era's new ideas and inventions by attending several international expositions; a journey to St. Louis's 1904 World's Fair culminated in a rather happy roller-coaster ride — "the finest thing I ever did in my life." Adams wished as well to know "expiring" peoples and places before they gave way completely to outside energies and economies. Such interest spurred his travels to the South Seas, Cuba, and Russia — the last "at least three generations behind us," he assured one correspondent. Similar elegies were conducted at home. Shortly after the 1890 federal census reported the closing of the nation's western frontier, he spent two months with a small party tramping around the Rockies, feasting, he wrote, "on elk-meat and trout," riding hundreds of miles "on ponies through . . . trailless country," and more generally imbibing the "illusion that we are the first white

19

men who ever crossed into" the disappearing wilderness.[4]

In sum, we can see much of the emerging world working on Adams — its tilt toward science, its growing commitment to capitalism, and its defensive response to changing ethnic demographics as a dominant Anglo-Saxonism gradually and somewhat grudgingly made way for other groups. Through it all, he sensed a new, uncertain America arriving right before his eyes. And perhaps this is our greatest point of access to Adams, recognizing in his curiously resonant life our own difficult struggles with the distempers and alienation, the churn and change of the unremitting modern condition.

For many readers who come to Adams primarily through the *Education,* it is easy to accept that work's underscored assertion that "failure" framed its author's life. Unable to emulate his ancestors' electoral success in an era owned by speculators and spoilsmen, Henry proved incapable, so he insisted, of making his backward-looking education in the great books, deeds, and dead languages pay. Of course he was striking a pose, instructing by paradox and chiding a nation that no longer knew what to do with its old gentry class. He employed "failure" thematically to question America's unreflective industrial development and the political system that served as its willing handmaiden. Through the *Education* he entered history itself, going beyond the mere compiling of facts to create a tragic vision of the past, to show how the modern age emerged in the United States following the Civil War, discarding a host of no longer germane traditions, values, and beliefs. Much more than an American story, this teeming book can profitably be read as a broader international statement on modernism's emergence alongside such classic household dramas as Thomas Mann's *Buddenbrooks* (1900), John Galsworthy's *The Forsyte Saga* (1906–21), and Tanizaki Junichirō's *The Makioka Sisters* (1943–48). All offer meticulously etched portraits of a fading high-bourgeois way of life.

Adams, equally comfortable before presidents and queens, apprehended easily this narrowing world. Though proud of his republican bona fides, he played a perfect Brahmin aristocrat, adhering to a host of morals, manners, and mannerisms conversant with his class. He knew how to dress and dine, casually occupied English summer houses and Paris apartments, and enjoyed horseback riding about Washington. He collected art (prizing Turner and Bonington watercolors), kept impressive libraries in two homes on two continents, and enjoyed medieval French chansons, Louis XV furniture, and good champagne. The very delicacy of his corporeal frame proposed a courtly air and polish. Self-conscious of a petit appearance — one acquaintance called his slight carriage "bird-like" — he cultivated an erect posture and exaggerated stride, both made to embellish proportion. His large, nearly bald head and dark, penetrating eyes suggested an acute intellectualism, as did a graying mustache and fashionable Van Dyke beard. A thin Adams nose contributed to an even expression behind which hid an occasionally playful, sometimes mischievous sensibility. Trim, proud, and a little vain, he dressed impeccably, wearing white in summer while otherwise sporting a black coat and trousers with a perpetually somber tie. Servant-prepared meals accentuated a long practice of donning formal dining attire.[5]

Such sartorial extravagance can conjure an image of Adams at odds with the democratic nation his ancestors helped to forge. Here, for all the world to see, is Henry the victim of fate, the heirloom aristocrat trapped in America's vulgar Gilded Age cage. A pattern of carelessly boorish behavior, unflinchingly advertised in a sprawling six-volume edition of his letters published in the 1980s, has reinforced this overdrawn impression. These full and elegantly crafted missives are tinctured with snobbery and self-pity, elitism and, particularly of those inscribed during the economic depression that followed the

Panic of 1893, Jew-baiting. They also contain, however, a raft of arresting observations, and readers will have to decide for themselves if Adams's insights on his country and its evolving cultural apparatus outweigh his arrogance. As a young man the historian Richard Hofstadter thought not, insisting to the literary critic Alfred Kazin in the early 1940s that Adams exhibited the mental tic of "a truly voracious anti-Semite." Kazin held a more positive view, admiring Adams's Boston Wasp backdrop and sense of historical place and possession, which Kazin, the son of Yiddish-speaking Russian immigrants, clearly coveted. In later years, he came to see the author of the *Education* as a neglected Cassandra, a major thinker who anticipated the spiritual and psychic victory of the coming industrial regime. Witnessing with increasing dismay the enthronement of a scientific-materialistic perspective in the West, Kazin wrote in 1980, "This country is going through the profound inner crisis that Marx and Henry Adams foretold: the technology of the future is already here and has outrun our existing social and economic relations."[6]

Sharing Kazin's concern, I have set out in this study to contribute a critical profile that interprets Adams as a significant if flawed American thinker. Structurally, the book is divided into halves, accentuating its subject's long and inventive life in the twin acts of

23

"becoming" and "performing." The former assays its subject from boyhood to the tragic 1885 suicide of his wife, Marian Hooper, called Clover. These chapters review Henry's early impressions, education, and influences and more generally reflect on familial expectations and the weight of the past pressing uncomfortably upon this "last" Adams, the most distinguished among the fourth and final generation of his relations to attain national recognition. Several key cornerstones were laid during this period: the enshrinement of rural Quincy, Massachusetts (the ancestral home), as the "better" America; the bitter reaction to partisan politics; and the maturing attraction to cosmopolitan Europe.

The sudden, violent end of his marriage opened a second, though by no means less vital path for Adams. He called it his "posthumous life," a floating world distinguished by the drift of persistent travel, darkening meditations on capitalism's quickening pace, and a taste for playing with personas — Henry the twelfth-century Norman, the Tahitian prince, and the progress-defying and -denying "conservative Christian anarchist," to name but a few. Perhaps too he turned away from the pressures of a history-laden patrimony, seeking anonymity of a kind in a fluidity of identity. And yet all the masks were connected in some quiet defiance of the modern condition, all were "primitive" and

24

skeptical of the automated age.

This suspicion became a defining feature in Adams's outlook. At times it threatened to distort his work, leading to caricature, doom-saying, and the uncritical elevation of those civilizations and peoples he often patronizingly regarded as antimodern. More fruitfully, however, it also opened to him an exceptionally wide range of perceptions and perspectives that yielded a harvest as rich, complicated, and varied as any American thinker at any time. He is our finest letter writer, our outstanding nineteenth-century historian, and, with the sole exception of Benjamin Franklin, our most iconic memoirist.[7] These searching articles of uncertain faith appraised an increasingly inventive, restless, and untethered world dominated, so Adams wrote in the *Education,* by the unknowable, uncontrollable "dynamo" of industrial development; it is a world we have inherited, a cultural spirit we have yet to shake.

PRELUDE: BACK TO BEVERLY

In the spring of 1917, less than a year before his death, Henry Adams returned to Pitch Pine Hill, a large, mansard-roof house in Essex County, Massachusetts, erected for him and his wife in 1876 and used as their summer residence. More than thirty years had passed since Adams last spent a night there. In December 1885 Clover, trapped in a mounting depression following the death of her father, had swallowed a vial of potassium cyanide in the couple's Lafayette Square apartment in Washington. From that point on, Henry made a monument of his grief. He destroyed Clover's letters to him, scarcely and then only enigmatically mentioned her name in public, and refused to reclaim Pitch Pine Hill. No doubt his sudden decision to haunt the house surprised those close to him. Perhaps unsure of how to proceed, he pled poverty, stating that a fear of U-boat attacks (Congress having declared war on Germany in April) had cooled the coastal rental market, leaving him no other choice than to take "possession of my poor old shanty."[1] Seasonally occupied over the years by family and friends — then-president William Howard Taft rented nearby during the summers of 1910 and 1911 — Henry's "shanty" sat on a hill covered by several acres of oaks and pines less than a mile from the village of Beverly. A comfortable structure capable of lodging several servants and guests, it featured French tiles, stained-glass windows in the dining area, and a fireplace in each room. One could hear the ocean from the house.

Adams's reappearance at Pitch Pine Hill proved to be something of a sentimental journey, though not without its occasional long shadows and late afternoons of unease. It brought to him a host of half-forgotten memories suddenly emancipated from an ancestral attic of odds and ends. Following an exhausting twelve-hour trip from Washington to Boston, Adams and Aileen Tone, his secretary-companion for the final five years of his life, dined at the elegant Copley Plaza Hotel. Clearly in an absorbed mood, Adams ordered gumbo soup and scrod, the latter of which, Tone reported, he "hadn't tasted . . . for 30 years." The following morning Henry received several callers in the Copley before motoring (in fur coat) on to Beverly, where he set up house, entertained "nieces and nephews and grandnieces and grandnephews by the score," and, in quieter moments, ruminated on the perishability of the past. "It all seems a very fantastic dream," he wrote of what could not be regained. "I wander every morning through the woods in search of something that I formerly knew, but it has been reformed out of existence."[2]

Even with such incoherencies, there were certain continuities to recover that summer along the shore. The recent American entry into the Great War reminded Adams of his own generation's circa 1860 crusade to subdue the slaveholders. Seeing now the young Beverly men and women in their khakis and Red Cross uniforms brought back distant memories suddenly made fresh. "I sit all alone wondering when I lived," he wrote in a sweet cloud of confusion. "I distinctly remember, some sixty years ago, being tumbled head over heels in the same way and everybody going to war and getting killed, or staying at home and getting abused for it, and whether that was now, or *now* was *then,* I haven't got clear in my mind."[3]

Perhaps this quiet encore is precisely what Adams desired in returning to Beverly. Aside from occupying Pitch Pine Hill, he used the house as a base to reconnoiter the surrounding area, which invariably connected him with layers of family history. On one chauffeured excursion, he traveled south to Quincy and walked a final time through the familiar halls of the Old House at Peacefield, built by a Jamaican sugar planter in the 1730s, purchased in 1787 by his great-grandparents John and Abigail Adams, and long the center of the family's domestic arrangements. Here, and in a host of other parlors and gardens, Adams indulged in a final education of the senses. He seemed drawn to reconcile with that fiercely tribalistic Quincy-Boston-Cambridge culture, equal parts puritan and patrician, that constituted his earliest and strongest references, and which he had tried to flee decades earlier by uprooting to Washington. Now, in his eightieth year, in what proved to be his last summer, Adams sought to make peace with the past.

■ ■ ■ ■

PART I
BECOMING
HENRY ADAMS

■ ■ ■ ■

■ ■ ■ ■

INHERITANCE

■ ■ ■ ■

For some remote reason, he was born an eighteenth century child.

Henry Adams, 1907

1
QUINCY

In the *Education*'s double-edged opening pages, Adams recalls a golden nativity: "Probably no child, born in the year, held better cards than he." From there, the narrative, interested in the price of privilege, moves on to an involved, ironic discussion surveying the special burdens of belonging to a pedigree of presidents. Henry knew well each hurdle before him. Raised, as he put it, in the long shadows cast by "the First Church, the Boston State House, Beacon Hill, John Hancock and John Adams," he internalized past glories, old prejudices, and dying traditions.[1] This demanding ancestor worship, as stifling as a posh sarcophagus, led eventually to a self-imposed Washington exile where, in the nation's capital city, he produced a vast nine-volume history of the early American republic, in whose final book he dedicated an epitaphic chapter to the "decline of Massachusetts." An efficient autopsy of the Bay State's imminent eclipse before the combined might of the slaveholding South and the democratic West, it might be said to have served as spadework for the one puzzling question never far from his thoughts: How did the prized child, the holder of so many "better cards," come to lose the hand?

To answer that query, it is necessary to dig a bit deeper into the circumstances, influences, and environments of Adams's youth. That will require at least a passing familiarity with family history and family homes.

In 1836, seven years into a marriage that united politics and money, Charles Francis Adams and Abigail Brown Brooks, Henry's parents, built a tidy six-bedroom colonial on Goffe Street in Quincy. Colloquially known as The House on the Hill or The New House, it featured oak floors and an arched entryway and sat within easy walking distance of the rambling Old House ("the President's place"), then occupied by Henry's grandparents, John Quincy and Louisa Catherine Adams. It was here, in the Goffe Street structure, that Charles Francis's growing family spent long summers, typically from the middle of May to the end of October. Winters were endured in Boston in a house on Mount Vernon Street purchased by Abigail's wealthy father, Peter Chardon Brooks, who kept its title and paid its taxes. Reported at the time of his death to be "the richest man in New England," Brooks, whose people arrived in the Bay Colony in 1631, possessed a parentage as deeply rooted in Massachusetts's soil as any Adams. For several generations it could claim no particular influence, but this changed with the swift financial ascendancy of the unusually industrious Peter Chardon. Apprenticed out in 1781 upon the death of his minister father, Brooks took up the business of marine insurance in 1789 and soon acquired a fortune. Following a brief retirement, he then assumed the presidency of the New England Insurance Company and accrued a second windfall. With characteristic dryness, Charles Francis once remarked that his father-in-law had "made enough money to turn any man's head."[2]

Peter Chardon's youngest daughter, Abigail (Abby), raven-haired and round-faced, married Charles Francis in 1829. Their union produced seven children, six of whom survived into adulthood. Louisa Catherine, perhaps Henry's favorite sibling, was the eldest (1831), followed by John Quincy Adams II (1833), and Charles Francis Adams Jr. (1835). These three constituted a distinct cluster unto themselves, connected not merely by age but by the fact that all were named in honor of previous Adamses: Louisa after her grandmother, John for his grandfather, and Charles for his father. With typical asperity Henry, the middle child, followed by Arthur, Mary, and Brooks, later described himself as "being of less account" in the order of extraction, and thus "was in a way given to his mother, who named him Henry Brooks, after a favorite brother just lost."[3]

This maternal tie took on added significance for Henry as the years passed. Taxed by a nervous, fretting temperament, Abigail found some vinegary satisfaction in sharing her many miseries with a captive household. As her son Charles once evenly observed, "My mother . . . took a constitutional and sincere pleasure in the forecast of evil. She delighted in the dark side of anticipation; she did not really think so; but liked to think, and say, she thought so. She indulged in the luxury of woe!" As Abigail aged and her anxieties grew more acute, Charles and his siblings became adept at managing their mother's up-and-down emotions, what someone in the family called her "unmeaning and loud nonsense."[4] Henry in particular proved to be an attentive and supportive son — out of genuine affection, though also in some service to his father, who recognized his calming influence on Abigail.

Charles Francis, by contrast, appeared to be almost forbiddingly placid. He knowingly called himself "grave, sober, formal, precise and reserved" — the retiring product of a famous family. In a memoir, Charles Jr. described his father as emotionally limited, a bland tutor blind to his children's juvenescence: "To us, it would . . . have made all the difference conceivable had he loved the woods and the water, — walked and rode and sailed a boat; been, in short, our companion as well as our instructor. The Puritan was in him, and he didn't know how!"[5] In a sign of respect — though perhaps with a certain chilly remove — the brothers took to calling their father "the Governor" and "the Chief." Preternaturally mature and something of a quiet island in a large and boisterous brood, Henry was the favorite of both parents.

Of course it was an even older generation that established the terms upon which these Adams siblings would long live. At the births of their grandchildren, John Quincy and Peter Chardon offered gifts to the infants symbolic of themselves: Bibles were handed out in chaste Quincy, silver mugs emerged from commercial Boston. On the respective deaths of these old men in the twin winters of 1848 and 1849, this process, in a sense, repeated itself. Peter Chardon's will left Abigail and Charles Francis approximately $300,000, a genuine fortune in antebellum America and equal in current dollars to something near $9 million. Such a sum, complemented by generous separate coming-of-age inheritances, secured the financial independence of their children. John Quincy, by contrast, most obviously assigned to his male heirs the singular cross of occupational expectation. Henry's brother Charles remembers their grandfather as "an old man, absorbed in work and public life. He seemed to be always writing — as, indeed he was. . . . A very old-looking gentleman, with a bald head and white fringe of hair — writing, writing — with a perpetual inkstain on the forefinger and thumb of the right hand."[6] A president and the son of a president, he fairly radiated the implication that certainly *his* sons — and grandsons — might one day lead the republic as well.

Weaned on such assurances, Henry lazily took his supposed fate for granted. He recalled in the *Education* being seated in Quincy's United First Parish Church "behind a President grandfather" and "read[ing] over his head the tablet in memory of a President great-grandfather, who had 'pledged his life, his fortune, and his sacred honor' to secure the independence of his country and so forth." This singular memory, or perhaps the hazy accumulation of numerous Sunday sittings, he paired with the surprising dig of "the Irish gardener" who dared to question the eternal order of the Adams universe: "You'll be thinkin' you'll be President too!" In just those few puncturing words lay shaken Henry's innocent faith in an assured future: "The casuality of the remark made so strong an impression on his mind that he never forgot it. He could not remember ever to have

40

thought on the subject; to him, that there should be doubt of his being President was a new idea. What had been would continue to be."[7]

Keeping in view Henry's impressionable youth, one must consider his unfortunate contraction of scarlet fever shortly before turning four. He later saw the illness as a definite turning point, writing, "This fever . . . took greater and greater importance in his eyes . . . the longer he lived." The infection, Adams came to believe, had stunted his growth, damaged his nerves, and destroyed his chances of turning a schoolyard fight into schoolboy glory. In a word, the fever had rendered him "delicate." Accordingly, he referred to his robust brothers as a coveted "type" while dismissing himself as a pallid "variation," by which he meant slightly framed and excessively intellectual.[8]

But this dichotomy emerged from an older man's mind; while still a summer child in Quincy, Adams lovingly indulged in the monastic practice of browsing the accumulated clutter of books and bric-à-brac, coin collections and memorials lodged in the Old House's grandly shabby study. These frail and yellowing artifacts filled the boy with a sense of destiny, connecting family history with the pivotal history of the Atlantic World during the Age of Revolutions. Here is where, in the heart of his youth, Henry saw great men gather, where he helped to organize generations of family papers, and where, on the sunlit second floor, in the weathered house's most inviting room, he enjoyed access to the eighteen thousand volumes that lined its hidden walls. *This* was Henry's real education, at least in his susceptible adolescence, and one uniquely supplemented by the stories, annals, and archives of his ancestors' various foreign service stays in England, France, the Netherlands, and Russia.

More formally, Henry attended a succession of schools; these included a small academy of sorts in the cold basement of the Park Street Church close to his Boston (winter) home and later the private Latin School on Boylston Place, where he studied Greek, Latin, history, composition, geography, declamation, and mathematics — essentially a curriculum to accommodate neighboring Harvard's entrance exams. These were important and formative experiences to be sure, but certainly no classroom could supplant for impact the Old House's study. Its association with generations of Adamses made an impression both deep and indelible on the boy; it seemed to invite a rich mental life to take root.

Much like the family library, Quincy assumed a sacred status in Henry's youth. He identified Boston with a host of lesser associa-

42

tions — "Town was restraint, law, unity" — that paled beside the native inducements of his summer home; "Country . . . was liberty, diversity, outlawry." In scale and aspiration Boston exuded a metropolitan, sophisticated, and, for its time, heavily peopled atmosphere; the 1840 census counted some ninety-three thousand Bostonians, making it the nation's fifth-largest urban area. Quincy, by contrast, contained fewer than thirty-five hundred souls. Situated barely ten miles below the erstwhile Puritan city, it seemed remarkably untouched by its great neighbor to the north. Charles Jr. recalled that "as late as 1850 Quincy was practically what it had always been — a quiet, steady-going, rural Massachusetts community, with its monotonous main thoroughfares . . . and by-ways lined with wooden houses, wholly innocent of any attempts at architecture, and all painted white with window blinds of green."[9] Farming still commanded much of the local economy, with artisans making shoes and boots in extensions built on existing homes. Not until Henry's eighth birthday did the railroad invade its environs.

The philosopher and novelist George Santayana (1863–1952), for several years a member of nearby Harvard's faculty, believed the civic-minded Adamses congenitally unfit for the big city, which he negatively associated with wealth-making:

43

In Boston, in the middle of the nineteenth century, no one who was ambitious, energetic, or even rich thought of anything but making a fortune; the glamour was all in that direction. The Adamses were not, and always said they were not, Bostonians; and the orators, clergymen and historians of the day, as well as the poet, though respected and admired, never dominated the community: they were ornaments and perhaps dangers.[10]

As a child Henry unabashedly embraced, even embellished upon Quincy's simple ways. Though the Old House creaked with colonial inconveniences, lacking the bathrooms, furnaces, and indoor plumbing found in Grandfather Brooks's Boston brownstone, he extolled its "ethical" superiority. "Quincy," he once swore, "had always been right, for Quincy represented a moral principle, — the principle of resistance to Boston."[11] Looking ahead to the *Education*'s striking historical duality, pitting the powerful modern industrial dynamo against the seraphic pre-industrial Virgin, it is difficult to escape the suspicion that its origin lies, to some imperative degree, in its author's youthful impressions of town and country. These recollections remained vivid and living memories, guiding Adams long after he had last basked in the Old House's familiar golden summer glow.

2
PARTY OF ONE

Though born in a free state, Henry Adams grew up in a republic conspicuous for its unfree. The first U.S. census taken after his birth showed some 2.5 million slaves in the United States, the vast majority, but by no means all, in the South. While a ruling by the Massachusetts Supreme Court effectively abolished chattel servitude in 1783, gradual emancipation laws in neighboring New Hampshire, Rhode Island, and Connecticut allowed New England slavery to survive into the 1850s. Abolitionists were quick to point out, however, that even Massachusetts, with its fleet of textile factories reliant upon southern cotton, remained linked to the slave system. This passive partnership between the "Lords of the Lash" and the "Lords of the Loom" produced a deep and ultimately ir-reparable rift within the Bay State's Whig Party, the chief opponent in national politics of the older Democratic coalition founded under Thomas Jefferson and later refurbished by Andrew Jackson. Conscience Whigs, those morally opposed to slavery's expansion, resided on one side of the divide, while a larger number of Cotton Whigs, eager to keep the profitable manufacturing mills of nearby Lowell churning out cloth and carpets, hosiery and other woven fabrics, occupied the other. Both Henry's father and Grandfather Adams were Conscience Whigs.

Charles Francis's interest in the slave question arose largely from circumstances surrounding the Mexican War (1846–48). Like many northerners, he worried that the conflict, which resulted in an American victory and the third-largest acquisition of territory in the nation's history following the Louisiana and Alaska purchases, might conclude in a vast new empire of unfree labor. Accordingly, in 1846, he purchased two-fifths of the *Boston Daily Whig,* took over its editorial pages, and turned it into a bulwark of Conscience Whig sentiment. This incensed more orthodox Whigs, who attacked both his paper and his judgment. Edward Everett, a prominent Boston pastor and politician, later to offer a two-hour oration at the same 1863 dedication ceremony of the Gettysburg National Cemetery made historic by Lincoln's two-minute address, thought the paper imprudent. Married to Charlotte Gray Brooks, an elder sister of Abigail Brown Brooks and thus Charles Francis's brother-in-law, Everett worried that the *Daily Whig* sought to poison Massachusetts politics by "plac[ing] the Whig party under abolition influences." Adams had no such designs. Like his father, now sitting in the House of Representatives, he believed that the federal Constitution provided certain and inviolable guarantees to slaveholders in slave states, though not in the nation's shared territories. "The [sectional] compromise of the Constitution does not require us to go thus far," he wrote at that time. "It does not bind us to approve of slavery . . . nor to look with composure upon a system of dishonesty practised to extend its limits to another and a new country, not infected by that blast."[1] As the country moved toward war with Mexico, Adams grew increasingly concerned that northern rights were being trampled. His resistance to slavery, in other words, had less to do with the peculiar institution's inherent inhumanity than with his belief that the interests of free men were under assault. His sons adopted this view as well, as did a good many in the North.

If not an abolitionist paper, the *Daily Whig* did propose a number of items designed to check the progress of the southern planter class. These included calls to end slavery in the District of Columbia, to terminate the interstate slave trade, and to make the exclusion of slavery a condition for future states entering the union. This last demand took on a particular urgency when the Mexican War promised through conquest to dramatically enlarge the United States — as indeed the subsequent cession by the defeated Mexicans of all or part of present-day Colorado, Utah, New Mexico, Arizona, Nevada, and California proved. John Quincy Adams, representing Massachusetts's 12th Congressional District (Plymouth), was one of only fourteen House members to vote against the war bill, and he remained an uncompromising critic of the conflict. He died in February 1848 from a massive cerebral hemorrhage shortly after collapsing during a war-related debate in Congress. Years later, Henry described how the old man's outlook had influenced his own, imparting an "education . . . warped beyond recovery in the direction of puritan politics."[2]

In June 1848, a few months after Henry turned ten, a Whig convention meeting in Philadelphia awarded Maj. Gen. Zachary Taylor the party's presidential nomination. Having commanded American forces in Mexico to victories at the battles of Palo Alto, Monterrey, and Buena Vista, Taylor, a career soldier with no prior political experience, received a hero's welcome on his return home. A Virginian by birth, he was raised in Kentucky and owned Cypress Grove, a nearly two-thousand-acre Mississippi plantation that produced cotton, corn, and tobacco; because he held slaves, Taylor proved an unpalatable candidate to antislavery Whigs. In early August some twenty thousand of the disaffected, including representatives from eighteen states, met under a massive tent in Buffalo, New York's city park to form a new coalition, the Free Soil Party. Walt Whitman served as one of Brooklyn's fifteen delegates, and Frederick Douglass, among others, addressed the gathering. Charles Francis presided over the convention and, in an opening speech, denounced the Whig-Democrat concert as archaic, stuck in past politics, and unable to contend with the brewing battle shaping up over slavery's future. These two parties, he argued, were "fighting only for expediency, and . . . expecting nothing but [patronage]."[3]

In reply, the Free Soilers nominated former president Martin Van Buren, a controversial maneuver that alienated many of the delegates. A longtime Democrat, he had captured the White House in 1836, failed to win reelection in 1840, and then watched with dismay as his party's presidential nominations went to other candidates in both 1844 and 1848. Now open to the idea of heading a third faction, Van Buren, so his enemies insisted, was nothing more than an opportunistic "Doughface" — a northern man with southern principles. As Andrew Jackson's vice president he had supported the first in a series of controversial "gag rules" that for several years accepted but forbade discussion on abolitionist petitions sent to Congress. Seeking regional balance on the ticket, the Buffalo convention gave western Free Soilers the second slot, but, instead of choosing one of their own, they surprised the assemblage by proposing Charles Francis. After the requisite hemming and hawing, he accepted. The party's plank recognized the legality of slavery where it stood — "We . . . propose no interference by Congress with slavery within the limits of any state" — but opposed its extension into the country's territories: "[The] history [of the Founding era] clearly show that it was the settled policy of the nation not to extend, nationalize, or encourage, but to limit, to localize, and discourage slavery; and to this policy, which should never have been departed from the government ought to return." Threatening to upend the tenuous sectional status quo, Boston's Free Soilers became pariahs on polite Beacon Street. Henry later argued that his father "could not help it. With the record of J. Q. Adams fresh in the popular memory, his son and his only representative could not make terms with the slave-power, and the slave-power overshadowed all the great Boston interests."[4]

In a tightly contested fall campaign, Taylor

narrowly defeated his Democratic opponent, former Michigan senator Lewis Cass, by a count of 163 electoral votes to 127; both candidates carried fifteen states. The Free Soil ticket captured no electors, though it took 10 percent of the popular tally — at that time the highest percentage ever for a third party in a presidential race. Additionally, Free Soilers sent fourteen representatives and two senators to Congress. "This political party," Henry later explained, "became a chief influence in [my] education . . . in the six years 1848 to 1854, and violently affected [my] character at the moment when character is plastic." He further described this critical period in the country's history as a "renewed war," meaning a resumption of the seemingly eternal Adams–New England Puritan fight against anything compromised, wicked, or wrong.[5] His subsequent efforts during the Gilded Age to combat various forms of political, financial, and corporate corruption can be tied directly to these heroic days of youth in which he observed his father and grandfather challenge the mighty Slave Power. Their defiance struck him as nothing less than an irrepressible family calling — and one that called him, too.

3
THE MADAM

Slavery's unresolved place in the western territories remained a crucial question in the spring of 1850, when Charles Francis brought Henry to the District of Columbia. On this, his first trip outside of New England, the observant twelve-year-old noticed a host of cultural and regional distinctions. Quincy's unspoken idolatry of order and structure gave way to Maryland's lovely "raggedness"; the casual warmth of southern manners and May sunshine put the boy, so eager to condemn the wicked slave drivers, unexpectedly at ease. Raised in the Revolution's shadow, he arrived in the capital city as the old republic entered its final phase. Congress was then in the midst of debating what proved to be the history-shaping Compromise of 1850 — a series of resolutions designed to address a host of post–Mexican War tensions between the free and slave states. All of the Senate's leading figures were there, and Charles Francis, as both a Free Soiler and an Adams, wanted to be there as well. The season's high political stakes, however, combined with yet another and more personal reason for his arrival in the capital. Here, against a backdrop of growing sectional discord and threats of disunion, he visited one final time his ailing mother, Louisa Catherine Adams.

Following her husband's death two years earlier, Louisa had left the Old House for good, making her permanent residence in Washington. Raised in cosmopolitan surroundings, she had never embraced rustic Quincy. Her father, Joshua Johnson, a handsome Annapolis merchant and the son of a prominent Maryland jurist and politician, had sailed for London in 1771 to represent an American tobacco firm; there he met Catherine Nuth (or Young), then still in her teens. They became partners, started a family, and in 1775, when Catherine was perhaps eighteen, welcomed a second daughter, Louisa. Without the conclusive proof of a parish record, it is uncertain if they ever wed. Their daughter Louisa was the only wife of a president born outside of the United States until Melania Trump in 2017, and she remains the only first lady apparently born out of wedlock. During the American Revolution, Joshua and Catherine, siding with the colonies, crossed the Channel with their young children and took refuge in the port city of Nantes on the lower Loire; there, Louisa learned to speak French and her parents entertained a number of Americans, including, in 1779, the visiting diplomat John Adams and his twelve-year-old son, John Quincy. After the war, the family returned to England, where Johnson served as the American consul general, assisting U.S. citizens in London. It was in that capacity, while holding a social gathering in his home, that his daughter again met the younger Adams, now U.S. minister to the Netherlands.[1] The following year, 1797, they married at the ancient Anglican parish church of All Hallows-by-the-Tower, established in 675 by the Anglo-Saxon Abbey at Barking and one of London's oldest churches.

Louisa's eclectic range of Anglo-Euro-American references made a powerful impact on Henry. Though a Brooks and most certainly an Adams, he identified strongly with the Johnson side of his stock — the "quarter taint of Maryland blood," as he evocatively put it. This pleasant blemish he came to regard as something of a saving grace as it represented a relaxed southern sense of protocol and politeness that he found altogether lacking in the less yielding New England conscience that otherwise dominated his outlook. At its best, this Chesapeake influence offered Henry a kind of double identity, for though he might fail to prove the mocking Irish gardener wrong and rise to the presidency, he more fully and perhaps more satisfyingly mimicked the life of Grandmother Louisa. Like "the Madam," as he and his siblings respectfully referred to her, Henry would come to appreciate the cultural amenities of London and, even more so, Paris, where he spent a considerable part of his life; also like her, he too escaped from cramped Quincy in search of a Washington situation. Her brave resistance to Boston proved a distinct inspiration. "He liked her refined figure," he wrote in the *Education,* and admired "her gentle voice and manner; her vague effect of not belonging there, but to Washington or to Europe. . . . Try as she might, the Madam could never be Bostonian, and it was her cross in life, but to the boy it was her charm. Even at that age, he felt drawn to it."[2]

Leaving New England that spring of 1850 to make his first journey to the South, Henry experienced the agreeably jarring sensation, as he later put it, of entering "a new world."[3] Boston gave way to New York, followed by Trenton, Philadelphia, Havre de Grace, and Baltimore, from which he entrained to Washington. He found Maryland wonderfully ramshackle and uncombed, an unexpected contrast to the tidy Puritan communities at home. Its fields were unfenced, its woods overgrown, and its streets indifferently shared with roving pigs and cattle. With a population of fifty thousand (some four thousand of whom were enslaved), Washington was little more than a medium-size city, about equal to Albany, New York. Entering the capital, Henry would have soon spied the incomplete Washington Monument, only two years into construction, inching slowly toward the sky. A September 1850 drawing by Montgomery Meigs, engineer for several District of Columbia facilities, shows the shrine's marble shaft barely fifty feet high, its tiered crown supporting a crane lumbering idly with no apparent purpose. Impeded by poverty, politics, and civil war, the monument remained unfinished until 1888.

Something of an Adams family fiefdom, Washington experienced a host of improvements since being torched by British forces during the War of 1812. Turnpikes, canals, and railroads bore evidence of progress, as did hospitals, colleges, and a secure water supply for the city. The appearance of sidewalks on Pennsylvania Avenue provoked much approval, as did the costly makeover of the old burned-out Capitol Building, as brick and freestone gave way to sleek, carved Italian marble. A few years before Henry's arrival, the British writer Harriet Martineau marveled at Washington's intensely fluid society, one "singularly compounded," she insisted, from a variety of influences, including "foreign ambassadors . . . members of Congress . . . flippant young belles, 'pious' wives dutifully attending their husbands, and groaning over the frivolities of the place; grave judges, saucy travelers, pert newspaper reporters, melancholy Indian chiefs, and timid New England ladies, trembling on the verge of the vortex; all these are mixed up together in daily intercourse like the higher circle of a little village."[4]

Combined, the buildings, pathways, and people of Washington furnished a comparatively "primitive" atmosphere that stirred Henry's adolescent imagination. Like many northerners he exoticized the South, emphasizing, he later wrote, its "want of barriers, of pavements, of forms; the looseness, the laziness; the indolent southern drawl . . . the negro babies and their mothers with bandanas; the freedom, openness, swagger, of nature and man." As an adult Henry traveled much of the world, including extended stays in Egypt, Japan, and Polynesia, which drew from his ever-present pen extensive descriptions of desert and island otherness. It was in the American South, however, where he first learned to romanticize the inscrutable locals and their untamed land. Here, he surrendered to the thick scent of catalpa trees, stared silently at the scattered congregations of dark-skinned slaves, and thought the unfinished District, with its dusty roads and rickety wooden homes amid the occasional clean white-columned government building, resembled nothing so much as a strange ruin from an ancient "Syrian city."[5]

Ultimately, the South presented to Henry a confusing contrast to Quincy. He *knew* what was right — education and free labor, piety and industry — yet he found himself undeniably attracted to the lack of southern institutional oversight, of church, state, and school, that pinched him at home. For the first time, he came upon a contradiction that he could neither solve nor shake. The South, he recognized from the parlor politics that held court in the Old House, represented the unhealthiest aspects of America — and of man. The region was choked with bad roads, and "bad roads," Henry knew, "meant bad morals." And yet here is where his grandmother had chosen — over Quincy, over the Old House — to live, and here, in a capital city conspicuous, even notorious for its slaves, he felt a kind of freedom unknown to him at home. "Though Washington belonged to a different world, and the two worlds could not live together," he later observed in the manner of confessing a heresy, "[I] was not sure that [I] enjoyed the Boston world most."[6]

Henry and his father stayed in Louisa's fashionable home at 244 F Street (now 1333–1335 F Street NW), just east of the Executive Mansion. John Quincy and Louisa had purchased the place — to be known for many years as the "Adams Building" — in 1820 during his tenure as secretary of state. Henry's aunt Mary, Louisa's niece and daughter-in-law, greeted them at the door. As Mary Catherine Hellen she had, following the death of her parents, moved in with her aunt Louisa and uncle John Quincy. In 1828 she married their son, John Adams II, in a small White House ceremony; an alcoholic, he died just six years later of what one member of the family stoically called "the scourge of intemperance."[7]

Using the Madam's house as a base, Henry and his father circulated through Washington, the Governor taking his son to the Capitol Building and shepherding him through the crush of congressmen. Sitting in the old Senate Chamber, neoclassical in style with a bright crimson and gold color scheme, they listened from the gallery to addresses made by the future Confederate president, Jefferson Davis of Mississippi, and Massachusetts's Daniel Webster, who, just three months earlier, had delivered his controversial "Seventh of March" speech in favor of what became known as the Compromise of 1850. Though its separate bills included several planks favorable to the North — making California a free state, banning the slave trade in the District of Columbia, and rejecting Texas's claim to New Mexico — it also contained a strengthened fugitive slave law that, under pain of financial penalty, required officials and citizens of free states, when summoned by a federal marshal, to cooperate in the capture of runaways and alleged runaways. Much of Massachusetts Whiggery had sharply denounced Webster's address, and Charles Francis was "appalled" by it. He called the senator "a mountebank . . . degraded by the lowest sensualities and by the upmost rapacity." Now, as Henry observed these celebrated figures in their fine blue dress coats making their long orations sprinkled with classical allusions, still more thoughts on regional variation came to mind. Though he knew all politicians to be pretentious, he was surprised to discover that "southern pomposity, when not arrogant, was genial and sympathetic, almost quaint and childlike in its simplemindedness; quite a different thing from the Websterian . . . pomposity of the north."[8]

Sometime during their stay, Henry and his father called upon President Taylor at the Executive Mansion, itself something of a presumed ancestral possession. The visit made a distinct impression on the boy, for this is where his father, grandfather, and great-grandfather had all once lived. John and Abigail Adams, leaving the comparative comfort of Philadelphia, the nation's second capital after New York City, were its original occupants, in November 1800. Henry remembered thinking he "owned it" and "should some day live in it." Taylor, who died of an ill-defined digestive ailment just a few weeks after entertaining the Adamses, left less of an impression. Presidents in the boy's family, after all, were common, something one might expect to see, so the boy later wrote, "in every respectable family."[9]

As a kind of ceremonial conclusion to what he called his "Washington education," Henry, driven with the Governor in a carriage and pair, visited Mount Vernon, still a private residence owned by the widow of George Washington's grandnephew John Augustine Washington II. There, he discovered an antique colonial world that bore a striking resemblance to Quincy: "It was the same eighteenth-century, the same old furniture, the same old patriot, and the same old President."[10] But as he ambled about the ancient plantation, its precincts redolent with historical suggestion, a puzzling contradiction began to wedge its way into the boy's ripening mind. For he had been taught to revere the great Washington — a man above all other statesmen, all other presidents. And yet this Roman among Romans had held slaves on the very grounds upon which the boy now trod, and Henry, the clean-faced Puritan who knew the difference between a good road and a bad one, knew slavery to be wicked. It was

a paradox that, in 1850, the entire country
began to wrestle with in earnest.

4
HEROES

Henry's journey to the capital overlapped an
extended period of literary labor in which he
assisted the Governor on a major editing
project, *The Works of John Adams.* Running
upon completion (1856) to ten fat volumes,
this collection of unearthed essays, letters,
and state papers required many hours of careful pruning and proofreading. Just entering
his early teens, Henry gave his eyes to the
enterprise. The finished product, one that fell
somewhere between historical documenta-
tion and filial piety, carried multiple meanings for its junior partner. Importantly, it suggested to Henry how biography could be
communicated over a large canvas filled with
narrative drama and color; his crowded history of the early republic, drafted a generation later and packed with masterful portraits
of Jefferson and Jackson, Madison and Monroe, picks up, in a manner, where *The Works*
leaves off. The apprenticeship further anticipated another and vital father-son partner-

ship: Henry's appointment as Charles Francis's private secretary in London, where the latter served as America's minister to Great Britain during the Civil War. And finally, combing through the House of Adams's seemingly endless archives offered Henry an intensive tutorial on the origins and "making" of his famous family. If, as he insisted in the *Education,* his historical perspective ran somewhat archaically to the colonial, *The Works,* a fife-and-drum hymn to the past, could only have nurtured that sentimental panorama.

Working closely in the Adams files with his father gave Henry an intensive line-by-line primer in the oft-disillusioning art of cross-generational comparison. He later confessed that Charles Francis's "mind was not bold like his grandfather's or restless like his father's, or imaginative or oratorical," though he did praise the Governor's stolid intellect for exhibiting "singular perfection, admirable self-restraint, and instinctive mastery of form" — before adding the inevitable Calvinistic caveat, "Within its range it was a model." In short, Henry esteemed the Governor's stable temperament even as he recognized it as something of a lesser virtue. And maybe this too — the bias toward balance — could be counted among Louisa Catherine's largely unrecognized legacies, giving to her son the soupçon of Maryland blood that helped him to withstand the passions, anxieties, and expectations that afflicted other Adams men. Charles Francis's uncle Charles Adams suffered from alcoholism and died at thirty; his two name-weighted brothers — George Washington Adams and John Adams II — died, respectively, at the ages of twenty-eight and thirty-one, having both struggled with drinking. Like Henry, Charles Francis was a lucky third son and thus not so obviously saddled with excessive expectations. Writing to his brother Charles some years after their father's death, Henry described the Governor in European rather than American terms, introducing yet again Louisa Catherine's influence: "His instinctive sense of form, combined with keenness of mind, were French rather than English. His simplicity was like the purity of crystal, without flash or color. His figure, as a public man, is classic, — call it Greek, if you please."[1]

If Henry admired his father's comparatively quiet constitution, he found such placidity in organized Christianity, another family formality, disappointing. He would look back with some puzzlement on the small role that religion had played in his life. Despite their formidable reputations, the great theologians, divines, and ministers who once commanded such prime cultural space in colonial New England, men such as Cotton Mather, the influential Puritan who supported the Salem witch trials, and Jonathan Edwards, a charismatic revivalist preacher central to shaping the First Great Awakening that helped create a common evangelical identity in American Protestantism, meant surprisingly little to him. Heroes were at home or in the statehouse; they resided not in the pulpit. Though Henry respected his father's poised temperament as a shield to certain inevitable family pressures, he thought less of that asset when practiced by Boston's influential Unitarian Church, which had rejected such ancient articles of faith as the Trinity, original sin, and biblical infallibility. He believed its prevailing "mental calm," modeled by a rational-minded Harvard-trained clergy, too distant, too analytical, and too self-satisfied. These learned men, he protested, "proclaimed as their merit that they insisted on no doctrine, but taught, or tried to teach, the means of leading a virtuous, useful, unselfish life, which they held to be sufficient for salvation. For them, difficulties might be ignored; doubts were waste of thought; nothing exacted solution. Boston had solved the universe; or had offered and realised the best solution yet tried. The problem was worked out."[2]

Henry and his siblings found little inspiration in such a stillborn theology. In youth they dutifully read their Bibles, marched off to church twice each Sunday, and outwardly followed the rituals of worship. And yet, he remembered, "neither to [him] nor to [his] brothers or sisters was religion real. . . . The religious instinct had vanished."[3] His brother Charles, late in life, wrote a rather caustic account of the generational disconnect behind that disappearance:

The recollection of those Sundays haunts me now. We always had a late breakfast — every one did; and we dined early — roast beef always for dinner; and I got a dislike for roast beef which lasted almost to manhood, because I thus had to eat it every Sunday at 1.30, after a breakfast at 9. Then came the Sunday hair-combing and dressing. After which, Bible reading, four chapters, each of us four verses in rotation. Then a Sunday lesson, committing some verses from the Bible or a religious poem to memory. . . . Then came the going to Church. . . . Twice a day, rain or shine, summer and winter. In town [Boston] we went to that dreary old Congregational barn in Chauncy Street — the gathering place of the First Church — where my uncle, Dr. Frothingham, held forth.[4]

Despite moving away from orthodox Christian belief, however, Henry retained throughout his life a searching attitude toward various cultural, intellectual, and aesthetic expressions of religious experience. Buddhism and medieval Catholicism, in particular, opened fresh avenues for making comparisons and contrasts with the modern West that found their way into his published work. Boston's liberal Protestantism, on the other hand, never made such a vigorous impression, and neither did the "eccentric offshoots" (as he called them) of Transcendentalism and Universalism, or the neighboring experimental communities — most famously Brook Farm (1841–47), satirized in Nathaniel Hawthorne's novel *The Blithedale Romance,* and Fruitlands (1843), a seven-month flop conducted by Bronson Alcott, father of *Little Women*'s author, Louisa May Alcott — that popped up and then promptly disappeared during his childhood. This utopic side of the New England conscience left Henry cold. Even with the old Calvinism no longer an encompassing cultural force, he felt intellectually at home with its skeptical view of humanity, a perspective that led him to suggest, with all due respect, that Mr. Ralph Waldo Emerson, the author, philosopher, and celebrated Concord sage, "was *naïf.*"[5] And as a harmless "eccentric," Emerson, no less than Boston's more conventional clerisy, failed to impress Henry as a compelling public figure. None among them would do as a hero, none could capture the boy's emotions, and none was Charles Sumner.

Henry's earliest memories of Sumner were in the family's Mount Vernon Street home, where the spirited discussions that led to the evolution of Whigs into Conscience Whigs and Conscience Whigs into Free Soilers ensued. At the age of ten or so Henry was given a desk in the large upstairs library to improve upon his Latin grammar. There, winter after winter, he toiled away at his studies, growing increasingly aware of the antislavery politics being practiced on the other side of the room. Though he admired each of his father's several associates (the historian John Gorham Palfrey "was to a boy often the most agreeable"; the lawyer-memoirist Richard Henry Dana "was . . . without dogmatism or self-assertion"), only Sumner held his attention. Here was a man, even more so than the measured Charles Francis, whom he clearly wished to emulate. Sumner's "superiority," he later wrote, came across as brilliantly real and incontestable; "he was the classical ornament of the anti-slavery party; their pride in him was unbounded, and their admiration outspoken. The boy Henry worshiped him. . . . The relation of Mr. Sumner in the household was far closer than any relation of blood. None of the uncles approached such intimacy. Sumner was the boy's ideal of greatness."[6]

Three years Charles Francis's junior, Sumner had made his mark in Massachusetts as a lawyer, a lecturer, and, following America's controversial annexation of Texas in 1845, a savage critic of slavery. A popular, gregarious figure who, at a towering six feet four inches, could look down upon lesser mortals, he had traveled in England and the Continent — still a rare thing — rolling up one social success after another. His attendance at Queen Victoria's Westminster Abbey coronation, intimacy with the Romantic poet William Wordsworth, and tales of Oxford friendships and Cambridge acquaintances only enhanced his reputation in status-conscious Boston. To the young Henry, Sumner had made the right friends and the right enemies; he was the Bay State's brilliant rising sun to the aging Webster's sinking star. When the latter left the Senate in July 1850, Sumner, a Free Soiler, claimed his seat. After several months of partisan wrangling, the legislature sent him to the upper chamber by a single vote on the twenty-sixth ballot in a tense session attended by an elated Henry. "He ran home as hard as he could," Adams later wrote of himself in the *Education,* "and burst into the dining-room where Mr. Sumner was seated at table with the family. He enjoyed the glory of telling Sumner that he was elected; it was probably the proudest moment in the life of either."[7]

In time, however, Henry came rather uneasily to equate Sumner with that other and more distant idol: the great Washington. If the latter had compromised his reputation by holding slaves, the former had played politics, only a slightly lesser sin in Henry's estimation. True, Sumner never overtly courted the opposition, the Massachusetts Democratic Party, but he had accepted a precious gift from its hand. With both a Senate seat and the gubernatorial chair open, the Free Soilers proved to be the balance of power in a state assembly dominated by Democrats and Whigs. Accordingly, they negotiated the Senate for Sumner in exchange for supporting the Democrat George S. Boutwell for governor. "Boy as he was," Henry recounted, "he knew enough to know that something was wrong." In fact, his disillusionment with Sumner had only just begun.[8]

A fierce moralist by nature, Sumner's rhetorical assault on the South drew the hatred of a cane-wielding South Carolina congressman named Preston Brooks who, eager to avenge the "honor" of his section, attacked him in the Senate Chamber on a spring day in 1856. Following a three-year convalescence (some below the Mason-Dixon Line accused him of "shamming"; the current view is that he may have suffered from posttraumatic stress disorder), Sumner returned and, in such baiting addresses as "The Barbarism of Slavery," fired upon the South with renewed vigor. By this point he had moved far beyond the moderate position on the slave question still held by Charles Francis. The Governor's reverence for the republic ensured his opposition to radical abolitionism, invariably souring his relations with Sumner. Siding with family, Henry could love the senator only as a fallen angel who had failed to put union first.

5

HARVARD

Late in the summer of 1854, sixteen-year-old Henry made the short pilgrimage across the Charles River and began taking classes at Harvard. Much like Quincy and the presidency, he recognized the College as something of a family fiat, all a part of being a male Adams. He was the fourth generation (and one of four brothers) to attend the school; his grandfather Adams had offered lectures as the Boylston Professor of Rhetoric and Oratory (1806–9) and sat on its Board of Overseers — as would the Governor and his son Charles. The Governor's eldest son, John Quincy II, served for a time on the Harvard Corporation, the smaller of the school's two superintending committees. Bending to family preference, not to say pressure, Henry himself returned to his alma mater in the 1870s to teach medieval and American history. "All went there," he later smiled with a deflating sarcasm, "because their friends went there, and the College was their ideal of social self-respect. . . . Any other education would have required a serious effort."[1]

Henry, in fact, gave his studies more than a passing glance, although, in the fuller sense that he meant, Harvard loomed as a tiresomely orthodox institution, a sheltered place for privileged sons to congregate with other privileged sons. The school's student body counted 340 undergraduates with an additional 365 in the divinity, law, scientific, and medical schools; its faculty consisted of thirty-nine professors, and its several libraries held fewer than 100,000 volumes; the young scholars, dressed in obligatory black coats, accepted a curriculum largely imposed on them by the administration and faculty. Total expenses for an academic year — room and board, instruction, and textbooks — came to $249, about $6,900 in current dollars.[2]

The school ranked its students on a complicated merit system, and Henry seemed willing to play the game before boredom and perhaps some resentment set in. He received no deductions for conduct his first year, but soon the penalties began to pile up — 70 as a sophomore, an additional 94 points as a junior, and a contemptuous 608 his senior year. Clearly he had little respect for Harvard's method of apportioning distinction.[3] He deliberately courted, rather, a number of small transgressions, including smoking in the College yard, cutting classes, and missing prayers. After absenting himself from one devotional service too many, the school sent Charles Francis a formal letter to acquaint him of his son's sins.

Combined, the penalties helped to bring Henry's final class rank down to a middling 44th out of 89 graduates. Even without these demerits, however, his chances of scholastic recognition were early and perhaps fatally compromised by a freshman-year illness (possibly mononucleosis) that caused him to miss a month of classes, thus dropping his first-term standing to 70th. Diligent work the following semester elevated him to 43rd. He inched up to 34th sophomore year and peaked at 21st as a junior. At that point, with but a year to go and no chance of cracking the top tier, he appears to have simply invited penalties. He rejected, in other words, a College model that policed private behavior, held out small rewards for congenial conduct, and treated undergraduates more like schoolboys than young men. In many respects, the institution existed less for the students than the students existed for the institution. Still socially informed by its proud colonial past, Harvard made few concessions to its clientele, who were fenced in a cramped quadrangle containing a few plain buildings. A ringing bell called students twice a day to morning and evening prayers, where, when seated, they were enjoined to refrain from fidgeting, whispering, and otherwise demon-strating a less than monastic reverence. One could conceivably cultivate an intellectual life apart from the school, though the merit system discouraged gestures in this direction. Henry's collegiate friend Nicholas Long-worth Anderson, the son of two distinguished Ohio families, complained to his mother, "Rank at college is determined not by a uniform elegance of recitation or by a knowl-edge of the subjects in hand, but by a confor-mity to the college rules."[4]

Henry's classroom performance varied by subject. He did well in languages (French, Latin, and Greek), labored unevenly in the sciences (taking higher marks in botany and astronomy than in physics and chemistry), and excelled in composition and elocution — the necessary skill set of pre–Civil War states-men. Ironically, considering his later success as an interpreter of the American past, he proved at this time a diffident student of his-tory. Disinclined to the lecture and recitation mode and perhaps unwilling to exert himself for something less than top place, there is evidence that he purposefully underper-formed. His peers considered him intellectu-ally formidable, and the College's chapter of Phi Beta Kappa made him an honorary member; one student, upon receiving an army commission, asked Henry to draft his letter of acceptance. Beyond a small circle of intimates, he more generally mixed well with his colleagues, who were possibly intrigued by his casual flouting of school rules. Apart from the academic routine, Adams contributed essays and book reviews to the student-run *Harvard Magazine,* made occasional forays into neighboring Boston for much needed dining alternatives, and was initiated into the Hasty Pudding Club, Harvard's preeminent student organization (and the country's oldest theatrical society). In its company he acquired the improbable moniker "Alligator" and appeared in several productions, including John Morton Madison's one-act farce, *Lend Me Five Shillings,* and *The Poor Gentleman,* a happy-ending five-act comedy by the British dramatist George Colman the Younger.[5]

Such episodes and activities drew from Adams a strong sense of camaraderie with several classmates, a bond captured well in his sentimental response, as an upperclassman, to leaving Holworthy Hall. After lovingly enumerating the dormitory's deficiencies as "the coldest, dirtiest, and gloomiest [quarters] in Cambridge," he wrote with feeling of how its frugal rooms held certain and special instances of unexpected friendships: "To me it will always be haunted by my companions who have been there, by the books that I have read there, and by a laughing group of bright, fresh faces, that have rendered it sunny in my eyes forever."[6]

Though Henry pertly disparaged Harvard in the *Education* as intellectually archaic, the school did offer certain amenities not to be found elsewhere in America. The English novelist and *Vanity Fair* author William Makepeace Thackeray, former longtime Missouri senator Thomas Hart Benton (who, with his brother Jesse, had years earlier nearly killed Andrew Jackson in a Nashville gunfight), and educational pioneer Horace Mann were a few of the notable lecturers brought to Cambridge during Henry's undergraduate years. The school's faculty, if uneven, did include several prominent dons, some of whom, like the Swiss-born naturalist Louis Agassiz and the versatile New England poet James Russell Lowell (replacing the nation's most famous bard, Henry Wadsworth Longfellow, at the beginning of Henry's sophomore year), made lasting impressions. Henry later remembered Agassiz's course on the glacial period and paleontology as "the only teaching that appealed to [my] imagination."[7]

Harvard's ability to draw students from across the country further earned Adams's appreciation. Nowhere else, outside of perhaps a military academy, was he likely to strike up a friendship with someone like William Henry Fitzhugh "Rooney" Lee, the ducal second son of then Lt. Col. Robert E. Lee. Many years after graduating, Henry supposed that a shared antipathy to the quickly approaching modern age — dominated by machines and accountants, bankers and bottom lines — made the two classmates temperamentally suited. He called himself "little more fit than the Virginians to deal with a future America which showed no fancy for the past. Already northern society betrayed a preference for economists over diplomats [Adamses] or soldiers [Lees], — one might even call it a jealousy, — against which two eighteenth-century types had little chance to live, and which they had in common to fear."[8] In Lee, Adams recognized a fellow aristocrat similarly burdened by the ghosts of history-laden ancestors. Lee's paternal grandfather, Maj. Gen. Henry "Light-Horse Harry" Lee III, had fought effectively in the southern theater of the American Revolution before serving as Georgia's ninth governor; his maternal grandfather, George Washington Parke Custis, was the step-grandson and adopted son of George Washington. Though an enemy of slavery, Henry nevertheless identified with the slaveholder as a powder-wigged fixture of the past, part of a southern system that, like black bondage, trembled on the edge of extinction.

In his later years, Adams came to see Harvard as performing a kind of intellectual evasion. Anchored in orthodoxy, the College seemed disinclined to grapple with fresh

80

discoveries in the social and hard sciences. Its emphasis on student attendance at religious services and a classics-heavy curriculum harkened back to its Puritan roots, but the next half-century unleashed upon the world — even the neatly trimmed Harvard Yard — Marxism, Fordism (the emergence of mass production in the automobile industry as elsewhere), and evolutionary theory. To be fair, Henry arrived in Cambridge at the tail end of an older scholastic tradition, before men such as Marx and Darwin had published their most influential works. Thus, when he later complained of "not . . . remember[ing] to have heard the name of Karl Marx mentioned [at Harvard], or the title of *Capital*," he was aiming for effect rather than accuracy.[9] The first volume of *Capital*, as he knew, did not appear until 1867; in any case Henry's copy, held at the Massachusetts Historical Society, has a number of uncut pages, indicating that they remained unread.

He more accurately indicted Harvard for seeking to inculcate its students with the liberal Protestant virtues — "moderation, balance, judgment, restraint" — that mirrored the character of the Cambridge Unitarian clergy.[10] This did nothing to prepare Henry and his peers for either the coming carnage of the Civil War or the age of industry and empire that followed. As a culture-shaping institution, Harvard seemed to play a part in a grand conspiracy to defend the idea of a New England conscience hardened in its quasi-Puritan convictions and indisposed to change. Had Henry taken his education, say, in the 1720s, it would likely have lasted him a lifetime, but to graduate as he did in 1858, on the cusp of a radical new age in science and economics, immigration and warfare, raised serious doubts about the very foundations of his training.

In this profoundly influential period (say, 1860–1905), x-rays, radioactivity, and electrons were discovered, and Einstein advanced the theory of special relativity; much of the Western world industrialized, which inspired a new era of imperialism evinced in the so-called scramble for Africa and incursions into Asia. A series of conflicts — the American Civil War, wars of German unification, and the Sino-Japanese War — demonstrated the efficacy of "modern" economies and technologies. Some twenty million immigrants, mainly from southern and eastern European countries, arrived in the United States during the last twenty years of Adams's life. No doubt he too severely condemned his college in the *Education* for failing to, in effect, predict the future. And yet, as a probing commentary on the insularity of scholastic institutions, the critique is worth considering.

Adams's single conspicuous triumph at Harvard came late, when his peers chose him to deliver their Class Day oration, a ceremonial occasion approximately a month before graduation. "This," he subsequently recalled, "was political as well as literary success, and precisely the sort of eighteenth-century combination that fascinated an eighteenth-century boy."[11] The recognition from his colleagues conformed to a traditional (and distinctly Adams-like) assumption of honor; presumably no horse-trading or special pleading from the penalty-mired candidate marred his elevation. His selection seemed an assurance that the "eighteenth-century" continuities would continue, and from the Quincy perspective that may have been a bigger prize than the oration itself.

A bit before noon, following an ice-cream repast, on a blazing late June day, an audience of faculty and families, students and guests packed into Cambridge's First Parish Church. "Here all hot — yes roasted, and dripping with perspiration," one of them wrote, "as we listened to the oration by Henry Adams and the poem by [George W.] Noble — both were good." Considering the convivial occasion, the address struck a decidedly critical note. Posing as a Puritan, Adams, decked out in de rigueur black gown and looking solemn and grave, attacked the age's — or at least Boston's — materialistic bent. And in doing so he vented too against the Unitarian mindset that, so he pressed, had done its best to dilute all wonder, mystery, and experimentation from the human experience. "Man has reduced the universe to a machine," he complained, and thus failed to recognize "that there are secrets of nature which have puzzled chemist and philosopher even in these days of science, and which still wait for a solution."[12] Conceding nothing to his captive audience, a happy gathering of the secure and the satisfied, he attacked the lazy intellectual assumptions of the New England way:

> Some of us still persist in believing that there are prizes to be sought for in life which will not disgust in the event of success. . . . There are some who believe that this long education of ours, the best that the land can give, was not meant to be thrown away and forgotten; that this nation of ours furnishes the grandest theatre in the world for the exercise of that refinement of mind and those high principles which it is a disgrace to us if we have not acquired.[13]

In effect, Henry subjected his audience to a sermon, one that raised the uncertain specter of a spiritual breakdown afflicting civilization. It proved to be an anticipatory statement, a minor jeremiad that he would rehearse and repeat over the course of his life in a number of literary genres.

More immediately, however, a newly commenced Adams was barely looking beyond the day and faced the nagging postgraduation problem of identifying a suitable profession; he simply saw no clear path. "Ultimately it is most probable that I shall study and practice law," he wrote in the class *Life-Book,* "but where and to what extent is as yet undecided."[14] He wished, in other words, for the rare gift of time before a decisive series of hushed parental conversations and maneuvers quietly cornered him into slipping on an occupational harness. "Law," like "Harvard," was reflexive, and he said "law" only because, for the time being, in his last, late collegiate spring, it offered the path of least resistance. More genuinely, if secretly, he had begun to formulate other plans and rather than saunter off to a local attorney's office to bow before the altar of apprenticeship, he broke in a decidedly different direction. The favorite son, desperate for independence, managed to make his way to Germany.

■ ■ ■ ■

EDUCATION

■ ■ ■ ■

New England boys. Mentally they were
never boys.

Henry Adams, 1907

6

GERMANY

Henry's postcollegiate journey to Europe signified, depending upon one's perspective, either a great break from family tradition or yet another pivot down a familiar path. His people, after all, had been sailing to the Continent ever since 1778, when John Adams, appointed as a special envoy by the fledgling U.S. government, boarded the frigate *Boston* with his preteen son John Quincy, bound for France. Over the next several decades, numerous European courts came to know one Adams or another. Henry, by contrast, sought not the clerical routine of an American mission but rather the leisure of unaccounted hours to consider carefully his next move and perhaps identify his *real* vocation. Brothers John and Charles were already admitted to the Suffolk County (Massachusetts) bar, a depressing concession, so Henry thought, to the gray ghosts of the Old House that he hoped to avoid. Hardly a renegade, the green graduate stood in solid company.

For the pressure to identify early an occupation figured prominently in the thinking, strategies, and evasions of many privileged young men disinclined to inflict upon the world yet more lawyers, politicians, and physicians. Under strain they might gesture in the direction of these rote professions only to later make their escapes. To note but two famous examples, the novelist Henry James, author of such classics as *The Portrait of a Lady* and *The Bostonians,* briefly attended Harvard Law School (1862–63) before launching a literary career; his brother William, the noted philosopher and psychologist, took the degree of M.D. at the Harvard Medical School in 1869 but never practiced medicine.

Negotiating for his short-term freedom, Henry asked his father for $2,000 for two years — about $55,000 in current dollars — promising upon his return to take up the duties of a "jurist," an authority and commentator, that is, on legal concerns.[1] He intended, so he told the Governor, to study civil law at Heidelberg and Berlin as well as in Paris. Naturally his language skills could only, he pointed out, be improved. The extent to which Charles Francis accepted the veracity of Henry's well-planned plea is a matter of conjecture, but there never seemed to be any real question about the young man's emancipation from Massachusetts. A third son and a

Brooks to boot, Henry considered himself eminently expendable and thus safe to be set free. There were, he supposed, already enough Adams men fingering musty law books and biding their time to claim the mundane political prizes they thought their due.

Still, parental doubts lingered. Neither Abigail nor Charles Francis were eager to let this much loved son go and took only small comfort in the fact that their eldest child, Louisa, then living in Italy with her husband of four years, Charles Kuhn, a former sugar broker, represented some vague shadow of American oversight. The Governor in particular took the separation hard. After seeing Henry off at the train station, Charles Francis confessed to his diary of an enveloping sadness: "My happiness is all at home, and he is on the whole that one of my sons who is possessed of the most agreeable home qualities. When we came home to our shortened evening table, I was under greater depression than I have felt for a long time."[2]

On October 9, eleven days after embarking on what one passenger called a "rough and tedious crossing," Henry and a small number of former classmates arrived in Liverpool aboard the RMS *Persia,* an iron side-wheeler reputed to be the fastest steamship in the world. From Liverpool, he set off for London, where he spent a few days sightseeing before crossing the Channel to Antwerp aboard the

91

steamer *Baron Osy;* a brief layover at Hanover prefaced his Berlin debut on the 22nd. Thus began a trying period for the young scholar, who perhaps read his difficulties — negotiating the language, loneliness, and lack of female company — into subsequent brittle appraisals of this period. "He loved, or thought he loved the people," he later wrote of these years, "but the Germany he loved was the eighteenth-century which the Germans were ashamed of, and were destroying as fast as they could. Of the Germany to come, he knew nothing."[3]

Part of Henry's troubles involved the after-tremors of an unrequited love. While at Harvard he had fallen quite completely for Caroline Bigelow, doe-eyed, trim waisted, and the daughter of a Massachusetts Supreme Court justice. A serious boy uninitiated in the ways of flirtation, he had perhaps opened his heart as never before. These still tender feelings followed him overseas. From a distant Germany he wrote to Charles of Carry's spell, "I wasted a good deal of superfluous philanthropy on her. It was my last and longest hit, that. Lasted me a matter of three years and might be still hanging round me if I'd remained at home, though I had pretty much found her out the Spring before I graduated. It cost me the hardest heart-aches ever I had before I could sit quiet under the conviction that she is — what she is. . . . By God, I grind my teeth even now to think how easily I let myself be led by that doll."[4] Years would pass before he let himself be led again.

Having begun his coursework in Berlin, Henry took an immediate dislike to the university's austerely formal academic environment. Professors lectured out of text-books, he later complained, and refused to engage undergraduates in discussion. He compared the system to an unsatisfying apprenticeship in which students paid for the credential of a degree but failed to acquire any useful knowledge. Turned loose on their own, he thought they might have a chance at self-education, but the regimented system of instruction worked against this. Their principal function, he once fumed, was to pay the salaries of a top-heavy professoriate. Defeated by the language and unable to follow his lessons, Henry quickly employed a "Dutch teacher" to come by each morning for conversation and look over his exercises. Needless to say, his first dispiriting weeks in Germany were humbling. "Here I am, then, in Berlin," he groaned to his brother Charles, "independent; unknown and unknowing; hating the language and yet grubbing into it."[5]

Though confused by the lectures — "I can't catch anything at all" — Henry maintained the polite fiction during these initial months abroad that a legal career beckoned. He sketched out plans for a two-year education in Europe, followed by two additional years back in Boston reading law, at which point, he somewhat arbitrarily proposed, he might abandon the East altogether, cross the Mississippi, and become a giant of jurisprudence in St. Louis. These were, of course, boyish reveries, part of Henry's stumbling search to find traction and offer, at least to his family, the semblance of stability. More generally, he spent a considerable amount of time in Germany organizing excursions and ruminating on his persistently thin finances. Concerts and theaters, wine shops and beer gardens were all temptations to be indulged. He saw Mozart's *Zauberflöte* and Beethoven's *Fidelio* at the Berlin Opera Haus, enjoyed a "remarkably well done" presentation of *Hamlet* in the local language, and sampled other Schauspielhaus performances of *Oberon, Don Juan,* and Wagner's *Rienzi.* Henry liked Maraschino liqueur and a nicely spiced Glühwein and more generally consumed Piesporter and Rhine wine. All of these entertainments and appetites added up. "But you see," he appealed to Charles (though he might just as easily have been showing off), "a single bat [spree], a single evening passed as is sometimes done, from six in the afternoon till three in the morning . . . may make necessary a week's economy." And while retrenching "on the heavy cheap," as he put it, the penitent scholar sat in Berlin cellars and quietly suffered "boiled sausages and a mug of beer."[6]

Pleasurable — if expensive — evenings out to the contrary, Henry's sense of duty kept him in the classroom, though not at the University of Berlin. Simply unable to fathom the lectures, he dropped his legal studies and in January enrolled as a special student in the Friedrichs-Wilhelm-Werdesches Gymnasium, which housed some 450 students. The boys in his class of forty-four ranged from ten to nineteen; most were under fifteen. Henry, the "older" American, obviously stuck out like a sore thumb. "One or two of the little fellows I am quite fond of," he wrote to Sumner back in America, "and you would split if you could see me walking away from school with a small boy under each arm, to whom I have to bend down to talk. . . . I am stared at as a sort of wild beast by the rest of the school . . . [although] they treat me with a certain sort of respect, and yet as one of themselves."[7]

Sitting in the third row, Henry struggled to absorb the language (his chief reason for being at the gymnasium) in which his lessons — Greek, Latin, history, and religion — were taught. With more confidence he took some critical note of his classmates' diet, complexion, and general physical countenance. He found them on the whole "pale, heavy, [and] dirty." This he chalked up to too much "sauer kohl and sausages" and a lack of exercise. He

95

reported that mere proximity to these pasty faces in the drab winter months "made [him] feel sick and low-spirited." He too, however, appeared to have picked up a bit of winter weight. "Adams has become a little fatter," observed Benjamin Crowninshield, a Harvard friend also tramping about Europe at this time. He noticed further that Henry, already battling an uncooperative hairline, had compensated with muttonchop sideburns cleanly kept off a still boyish lip and chin.[8]

By March Adams had had enough and sought an honorable and all-encompassing retreat from the law, from language training, and most especially from Berlin. In a letter to Charles he happily granted, "For my own part I feel as certain that I never shall be a lawyer, as you are that I'm not fit for it." But this confession only begged the question: If he were not to study law, what would constitute his reason for remaining in Europe? A number of answers came conveniently to hand: he wanted, like a number of his fellow Harvard alums, to experience the Continent's outstanding cultural amenities; continued language training augured well for future diplomatic service; and exposure to Europe traditionally benefited Adams men, broadening their education and making them more suitable for public careers. Years later, Henry framed those drifting days abroad in a brief admission that may contain multiple meanings: "Adams stayed because he did not want to go home."[9]

Neither, however, did he wish to remain in Berlin, a city in which, Crowninshield contended, "he look[ed] like a beaten dog with the tail between the hind legs." In early April he left the Prussian capital for a holiday in Dresden, the center of the Kingdom of Saxony some 115 miles to the south. His letters to family up to this time suggested a blending of youthful confusion, occupational frustration, and perhaps a trace of depression. The escape promised a clean start, as did the end of an oppressive central European winter. In the hopeful light of spring, he wrote to Charles of his altogether more radiant surroundings: "Sun doesn't set till after eight and I tell you, sir, that a sunset concert on the Brühlsche Terrasse at Dresden, sitting under the trees and smoking with a view down the Elbe at the sunset, and a view up the Elbe to the pine hills above, is something jolly. I don't deny it, Sir, I enjoy this life." If still troubled by having to solicit the Governor for financial assistance, Henry nevertheless took advantage of his altogether brighter Dresden days to scour the city and neighboring countryside. He paid a call on the Königstein Fortress — a medieval castle that dated back to the thirteenth century — and pronounced its valley environs "deuced pretty." He adopted a less generous line regarding the region's much admired artistic holdings, posing as something of a seasoned if sniffy connoisseur. After touring the vast Grünes Gewölbe (Green Vault) museum in Dresden, one of the oldest collections of treasures in the world, he smugly declared the gallery "rather a bore . . . [just a] lot of old knick-knacks, precious stones and all that; decided bore. Palace, frescoes, rather good but no[t] great." He further adopted a rather inelegant attitude toward the "too coarse complexioned and dowdy . . . German women," who, he idly swore, didn't "please" him. Of course such insecurity-driven assertions allowed Henry to rationalize his annoyingly persistent lack of female attention. With varying degrees of gallows humor and self-pity he wrote Charles, "No one has taken the trouble to fall in love with me."[10]

Inevitably, Henry's Dresden holiday — with its offshoot journeys to Nuremberg and Thun — turned into an extended stay. Returning briefly to Berlin at the end of summer, he realized the impossibility of enduring another long and isolating winter in the capital. Concerned, as he put it to Charles, that he was about to "sink into a chronic melancholy here," he made other plans. Writing to his mother, he stated simply, "Berlin is too much for me. The city itself, the mode of life here, the American society and the climate have all disagreed with me so much that . . . I didn't care to go through it all again." After petitioning his "papa," Henry received permission in late October for a permanent removal to Dresden. There, over the next several months, he gave himself up to the luxury of riding lessons, continued to work on his German, and more generally took in the stray books, ideas, and conversations orbiting about him. He also discovered that to be an Adams meant something even overseas. Of the mistress of the house in which he was staying Henry related to Charles with ill-concealed pride, "[She] has once or twice spoken of my 'historical name' &c so that I suppose some one has told her my grandfather was president. She has tact enough however to leave me alone."[11]

In April he uprooted once again, leaving Dresden for a series of stops in Germany, Austria, and Switzerland. Making his way, finally, to northern Italy, he joined his sister Louisa and her husband. There, he became intensely interested in the Italian Risorgimento, the Resurgence or "rising again" then contesting papal and Austrian authority on the way to creating the Kingdom of Italy. And simply by virtue of being an Adams, even a third son, he discovered that he might have access to some of the major figures of the movement. Compared to his gray German days, Henry took easily to Italy, which touched off all sorts of historical and aesthetic associations in the young man. From its powerful influence would be planted the seed of perhaps his greatest work.

7

ITALY

Brotherly inspiration and perhaps a bit of brotherly rivalry resulted in Henry's first published commentary, a series of Italian letters touching upon his travels, hasty impressions of the Peninsula's politics, and callow reflections of the Risorgimento. The letter's origins can be traced to a number of winter 1860 *Boston Advertiser* articles by Charles attacking Congress's spoils system. Writing under the prim pseudonym "Pemberton," he praised a small group of House Republicans, including the Governor, for contesting their party's politics-as-usual choice, one Mr. Defrees, for House printer. The nominee, the reformers claimed, bought the recommendation "on a promise of future campaign funds." After a number of inconclusive ballots, the tainted candidate retired from the field and a presumably more reputable Mr. Ford from Ohio claimed the position. Charles predictably touted his father's efforts in the *Advertiser* as nobly disinterested and above politics, precisely the kind of leadership needed by a nation suddenly on the edge of separation.[1]

Slavery, the principal source of this sectional discord, was long subject to a series of settlements and compromises now coming undone. In 1857 a Supreme Court comprising mainly southerners controversially affirmed the rights of slaveholders to take their chattel into the western territories. Two years later, in something of a violent counterstroke, nearly two dozen abolitionists led by John Brown captured the federal arsenal at Harpers Ferry, Virginia, in a bid to initiate an armed revolt among slaves. The assault began on October 16, 1859; two days later marines under the command of Robert E. Lee killed or captured several of the raiders, and on December 2 Brown, convicted of treason, murder, and inciting slaves to rebellion, was taken to a scaffold surrounded by soldiers and hanged in Charles Town, Virginia.[2] On that very day, an in-transit Governor neared the nation's capital, on his way to taking his place in the U.S. Congress.

His family, surrounded in Quincy by sundry memories and memorials of their kin's service to community and country, wondered if some intricate destiny now called upon the Governor. Henry seemed to believe so. Across the Atlantic, he declared Charles's articles "a great success," thinking they augured well for their father's rising political profile. Currently the occupant of a mere congressional seat, the Governor, only in his early fifties, appeared to be coming into his own. Perhaps now, in the uncertain electoral climate of 1860, might he find his way back to the White House? And might the Adamses, after a generation of slaveholder ascendency and Jacksonian Democracy, matter once more? "We must all feel the importance of this start," Henry wrote to his mother shortly after learning of the "Pemberton" letters. "It's the first declaration of the colors we sail under. . . . We young ones don't count much now, but it may at least please papa to know that those who are nearest and dearest to him, go heart and soul after him on this path."[3]

Ready to take leave of Dresden and stimulated by Charles's example, Henry proposed now to see his own work in print. Moving south, he planned to pass through Vienna, Bologna, Florence, Rome, Naples, Palermo, and Sorrento, eager to record his impressions of people, places, and politics. He carefully, somewhat shyly, and a bit self-consciously spelled out to Charles what he hoped to do:

As you know, I propose to leave Dresden on the 1st of April for Italy. It has occurred to me that this trip may perhaps furnish material for a pleasant series of letters, not written to be published but publishable in case they were worth it. . . . Now, you will understand, I do *not* propose to write with the wish to publish at all hazards; on the contrary I mean to write private letters to you, as an exercise for myself, and it would be of all things my last wish to force myself into newspapers with a failure for my first attempt. On the other hand if you like the letters and think it would be in my interest to print them, I'm all ready.[4]

Charles liked the letters.

Traveling through a succession of Italian states convulsed by revolution, Henry forwarded to his brother nine communications that were, with some slight editing, published in the *Boston Courier* between April 30 and July 13. The pieces included touristy reflections on art, architecture, and cuisine, mingled with weightier if understandably uneven observations on the Italian drive for unification. These were historic weeks in which the Italian nationalist Giuseppe Garibaldi led a small corps of volunteers (the famous Expedition of the Thousand) from Genoa to the port of Marsala on the westernmost point of Sicily; its improbable victories culminated in the taking of Palermo, the island's largest city, and in the subsequent collapse of the Bourbon-ruled two Sicilies. The creation of the Kingdom of Italy came as a result the following year. For a brief time, the little *Courier* could claim some journalistic distinction in having an American observer reporting firsthand on the birth pangs of a new nation.

Henry's initial letter to Charles, dated April 5 and published on the 30th, detailed its author's last and altogether enjoyable evening in Dresden. What stands out is Henry's obvious infatuation with the colorful pageantry of high Court culture. While assuming the skeptical tone of the seasoned traveler, he more clearly took pleasure that night in performances of Mozart's *Requiem* and Beethoven's Ninth Symphony; the city's Royal Orchestra (founded in the 1540s and conducted that evening by Carl August Krebs) partnered with a chorus, Henry estimated, of some three hundred. In the royal box sat King John of Saxony and his handsome wife, Amalie Auguste, Princess of Bavaria and Queen of Saxony. Henry's admiring, though not uncritical, interest in monarchical privilege marked several of his *Courier* communications that spring — a curious absorption for a supposedly rock-ribbed New England republican.[5]

The aristocrat pitch of the first letter, written from Vienna, is further evident in Henry's stumbling understanding of the polyglot Austro-Hungarian Empire. Its apparent success melding peoples of differing nationalities (Germans, Magyars, Poles, etc.), languages

105

(Hungarian, Croatian, Czech, etc.), and religions (Roman Catholic, Eastern Orthodox, Islamic, etc.) seemed to him argument enough to justify the Hapsburg Monarchy's hold over such a vast territory. Only surface-sensitive to the many and intricate tensions that underlay the conservative regimes in Vienna, Prague, and Budapest, he thought the empire likely to reform itself and doubted democracy's capacity to do better. As he put it, "The Austrian government is a mass of faults and evils, but even republics are not always wholly pure. It is fairer and pleasanter to trust that under the long and steady pressure from within and without, the nation and the government may gradually be forced forward step by step without marking its course by more blood."[6] Henry's "trust" in a benign process of central European liberalization turned out, of course, to be colossally misplaced. Continued ethnic tensions in the sharply divided Hapsburg Empire proved to be, with the assassination of the Archduke Franz Ferdinand of Austria and his wife by the Bosnian Serb Gavrilo Princip in July 1914, the immediate catalyst for the First World War, the collapse of several empires, and the spilling of far "more blood" than any late nineteenth-century American could have imagined.

Adams's second letter, also carrying a Vienna dateline, reviewed his travels to

Trieste and Austrian-occupied Venice. In the interest of capturing local color for his Anglo Boston readership (and perhaps exercising his untried hand at humor), he chastised the small navy of noisome gondoliers who "quarreled" over customers "as badly as Irish hackmen." Visiting the obligatory Venetian retreats, Henry trooped about stately palazzos and crumbling churches, took in Titians and cool evening crypts. And like a good countinghouse Puritan, he marveled a little dubiously at the city's apparent lack of economic initiative, which he identified in its leisurely pace. "The idea that I got," he informed *Courier* readers, "was that every man in Venice keeps a shop, and every one of them loses money by it. And this must be tolerably near the truth. . . . All hard at work doing nothing . . . all lazy as they well can be." Despite holding such an unabashedly Beacon Hill opinion on the unsure virtues of "doing nothing," Henry took rather easily to the relaxed environment, spending his days sitting in the warm Adriatic sun, sipping chocolate, smoking cigarettes, and listening to regimental bands while watching the inevitable beggars shuffle along the charming Riva degli Schiavoni quay.[7]

From Venice, Adams passed through Padua, Ferrara, and Bologna en route to Florence, where he moved once more in the privileged company of kings and counts. Enjoying the horse races on a track just outside the city, he saw the arrival of royals in a bright show of carriages and heard the rhythmic clapping of hands accompanied by shouts of "Evviva Vittorio Emmanuele!" when King Victor Emmanuel II appeared dressed in a shooting jacket and looking, so Henry told Charles, "like a very vulgar and coarse fancy-man." The following day, while attending the opera, Adams caught site of the Count of Cavour, "the greatest man in Europe," he boasted, and certainly one of the unification movement's acclaimed statesmen. He stared in respect "through [his] glass for five minutes steadily."[8] These leading figures of the Risorgimento impressed Henry as modern statesmen who personified the kind of first-family ruling regime he wished for his own country.

While in Florence, Henry visited his sister Louisa (Loo) and her husband, Charles Kuhn, then in the midst of a prolonged grand tour of the Continent. Having taken easily to European manners, customs, and certain social freedoms, Loo loved Italy, lived in the handsome Piazza Santa Maria Maggiore, and, as a privileged Victorian, surrounded herself with a staff of smartly attired servants. "I am thought very French," she bragged at this time of the Anglo Florentine community's response to her fine Paris-made apparel. "She was not meant for America,"

Henry once said of his sister. "She ought to have been an English aristocrat." Though Loo, too, had grown up in the Adams hothouse, her sex guaranteed a different set of experiences than her brothers'. Despite a lively intelligence, she would not go to Harvard, would not train for a profession, and would never write for the Boston papers. She found herself, rather, maneuvered into something of an idler's existence, spending money, decorating apartments, and ordering about the help. That Henry recognized the fundamental unfairness of his sister's inert condition is evident in his anxious comment to their mother, "To me hers seems a life thrown away. That is, she has no object to it."[9]

Calling on Loo for a week in April, Henry commented favorably to their mother on the couple's convivial Florentine routine: "They've charming rooms, and seem to have acquaintances in abundance." Perhaps reflecting on his own desire for flight, he defended his sister's choice to live abroad: "I have no doubt she is and always will be happier here than anywhere else, not because it's gay or because it's amusing, but because one is free and one's own master." In his later years, Henry remembered this brief Italian interlude as having enlarged his view of women. An ocean from home, he realized Loo for the first time as an adult and reveled in her presence. "She was the first young woman he was ever intimate with," he wrote in the *Education.* She was "quick, sensitive, wilful, or full of will, energetic, sympathetic and intelligent enough to supply a score of men with ideas, — and he was delighted to give her the reins; — to let her drive him where she would. It was his first experiment in giving the reins to a woman, and he was so much pleased with the results that he never wanted to take them back."[10]

Reluctantly parting with Loo, Henry moved on to Rome, where he wrote his fifth *Courier* letter. It was now mid-May and the ancient city's eloquence heightened before the deepening colors of a delicious spring. Succumbing willingly to its many charms, Henry remembered his fortnight in Rome as "the happiest fourteen days known ever to have existed." His interest in the Gothic world, most apparent in the last decades of his life, appears to have first stirred during this magical season. "The lights and shadows were still mediaeval, and mediaeval Rome was alive," he later wrote. "No sand-blast of science had yet skinned off the epidermis of history, thought and feeling." Strolling about the city he encountered a splendid medley of unearthed ruins and decaying churches so agreeably different from the scrubbed spirituality of Puritan New England. Here he felt at ease, able for a few days to drop the Adams pretense and sun himself in a weightless

110

anonymity. "One's emotions in Rome," he observed, with a mixture of peace and relief, "were one's private affair."[11]

Rome held one further virtue for Henry: it coaxed him to read Edward Gibbon's sublime *History of the Decline and Fall of the Roman Empire* (six volumes, 1776–89). A visit to the Eternal City in October 1764 inspired Gibbon to take on the tome. At first he contemplated writing a history of Rome, later shifting his perspective to the empire. Henry carried with him a popular *Murray's Handbook* that contained a selection from Gibbon's autobiography, *Memoirs of My Life,* in which the Englishman recounted (after a bit of doctoring for dramatic effect) his sudden decision to write the *History.* The moment arrived, he recalled, "in the close of the evening, as [he] sat musing in the Church of the Zoccolanti or Franciscan Friars, while they were singing Vespers in the Temple of Jupiter, on the ruins of the Capital." Henry absorbed these affecting words amid Rome's arresting backdrop and wrote to Charles of their power: "I read Gibbon. Striking, very. Do you know, after long argument and reflexion, I feel much as if perhaps some day I too might come to anchor like that. Our house needs a historian in this generation and I feel strongly tempted by the quiet and sunny prospect, while my ambition for political life dwindles as I get older. This came up once before in our discussion. What do you think? Law and literature."[12]

Leaving Rome, Adams continued south to Naples, where he improbably met Garibaldi. An audience with Pennsylvania Whig Joseph Ripley Chandler, the American minister to the Kingdom of the Two Sicilies, won Henry a seat on the USS *Iroquois,* an American sloop-of-war embarking for Palermo to protect the lives and property of U.S. citizens. "He was kindly treated," Adams candidly wrote of himself, "not for his merit but for his name."[13] Given the nominal task of delivering dispatches to the *Iroquois*'s commander, James Shedden Palmer, Henry accompanied the ship and its crew to Palermo, where, presumably "for his name," he managed to finagle an interview with the great Garibaldi himself. In the eighth *Courier* letter, he evenly assessed the man:

The party was five in all, officers and civilians, and the visit was informal; indeed Garibaldi seems to discourage all formality and though he has just now all the power of an Emperor, he will not even adopt the state of a General. . . . He rose as we came in, and came forward shaking hands with each of the party as we were introduced. He had his plain red shirt on, precisely like a fireman, and no mark of authority. His manner is . . . very kind and offhand, without being

112

vulgar or demagogic. He talked with each of us and talked perfectly naturally; no stump oratory and no sham.[14]

But what did Garibaldi, speaking in French with a few words of broken English dropped in, actually say? What striking observations on war and revolution did he have to share? According to Henry the conversation never lifted beyond the pedestrian: "As for what he said, it was of no particular interest to anyone, at least as far as it was said to me."[15] In another respect, however, the evening proved for Henry unforgettable. Wandering through Palermo's mess of barricades and broken streets, shouting crowds and celebratory cannon fire, he witnessed a revolution as something more than a textbook recitation blandly devoted to an antique Boston and peopled by an antique ancestor.

That May, while Henry ambled about Italy, Republicans gathered in Chicago and awarded their party's presidential nomination to the Illinois lawyer Abraham Lincoln. The Adamses, having supported New York's Senator William Henry Seward, a protégé, as a young Whig, of John Quincy Adams, were greatly disappointed. The Governor and his sons looked upon Lincoln as a novice from nowhere, too "small" to tackle the immense task ahead. "In '56," Henry reported to *Cou-*

rier readers with thick sarcasm, "we had the satisfaction of rejecting our Garibaldi [John C. Frémont, opposed to slavery's extension, lost that year's presidential election to James Buchanan], and now in '60 we have done still better; we have deserted our Cavour [Seward]."[16]

On this snappish note did Henry's Italian letters come to an end. Leaving the Peninsula he returned north, spending much of the summer in Paris. "It's a great life," he glowed to "dearest mamma" of his daily round of restaurants and theater, "varied, exciting and elevating."[17] From Paris, he made his way to the coast and from the coast finally back to Quincy. In a few weeks there would be a presidential election and shortly after that a growing momentum among several of the southern states to leave the Union. Moving about Italy, Henry had watched a nation being built; in America he witnessed one coming undone. What his future held that autumn of 1860 he could not divine. Even as a third son his days and choices were not yet his own.

8
WASHINGTON

Back on American soil for the first time in two years, Adams returned to a nation in flux. Much, including the emergence of Free Soil Republicanism and Lincoln's election, had redefined the political landscape. But Henry had little time to take it all in. He briefly read law in Boston before migrating to Washington as the Governor's private congressional secretary. All of this transpired over a single dramatic winter in which, shocked at the prospect of a Republican administration, seven Deep South states left the Union. With an unprecedented crisis at hand, these proved to be anxious months for the House of Adams, whose gilded reputation rested on past deeds. As congressional discussions over the country's future heated up, Charles Francis, now representing Massachusetts's 3rd District, spoke not simply for his constituents but for his family and, looking especially down the line at Henry and his brothers, its uncertain prospects as well.

The Adamses' dwindling political status took on a particular resonance during this contentious winter, when Henry and his brother Charles crossed the Potomac one late February day to dine at Arlington House, the plantation home of (an absent) Robert E. Lee and Henry's Harvard classmate Rooney. Charles later remembered thinking the general's third daughter, Eleanor, "extremely attractive," though more significant is the symbolism of these two distinguished antebellum families, gathering on a "dull, murky day," each approaching the precipice of its own particular oblivion.[1] As Henry so attentively noted in the *Education,* the shifting cultural, economic, and political energies that undermined the nation's old ruling elite were already at work. This breaking of bread among declining ducal clans gave the day an altogether secular Last Supper dynamic.

The Adams family's encroaching obsolescence might be equally measured in the Governor's vain efforts to lead the moderate wing of the Republican Party. If eager to bar slavery from the nation's western territories, he nevertheless annoyed more radical Republicans like Charles Sumner by proposing conciliation with the South. Putting the Union above all, he worked ceaselessly during the secessionist debates to avert the rise of a southern Confederacy. To Sumner, however, there could be no more compromises. Lincoln had fairly won the White House, carrying eighteen states and capturing nearly 60 percent of the electoral vote. Better to see the slave drivers leave, Sumner believed, than to prop up their long-standing power over the American political system. "If the secession can be restrained to the 'Cotton States,' " he wrote an English friend shortly after the election, "I shall be willing to let them go."[2]

Rejecting radical Republicanism, the Governor regarded William H. Seward, Lincoln's secretary of state–designate and a fellow moderate, as the party's most distinguished statesman. "Alone of all others," he maintained, "[Seward] had most marked himself as a disciple of the school in which I had been bred myself."[3] Both presumed that most southerners were unsympathetic to secession and given time would make their voices heard. Both believed the border states' responses were key. Without Kentucky, Maryland, Delaware, Missouri, Arkansas, Tennessee, and particularly Virginia, they reasoned, there could be no Confederate nation.

In December 1860 a House committee made up of a single representative from each state was charged with finding a solution to the tangle of issues dividing the sections. Charles Francis, one of the body's thirty-three members, promptly joined other moderates in proposing a series of concessions to

117

the South. These included admitting the New Mexico Territory into the Union as a slave state, ratifying a constitutional amendment to protect slavery in those states where it currently existed, and vigorously enforcing the country's controversial fugitive slave laws — which, as noted earlier, bound the citizens of free states to participate in the capture and return of runaways. Considering that the party's appeal in the North depended on its Free Soil promise to exclude slavery from the territories, the Governor appeared to be asking his fellow Republicans to repudiate their recent victory, indeed their identity. Believing that a series of accommodations would, as he put it, show "sympathy with the hesitating and timid but honest citizens of the slave states," Charles Francis badly misread both the South and his own party.[4]

But young Henry, full of family pride, thought just the opposite, supposing his father to be, in this darkening hour, the country's one essential man — if only he could learn to perform like a politician. "Papa has got to make himself indispensable," he wrote his mother, Abigail, "not only in the wild-beast pen [of politics], but out of it too. . . . He doesn't like the bother and fuss of entertaining and managing people who can't be reasoned with, and he won't take the trouble to acquire strength and influence that won't fall into his mouth." Now, as the

118

republic teetered on the verge of collapse, Henry believed the Governor's moment had suddenly arrived. "He's a growing man," he confidently wrote his brother Charles in early January, "and will soon have a national fame and power inferior to no one unless it be Seward."[5]

In fact, the Governor's conservative response to the secession crisis spoke of an inability to recognize that the questions of race, regionalism, and states' rights had grown beyond the control of Congress. He hoped to revisit the old politics practiced in the compromises of 1820 and 1850, as though that sectional status quo still existed. Rather, the determination of southerners to see slavery expand and the refusal of an increasing number of northerners to allow that to happen argued otherwise. Confronted with circumstances they could neither direct nor even fully fathom, the moderates fell into paralysis. Charles Francis later and somewhat lazily blamed the bitter outcome of that winter on an inconvenient calendar: "Our only course in the defenceless position in which we found ourselves was to gain time." His son Charles, a proud veteran of the war that could not be negotiated away, however, took a different, harder, and more personal line. "My father," he wrote some years after the Governor's death, "favored the abandonment of [Fort] Sumter. His horror of civil war was such that I find myself at a loss to fix the point at which he would have made a stand. I am not at all sure he would not have concluded that a peaceable separation was best."[6]

If Henry doubted the Governor's course in Congress, he kept it to himself. It was Sumner, once a dear family friend, now a radical, who epitomized to Adams all that had gone wrong on the Republican side. He subsequently conjectured, and some scholars have followed suit, that the senator's unwillingness to compromise with the South resulted from the brutal caning he had suffered several years earlier: "his nervous system never quite recovered its tone." But Henry's reproach of Sumner more distinctly suggested his own failure to grasp the ethical struggle over slavery. He knew the institution to be wrong, hoped for its eventual extinction, and yet, along with many others, to be sure, drew back from abolitionism's moral severity and the heightened emotional pitch frequently attending its arguments. One might say that to Henry slavery was a distant sin, while Sumner had formerly been a very real friend. "Not one rebel defection — not even Robert E. Lee's — cost young Adams a personal pang," he later wrote, "but Sumner's struck home."[7]

Sumner's "defection," however, only accentuated the fact that some few years earlier the Adamses' political support had shifted to

Seward. Like many Republicans, Henry had hoped to see the New York senator elected president in 1860, believing him capable of reaching a binding agreement with the South short of war. Successful leadership on Seward's part promised further to validate the moderates' course — and Charles Francis stood second only to Seward, his son supposed, as the exemplar of that school. "If the Governor weathers this storm," Henry wrote Charles, "he has a good chance of living in the White House some day . . . [and] the house of Adams may get [its] lease of life renewed."[8] This roseate speculation failed to reckon, however, with several crucial factors: the emergence of Lincoln, the rising political importance of the Middle West (whose favorite sons captured the presidency in every campaign from 1860 to 1880), and the unwillingness of the white Lower South to remain in a Union dominated politically by Republicans.

Fresh off his Italian letters and eager to advance the moderate cause, Henry proposed to write on Congress's doings during these critical months. Accordingly, family friend and *Boston Advertiser* publisher Charles Hale agreed to print the opinions of this unusually well-connected if otherwise untried "Washington correspondent." As the Governor's private secretary, privy to confidential information, Henry requested anonymity, so the articles were innocent of even the "H.B.A." byline appended to his Mediterranean dispatches. Thinking about his journalistic role and possibly of other and more consequential roles to come, Henry decided that despite certain benefits in passing as a Brooks or a Johnson, he wished perhaps more than these to be an Adams — he wanted, that is, to count. "I fairly confess that I want to have a record of this winter on file," he wrote Charles in December. "I . . . would like to think that a century or two hence when everything else about us is forgotten, my letters might still be read and quoted as a memorial of manners and habits at the time of the great secession of 1860."[9] He then proceeded, between early December and early March, to produce twenty-one epistles for the *Advertiser.*

Henry, just two years out of Harvard but already eager to engage in public affairs at the highest level, predictably used Hale's paper to both clarify and amplify the moderate position in Congress — sometimes without much regard for reality. He claimed in one commentary that a southern confederacy under the "moral opposition . . . of the whole world" promised to implode "before a year was over." This wild guess of global opprobrium might be dismissed as mere inexperience, though on occasion Adams crossed over into outright fiction. He disingenuously

122

assured his Boston audience, for example, that "the republicans in Congress [were] said to be unanimous" on a policy of "kindness and forbearance to the South, short of a sacrifice of principle." Certainly this view misrepresented the vital Sumner strain of Republicanism, now deeply involved in shaping party policy. Henry, in fact, promised readers that no fundamental differences separated Seward and Sumner. "So long as the republicans remain united, temperate, and forbearing in tone and manner," one December editorial argued, "it is thought that there is no real danger for the country." In other words, if the Republican Party did not split, then neither would the Union. Adopting an equally fantastic attitude, one late January column declared, "The tide is certainly turning . . . the disunionists are checked and wavering, and it would not take much to turn the scale against them."[10] Actually, five states had already seceded from the Union, with Louisiana and Texas to follow within a few days.

If Henry's two years abroad offered valuable insight into European conditions, they did nothing to improve his understanding of America's rapid race to separation. His fealty to the moderate approach staked out by Charles Francis, moreover, dimmed the darkened lens through which he imperfectly read both Sumner and the secessionists. As a historical document, Henry's contributions to the *Advertiser* tell us more about moderate Republicanism's confusion in an increasingly radical period than they do about the intentions, motivations, and maneuvers of the major players who set the terms of debate; among this small circle, Lincoln undoubtedly mattered most.

Accustomed to elite rule in the republic, a snobbish Charles Francis took one look at the new president and his plain wife, Mary Todd, and ran to his diary. "Neither of them," he wrote, "is at home in this sphere of civilization." Nominated in March to serve as U.S. minister to the United Kingdom, the Governor, back in New England, returned to Washington to acknowledge his benefactor. Some years later Charles Francis Jr., privy to his father's private remembrances, recorded the strained interview between the Boston Brahmin and the prairie politician. His account stressed Lincoln's supposedly awkward and ungainly carriage before the poised Governor, whose education, experience, and patrimony, the younger Charles suggested, deserved a better reception then they received:

Presently a door opened, and a tall, large-featured, shabbily dressed man, of uncouth appearance, slouched into the room. His much-kneed, ill-fitting trousers, coarse stockings, and worn slippers at once caught the eye. He seemed generally ill at ease, — in manner, constrained and shy. The secretary [Seward] introduced the minister [Charles Francis] to the President, and the appointee of the last proceeded to make the usual conventional remarks, expressive of obligation, and his hope that the confidence implied in the appointment he had received might not prove to have been misplaced. They had all by this time taken chairs; and the tall man listened in silent abstraction. When Mr. Adams had finished, — and he did not take long, — the tall man remarked in an indifferent, careless way that the appointment in question had not been his, but was due to the secretary of state, and that it was to "Governor Seward" rather than to himself that Mr. Adams should express any sense of obligation he might feel; then, stretching out his legs before him, he said, with an air of great relief as he swung his long arms to his head: — "Well, governor, I've this morning decided that Chicago post-office appointment." Mr. Adams and the nation's foreign policy were dismissed together![11]

Appropriating the family view, Henry thought Lincoln clumsy, rustic, and decidedly too western. The Harvard in him scorned what he called the "stump oratory" and crabbed education that he associated with Ohio Valley politicians. Seeing Lincoln only once, at the Inaugural Ball, he scored the sixteenth president as anxious, overmatched, and lacking in "apparent force," nervously clasping at his "white kid gloves." The future of the republic seemed to Henry a very uncertain thing that evening. By the end of the war, however, he had come to appreciate Lincoln as a vigorous and resolute leader — an attitude subsequently embellished by his deep friendship with John Hay, Lincoln's private secretary and biographer. "Had young Adams been told that his life was to hang on the correctness of his estimate of the new President," Henry later admitted, "he would have lost."[12]

A few weeks after Lincoln's inaugural, Charles Francis, duly confirmed by the Senate, boarded the *Niagara* at East Boston and along with Abigail and their three youngest children, Henry, sixteen-year-old Mary, and twelve-year-old Brooks, steamed to England. The increasingly indispensable Henry retained his role as private secretary. Like his ancestors who had served their country in an age rocked by revolutions, the fortunes of war and diplomacy now moved him far from home. Not long returned from his European travels, he again crossed the Atlantic, and would not cross again for seven long years.

9
LONDON

Charles Francis must have wondered what the London appointment meant for his future. Reelected to a secure House seat just a few months earlier, he might conceivably have remained in Congress, served its Republican majority with distinction, and risen in its ranks. The diplomatic post, however, also suggested a perfectly respectable path to higher office. No fewer than five American ministers to the Court of St. James's, including two Adamses, had subsequently captured the presidency. The Governor's fortunes, in any case, were much on Henry's mind. His correspondence with Charles, now in the army and quartered on Castle Island in Boston Harbor, indicates a shared scrutiny of their father's prospects, a natural curiosity considering that the older man's reputation and connections might well determine their own.

On the very May day the Adamses arrived in London, Queen Victoria issued a proclamation of neutrality "between the . . . contending parties" that cautiously recognized the belligerent rights of "certain States styling themselves the Confederate States of America." Henry and his father probably learned of the Queen's actions the following day as they breakfasted and perused the city's newspapers from their rooms at Maurigy's Hotel.[1] Combined with the Confederates' bombardment of Fort Sumter near Charleston, South Carolina, in early April and the Second French Empire's ensuing issuance of its own neutrality declaration in June, Charles Francis's role quickly narrowed to a single supreme aim: preventing England from extending recognition to the Confederate nation. If that happened he might be instructed by the Lincoln government to break diplomatic relations with London, a move likely to lead to hostilities. In short, the outcome of the war between rival republican armies in North America depended not merely upon soldiers and generals but on the adroitness with which Charles Francis, suddenly the country's most vital diplomat, serving in its most crucial diplomatic post, conducted his affairs.

In working to prevent Britain from recognizing the Confederate government, the Governor sought to keep both an old and a new threat to the United States from making common cause. This proved immensely difficult during the first year and a half of the war as the cautious Palmerston ministry in London inched toward intervention. The sympathy often expressed by Britain's governing classes for the southern slaveholding oligarchy indicated, to both Charles Francis and Henry, its fundamental and long-standing contempt for representative government. In some ways it must have struck both men as a revisitation of earlier Anglo-American conflicts — the Revolution of 1776 and the War of 1812 — in which the emerging strength of New World democracy threatened the staying power of Old World aristocracy. Henry's enmity easily fixated on Britain, with its unsinkable navy and its bullying colonial system, as a familiar, traditional foe. "Young Adams," he wrote years later, "neither hated nor wanted to kill his friends the rebels, while he wanted nothing so much as to wipe England off the earth."[2]

Henry's resentment may perhaps be further understood as a shadowy extension of his embarrassed inability to ease his way into polite English society. How many times had he arrived at late evening balls in his best dress only to be indifferently announced, dully received, and duly cut adrift into the greater pell-mell, to linger conversationless for a few humiliating hours until slipping away unnoticed? Exasperated, he described these occasions as "beastly repulsive" and

129

"solemn stupid crushes." He thought them mere "matters of necessity" among London's elite, simply "one of the duties of life" and thus lacking "the gaiety of our balls" in America. Neither did he appreciate having to shell out "upwards of $200.00" — some $5,500 in current dollars — for a sober Court suit. Accustomed at home to the privileges of a sparkling pedigree, Henry discovered in his new environment that his name counted for very little. "London society is so vast," he complained to Charles, "that the oldest habitués know only their own sets, and never trouble themselves even to look at anyone else."[3] Something of a practiced snob, Henry realized in London what *real* snobs were and felt unusually common in its immense, intricate, and capricious hierarchy.

His discontent with English society almost certainly had something additionally to do with his awkward invisibility before its women. As in Germany, he seemed unable to enter into light, playful, flirtatious situations — a limitation suggested in the way he habitually intellectualized problems and analyzed personalities. He inclined to dissect first and indulge afterward. "From the educational point of view," he later wrote of this period, the women of London "could give nothing until they approached forty years old. Then they became very interesting — very charming, — to the man of fifty. The young

American was not worth the young English-woman's notice, and never received it."[4]

Henry's mood in London only darkened after learning that a Union Army under Brig. Gen. Irvin McDowell suffered a humiliating defeat in late July at the Battle of Bull Run in Fairfax County, Virginia. The largest and costliest contest in American history to this time — the engagement featured some thirty-six thousand poorly trained and in some instances badly led troops — demonstrated the Confederacy's ability to sustain an army in the field and to protect its government. Suddenly it seemed possible, perhaps even likely, that hostilities might last for months if not years. "If this happens again," Henry wrote shortly after the battle, "farewell to our country for many a day."[5]

Unsure of his still vaguely defined role as the Governor's private secretary and eager — so he supposed — to enter the fight, Henry implored Charles to secure him a commission. "I am the youngest and the most independent of all others," he wrote his brother, "and I claim the right to go as younger son if on no other grounds." But Henry's moods waxed hot and cold during this anxious period, and just a month later he asked Charles to ignore his earlier note. Now he thought it entirely likely that the Lincoln government, with evidence that the British consul at Charleston had quietly conducted negotiations with the Confederacy, might threaten to make war on Britain, and that possibility amplified the importance of the American minister's position. The pace at the Court soon picked up and along with it Henry's spirits. "I am," he then beamed to his brother, "absolutely necessary here."[6]

While working closely with the Governor, Henry assumed a growing role in the American legation, and this caused no little irritation on the part of Benjamin Moran, a career official stationed at the embassy since 1853. Eighteen years Henry's senior, Moran thought the young man little more than a well-petted arriviste. In February 1863 several English cities sent addresses to the American delegation supporting Lincoln's Emancipation Proclamation, which had declared the freedom of "all persons held as slaves" within rebellious states, excepting those areas already under northern control. Believing that the embassy's old hands should have acknowledged the communiqués, Moran fumed when they were given to Henry. "It is quite evident that Mr. Adams has determined to push his son to the front whenever he can," he informed his journal, "and this is the first open move. The boy has no business to do these things and Mr. Adams knows it." Moran goes on in the diary to detail with some unfiltered acerbity Henry's constant "meddling" into the delegation's affairs, calling him "pompous" and "assuming" and insisting that if "there is much discontent [in the embassy] . . . it all comes from [the minister] having his son here."[7]

Not above belittling Henry's evident social aspirations, Moran gaily noted his adversary's embarrassment when uninvited to a London city ball in honor of the Prince of Wales. He described Henry as something of a sneering tourist who had misread the cordial hospitality extended to him by the city's elite and, having let his petty irritation show, now found himself understandably dropped. No doubt Moran had an axe to grind, and yet a perusal of Henry's correspondence at this time gives every indication that he struggled with competing impulses, finding himself both attracted to and wary of English aristocratic life. "The tone of people here is insufferable to me," he wrote Charles in early 1862. "I lose my temper, or get sulky, and as for pleasure, don't know what it is. How is one to make friends when friends are only ballroom acquaintances. Such friends bore me."[8]

But this rich, sprawling, and complex environment more favorably produced a thousand bright amenities that soon drew, after a fitful and uneven start, Henry's interest. Dining and concerts — a table at the Star and Garter, a convivial few hours at the Argyll Rooms — offered special opportunities to congregate among the city's elect and to measure one's progress. Adams shared crowded conversations with Charles Dickens and Robert Browning, met the narrative painter Edward Matthew Ward, and ran into the occasional exiled revolutionary — the French socialist Louis Blanc, for one. Reflecting on a particularly joyful spring 1863 gathering, he wrote Charles, "All were people of a stamp, you know; as different from the sky-blue, skim-milk of the ball-rooms, as good old burgundy is from syrup-lemonade. I had a royal evening; a feast of remarkable choiceness, for the meats were very excellent good, the wines were rare and plentiful, and the company was of earth's choicest."[9]

Such associations Adams embraced fully, freely, and perhaps a little naïvely. He enthused over a several-day stay at Cambridge ("It is astonishing what good fellows these gowned individuals may be, and how well they do live"), joined the small St. James's Club ("I have at last become a Club man"), and more generally took to a routine of sociable pleasures. He accompanied his sister Mary to Ascot "and did the races," made the acquaintance of numerous "stray Americans and stately English," and attended any number of balls, fêtes, and house parties. Vacations were opportunities for travel, and Henry, typically with his mother and junior siblings in tow, "did," over a number of

134

seasons, Scotland, Paris, Rome, and Baden-Baden. The first he disagreeably declared "too uniform in its repulsive bareness"; the last, an ancient spa town in southwestern Germany, he called "morally . . . delicious. The females one sees, are enough to make one's hair stand out in all directions."[10]

At its best, London's throbbing multiplicity gave Adams an attractive alternative to Boston, to lawyering, and to pragmatic America's suspicion of artistic aptitude and literary ambition. The city positively *moved.* Its insatiable appetite for urbanization absorbed neighboring boroughs, including Bromley and Sutton, Harrow and Havering; its railways spread about the countryside, and in 1863, during Henry's second London year, the first lines of its Underground — using gaslit wooden carriages to convey passengers by steam locomotives — opened. With some three million residents, London more than trebled the number of New Yorkers.

Amid all of this eclectic energy Adams's friendship with Charles Milnes Gaskell, a highly educated gentleman and Liberal Party politician, proved perhaps most instructive, most satisfying. Four years Henry's junior, Gaskell had read classics at Cambridge, moved easily among lettered circles, and, as one source notes, "took his place in the British liberal establishment with an ease and assurance that contrasted with the chanciness of American careers."[11] Adams appears to have instantly appreciated Gaskell — whom he met in 1863 at a breakfast given by Sir Henry Holland, formerly physician extraordinary to Queen Victoria — and the two began a warm friendship spanning a half-century. Their reunions sometimes transpired at Wenlock Abbey, a restored late fifteenth-century prior's house now the Gaskell family's Shropshire seat in the West Midlands. Henry reported to Charles of his first impressionable visit to the place:

Such a curious edifice I never saw. . . . I dined in a room where the Abbot or the Prior used to feast his guests; a hall on whose timber roof, and great oak rafters, the wood fire threw a red shadow forty feet above our heads. I slept in a room whose walls were all stone, three feet thick, with barred, square Gothic windows and diamond panes; and at my head a small oak door opened upon a winding staircase in the wall, long since closed up at the bottom, and whose purpose is lost.[12]

Recalling his entrée into the charming social world inhabited by "Carlo" (as he came to call Gaskell), Adams later described this period as "a golden time for me," one that "altered my whole life."[13]

136

■ ■ ■ ■

More than one-third of Henry's Harvard class fought in the Civil War, and there were sober moments in London when a guilty conscience gnawed upon the safely placed private secretary. In the early summer of 1863, with Grant's frustrated army stalled during a long siege at the gates of Vicksburg, Mississippi, and Lee's Confederates marching north into Pennsylvania, Henry lamented to Charles, "I am becoming more and more uneasy and discontented. It hardly seems consistent with self-respect in a man to turn his back upon all his friends and all his ambitions, during such a crisis as this, only for the sake of conducting his mother and sister to the opera."[14] But Henry's idle musings of military duty, let alone glory, were emotions of the moment. Despite the random pang of self-reproach, he had fallen in love with London, enjoyed its outstanding energy, and would have a difficult time readjusting to the comparatively unpolished American arena, let alone stumbling about the muggy Virginia wilderness in an ill-fitting blue flannel sack coat hoping very much not to be shot. He acknowledged all of this to Charles in a string of mocking exclamations:

Though I grumble at my position here and

want to go home, [I] feel at times that I don't know what I say, in making my complaints. I want to go into the army! to become a second lieutenant in an infantry regiment somewhere in the deserts of the South! I who for two years have lived a life of intellectual excitement, in the midst of the most concentrated society of the world, and who have become so accustomed to it that I should wither into nothing without it! Why, the thing's absurd! Even to retire to a provincial life in Boston would be an experiment that I dread to look forward to! But for me to go into the army is ridiculous![15]

No doubt Charles agreed with his brother's self-important self-assessment. Introverted, intellectual, and indoor-minded, Henry seemed well suited to the patient parlor game of diplomatic service. It strains the imagination to place him in Charles's position during these critical years, that of a cavalry officer commanding men and barking out orders. Even so, one might make a case that Henry's London years, for all of their "concentrated society" appeal, did the young man at least some small harm. He took, that is, perhaps too easily to British airs, snobberies, and social graces. The strong inborn sense of Boston-based superiority already in his possession only ossified during this period, hardening into a pronounced and not al-

138

together attractive facet of his personality.

Perhaps this is the reason why Charles, making his first tour of London in 1864 while on military leave, worried for Henry's future. The day after the brothers strolled about St. Paul's Cathedral and enjoyed "the excellent stout" at the Mitre Tavern, Charles, writing to a family friend in Boston, described Henry, whom he had not seen for three years, as "a very aged man. He is more changed than any of the rest of the family. . . . [He] philosophizes, and seeks the society of the profound and had better return to America as soon as my father can spare him."[16] Only in his late twenties, Henry had grown prematurely bald, his beard already graying, and Charles noted each change of face and feature. He seemed even more struck by his younger brother's fascination with the better sort, perhaps concerned that London had proven after all a corrupting influence, an emphatic temptation to simple Quincy's polite pieties.

10
THE CORRESPONDENT

The call of multiple missions — to aid the Governor, to commence a career, and to save war-torn America — gave form to Henry's English existence. As an Adams he naturally sought the knight's armor of a sufficiently sharpened pen. Invited by *New York Times* editor Henry Jarvis Raymond to serve as the paper's London correspondent, he tirelessly sent more than thirty dispatches across the Atlantic between June 1861 and January 1862. Because of his sensitive position as the private secretary–cum-son of the American minister, Henry concealed his dangerous authorship. The essays, emphasizing political and diplomatic affairs, typically carried generic titles — "American Topics in England," "American Questions in England," and "Matters at London" — that belied the strained nature of U.S.-British relations. Collectively they somewhat wishfully argued that liberal Britain, having emancipated its immense West Indies empire a generation earlier

(1833), must now support free labor in the United States. But as the first year of the war closed with southern armies as yet unsubdued, Henry grew increasingly disappointed in England's willingness to entertain the prospect of planter independence. "Neutrality in a struggle like this," he wrote in one provocative dispatch, "is a disgrace."[1]

Adams's seven-month run as a *Times* contributor ended abruptly after his name appeared in the byline of an independent piece — "A Visit to Manchester: Extracts from a Private Diary" — published in the December 16, 1861, *Boston Daily Courier.* Encouraged by Charles to "look into the cotton supply question . . . and try to persuade the English that our [Yankee] blockade [against southern shipping] is their interest," he had traveled north to Manchester, interviewing the city's textile barons but seeking more generally to register the working classes' support for the Union cause. In the article, however, a jejune Henry, only twenty-three, indulged in a rather gratuitous swipe at London, the glittering oasis so often indifferent to his existence. "It is still the fashion" in Manchester, he wrote, "for the hosts to see that their guests enjoy themselves," while in London "the guests shift for themselves, and a stranger had better depart at once so soon as he has looked at the family pictures."[2] He supposed this invidious comparison to be

141

anonymous, but the *Courier*'s editor, oblivious to the delicacies involved, artlessly blew his cover. London's journalists promptly filed their knives.

Most notably, a *London Times* editorial made sport of Henry, suggesting that the workings of a truly cosmopolitan society were as yet beyond his untutored acuity. Perhaps, the writer purred, if young Adams but "persevere[d] in frequenting *soirees* and admiring 'family pictures' " he might someday come to appreciate "the gay world of our metropolis." Outfoxed, Henry complained to Charles, "The Courier in putting my name to my 'Diary' has completely used me up. To my immense astonishment and dismay I found myself this morning sarsed through a whole column of the Times, and am laughed at by all England."[3] One wonders, however, if the "sarsed" diarist might have privately relished the attention — noticed at last, important enough to briefly be the object of a London editorialist's sarcasm.

For good measure, a few Americans piled on as well. Moran, his critic at the legation, delighted in the public drubbing: "We have had a little fun at his expense, and I have told him that it is not every boy . . . who can in 6 mos. residence here extort a leader from *The Times.*" More than a momentary humiliation, Henry feared that some inveterate scanner of English newspapers, sensitive to

142

language, might connect the author of the Manchester essay to the *New York Times* dispatches. Such a revelation would, he feared, compromise Charles Francis's London labors while forcing an awkward *père et fils* encounter — the Governor having known nothing of his son's moonlighting. "I have wholly changed my system," a reformed Henry anxiously assured his brother, "and having given up all direct communication with the public, am engaged in stretching my private correspondence as far as possible."[4] No more dispatches left London.

While writing for the *Times,* Henry's thoughts frequently turned to the question of emancipation in America. "I am an abolitionist," he imprecisely wrote Charles in October 1861, making no distinction between gradualists (his position) and immediatists (the position of Sumner and other radicals). "We must wait," he radiated a patrician smugness, "till the whole country has time to make the same advance that we have made within the last six months." Wildly overestimating the efficacy of Union military forces operating in the Chesapeake, he thought a "dispersed or captured . . . main southern army" in Virginia quite likely quite soon. But what then? — what to do with Virginia's slaves? He feared "a new explosion" between the sections if the "extreme abolitionists," as he called them, insisted on black freedom. "Emancipation," he told one correspondent, "cannot be instantaneous."[5]

In place of immediatism, Henry thought that the Lincoln government would do well, following military victory, to "found free colonies in the south," thus emulating the Port Royal Experiment in which thousands of former slaves worked the captured Sea Islands cotton plantations off the South Carolina coast. He envisioned a great colonizing wave of Yankee power and purpose somehow erasing the racial caste past. "The old soldiers with their grants of land, their families, their schools, churches and Northern energy," he wrote Charles in early 1862, would surely make "common cause with the negroes in gradually sapping the strength of the slave-holders." He believed that "year after year" the impact of "new industry and free institutions" linking "the Atlantic, the Gulf, the Mississippi and the Tennessee" promised to make slavery but a bitter memory: "and the old crime shall be expiated and the whole social system of the South reconstructed."[6] Never did he imagine — from a plush London lodging — the desperate years of battlefield campaigning to come or the brutal Jim Crowism that proved impervious to the grand plans of "Northern energy."

Beyond the practical implications of emancipation, another and seemingly more distant southern question captured Henry's attention while in London: the problematic narratives of John Smith (1580–1631). Soldier, explorer, and colonial governor, Smith, as every ten-year-old knew, helped establish Jamestown, the first permanent English settlement in North America. More than simply conducting an exercise in textual analysis, Adams took aim in his research at one of the South's original icons. To reduce Smith's reputation might vicariously diminish the status of all "cavaliers" who claimed him as a patriarch of sorts. The idea came to Henry after the Boston historian John Gorham Palfrey raised doubts about Smith's famous account of his rescue in 1608 by Pocahontas, daughter of Powhatan, a leader of the Algonquian-speaking Virginia Indians. Presumably the young princess threw herself between Smith, his head pressed down upon a stone, and a warrior about to club him to death in a ritual ceremony. Impressed, her father spared the lucky Englishman's life. After a few hours of research at the British Museum in October 1861, Henry began preparing a paper designed to demolish Smith's credibility — "the ancient liar," he called him. "I hardly know whether I ought not to be ashamed of myself for devoting myself to a literary toy like this, in these times," he wrote Palfrey, "when I ought to be helping or trying to help the great cause." But as a self-ascribed "social failure" unable to fire off any more dispatches to New York, he had time on his hands. "So perhaps the thing is excusable, especially as it is in some sort a flank, or rather a rear attack, on the Virginia aristocracy, who will be utterly graveled by it if it is successful."[7]

Henry sent a copy of the completed essay, "Captaine John Smith," to Palfrey in early 1863; due to authorial second thoughts it remained unpublished until, under Palfrey's prodding, appearing four years later in the *North American Review*. The piece, propagandistic in temper and intent, opens with a predictably deflating contrast: Smith is dismissed as a poor composite of the piratical line, a Sir Walter Raleigh redux "on a much lower level." Adams then launches into a comparison of Smith's memoir, *A True Relation by Captain John Smith* (1608), with his later study, *The Generall Historie of Virginia, New England, and the Summer Isles* (1624). It is in the second manuscript that Smith included the dramatic Pocahontas story, and its absence in the first history led Henry to reject it outright as a tall tale. His antisouthernisms come through in various pointed remarks — "Smith's character was always a matter of doubt," "his career in Virginia terminated disastrously" — and in a derisory

146

observation: "Families of the highest claim to merit trace their descent from the Emperor's daughter that saved the life of Captain John Smith." Presumably the members of these high-tidewater clans could connect their blood to the celebrated young Indian sovereign and her English husband, John Rolfe. Of course in attacking Smith's character and questioning Pocahontas's posterity, Henry more broadly undermined the founding article of southern history — the story of the noble "savages," the beautiful princess, and the brave Elizabethan adventurer — as a mere creation myth. Pocahontas's 1616 "visit to England," he insisted, "made her the most conspicuous figure in Virginia, and romantic incidents in her life were likely to be created, if they did not already exist, by the exercise of the popular imagination."[8]

Though Adams took an occasional slap at southern sensibilities while in London, he devoted far more of his time and energy to the study and criticism of America's representative form of government. In this endeavor his primary tutors included the slightly built French gentleman-scholar Alexis de Tocqueville (1805–1859), best remembered today for authoring the influential treatise *Democracy in America,* and the British philosopher John Stuart Mill (1806–1873), whom he once called "about the ablest man in England."

Writing to Charles in the spring of 1863, Henry described these theorists as "the two high priests of our faith." He agreed with their shared conviction that democratic societies require a small elite — primarily of the best educated — to add distinction, expertise, and tone. In Tocquevillian terms, the "best government is not that in which all have share, but that which is directed by the class of the highest principle and intellectual ambition."[9] No doubt Henry imagined himself a future elect in this select club. Something of a backward-looking faith, it harkened to the deferential politics once the bread and butter of the early American republic, when men like Washington, Adams, and Jefferson could count on being recognized and rewarded as the "better sort." The rise of a more inclusive democratic sprit, beginning in the 1810s with a rising suffrage in the new western states and running through the populistic age of Jackson, pointed to a shifting direction in statecraft that never sat well with Henry.

Like Tocqueville and Mill, Adams understood the emergence of large-scale democracies as an inevitable historical outcome. Accordingly, he read the American Civil War as positive proof that representative government's triumph over a pecking order of planters demonstrated the resilience and self-correcting nature of a people's republic.

Under proper guidance, he presumed, America might yet fulfill the promise of its Revolution. But this would necessitate the cultivation of a learned, disciplined, and disinterested civil service class that stood outside the ugly scrum of sectionalism, moneymaking, and partisanship. Henry put his finger on the problem when he wrote Charles, "What we want, my dear boy, is a *school.* We want a national set of young men like ourselves or better, to start new influences not only in politics, but in literature, in law, in society, and throughout the whole social organism of the country. A national school of our own generation." Existing cultural and educational institutions had failed to cultivate such an elite. Harvard proved too parochial, Washington too political, and New York too commercial. Henry sensed the impossibility of his plea when he acknowledged to Charles that such a school was precisely "what America has no power to create."[10]

Much influenced by the tenor of what he took to be London's aristocratic public-spiritedness, Henry drafted an article lamenting the lack of such patrician resolve in his native land. Titled "Men and Things in Washington" and published in the November 1869 *Nation,* it conveyed his disappointment that the American capital city remained, nearly seventy years into its existence, a sleepy, provincial, and altogether dull center of arts, letters, and society. One could find no satisfactory salons or clubs, no distinguished symphonies or theaters; the talk remained tenaciously political, and those who might conceivably raise the cultural conversation lingered about, dispersed and fragmented. Reaching desperately for a solution, Henry called for a kind of social congress, what he termed a "cosmopolitan club."[11] Left to itself, this lofty body of legislators and lawyers, diplomats and editors might quietly convene, screened from the public's prying eyes, and discreetly decide on what must be decided. Bankers, Irish bosses, and prairie politicians were welcome to wait outside. The article betrayed Adams's infatuation with the London civil-electoral elite while offering an indication that, like his aging mother, he too sometimes indulged in the luxury of a well-petted woe.

While Henry mused a little abstractly in the 1860s on the perils of representative government, the clock of history refused to stop. Grant's victories in Virginia, the assassination of Lincoln, and the collapse of the Confederacy remade America, though Adams experienced all of this only vicariously in the pages of *The Times*. He missed as well the rise of a new Trans-Mississippi West. The decade saw three new states, including Nevada and Nebraska, enter the Union, the

150

Alaska Purchase, and the emergence of Jesse James into a folk legend. In a Philadelphia factory, John B. Stetson began to make a fortune producing "Cowboy" hats; and in Wyoming women were granted the right to vote.

Even old Washington, so familiar to the Adams family, underwent a great change during the war years. Though still burdened by dirt roads and insufficient sanitation, the capital ceased to be a sleepy southern village. Its population, despite the exodus of many Confederate-minded, increased considerably in the 1860s, from 75,000 to over 130,000. "Washington is perfectly thronged with strangers," one recently transplanted Iowan noted during the war. "Every nook and corner is occupied with officers and their families, and with lookers-on at this swiftly moving Panorama of life."[12] The completion of the U.S. Capitol Building's iconic cast-iron dome in 1866, establishment of Howard University (conceived as a theological seminary for African Americans) the following year, and founding of the Corcoran Gallery of Art in 1869 suggested an evolving attitude in the nation's relationship to race and education, art and architecture. Such improvements, Adams may have appreciated, though they hardly offered hope for a "cosmopolitan club."

Henry's decided commitment to the declining patrician order is fully evident in a solicitous December 1869 letter to George Adams, his six-year-old nephew. In this playful communication, Henry promised to connect his young charge to the old Washington scene: "One of these days, when you are twelve or fourteen years old, and your mamma lets you travel . . . I will take you up to the Capitol where all the Senators and Judges are sitting in great rooms; and you shall call on the President and ask him how he likes it, and you shall go down to Mount Vernon and see where the great General Washington lived; and you shall know all the great people who are going to live when the time comes."[13] One hears clearly in this sentimental overture the echo of Henry's own boyhood journey to Washington in 1850. In that lost antebellum world he had met President Taylor, observed the "great people" entering and exiting the "great rooms," and soaked in an atmosphere thick with national and family history. But this type of personalized politics, one with all the fragrant redolence of a Quincy summer, no longer held court. It was an illusion that Adams gave up with great reluctance — and mourned long thereafter.

■ ■ ■ ■

ILLUSIONS

■ ■ ■ ■

Adams was young and easily deceived.
Henry Adams, 1907

11
GOING SOUTH, COMING HOME

On a sweltering July evening in 1868, Henry Adams entered New York Harbor aboard the Cunard steamer *China* from London. His altered appearance, conspicuously aged ("I am . . . very — very bald"), hinted at a broader attitude of adjustment.[1] Returning to the Old House in Quincy, he encountered a "colonial" setting suddenly juxtaposed against the metropolitan backdrop of his seven years overseas. Back home at last, the native discovered a country much challenged, much changed. Formerly obscure towns, hamlets, and crossroads, including Shiloh and Antietam, Gettysburg and Cold Harbor, were now enshrined in national memory; the country's conception of freedom had suddenly, radically enlarged with slavery's violent end; and the Old South's once powerful political voice no longer boomed through congressional corridors. Despite all that had passed, however, a post-Appomattox peace proved elusive. Fresh issues, rather, regarding

155

the educational, economic, and civil rights of the former slaves now took center stage. In a word, the southern states were undergoing Reconstruction, the long and incomplete effort to forge a new era of emancipation and industrialization under Republican rule.

Political moderates during the secessionist winter of 1860–61, the Adamses showed a similar restraint in advocating an easy reconciliation with the former Confederates. John Quincy, Henry's eldest brother and the occupant of a lower house seat in the Massachusetts legislature, conspicuously broke with the country's congressional radicals in the postwar period. For this apostasy the U.S. Senate rejected his pending appointment to the Boston Customs House in 1867. Arrogant and aggrieved, he switched party allegiances, becoming a Democrat — the party of Jefferson, Jackson, and much of the old planter elite. Over the next five years the Massachusetts Democratic Party conferred its gubernatorial nomination upon John Quincy five times (terms lasted only twelve months), and each year he went down to a predictable defeat. Possibly sensing a way to "respectfully" evade the kind of difficult political life endemic among his ancestry, "John," writes one historian, "wanted to lose." Like other Adamses — proud, certain, and sometimes sanctimonious — he seemed reconciled, even determined, so his daughter

156

Abigail later remembered, to break from majority opinion. "He was a lone wolf," she wrote, and switching to the Democratic Party, "however ill-advised, was very characteristic of his independent spirit."[2]

John's electoral struggles only underlined for Henry the House of Adams's chronic decline. The senior John Quincy had captured the presidency, his son occupied a more modest congressional seat, and now his namesake grandson failed repeatedly to win even a state race. These political reversals exemplified both the rise of popular politics in the republic and the wisdom — or rationalization — in Henry's insistence that as a third son and a Brooks, he need not master the dubious arts of glad-handing, stump speaking, or wire pulling. What, after all, was the point? Voters seemed disinclined, so he concluded, to recognize and reward talent, blindly ratifying the cynical strategies of party bosses to elevate party hacks. He thought it a far more attractive prospect to shape policy than to play politics. If unelectable, he still wished to have a say, and if Reconstruction failed to win his sympathy, other national issues, including the need for civil service reform — stressing proficiency over patronage when appointing government employees — most emphatically did.

Creating an "independent" civil sector class, Henry reasoned, promised to undermine partisanship's noxious power. Who could disagree that expertise, rather than blind loyalty to a faction, should decide who served and where? He seemed less aware of the obvious self-interest in recommending the maintenance of a meritocracy, for he, the beneficiary of Adams privilege, Brooks wealth, and a Harvard education, might expect to do reasonably well on any exam that any government office or agency happened to pass his way. Thus, by outpointing his peers, he might yet see a way to resurrect the Adams family's fortunes. If the family no longer commanded a national, or even, as John Quincy repeatedly demonstrated, a state constituency, perhaps it could avoid the electorate altogether as part of a unique American Mandarin class, above politics, above democracy.

Seeking national influence Henry, now thirty and having outgrown the provincial city of his youth, prepared to exit Boston. In vibrant Britain, he had made friends among the country's aristocratic liberals, discovered Tocqueville's and Mill's stimulating criticisms of representative government, and demonstrated a budding talent for historical research. A nebulous New England situation, by contrast, struck him as perfectly impossible. "Boston seemed to offer no market for educated labor," he later remembered. "A peculiar and perplexing amalgam Boston always was, and although it had changed much in ten years, it was not less perplexing. One no longer dined at two o'clock; one could no longer skate on Back Bay; one heard talk of Bostonians worth five millions or more as something not incredible. Yet the place seemed still simple, and less restless-minded than ever before."[3] Only one American city excited Henry, and that was Washington. His enthusiasm for the capital, awoken in childhood and abetted by family folklore, remained firmly in place. If no London, it did offer certain offsetting urbanities, including a front-row seat to national affairs and the promise of a more cosmopolitan social order than Boston's incestuous nest of bankers, lawyers, and professors. It included, finally, the added and certainly much appreciated virtue of harboring none of his kin. In a city that many Americans associated with one Adams or another, Henry would be on his own.

The not unrelated questions of occupation and ennui that prompted his Boston withdrawal had been building. Having given up on two deeply rooted paternal professions — law and international relations — he seemed at something of a loss to reconcile with his future. "Anyone who had held, during the four most difficult years of American diplomacy, a position at the centre of action," he once explained his refusal to consider a career

159

in the State Department, "could not beg a post of Secretary at Vienna or Madrid in order to bore himself doing nothing until the next President should do him the honor to turn him out."[4] No doubt Henry's financial independence, family connections, and quick intellect offered several possible paths, though the decision to become a writer and critic seems in retrospect inevitable. His Italian letters, Secession Winter articles, and London dispatches all pointed to something more autonomous and privately ambitious than a cozy but constraining sinecure in Boston — or in Bolivia.

By late September, less than three months after returning to America, Henry's plans to relocate to the capital were secure. On the 25th he wrote to Gaskell, "I am still here [in Quincy], waiting till the first frosts shall have made Washington habitable." Seventeen days later, he departed. Stopping off in New York he met William Evarts, recently appointed U.S. attorney general and, like Henry, the progeny of an old patriot. For a few weeks in the early summer of 1776 Evarts's grandfather, the Connecticut statesman Roger Sherman, had served with John Adams, Benjamin Franklin, Thomas Jefferson, and Robert R. Livingston on the Committee of Five assigned to draft the Declaration of Independence. Making a more modest kind of history, Evarts was Andrew Johnson's chief counsel during the recent (March–May) impeachment trial in which the president survived, by a single vote, charges of obstructing the War Department's attempts to carry out various Reconstruction programs in the southern states. Henry thought him "a great man" for "saving the President."[5]

In Washington, Adams stayed briefly at Evarts's home, during which time the attorney general took his guest to meet Johnson, "who," Henry wrote Gaskell, "was grave, and cordial, and gave me a little lecture on Constitutional law." Adams also rekindled an old family friendship during his early days in the capital by visiting William Seward, now in his final months heading the State Department. Anticipating that the autumn elections would usher in a new generation of Republican power brokers, men shaped by the realities of war and Reconstruction, Henry recognized the cessation of his father's political influence and, more broadly, whatever attenuated White House connections his people still possessed. "This whole cabinet goes out on the 4th of March," he told Gaskell, "and in the next one I shall probably be without a friend."[6]

Bidding Evarts adieu, Henry moved on to the house of his aunt Mary Catherine Hellen Adams. This constituted but a brief stay, a question of propriety rather than budgetary convenience. In November, having made arrangements to contribute to the *Nation* and the *New York Post,* Henry informed the London barrister Ralph Palmer of his "full determination to make Washington [his] home," while disclosing to Gaskell both pride in his escape — "The great step is taken" — and the hope that after a decade of drifting, he had encamped at last: "Here I am, settled for years, and perhaps for life."[7] And so, given an interlude or two, he was. Over most of the next half-century, until his death in 1918, Adams enjoyed the social energy and proximity to power offered in the growing American seat of government. If not London, it nevertheless attracted a richer and more eclectic range of minds, opinions, and politics than Boston's inevitable inbreeding permitted. It might further be the case that in coming to the capital city he wished to resume an indelible family fiefdom. Washington retained for Henry both the magic of his first visit and the inviting idea that if Adamses could no longer capture elections, they might yet find a path to appointed success in a city built, in some small sense, upon their talents. In going south, he unquestionably advertised himself as an available man, open to assuming his share.

12
THE RACE QUESTION

As Adams arrived in Washington in the autumn of 1868, a new form of racial hierarchy, eager to overturn emancipation, took hold in the South. A series of recently passed black codes sought to regulate the movement, labor, and behavior of African Americans; newly enacted convict laws, selectively applied to blacks, permitted prisoners to be hired out to local farmers and private companies. "The Codes spoke for themselves," W. E. B. Du Bois later wrote. "No open-minded student can read them without being convinced they meant nothing more nor less than slavery in daily toil."[1] Republicans responded to the codes with constitutional amendments securing the freedom and citizenship of the former slaves and by passing a series of Enforcement Acts (known also as the Ku Klux Klan Acts) in 1870 and 1871, which punished efforts to interfere with voting and made the infringement of civil rights a federal crime. Accordingly, President Ulysses S. Grant suspended the writ of habeas corpus in nine South Carolina counties affected by Klan violence and sent in federal troops and marshals. Though Klan power declined throughout the South, the region's whites remained opposed to black equality.

Such vital federal oversight on the questions of race and reunion ultimately proved ephemeral. The 1877 removal of the last occupation troops in the South — "Redemption" to the unreconstructed — coincided with the creation of a caste system sanctioned by poll taxes and literacy tests, sharecropping and tenant farming. Jim Crow — the assemblage of state and local statutes designed to legitimize racial segregation — became the law of the land. In its name, nearly three thousand blacks were lynched in America between 1885 and 1915.[2]

To Henry, the newly freed peoples, like the Civil War battles he had read about in Britain, were little more than abstractions; he thus innocently insisted that the nation's constitutional system, which offered scant direction and no precedent on bringing states back into the Union, be respected. In effect, this meant no congressional Reconstruction, radical or otherwise. He thus joined his father and older brothers in warming to the attractively besieged Andrew Johnson, like them a quixotic outlier in the either/or partisan pattern. Elevated to the presidency upon Lincoln's

164

death, Johnson, direct in manner, blunt in opinion, and intolerant of others' views, was a Tennessee Democrat utterly at odds with the radical Republican agenda. His list of (congressionally overturned) vetoes included the Freedmen's Bureau Bill, the Civil Rights Bill of 1866, and the First, Second, and Third Military Reconstruction Acts. Combined, these crucial legislative achievements extended federal assistance to the freed peoples, defined citizenship to include African Americans, and established the requirements by which Rebel states could reenter the Union. Not insignificantly, this pivotal reordering of American law enlarged appreciably the powers of the central government.

Taking a strict constructionist line, the Adamses joined Johnson in looking to the South to restore itself. For a while Charles Francis doubted even the legality of slavery's elimination. Though he believed black bondage an obvious evil, he pedantically questioned Lincoln's presidential powers to end the institution. Having spent the terrible war years overseas, he appeared upon his return punctilious, tone deaf, and unable to grasp the great and permanent changes brought about by the conflict. Writing shortly after the war to the Massachusetts lawyer Richard Henry Dana, author of the popular memoir *Two Years before the Mast,* he raised serious doubts about the Emancipation Proclamation's juridical standing and Congress's right to determine the fate of the defeated Confederate states: "The President's proclamation as well as most of the plans of reconstruction of the state authorities which were offered in Congress seem to me to rest upon a mistaken idea of the powers vested by the Constitution. As President, Mr. Lincoln unquestionably had no power to emancipate a single slave. Neither had Congress the smallest right in my mind to meddle with the reconstruction of a single state."[3] Such an idle, inert response on the Governor's part to southern secession and the futures of some four million former slaves lacked verve, courage, and imagination. Shamelessly stubborn, it conformed, rather, to the by now cast-off compromise politics of the not so distant past.

The Adamses' irrelevance in Washington almost certainly abetted Henry's decision to position himself as a political critic. "When I think of the [Reconstruction] legislation," he wrote to Charles, "my blood boils," and he promised Gaskell that even though the Governor and his sons were now on the outside looking in, they "mean[t] to be seen and be heard."[4] What seems to be most conspicuously lacking from the Quincy perspective is simple compassion. To a man, the Adamses appeared curiously incapable of recognizing the humanity of the former slaves. Their sympathies and energies, rather, were invested

166

in "defending" the Constitution from presidential emancipation and "extra-legal" congressional legislation affirming African American citizenship and equal protection under the law. At bottom, and for all their education, erudition, and reputation as men committed to liberty, they lacked the moral vision to grow beyond their now dated prewar principles. In effect, they were championing an older interpretation of the Constitution, one that had allowed the southern planter class to pilot the Union for the three generations bookended by the elections of Jefferson (1800) and Lincoln (1860). But in destroying such southern articles of faith as the Three-Fifths Compromise (by counting slaves for purposes of representation, the South received additional congressional seats and electoral votes), the Fugitive Slave Law (requiring northern participation in the capture of runaways), and the *Dred Scott* decision (the infamous 1857 Supreme Court case that denied both black citizenship and Congress's capacity to keep slavery out of the nation's territories), the Civil War had also destroyed *that* Constitution and given rise to another, codified in the passage of three freedom-enlarging amendments between 1865 and 1870.

Ironically, many scholars today remember Adams as a remarkably capacious historian, one comfortable gauging the grand sweep of time from the medieval Virgin to the modern dynamo. Yet on the race question he made far too little of slavery's corrosive and all-pervading impact on America. Lincoln, by contrast, acknowledged with a sharp clarity the country's immeasurable involvement — economically, spiritually, and psychologically — in slavery and had warned his fellow citizens on the occasion of his second inaugural in March 1865 that they were now most assuredly settling with the cosmic order for centuries of injustice: "Yet, if God wills that [the war] continue, until all the wealth piled by the bond-man's two hundred and fifty years of unrequited toil shall be sunk, and until every drop of blood drawn with the lash, shall be paid by another drawn with the sword, as was said three thousand years ago, so still it must be said 'the judgments of the Lord, are true and righteous altogether.' "[5] Adams's far narrower outlook reduced slavery to a repercussion-less fact, a wicked act now mercifully ended. It lacked a living, concerned realization of tragedy.

Henry's inability to read congressional Reconstruction as a moral struggle rather than a political blunder testified to a deeper private indifference in regard to race. While still in London, he mused somewhat crudely over the prospects of Africans in America. "I fancy white is better breeding stock," he wrote Charles. "I doubt about black states."[6]

168

Returning to America after the war, he adopted a distinctly negative attitude to the proposed Fifteenth Amendment, which excluded "race, color, or previous condition of servitude" as categories for denying black men the ballot. He coolly dismissed the Amendment as having "small practical value" and showed a greater concern that Congress might overstep its powers while applying the law. No doubt much of Henry's myopic outlook on race can be chalked up to the composite workings of an ingrained elitism nurtured in the precincts of presidents, the dining halls of Harvard, and the country houses of England. Reconstruction's challenge to the vanishing old republic attracted him as last stands had always attracted Adamses — he thought himself contesting yet another errant majority.

It should further be remembered that, like his father, Henry experienced the war as a spectator, rendering, to be sure, an important service in London, yet fundamentally away from the fray. His fanciful 1868 letter to the British merchant banker Thomas Baring (whose elegant Upper Grosvenor Street dinners he enjoyed), claiming, "The southern States promise soon to be richer than ever and the questions resulting from the war are practically settled," exhibited an astonishing lack of awareness.[7] His equally starry-eyed vision of the overmatched Johnson "saving" the Constitution as a white-led biracial South moved promptly toward prosperity showed a fundamental inability to grasp the complexities of the Reconstruction process — not to mention the formidable and deeply entrenched power of racism. Henry's long London detour had done little to shake his settled Victorian attitudes.

In sum, he seemed certain that, left on their own, northern and southern leaders might yet arrive at a gentlemen's agreement on the vital issues that divided them, though this is precisely what they had failed to do in either the contentious Secession Winter of 1860–61 or the anxious war years that followed. He thus underestimated the degree, rapidity, and ferocity to which the white South had begun to reassert its control in a dawning age of postwar apartheid. Eager while in London to dismantle the Pocahontas myth, Henry now harbored a new delusion. For in denying the concerns of radical Republicans, he paradoxically affirmed a fresh southern self-image — that of a virtuous people unfairly subjugated by a combination of Yankee carpetbaggers, black congressmen, and unscrupulous scalawags. Such problematic opinions left him ill prepared to take on the reform agenda for which he went to Washington. Principally interested in the Herculean task of cleaning out the congressional Augean stables, to free, that is, the national legislature from the cor-

rupting influence of corporations and lobbyists, he failed to appreciate the problem of
race in America with any urgency, insight, or
empathy.[8]

13
WAITING ON ANOTHER
WASHINGTON

Long before the Civil War, the idea of elite-
born rule had ceased to stir American politics.
Weaned on a diet of Vox Populi, Vox Dei
("The voice of the people is the voice of
God"), several millions came by the 1820s to
embrace the idea of common man democracy. In company with a host of
Reconstruction-era Brahmin reformers,
Henry hoped to arrest this egalitarian trend.
The recent war exposed, so he believed, the
inherent perils of popular partisanship as two
"extremist" groups — the southern plantocracy and northern abolitionism — came to
dominate the political landscape with devastating results. In coming to Washington, Adams determined to make the case for the
country's haute bourgeoisie as a hedge
against the next gathering storm of special
interests. Its patriotic pedigree, educational
advantages, and cultivated sense of civic
responsibility promised to transcend narrow
regional, economic, and ideological concerns

encased in one-sided party planks. He knew, however, that the patricians faced an uphill and perhaps insurmountable struggle. America's growing suffrage prompted a type of professional electioneering and vote begging that easily eclipsed the comparatively minor-key canvassing of Jackson's day. Public policy, rather, now moved to the beat of the urban bosses and their patronage-as-usual politics.[1]

In several of the nation's larger metropolitan areas, including Boston and Chicago, Cleveland and Kansas City, the great machines dominated daily affairs. New York's Tammany Hall, once governed by the notorious William "Boss" Tweed, controlled immense assets in money and jobs, housing and administration; the investigative journalist Lincoln Steffens, author of *The Shame of the Cities,* a 1904 exposé of municipal government malfeasance, famously called Philadelphia's Republican faction "the most corrupt and the most contented" in the country.[2] While it is true, as Adams duly noted, that these organizations engaged in graft as well as more inventive forms of criminality, they also (in exchange for loyalty at the polls) supported immigrants, helped cut through ribbons of bureaucratic red tape, and aided often poorly structured city governments. They were shady but efficient, autocratic but responsive.

Henry, of course, hoped to see them

173

doomed, anticipating in their demise the rise of a partisan-free civil service corps and an independent president. For a brief period in the winter of 1868–69 he thought the great patriot king of the past, George Washington, might be approximated in the whiskered visage of Ulysses S. Grant, the latest in a not so small line — five at the time, including Jackson, Harrison, and Taylor — of American army generals to occupy the White House. Smitten by Grant's successful turn defeating the secessionists and eager to believe that a military man might share the patricians' contempt for political parties, Henry thought the republic soon to be in capable hands. Arriving in Washington just weeks before Grant captured the presidency, he indulged in a romantic sense of shared destiny. Years later he wrote of his — and what he somewhat dubiously described as the nation's — hope for a golden Grant era:

At least four-fifths of the American people, — Adams among the rest, — had united in the election of General Grant to the Presidency, and probably had been more or less affected in their choice by the parallel they felt between Grant and Washington. Nothing could be more obvious. Grant represented order. He was a great soldier, and the soldier always represented order. He might be as partisan as he pleased, but a

General who had organised and commanded half a million or a million men in the field, must know how to administer.

With characteristic morbidity, Henry concluded this retrospective account of his initial dip into presidential politics with the double-damning line, puncturing both himself and Grant, "Adams was young and easily deceived."[3]

The general proved human after all, presiding, despite his own personal integrity, over a scandal-ridden administration that mirrored the new era's growing reputation for plunder, spoils, and shakedowns. Its more conspicuous examples include the Whiskey Ring (a conspiracy of distillers to bribe government officials and to defraud the government of excise taxes on alcohol), the Crédit Mobilier scandal (government officials accepted payoffs from a construction company building part of the first transcontinental railroad), and the Belknap bribery (Secretary of War William Belknap collected kickbacks for licenses to sell supplies on Indian lands). Other instances of corruption occurred in various federal departments, resulting in a broad if somewhat amorphous cry for reform.

Henry's mature observations of Grant contain all the scorn of a betrayed lover embarrassed by his former infatuation. He designated the general in the *Education* as

175

"pre-intellectual, archaic," and more primitive than "the cave-dwellers." Sporting with Darwin, and his own callow conflation of war heroes, Henry insisted that the sharply *descending* line linking the great Washington to the assuredly less than great Grant made ridiculous any suggestion of executive evolution. And for several decades scholars more or less agreed, ranking the general in one presidential poll after another near the bottom of the bottom. The making of Lost Cause mythology (celebrating the Confederacy's cause as heroic), the deification of Gen. Robert E. Lee, and the Redemption of the white South from northern occupation armies contributed to a long-standing tendency to downgrade the eighteenth president. The historiography of our own day, however, influenced by the long civil rights movement, has offered a far more positive interpretation of Grant, emphasizing his efforts to defend black rights in the South.[4] But this is a contemporary consensus. Deferring to his cultural education and constitutional scruples, Henry, as noted, could muster only indifference to the situation of the newly freed peoples, and this negatively impacted his view of Grant, whose efforts to enforce the Reconstruction revolution in southern states he sometimes criticized.

It was Grant's willingness to play the partisan game, however, to defer to the interests and the bosses, that really broke Henry's heart. Adams had looked to the general to tame the Senate (having dangerously overreached, he claimed, in its efforts to remove Johnson from office), rein in the emerging postwar money power (southern agrarianism no longer in vogue), and more generally model for the country a spirit of public service and high-mindedness. None of this happened. Adhering to the realities of American electoral politics, Grant's cabinet predictably included its share of political appointees. "It is the old régime," Henry fumed to Charles shortly after the new administration took power in March. The following month he unleashed his disappointment in "The Session," a stinging but very able essay that appeared in the *North American Review.* It detailed the previous December's assembly of the Fortieth U.S. Congress, while more widely expressing its author's doubts about the government's failure to move the nation forward. Inspired by Lord Robert Cecil's "review of politics" articles in the *London Quarterly,* Henry sought to elevate the quality of American political discourse, primarily by exposing its present deficiencies. He argued that several key issues, including Reconstruction, revenue and monetary reform, and the restoration of presidential power, demanded address, only to receive, as he put it, "superficial attention." In a provocative censure of democratic politics he observed, without a trace of irony, "The system itself is at fault."[5]

Most emphatically, the evident need for financial reform captured Adams's attention. As the growing nation's money supply remained constrained in the postwar period, major creditors did well, for this increased the value of their every precious dollar. Debtors, by contrast, were obviously injured by the lack of cash. In the not too distant future the Greenback (1874–89) and Populist parties (1891–1908), two debtor-oriented coalitions, would put the currency question near the forefront of American elections. Henry identified the northern plutocracy — the creditor class — as the new driving force behind national policy, in effect replacing the old southern gentry. Thus, his observation to the Boston economist Edward Atkinson that "the whole root of the evil is in *political* corruption" stressed big money's power to purchase public policy. This he thought it did altogether effectively, and he held out little hope that the patricians might manage Wall Street's rising titans. "Our coming struggle is going to be harder than the anti-slavery fight," he predicted. "I fear we shall be beaten on the wider field."[6]

The solution to the currency question, and so many other challenges, seemed obvious to Henry: the country must learn to elevate the "right" men to office. Condemning mere

politicians, he argued that an attentive electorate could always replace spoilsmen with
men of high character and expertise. His appeal clearly bristled with self-interest: "To
conduct the Government without the aid of
trained statesmen is as dangerous as to
conduct a war without the aid of trained
generals." Presumably Harvard '58 and the
like were waiting in the wings. But just how
such competent men were to overcome the
marching orders of national parties he left an
open and perhaps unanswerable question. A
host of interests or "rings," he conceded,
dominated Congress and were alert to the
wishes and winks of various railroad, whiskey,
and iron barons. All depended on reducing
the power of the parties, for that would
reduce the power of their paymasters. And
yet most Americans, as Henry knew, identified closely with the country's partisan
culture; turnout in presidential elections averaged nearly 80 percent during this period.
Raised on Quincy's Old House homilies, he
seemed unable to appreciate why this was so
— why, say, former slaves and Union Army
veterans so uncritically embraced the Republican Party and urban-based immigrants so
often supported Democrats. Thus, when he
wrote, "The system of protecting special
interests should be reformed," he failed to
reckon that many Americans were willing to
accept a certain surplus of commonplace cor-

ruption as long as their own concerns were among the protected. They, of course, had precious little privilege to fall back upon.[7] He seemed further to have never entertained the idea that the Brahmins themselves constituted a kind of special interest.

Despite its author's caste-bound shortcomings, however, "The Session" offered an intelligent if unsparing critique of contemporary political life. It not unfairly admonished the "curiously ill-informed" public, the shrewd capitalists who pocketed politicians, and, of course, the quite-willing-to-be-bought politicians themselves. In demanding good government, Henry might be said to have anticipated the Progressive reformers of a later generation (1890–1920), including the socialist Eugene Debs and the social worker Jane Addams, who were also disturbed by the power of money in politics. But this putative connection, if suggestive, is also imperfect. The eclectic Progressives — muckrakers and modernizers, social scientists and suffragists — tended to believe that *more* democracy meant better governance and worked for the Sixteenth, Seventeenth, and Nineteenth Amendments which, by allowing for the taxation of the highest incomes, the popular election of U.S. senators, and "votes for women," provided the framework for a more egalitarian century.

Henry, as noted, thought the republic safest when governed by fewer hands — those presumably belonging to the men thumbing through his essay. "For once," he wrote to Gaskell shortly after "The Session" appeared, "I have smashed things generally and really exercised a distinct influence on public opinion by acting on the limited number of cultivated minds."[8] And to be sure, some among the would-be meritocracy took notice. The *Nation* called "The Session" "statesmanlike," while Samuel Bowles, an old ally of the Governor's and editor of the *Springfield Republican,* predicted a bright future for its young author:

Among the officers of the new "Reform League" at Boston may be found the names of three Adamses — all sons of the late Minister to England, and great-grandsons of the second president of the United States. Two of these names are well known to the people of the country, both in the present and the past generations, — John Quincy Adams and Charles Francis Adams. But the third — Henry Brooks Adams — designates a young gentleman who has quite as good a chance of becoming prominent in the future politics of the country as either of his brothers, although he is yet but little known. . . . The fruit of his winter's studies in Washington now appears in the April *North American* — a long and brilliant paper

181

on "The Session," in which, with some conceit and some pedantry, but with more ability than either, he reviews the doings and omissions of the last session of the Fortieth Congress.[9]

Bowles's generous editorial made for Henry a pleasant period of possibilities. Just removed to Washington and already the talk of the town, he might have fairly considered himself a coming man among the men who mattered. Anticipating another "Session" and perhaps still another, he sought to make the format a formula for authority. In fact, just what little clout he actually carried soon became apparent.

With the onset of "Grantism" — an acidic shorthand coined by Sumner in 1872 and broadly appropriated to construe the era's cronyism and political corruption — Henry saw the extent of his illusions. Though greatly disappointed by the new administration, the arch-contrarian in him rather enjoyed being on the outside looking in. It felt like home. Thus, when he wrote to a friend, "My family is buried politically beyond recovery for years. I am becoming more and more isolated," he predictably finished the thought on a defiant note: "But I rather like all this, for no one can touch me and I have asked nothing of any living person."[10]

Rather than a private cri de coeur, however,

Henry's conspicuous independence and wishful plans for a rule-by-the-better-sort republic telescoped the aspirations of an entire class of liberal Victorian reformers. Its members — including the author George William Curtis, the poet James Russell Lowell, and the art historian Charles Eliot Norton — were raised in the Unitarian persuasion, spoke New-Englandese, and sought to upend the boss-and-party system. Together they occupied a shrinking stage. From the vantage of the 1890s, E. L. Godkin, editor in chief of the *New York Evening Post,* a reform mouthpiece that Henry once contributed to financially, looked back upon Grantism's victory with a cutting candor. "When I think of what I hoped from America forty years ago, and see what is coming," he wrote Norton, "I see that we all expected far too much of the human race. What stuff we used to talk!"[11]

Henry too liked to talk, and though long attracted to the idea of civil service reform, he never committed himself to the practical business of trying to bring it about. Belonging even to a minority faction aroused in him a palpable unease. His family's prized political autonomy merged with an innate distrust that expected the rough game of modern partisanship to be carried by influence peddlers and crowd pleasers. To fail in such a rigged arena, in other words, held certain charms. It confirmed for Henry the problematic nature of unwieldy democracies, excused the House of Adams's ebbing influence, and suggested the neglect of those talented but superfluous and no longer quite so young men idling about in the better Washington, London, and Paris hotels. Understanding well his own discounted value in the land of Grant, he seemed almost eager to mock the shambling political system and to heap scorn upon those who made it pay. In a gesture to be repeated many times over the years, Henry reached confidently for the martyr's cross. "But my opinions and dislike for things in general will probably make my career a failure so far as any public distinction goes," he wrote to Gaskell in the summer of 1869, "and I am contented to have it so."[12]

14
THE HIGH ROAD TO REFORM

Despite Henry's occasional bouts of occupational uncertainty, the success of "The Session" illustrated its author's growing reputation as a pundit or even, as might be said today, a public intellectual — a fresh profession in America. There were distinguished historians (the Boston products George Bancroft and Francis Parkman, author of *The Oregon Trail,* stood out), a few unbuttoned voices (Bret Harte and Mark Twain come to mind), and a sage or two (Emerson most notably), but scribbling about political affairs, unless done in the routine of journalese, hardly counted as a career. And for Henry, having turned thirty-one in February 1869, the month before Grant took office, the career question loomed large. He never dropped completely the idea of government service, almost a mechanical reaction for an Adams, but recognized that life as a lowly congressman held no appeal, particularly when men he considered far inferior to himself — party managers, industrialists, and financiers — wielded power. Better, he believed, to educate and influence such men than to merely serve them. But could such a situation be fashioned? "I should be . . . pleased if I could only find out what I myself wanted," he wrote to Gaskell that July. "Certainly not office, for except very high office I would take none. What then? I wish some one would tell me."[1]

The answer, in fact, was becoming increasingly obvious. While summering in Quincy, Henry drafted "Civil Service Reform," published in the October *North American Review* and intended to serve as a companion piece to "The Session"; it "was really a part of the same review," he later remembered. Still unable to take his efforts in journalism seriously, he affected a casual, dismissive air when discussing the essay, describing it as "another ponderous article." But even when joking to Gaskell that his "impudent" tone and "abusive" tongue would surely bring him trouble, Henry relished the prospect of shearing Washington's power brokers down to size. In a blunt moment he described the piece as "rather bitter, rather slashing, [and] very personal."[2]

"Civil Service Reform" opens on a family note. Concerned with preserving a strong presidency in an age of congressional Reconstruction, Henry quotes passages from the

Massachusetts Constitution (1780), a document principally authored by John Adams that emphasizes the critical importance of shared governance. Like many of the Founders, the senior Adams believed that no single social class could be entrusted to rule without trampling on the rights of others. Representative government thus required a careful distribution of authority and of checks and balances. Reflecting on both Johnson's recent near conviction by the Senate and special interests' growing influence in Washington, Henry arraigned the rise of congressional supremacy and its appropriation by legions of lobbyists as complementing cancers. A weak executive lacked the resources to combat such shenanigans — or even to protect the executive office.

Not yet disillusioned with the new administration, Henry depicted Grant in "Civil Service Reform" as "non-partisan" while praising his nationalism, military background, and "frank expressions of opinion." Hitherto, so he argued, only Generals Washington and Jackson had fully asserted the constitutional prerogatives of the presidency; Lincoln's vigorous use of executive power he apparently supposed a wartime anomaly. Ignoring the dynasty of Democratic presidents from Virginia — Jefferson, Madison, and Monroe — who had furthered the interests of the antebellum plantocracy, Henry curiously claimed that through Jackson's reign (1829–37), "the President represented, not a party, nor even the people either in a mass or in any of its innumerable divisions." But since then, he continued, the rapid growth of factions had chipped away at executive authority. Most recently, Republicans sought to control patronage absolutely and in the Senate had supported the 1867 Tenure of Office Act that denied Johnson the right to remove certain officeholders without the consent of the upper chamber. Perhaps Lincoln's death proved the tragic catalyst for "bringing the evil [of legislative supremacy] to a head," Henry argued, but congressional efforts to undermine the constitutional rights of the executive had long, so he believed, been in the works.[3] He hoped now to see Grant join Washington and Jackson as commanding generals who ascended to commanding presidencies.

The cult of partisanship and the problems it raised, Henry persisted, extended far beyond the sphere of electoral politics. The culture, he claimed, looked to officeholders to set the bar for civility, integrity, and fair play. When the less ethical among them were caught taking bribes, diverting tax revenues, or selling government sinecures to the highest bidders, the public internalized these lapses and began to reorder their own lives, families, and civic expectations to meet the lessened expectations. They noted how corrupt postal contractors suborned postal officials and overcharged for rural western routes; how states like Michigan and Montana were ruled, respectively, by lumber barons and copper kings; and more generally how, as one liberal reformer insisted, it seemed as though "every business firm, trade, profession, and calling is in constant conspiracy against the public." Some among the new movers and shakers saw no reason to apologize for their actions. As Roscoe Conkling, a congressman, senator, and controller of patronage at the New York Customs House, once candidly put it, "Of course, we do rotten things in New York. . . . Politics is a rotten business." Such plain-spoken spite, Adams alleged, promoted "in the country an indifference to strict rules of wrong and right, a contempt for personal dignity, a cynical assumption of official dishonesty, and a patient assent to the supposed necessity of corruption."[4] In arguing for a "return" to the presidential powers of a Washington, Adams more precisely called for a recovery of the kind of character he ascribed to Washington. Good men, after all, made for good politics.

But far too many of the good men, Henry claimed, were now altogether contemptuous of the political scene. In refusing to "lower themselves to this struggle for patronage," he observed, elites in effect went on a kind of public service strike. Leaving the game of governing to the bosses and the party managers, they retired in some disdain or detachment to their clubs and salons, to their reform-minded (and low-circulation) reviews and journals. With old money still in their pockets, they could afford such high if private morals. Proud, superior, and unwilling to fight for political scraps, they made a virtue of absenting themselves from the offices and appointments once the calling of their class. As a result "the baser type of professional politicians" enjoyed, so Adams averred, a clear field and all but dropped the hypocrisy of emoting over a troubled conscience. Accepting favors and buying votes, rather, enjoyed a certain vogue, even, one might say, a kind of respectability, for these tactics simply constituted the price one paid for conducting business. As the railroad magnate Collis P. Huntington advised a political agent, "If you have to pay money to have the right thing done, it is only just and fair to do it. . . . I would not hesitate."[5] And if one played the game particularly well, the politics of appointment might be handsomely rewarded with a long career and an agreeable income.

The only solution to the patronage problem, Henry concluded, involved the resurrection of presidential power and the employment of competitive exams to foster independent officeholders. These would have the effect, he conjectured, of reducing the authority of Capitol Hill and thus the importance of congressional elections. Embedded in this prescription is a transparent pining for an imagined political past — one in which intellectuals, reform journalists, and gentlemen were to inhabit a sanctuary of their own, immune from pols and polls.

By the time "Civil Service Reform" appeared, Adams had evolved a psychological tactic that allowed him to write from the heart even as he fully expected to be ignored. The stratagem involved making ironic or dismissive comments to a few close correspondents in order to show that he grasped the futility of his efforts. Thus he laughed to Gaskell of his essay, "I expect to get into hot water, and shall be disappointed if no one retaliates on me." But reaction and perhaps even a bit of retaliation are precisely what Henry wanted. Newly settled in Washington, he slowly began to earn through his writings a reputation independent of family connection. Having sounded the trumpet for congressional reform, he now planned to maintain his momentum by going after the single greatest interest behind the age's casual corruption: the money power.

15
FOLLOWING THE MONEY

"The world, after 1865," Henry once wrote, "became a bankers' world," and he confessed without apology to finding "the banking mind . . . obnoxious." The era's omnipotent financier, J. P. Morgan, mastered the art of moneymaking, bringing industry, communication, and transportation into a vast empire of enterprises and trusts. One year older than Adams, the rotund Pierpont dominated the landscape of American business; his banking house, J. P. Morgan and Company (established in 1871), organized or underwrote dozens of firms and railroads, including General Electric, United States Steel, and American Telephone & Telegraph. More broadly, Morgan embodied a new monopolistic age in the nation's economy, for which Henry accused him of "trying to swallow the sun."[1] Following the Civil War, a great industrial renaissance transpired, predicated upon the availability of land and labor, technology and capital. The opening of the

West, freeing of southern slaves, and influx of immigrants mainly in the North all came together to make possible the continent's commercial conquest. This process dominated, as Henry noted, "the world," and its legacy remains to this day contested. Undeniably, the House of Morgan replaced the House of Adams as a historical focal point, embodying the ascendance of corporate consolidation over a waning political class.

Henry by no means stood alone in his skepticism of the period's fluid political and moral mood. "The great cities reek," Walt Whitman complained in 1871, "with . . . robbery and scoundrelism," while the economist Henry George wrote in *Progress and Poverty* (1879), an influential study of inequality in the United States, "Where population is densest, wealth greatest, and the machinery of production and exchange most highly developed — we find the deepest poverty, the sharpest struggle for existence, and the most enforced idleness."[2] More than an American circumstance, this radically altered economic environment produced a series of dislocations encapsulated in the Panic of 1873, a financial crisis that first hit Europe and quickly spread to the United States, South Africa, the West Indies, and Australia. Prompted in part by rampant speculation in railroad stock, the downturn — lasting some six years in America, where it caused the bankruptcy of several thousand businesses — demonstrated conclusively the increasingly integrated nature of world markets.

Henry came of age during this profound process, eager to trace its impact on his family and his country. He took up the money question shortly after arriving in Washington, clearly interested in finance capitalism's power to impose itself on both politics and culture. His earliest published work on the subject responded to the controversy surrounding the greenback dollars, the irredeemable paper currency made lawful by the Legal Tender Act of 1862. Regarded as a critical wartime measure to pay for the Union effort, the Act put over $400 million of greenbacks into circulation. Henry, a hard-money man like his father (who sternly declared any other kind of currency "gambling"), feared the inflationary potential of paper notes and began to focus his writing on monetary management. The fruits of these researches included "The Argument in the Legal Tender Case" (*Nation,* December 1868) and "American Finance, 1865–1869" (*Edinburgh Review,* April 1869). Combined with "The Session" and "Civil Service Reform," his essays were beginning to attract notice in the nation's capital. "So I come on," he informed Gaskell with no little satisfaction, "and the people here are beginning to acknowledge me as some one to be considered."[3]

A potent blend of pedigree and ripening talent brought Henry to the attention of those in a position to aid his diagnosis of American finance. The Adams name, if somewhat discounted, still counted for something — a convenience Henry happily acknowledged when deadpanning to Gaskell, "I . . . am held up solely by social position and a sharp tongue." The sharp tongue made him a favorite of the reformers, for his essays were not merely lucid pieces, they were also decidedly pungent, devilishly cutting, and occasionally "wicked" — they flirted, that is, with borderline libelous descriptions of the principals he sought to skewer. The Grant administration did its best to mirror "an absolute despotism"; the public had "been robbed" by railroad directors Daniel Drew and Cornelius Vanderbilt; and New York Supreme Court judge George C. Barnard (subsequently impeached on various charges of corruption) paraded before his Tammany Hall paymasters with "a silken halter round the neck."[4] Rather quickly, Henry's acidic brand of satire won its share of well-situated readers. Aside from political-minded literati, he counted congressmen and cabinet members among his connections and placed his work repeatedly in the respected *Nation* and *North American Review.* Perhaps he would never lay claim to the elected or appointed offices of his ancestors, but he could break new ground, forging a respectable Washington situation of his own.

On the topic of American finance, Francis A. Walker, a fellow Bay State reformer, proved an invaluable ally. Formerly chief of the Bureau of Statistics, Walker conducted and furnished for Adams the detailed research used in "The Legal Tender Act," a scathing assessment of recent monetary policy published in the April 1870 *North American Review.* The timing of the essay proved auspicious. In February the U.S. Supreme Court had declared unconstitutional those parts of the 1862 Act permitting the use of greenbacks for payment of debts assumed *before* the Act became law. If not a sweeping condemnation of irredeemable paper money (currency made legal tender but not redeemable in gold or silver), the Court's ruling nevertheless limited the scope of the Act and offered something of an entrée for Henry's essay. The decision was sure to attract criticism in some quarters and "Legal Tender Act," conceived by its author as an expository exercise, would now double as a defense of the Court's findings. Armed with Walker's statistics, Adams savored having a "big" topic all to himself. "I have been busy as a Roman flea in May," he wrote Gaskell, "and have written a piece of intolerably impudent political abuse."[5]

Avoiding empty pleasantries, the essay opens with a ringing condemnation of Congress. That body, Henry wrote, had organized countless committees of inquiry to scrutinize a lost Civil War battle here, a failed army strategy there, and yet it remained oblivious to a "disaster" whose "effects have extended far beyond the period of the war" — that calamity evident in the flood of greenbacks currently floating through the American economy. Casting about for blame, Henry proceeded to ridicule the men responsible for seeing the Act pass. Thaddeus Stevens, chairman of the House Committee on Ways and Means, merited special aspersion. Formerly the face of the congressional Reconstruction efforts that Adams believed unconstitutional, the Pennsylvania congressman once again came under Henry's unsparing gaze. "That Mr. Stevens was as little suited to direct the economical policy of the country at a critical moment as a naked Indian from the plains to plan the architecture of St. Peter's or to direct the construction of the Capital," he caustically wrote, "expresses in no extreme language the degree of his unfitness."[6] Ignorant on the greenback question and more broadly bereft of any special knowledge or experience in matters of national revenue, Stevens all but handed his rather large chairman's powers over to the champions of the Legal Tender Act, men who believed that only through the expansion of the country's currency could the war be financed and the Union preserved.

One of them, Elbridge G. Spaulding, invited Henry's particular spite. A former New York congressman and chief architect of the Act, Spaulding had recently authored *History of the Legal Tender Paper Money Issued during the Great Rebellion* (1869), a trenchant defense of currency policy during the war which, Spaulding insisted, was "indispensably necessary, and a most powerful instrumentality in saving the government and maintaining the national unity." In reply, Adams resorted to name-calling, snobbishly describing the Buffalo-based Spaulding as "a provincial banker" who had learned his trade "shaving notes at a country bank." Henry never accused Spaulding of malfeasance, but he thought the Act unnecessary and, in its augmentation of congressional power, detrimental. The government, he concluded, enjoyed two legal means to acquire finance: taxation and loans via the selling of bonds. In his opinion no financial emergency existed, and thus when "resorting to a forced paper circulation," as he put it, Congress had overstepped its powers.[7]

Adams pointed out that in December 1861 Secretary of the Treasury Salmon P. Chase had briefly flirted with the idea of employing irredeemable paper money, only to quickly quash the idea. But soon after, a looming urgency for $1 million to continue running the government produced a crisis-like atmosphere in Washington. "The vague notion that sooner or later legal-tender paper was inevitable," Henry observed, clinched the case in its favor.[8] He acknowledged both the real need for the $1 million and the vast sums subsequently eaten up in the war effort, though he remained stubbornly insistent that the existing power of Congress to tax and sell bonds could raise the necessary funds. On this critical point he deferred to the judgment of James Gallatin, president of the Gallatin National Bank of the City of New York and the son of Albert Gallatin, secretary of the Treasury under Presidents Jefferson and Madison. James had testified during the legal tender debates of 1861–62 that the U.S. Treasury need only sell more bonds to meet its obligations. And who, Henry scoffed, was a mere Buffalo note shaver to argue with a Gallatin?

Uninterested in debating the fruits of family trees, Spaulding offered a rejoinder to Gallatin's position, emphasizing the efficacy of legal tender to quickly provide the sums required by a war-pressed Congress. This logic led Henry to presume in "Legal Tender Act" that Spaulding conceded Gallatin's point and simply put convenience above necessity. Believing his opponent bested, Adams subsequently referred to Spaulding as "a man whose scalp I took." But it seems likely that in the winter of 1862, in the midst of a violent civil war only beginning to expand in its scope and intensity, Spaulding and other supporters of the Act regarded the turn toward greenbacks as very much a necessary prerequisite to victory. T. J. Stiles, the author of a recent Pulitzer Prize–winning biography of Cornelius Vanderbilt, has argued that Spaulding "performed a true miracle: he conjured money out of nothing, and so contributed more toward the Union victory . . . than any single battlefield victory." Stiles goes on to contradict Henry's claim that "absolutely no evidence proves that the government might not have carried the war to a successful conclusion without the issue of legal-tender paper."[9]

As a rumination on American finance, "Legal Tender Act" proved to be something of a primer, for six months after its publication, Henry's formidable essay "The New York Gold Conspiracy" appeared, though not in one of his customary outlets. The periodicals he typically patronized deemed the topic too hot to handle, a piece of libel looking to incite a lawsuit. Briefly, the essay took as its centerpiece "Black Friday," September 24 of the previous year (1869), on which date the railroad developer and speculator Jay Gould and Wall Street financier James Fisk, with the aid of President Grant's brother-in-law, Abel Rathbone Corbin, sixty-one and very recently and opportunistically married to the President's thirty-seven-year-old spinster sister, Virginia Grant, sought to corner the New York Gold Exchange. When gold prices soared Grant realized the gambit at hand, which he countered by releasing some $4 million in government gold onto the market; many of the investors, though neither the nimble Gould nor Fisk, were wiped out. The episode riveted Henry's attention to the rising power of finance capitalism in America. Since the end of the Civil War fresh markets, regions, and raw materials were opened to both development and exploitation. A spirit of garden-variety greed met with unparalleled opportunities to tempt investors, financiers, businessmen, and industrialists as never before. In writing up the drama of the gold battle, Henry more generally attacked the emerging corporate money culture and its sudden challenge to traditional values.

Initially concerned that Congress might "suppress the scandal" of the bullion run, involving as it did the president's brother-in-law, Henry, to his surprise, discovered that he "soon knew all that was to be known" about the affair. Future president James A. Garfield, an Ohio congressman and chairman of the House Committee on Banking and Currency, led an inquiry into the "conspiracy" and, aside from the published report, offered other materials to Adams, whom he had befriended.

Though Henry often moaned about his family's lapsed status, he now enjoyed the independence to make contacts and publish criticisms that would have proven impossible had he held an elected or appointed office. His playful promise to Gaskell, "I am about to write an article on a very curious and melodramatic gold speculation . . . [and] it involves a good deal of libelous language," is true enough and underlines the fact that, patrician instincts aside, Henry enjoyed a good (print) brawl, particularly when he considered his targets upstarts and arrivistes.[10] Long before the investigative journalist Ida Tarbell published her famous attack on John D. Rockefeller's oil empire, *The History of the Standard Oil Company* (1904), Henry had already torn into the new money power. He proved to be both a blue blood and a muckraker, unwittingly helping to pioneer a profession that anticipated the progressive presidency of the Knickerbocker reformer Theodore Roosevelt.

Henry argued in "The New York Gold Conspiracy" that beyond Gould's and Fisk's rascality, the nation at large had quite promiscuously flung itself into the Stock Exchange. Anyone with a little cash, he somewhat exaggerated, from farmers and merchants to druggists and dentists, began to push dollars into the swollen market.

It seems that for Gould and company the

"conspiracy" was less an inspired bit of buc-
caneering than the inevitable outcome of a
country looking to make a killing, even if it
meant buying on margin. And yet it humored
Henry to assemble a host of questionable assumptions regarding the psychology and
ethnic makeup of the major players involved
in this failed caper. He tended, as noted, to
personalize crusades. Appealing to the age's
casual anti-Semitism, he supposed, errone-
ously, that Gould betrayed "a trace of Jewish
origin," this fanciful detail apparently giving
some insight into why the speculator "had
not a conception of moral principle." Adams
simply dismissed Fisk as "noisy, boastful,
[and] ignorant," a shifty-eyed mercenary who
resembled "a young butcher in appearance
and mind."[11]

These dark princes of finance, Henry continued, suddenly found themselves climbing
in the new financial order, unexpectedly
armed with unprecedented power. Their
interests in the Erie Railway — connecting
New York City to Chicago — alone set them
above, in certain vital aspects, even the reach
of government. Holding capital stock of some
$35 million (roughly $700 million in current
dollars) and employing fifteen thousand
workers, the company, Henry argued, had set
itself up as "an empire within a republic."
Who enjoyed more influence than the execu-
tives of this line? What mere king could claim

the cash resources sitting in the company's brimming coffers? With the national legislature and judiciary more than willing to abet the great financial titans and railroad barons, "Gould and Fisk," Henry observed, "created a combination more powerful than any that ha[d] been controlled by mere private citizens in America or in Europe since society for self-protection established the supreme authority of the judicial name." Such immense advantage in private hands disturbed Adams, who called it "far too great for public safety either in a democracy or in any other form of society." Compounding matters, Gould and Fisk constituted a new type of power broker that Henry found especially distasteful. What could be worse, after all, than to cede authority to equivocal genealogies? "Both these men," he sneered, "belonged to a low moral and social type."[12]

Proud of the article, Henry described it many years later as part of his early oeuvre and, on those terms, "the best piece of work" he had done.[13] And this raised the question, might Henry's true literary gifts reside in the recovery of the past rather than in the micro-scrutinizing of modern Washington politics? His greatest labors — the nine-volume history of the early American republic, the *Education,* and his meditation on medievalism, *Mont-Saint-Michel and Chartres* — all point to their author's talent for taking a small subject (a president, a private citizen, a song, or a cathedral) and connecting it to larger social, economic, and cultural forces. Accordingly, "The New York Gold Conspiracy" might be read as an apprentice piece for Adams's more mature works. Clearly it displayed a distinctive historical voice.

Getting the essay published, however, proved difficult. Henry did more than offer a grand narrative of a failed gold conspiracy; he named names, and that made editors fear defamation suits. His hopes for finding a warmer reception among magazines outside of America also proved elusive; both the *Edinburgh Review* and (London) *Quarterly Review* declined the essay. One London editor, James Froude of *Fraser's Magazine,* called the piece "prima facie actionable." The article finally found a home in the influential left-leaning British quarterly *Westminster Review,* appearing in October 1870. The cautious publishers were right; to Henry's delight the article made a lot of people mad. In separate communications to Gaskell, Adams boasted that Cyrus Field, the brother of David Dudley Field, attorney to Fisk and Gould, was "after" him, and that James McHenry, a British financier accused in the essay of advancing the gold scheme by planting a misleading article in the *New York Times,* "want[ed] to sue [him] for a libel." Sure of his impeccable government sources, Henry declared himself eager to confront McHenry: "[A court case] would bring me over to England again as I mean to hurt him if he gives me a chance."[14]

A year after publication, "The New York Gold Conspiracy" was reprinted, along with seven other articles, in *Chapters of Erie: And Other Essays,* a sort of omnibus of robber baron mischief. Henry authored most of the offerings, while his brother Charles, having given up law and now occupying a seat on the Massachusetts Board of Railroad Commissioners, contributed three studies on the chaotic struggle among financiers — including the ubiquitous Gould and Fisk — for control of the Erie Railway. Combined, the Adams men made the case that a rising plutocracy threatened to upend the republic. Not that such grave concerns kept Henry from enjoying Washington. Comfortable in his bachelor's life, he circulated among cabinet members and power brokers, rapidly building a reputation as a formidable freelance journalist. That spring of 1870, with "Conspiracy" about to shame a slew of knaves, may have been one of the most satisfying seasons of his life.

As a reward for his recent literary labors, Henry left for England in May, eager to see Gaskell, visit London, and, so he said, take a "moral bath" after plunging into the brackish pool of American politics. All did not go as planned. A few weeks into his holiday Henry received disturbing news from the Continent that his sister Louisa lay seriously ill at Bagni di Lucca, a small commune in Tuscany known for its therapeutic thermal springs. Slightly injured in a carriage accident, Loo had subsequently contracted tetanus. Rushing to her sickroom, Henry could only witness the shocking end of her suffering. "It is all over," he informed Gaskell on July 13. "My poor sister died this morning. I will tell you about it some day or other, but now I am fairly out of condition to write details. The last fortnight has been fearfully trying and the last few days terribly so."[15] Louisa received burial in Florence's English Cemetery at Piazzale Donatello, resting place of the city's Anglophone communities. Henry's stabbing memory of Louisa's last days, captured so graphically some thirty years later in the *Education,* is an admission that, beyond Grant and Gould, beyond even the omnipresent industrial dynamo, his distinctive fatalism could be partially traced to deeper and more personal losses: the death of a sister, the suicide of a wife. In such acutely felt tragedies did an already defensive and satirical exterior stiffen. Louisa's alarming passing proved to be her brother's first great blow:

He had never seen nature, — only her

surface, — the sugarcoating that she shows to youth. Flung suddenly in his face, with the harsh brutality of chance, the terror of the blow stayed by him thenceforth for life, until repetition made it more than the will could struggle with; more than he could call on himself to bear. He found his sister, a woman of forty, as gay and brilliant in the terrors of lock-jaw as she had been in the careless fun of 1859, lying in bed in consequence of a miserable cab-accident that had bruised her foot. Hour by hour the muscles grew rigid, while the mind remained bright, until after ten days of fiendish torture she died in convulsions.[16]

In his grief Henry understandably failed to mention to Gaskell a letter that he had received some days prior to Louisa's passing. The communication, from Harvard president Charles W. Eliot, invited him to accept an assistant professorship of history. On the third of July Henry wrote back, calling the offer "not only flattering but brilliant," before tendering a polite refusal. He had a career or, as he put it to Eliot, an "experiment" just beginning and was "determined to go on in it as far as it [would] lead [him]."[17] There is no evidence that he informed his family of the offer and most likely presumed the matter to be over. In fact, he remained vulnerable to parental appeal. The summer's end would send him back to America, a reluctant professor, uncertain of what he might profess.

■ ■ ■ ■

BOSTON

■ ■ ■ ■

Boston is not big enough for four Adamses.
Henry Adams, 1867

16
THE PROFESSOR

Henry's July refusal to Eliot constituted his second Cambridge-related rebuff in three months. Earlier that spring Ephraim Whitney Gurney, Harvard professor of ancient history and editor of the *North American Review,* received a new appointment as the College's first dean of the faculty. As a consequence, he offered Henry, without success, editorship of the magazine. Having published several of his articles and reviews, Gurney obviously thought highly of his talents, though more personal considerations may have been at play. Nearly two years earlier, in the fall of 1868, Gurney had married Ellen Hooper, connected advantageously on both sides of her family to banking and seafaring fortunes. The nuptials, which lifted the then thirty-nine-year-old Gurney's profile considerably in Cambridge, owed something to an unlikely matchmaker: Charles Francis. While visiting London in 1866 the Bostonian Dr. Robert Hooper, Ellen's father, had asked the Governor for the name of a scholar to tutor his daughter in Greek. Pleased with Gurney's efforts instructing his youngest child, Brooks, the Governor passed on the professor's name.[1] Possibly in reaching out to Henry, Gurney hoped to return the favor. If so, he soon learned, like Eliot, that honoring an Adams required patience, humility, and a bit of luck.

In August, about a month after Louisa's death, Gurney opened negotiations with E. L. Godkin, then editing the *Nation,* to take over the *North American Review.* Despite the promise of a considerably higher salary than that offered to Adams in the spring, Godkin turned him down. At this point, both Gurney and Eliot, perhaps allied, renewed their respective interest in Henry and appear to have successfully made their plans known to a higher power. Adams's earlier refusals to edit and to teach were launched safely from a distant Europe, but now back in America he felt the gentle if persistent pull of family pressure. He must have wondered with some embarrassment if Eliot's offer in any way constituted a quid pro quo. The Governor, as everyone knew, counted at Harvard; he occupied a seat on the College's Board of Overseers, which had proffered him the school's presidency shortly after he returned from London. His decision to decline the post opened the door for Eliot, who remained in the office until 1909, a remarkable forty-year tenure that remains the longest in the University's history. Whether or not Eliot felt an obligation to Charles Francis, he again offered Henry a professorship — and this time the Governor weighed in. Reasoning that Harvard occupied "now the field of widest influence in America," and thus presented its more gifted instructors with every opportunity to make "the greatest mark" in scholarship, Charles Francis encouraged Henry to reconsider. The head of the family having spoken, others — brothers — piled on. Petitioned on all sides, a laconic Henry wrote to Gaskell in late September of his inevitable capitulation: "On my return home I found the question of the professorship sprung upon me again in a very troublesome way. Not only the President of the College and the Dean, made a very strong personal appeal to me, but my brothers were earnest about it and my father leaned the same way. I hesitated a week, and then I yielded. Now I am, I believe assistant professor of history at Harvard College."[2]

In truth, he yielded twice. Exposed to Dean Gurney's "very strong personal appeal," he agreed not merely to instruct students but to take over the editorial duties of the *North American Review.* That last task made sense. He had written for the *Review,* as well as several other magazines, and could thus claim some journalistic expertise. But the idea of lecturing on ninth-century witch cults before an audience of nineteen-year-olds seemed absurd — until it happened. Assigned to teach medieval history, a doubtful Henry observed to Gaskell, "I gave the college fair warning of my ignorance, and the answer was that I knew just as much as anyone else in America knew on the subject, and I could teach better than anyone that could be had." This dry report captures Adams's appreciation of historical training's low status in America. The professionalization of history had yet to occur, so the past still remained in the hands of patrician scholars. Indeed, more than a decade after Henry's appointment, Ephraim Emerton, an Adams student who later returned to Harvard to teach German history and language, condemned the still common assumption that "any 'cultivated gentleman' could teach European history."[3]

If Henry sported with the offer (he later swore that "Harvard . . . made him Professor against his will"), it nevertheless arrived in an appealing fashion. Throughout his life Adams took great pleasure in being courted, even if he sometimes found the prizes unpalatable, as he seemed to in this case. Returning to Washington in late September to "break up" his lodgings before heading north, he described himself to Gaskell as "very hot, very lonely, and very hard run." So many of his political friends had deserted the "corrupt" capital, and only this, so he insisted, "reconcile[d him] to going away." But the note betrays the inference of exile, and his explicit coda — "I hate Boston and am very fond of Washington" — seems closer to the mark. Adams probably knew, as he reluctantly packed for Cambridge, that his long-term future lay elsewhere. "My engagement is for five years," he wrote, sounding like a prisoner, "but I don't expect to remain so long." For now, he had decided to bide his time and appease his family; the prodigal son would make his mother happy — which is precisely what transpired. Having learned of Henry's plans, Abigail wrote with a mixture of gratitude and relief in her diary, "Very glad, we shall not only have him with us . . . but I think his life will be more useful and settled."[4]

It is difficult to say which of Henry's positions promised more prestige. As a Harvard professor he taught at America's best college, and as the editor of the *North American Review* he ran one of its most important literary magazines. To be sure, the combined outlay of effort and hours proved considerable. The editorial post alone must have seemed to Henry a full-time office. Published quarterly, the *Review* appeared each January, April, July, and October; anxious to fill a raft of empty pages, he called upon Adamses young and old to contribute. Along with Charles,

Brooks, and the Governor, he wrote dozens of unsigned essays and reviews, sketches and notices. In all, Henry edited over one hundred articles during his six-year tenure (1870–76), the ever-present load lightened somewhat by the assistance of his doctoral student Henry Cabot Lodge.

At Harvard, Henry joined a small cohort of historians. Dean Gurney and Henry Warren Torrey, the McLean Professor of Ancient and Modern History, were his colleagues. With a bemused attitude, he recalled his impossible pedagogical obligation to the sons of the College: "Between Gurney's classical courses and Torrey's modern ones, lay a gap of a thousand years, which Adams was expected to fill." Given free rein to teach what he pleased within the period 800–1649, he began to work up lecture material and discovered an unexpected interest in medieval building and design that deepened over the years. His classic studies *Mont-Saint-Michel and Chartres* and the *Education* juxtapose the moral imagination of medievalism with the rush and anomie of modernity. Henry may have come to this signal cultural comparison without the spur of performing in a Harvard lecture hall, though this initial immersion in Gothic forms proved memorable, what he called at the time "a new interest in architecture."[5]

Adams's students are adamant that he rejected a classroom of "facts" for one of critical engagement. Lindsay Swift, later to serve as editor of library publications at the Boston Public Library, remembered Henry characteristically pacing in front of his young scholars, hands in pockets, and carrying on as though he were in conversation. He seemed genuinely concerned with his students' welfare and almost certainly identified with the pressures that many of them faced as the sons and grandsons of "great" men. Just a dozen years earlier he had been of their number, and now he again lived in their midst. For two years Henry resided "on-campus," occupying two ground-floor rooms in the gambrel-roofed Wadsworth House, which had previously sheltered nine Harvard presidents, briefly served as Washington's headquarters during the Revolutionary War, and once lent Andrew Jackson its parlor to receive students. One of Harvard's more iconic buildings and an excellent example of early Georgian architecture in America, its five-bay façade sits conspicuously on Massachusetts Avenue and looks, in all its circa 1720s splendor, suitably sage-like.[6]

A reflective instructor, Henry embedded his personal educational philosophy in a long essay on Cambridge and its college in the January 1872 *North American Review*. One passage in particular, though relating to the late eighteenth century, made a more general observation on the importance of respecting, engaging, and listening to students:

> The College records . . . tell a somewhat stiff and often ludicrously formal tale of boys' experiences and petty discipline, without in the least entering into boys' feeling. For after all it is primarily with students that education deals, and the opinion of students is therefore an essential part of all successful education. One wishes to know what the student, at any given time, thought of himself, of his studies and his instructors; what his studies and his habits were; how much he knew and how thoroughly; with what spirit he met his work, and with what amount of active aid and sympathy his instructors met him in dealing with his work or his amusements.

Clearly Henry's sympathies ran to the "boys," and he seemed eager to know their occasional nonsense as a way of fostering trust and keeping clear the lines of learning. Professors, he poked, were dry reeds without the provocation of their students. "A skilful instructor ought," he suggested, "to derive as many ideas from the absurdities or extravagances of the scholars who are in his charge, as he does from their better qualities."[7] Adams's openness and intellectual charisma in the classroom became the stuff of Harvard

Yard lore, and over the years a number of alumni wrote of his impactful manner. Lodge observed that Adams "had the power not only of exciting interest, but he awakened opposition to his own views, and that is one of the great secrets of success in teaching"; Stewart Mitchell maintained that "he was a new type of man"; and Edward Channing, himself a distinguished Harvard historian, remembered Adams as simply "the greatest teacher that I ever encountered." As one might guess of such a protean thinker, Henry continued to inspire young scholars long after retiring from the classroom. In 1884 Johns Hopkins instructor John Franklin Jameson, a critical force behind the professionalization of history in the United States as the longtime managing editor of the *American Historical Review,* wrote appreciatively of Adams to one correspondent: "His abilities impress me greatly; I would give a great deal to be under him, as some of those Harvard fellows were."[8]

One of those fellows, J. Laurence Laughlin, later an economist at the University of Chicago, remembered Adams as unmistakably aristocratic, a dapper man indelibly marked by descent:

At the time when I was a Harvard undergraduate, examinations were held in Lower Massachusetts Hall, then hung with the college portraits. In the intervals of writing,

when I looked up, I was struck by the like-
ness of Henry Adams to the full-length
portrait of John Quincy Adams on the eastern wall. Henry was small, short, bald, with
a pointed clipped beard, a striking brow, but
he was not as stout as his grandfather.
There was in both the same air of self-
contained strength. . . . His manner was
animated and brusque, but kindly. Although
short in stature and unconventional in manner, he never lacked dignity.[9]

Laurence described Adams's teaching as
"original, unexpected, and even explosive,"
the raw qualities of an iconoclast intent on
being something more than merely "faculty."
Delighting in resistance, "he was satirical,
heterodox, and sweeping in his comments . . .
chiefly from a sense of humor, a desire to
shake up established commonplace, to start
others to think."[10]
Brought in to teach the "gap of a thousand
years" between the ancient world and modern
Europe, Henry soon moved his courses
beyond the Frankish Middle Ages. In 1874
he offered a section on "colonial history of
America to 1789" and initiated that same
year a seminar on Anglo-Saxon law for
doctoral candidates — the first history seminar at Harvard. Two years later he pioneered
the course History of the United States from
1789 to 1840, shorthanded in the College's

catalog as "History 6." Facing his students the first day of class, he acknowledged that some of them descended from the public men they were about to study. As one undergraduate remembered, Adams delicately allowed "it was probable that some toes would be trodden on uncomfortably."[11] Of course Henry, with all the prerogatives, controversies, and dead weight of an ancient family name, had no need to remind his audience that his own toes were likely to be trampled on, too. Swift, a student in the section, recalled Adams as a fraternal, available presence rather than a distant man speaking down to ignorant boys:

Mr. Adams . . . was wholly unacademic; no formality, no rigidity, no professorial pose. . . . We faced a friendly-disposed gentleman some twenty years older than ourselves, whose every feature, every line of his body, his clothes, his bearing, his speech were well bred to a degree. . . . In our course, he would select various topics, incidental to the periods covered, and assign one side to one student and the opposing to another. Thus we had under discussion all the important phases of American history for about fifty years — the formation of the Constitution, Jay's Treaty, Genet's Mission, the Alien and Sedition Laws, the trial of Aaron Burr, the Hartford

223

Convention, etc., etc., down through the Administration of Van Buren. . . . The point of it all was that we moved in a perfectly free intellectual atmosphere; no constraint, no didacticism, and really no partisanship.[12]

Adams's views on the success of History 6 were more qualified. He offered in the *Education* an affectionate regard for his students, describing them as "excellent company," even as he insisted that only one in ten demonstrated an original intelligence. More typically he listed Harvard's shortcomings — the packed lecture halls, the pressure to make history fit into neat patterns, the gentlemen's agreement among the professors to avoid intellectual disagreement — and a little unfairly claimed that his Cambridge days amounted to a handful of lost years.[13] This pregnant period fills only a few pages of the *Education* in a chapter casually called "Failure."

In truth, Henry's Harvard turn contributed greatly to his growth as a historian. Though he unapologetically neglected to build the College into a center of medieval studies, other and more personal accomplishments were attained. Working in the classroom forced him to consolidate and arrange material for a lay audience; turning students loose on competing historical debates brought to his own writing an enlarged and questioning perspective; and identifying as a Harvard scholar helped him to make the transition from serious magazine work on the *North American Review* to longer and more specialized studies of the past. In terms of prompting Henry to reflect and develop a historical methodology, these were vitally important years. They gave him the apparatus of "scientific" learning without encumbering his developing manner of clear and occasionally elegiac expression. "Learn to appreciate and to use the German historical *method*," he once wrote Lodge, "and your *style* can be elaborated at leisure."[14]

17
THE INSURGENT

Despite settling in at Harvard, Henry remained an active combatant on the political reform front. His "Session" essay, as well as those on finance and government corruption, may have irritated congressmen and singed a spoilsman or two, but they changed nothing. As editor of the *North American Review,* however, he possessed the means to carry on a more concentrated effort in upscale muckraking. He wrote confidently to Gaskell in the late autumn of 1870, "Retirement from Washington has by no means thrown me out of politics. On the contrary, as editor I am deeper in them than ever, and my party is growing so rapidly that I look forward to the day when we shall be in power again as not far distant." By "my party," he meant the self-styled liberal wing of the GOP. In this late nineteenth-century sense, "liberal" did not connote sympathy for minorities, immigrants, or organized labor. When applied to Grant's critics within the Republican Party, rather, it meant rooting out the special interests, seeing the nation steered by the "Best Men" (themselves, naturally), and more generally elevating the character of American politics. Remarkably Adams, seldom one to erect air castles, believed rule by robber baron to be in his sights. "Two or three years," he innocently unfurled the family banner, "ought to do it."[1]

This fleeting Liberal Republican movement to which Henry offered his assistance began in 1870 under the leadership of Carl Schurz. A German-born American who came to the United States shortly after the failed European revolutions of 1848 (a series of republican revolts against monarchies), Schurz settled in Wisconsin, joined the antislavery movement, and gained a reputation among Republicans as an important spokesman for German Americans. Rewarded for his exhaustive canvassing in the 1860 presidential campaign, he was appointed U.S. ambassador to Spain. Stopping in London on his way to Madrid, Schurz met Charles Francis Adams and his son Henry. His European tenure ended not long after. Having convinced Lincoln to make him a brigadier general of Union volunteers, he saw action at Chancellorsville, Gettysburg, and Chattanooga before accompanying Sherman's army on its destructive march into the Carolinas. With the war's end, Schurz briefly edited the *Detroit*

Press before uprooting to Missouri, where, in 1868, he won election to the U.S. Senate.

The success of Missouri's "insurgent" Republicans over the state's regular Republicans led to the development of a national, if somewhat unruly, reform movement within the party. Its mouthpieces included Henry's *North American Review* as well as Horace Greeley's *New York Tribune,* Horace White's *Chicago Tribune,* and Murat Halstead's *Cincinnati Commercial.* Really a loose collection of concerns and interests, Liberal Republicanism found common ground in its disdain for Grantism, which it associated with political corruption and the overextension of federal power in the states. Schurz and his supporters sought to end Reconstruction, amnesty disenfranchised former Confederates, promote free trade as a way to attack the trusts, and advance the cause of civil service reform. Most had joined the Republican Party in the 1850s in opposition to slavery's expansion, and now, with slavery ended, inclined toward a more traditional limited government orientation. Along with the vast Reconstruction apparatus, Johnson's near impeachment convinced them that traditional constitutional norms were directly endangered. Henry actively courted Schurz from Boston, inviting the senator on at least two occasions to write for the *North American*

Review. "I would like to support your course, and make known to the eastern people the true nature of the contest you are engaged in," he explained. "I want the public to know, if possible, how far you and your party represent principles which are of national interest; how far free-trade and reform are involved in the result; and what influences have been at work to counteract success. . . . I would be glad to extend the range of your influences so far as is in my power."[2]

In January 1872 Missouri's Liberal Republicans issued a call for a national convention to meet in Cincinnati on the first of May. Some of their number hoped this gathering of the disaffected might prompt regular Republicans to refuse to run Grant in the fall election; others wanted to form a third faction or, perhaps, lay the foundation for a partnership with the Democratic Party. Massachusetts's Liberal Republicans arrived in Cincinnati determined to go the third-party route and to engineer the nomination of Charles Francis Adams. The Governor's appeal beyond the Bay State, however, proved thin. In the post-war decades national elections generally went to Civil War veterans, and Charles Francis's wartime diplomatic service in England, though important, stood outside this trend.[3]

Regionally the Governor could point to

little popularity outside of New England. Southerners, particularly those with long memories, saw all Adamses as defenders of federal power, while westerners were turned off by his aristocratic mien. Even his appeal in the East extended only so far. Marcus Morton, who served as chief justice on the Massachusetts Supreme Court, indelicately described Adams as "the greatest Iceberg in the Northern hemisphere," and one Liberal Republican complained that the Governor "represent[ed] too much the anti-popular element — the sneering and sniffling element."[4] The large concentration of Boston's Irish voters, moreover, distrusted Charles Francis's Anglophilia (suggested by his long London residency), while his former colleague Charles Sumner would almost certainly offer no support. And perhaps most important, the presumptive nominee shared his father's and grandfather's now dated hesitation for actively pursuing public office. He would accept, but not grasp.

Neither would he be within four thousand miles of Cincinnati that spring. The Governor had been called to Geneva, where he led the American delegation before an international arbitration commission designed to settle claims for damages inflicted on Union shipping during the war by British-built Confederate commerce raiders. When asked if he might offer assurances of his views before the

Cincinnati convention, the old diplomat demurred. In the absence of clear signals his sons were reduced to making coy assurances on their own. Some two months before the convention met, former Ohio governor Jacob Cox wrote to one correspondent that Henry had vaguely "inferred" to him that the Governor "was cordially with us."[5]

The three-day convention proved to be a curiously disharmonious affair for a group of insurgents supposedly united by the goal of toppling Grant. But a common enemy is all they shared. The historian John Sproat has written, "One great weakness was the gathering's heterogeneous composition: it was as motley a collection of politicians and reformers as ever tried to form a political party in the United States. Among the delegates were free traders and protectionists, conservative New England patricians and agrarian radicals . . . advocates of Negro rights and Southern Redeemers." Enough of a consensus existed, however, for the hammering out of a party platform; it emphasized civil service reform to break up the old patronage politics, a return to "the constitutional limitations of power" that prevailed before the war, and a reversion to specie payments paired with the retirement of inflationary greenbacks. Next, the convention moved to nominate a presidential candidate. Despite his absence, Charles Francis surged ahead as the early front-runner, but following six ballots (four of which the Governor led) Greeley captured the prize. It proved to be a divisive choice in an already divided party.[6]

A former Whig, the fiercely independent Greeley had been a strong critic of Lincoln, opposed keeping federal troops in the South, and signed a bond in the spring of 1867 to help former Confederate president Jefferson Davis — locked up in Hampton, Virginia's Fortress Monroe — make bail. Many northerners considered him a traitor. When the Democrats, still damningly associated with secession, met at Baltimore two months after the Liberal Republican convention and, determined not to split the anti-Grant vote, chose Greeley to lead *their* ticket, more than a few Yankees thought their suspicions confirmed. As the fall campaign shaped up, Henry backed away from the sinking Liberal Republican cause. Putting on a brave face, he defiantly insisted to Gaskell that the Governor, after all, had gotten lucky: "My father narrowly escaped being the next President, but has come out of the fight very sound and strong, while his successful rival is likely to be not only disgraced but beaten."[7]

The beating arrived soon enough. Come November Greeley captured not quite 44 percent of the popular vote while carrying only three border states (Maryland, Kentucky, and Missouri) and three former Confederate states (Texas, Tennessee, and Georgia). It perhaps struck some Americans as morbidly fitting, then, when, following the election but prior to the meeting of the Electoral College, Greeley suddenly died on November 29. The passing of the man prefaced a passing phase in postwar reform politics. Liberal Republicanism's view of the war as a tragedy and its belief that corporate power threatened the country's independent yeoman heritage failed to convince a growing northern electorate that now dominated national politics. Instead, Grant's "blood and iron" vision of a strong nation united by its railroads, commerce, and industry proved compelling; as an organizing principle it more or less ruled America's political roost until the Great Depression.

Neither Henry nor his father was in America to witness regular Republicanism's predictable triumph. They thus shared a peculiar connection with earlier Adamses who had also avoided the public after difficult political defeats. John Adams and John Quincy Adams, both trounced in reelection bids, were the first retiring presidents to abstain from their successor's swearing-in ceremonies; a handful of others, including Andrew Johnson and Richard Nixon, inconveniently entangled in issues of impeachment, followed. Charles Francis left Geneva in late September following the successful conclusion of the arbitration discussions and toured Europe with his family for several weeks thereafter. He sailed for home on November 3; Grant won reelection on the 5th. Altogether different circumstances ensured Henry's removal from the American scene. Much to his family's surprise he had married earlier in the year and Election Day found him and his bride, Marian (Clover) Hooper, honeymooning in an "empty" Florence, far away from Greeley and Grantism.[8] For the moment he had no room for politics, for Harvard, or even for other Adamses. The dutiful son had stolen a march, taken a wife, and slipped away.

18

CLOVER

Marian "Clover" Hooper lived in Boston and, as a Sturgis on her mother's side, circulated in the same genteel circles and urban spaces as the Adamses. She probably met Henry in the spring of 1866, when she and her father, Robert Hooper, began a tour of Europe. The Governor maintained something of an open-house policy for visiting Americans, and a number of Bostonians, including the Hoopers, showed up at the U.S. legation in London. It would be convenient to report on Henry and Clover's immediate and mutual attraction, though on this day neither of the interested parties seemed particularly interested. Nearly five more years passed, rather, before their courtship commenced in the house of Henry's Harvard colleague, Ephraim Whitman Gurney, the spouse, as noted earlier, of Clover's sister, Ellen. At thirty-three the by all appearances celibate Henry gave every indication of entering the ranks of confirmed bachelorhood. He seemed unshakably wedded to his work, looked older than his age, and suffered from delicate nerves, a "weakness," he later recalled, "exaggerated" as the years passed. Photographs of Clover (the very few that she allowed to be taken), accentuate a prominent nose, rounded chin, and heavy cheeks. Her refusal to sit for the camera suggests that she may have suffered the insecurity of many plain-looking girls born to pretty mothers. Clover and Henry were cerebral, self-conscious, and no doubt aware that their respective windows for marriage and children, if still open, were quietly closing. They developed a strong rapport based on mutual sympathy and respect; they were intelligent, occasionally caustic, and not a little snobbish.[1]

To many who knew them, however, Clover and Henry must have seemed a curious pairing. The Adamses were a "political family," while the Hoopers, with connections to Concord's fading Transcendentalist tradition, claimed a slender place among New England's literary elite. Clover's mother, Ellen Sturgis Hooper, who succumbed to tuberculosis in 1848, when Clover was five, had won a reputation as a regional writer of some note. A friend of Emerson, she published her poetry in the *Dial,* the chief Transcendentalist publication; Margaret Fuller, author of *Woman in the Nineteenth Century* and a *Dial* editor, said of Hooper, "I have seen no

236

woman more gifted by nature than she," while an impressed Henry David Thoreau quoted the final stanzas of her verse "The Wood-Fire" in *Walden*. The Adamses, by contrast, were habitual writers, fillers of diaries and daybooks, authors of numerous volumes of letters, memoirs, and public papers, but they lacked, and knew they lacked, and made no apologies for the lacking, a finer appreciation of words as the means to convey complex emotions. Henry's engagement gift to Clover, a copy of novelist William Dean Howells's *Their Wedding Journey,* which he had recently assayed for the *North American Review,* seems an oddly impersonal tribute. In such innocent if unclever gestures, he understood that to the old Concord circle, "all Adamses were minds of dust and emptiness, devoid of feeling, poetry or imagination; little higher than the common scourings of State Street; politicians of doubtful honesty; natures of narrow scope."[2]

If equipped with differing sensibilities, the Adamses and Hoopers more assuredly shared the outlook of an ebbing New England gentry. The Sturgises were once an immensely wealthy clan whose original success their offspring might exploit, though never repeat. Clover's maternal grandfather, William F. Sturgis, had made a fortune as a trader and sea captain; his ships plowed the Pacific from Alaska to Macau fending off

Chinese pirates and trafficking in otter skins and other commodities. In 1810 the twenty-eight-year-old Sturgis returned to Boston a merchant prince, married Elizabeth Davis, and established a trading partnership, Bryant & Sturgis, that dominated America's Pacific trade for a generation. But what were succeeding Sturgises to do except to manage the wealth they played no role in accruing? The philosopher George Santayana, author of *The Last Puritan,* which details the decline of the old Boston gentry and became the second-best-selling novel of 1936 behind only *Gone with the Wind,* observed this family from an unusually close perspective. His mother, Josefina Borrás y Carbonell, was first married to a second-generation Sturgis, George, who died in 1857 at the age of forty. The younger George, the product of Josefina's second marriage, to Agustín Ruiz de Santayana, was brought to Boston at the age of nine to live with the Sturgises. He came to see his adopted family as a spent historical force. Their "type," he insisted, "ha[d] since been replaced by that of great business men or millionaires, building up their fortunes at home." Resolved to lives of "romance and tragedy," these once "great merchants," he continued, inevitably succumbed to the industrial age, making "their careers and virtues impossible for their children."[3] Henry, of course, felt a similar sense of displacement by the same men and by the same process. In deciding to marry, he and Clover produced a union of dynastic New England names — ancient, respected, but inescapably bleaching into the background.

Cautiously keeping his nearly yearlong courtship with Clover a secret, Henry apprised Brooks, the youngest Adams, of his impending wedding in a March 1872 letter, waiting until the fourth paragraph to announce the news: "And now prepare yourself for a shock. I am engaged to be married. There!. . . . I have had the design ever since last May and . . . threw myself head over heels into the pursuit, and succeeded in conducting the affair so quietly that this last week we became engaged without a single soul outside her immediate family suspecting it." Henry closed by warning Brooks to refrain from adopting a judgmental (that is to say, Adamslike) attitude: "I shall expect you to be very kind to Clover, and not rough, for that is not her style."[4] He had yet to tell his older brothers and pointedly communicated this fact to Brooks.

Some three weeks later Henry acquainted Gaskell of his decision. In describing Clover he seemed almost eager to reduce her that others not. "She is certainly not handsome; nor would she be quite called plain. . . . She dresses badly." His facetious candor then lit upon those qualities in Clover that he admired most — and that he knew Gaskell would also respect: "She knows her own mind uncommon well. She does not talk *very* American. Her manners are quiet. She reads German — also Latin — also, I fear, a little Greek, but very little. She talks garrulously, but on the whole pretty sensibly. She is very open to instruction. *We* shall improve her. . . . She decidedly has humor and will appreciate *our* wit." There is embedded in this prescription for improvement the suggestion that her husband and his friends could aid Clover in more than intellectual ways. Henry likely entered their marriage with some slight concern for his fiancée's mental health ("I know better than anyone the risks I run," he confessed to Brooks), perhaps imagining that an active social regimen might ward off any neurotic tendencies and provide stability. The Sturgises were rumored to suffer from depression; in 1853, when Clover was nearly ten, her aunt Susan Sturgis Bigelow ended her life and that of her unborn child by taking arsenic. Upon learning of Henry's engagement his brother Charles unmindfully chimed in, "Heavens! — no! — they're all crazy as coots. She'll kill herself, just like her Aunt!"[5] Henry's mother, by contrast, welcomed news of the engagement, while the Governor restrained whatever trepidation he may have held and, from the uncritical distance of

Geneva, approved of the union.

The intimate wedding (numbering, including the minister, an auspicious baker's dozen) took place at the Hoopers' North Shore summer cottage on June 27. A fussy Charles made light of the occasion when describing the day for his absent father:

The only persons present were the bride's father and fair brothers and sisters, by nature and in law, the groom's two brothers and their wifes, a clergyman and an old family servant, — thirteen human beings in all, including the unfortunate victims themselves. The ceremony lasted in the neighborhood of two minutes, after which we all trundled into luncheon and sat down anywhere and the bride, at the head of the table, proceeded to calm her agitation by carving a pair of cold roast chickens. John and I dished out the bread and labored hard [to] stimulate an aspect of gaiety, but the champagne wasn't cool and made its appearance only in very inadequate quantities, and the aspect of affairs tended toward the commonplace.[6]

More generously, Clover trusted that the "wedding lunch went off charmingly," while a day after the ceremony Henry offered a gallant promise to his father-in-law: "I wish it were in my power to make the loss of Clover

241

less trying to you, but I know of no way of doing it than by making her as happy as I can." After several quiet days at Cotuit Port on the Cape, followed by a quick respite at Quincy, the couple embarked on an extended honeymoon in Europe and Egypt. Sailing on the gravely named *Siberia* they were joined by a host of Brahmins — including the James Russell Lowells, Francis Parkman, and John Holmes, a brother of the poet Oliver Wendell — all heading toward various summer sanctuaries. It proved to be an awful voyage. Only three days after departure Henry confided in an anxious letter to Clover's father back in Beverly of her longing to be with the Hoopers. "Wishes she had staid at home," he wrote. "Much sleep. An hour or two walk on bridge. Wretchedness aggravated by the idea of a week more of it. Can't read. Can't talk. Homesick for Cotuit. For Beverly." Three days later Clover offered her own sullen perspective of their journey, reporting the deck to be "nasty damp" and relating her unwelcome discovery in steerage of a coffin under construction for a fellow passenger just passed. She declared herself eager to see all that the Continent had to offer on what she vowed would be the couple's "last trip to Europe."[7]

Following a brief stay at Wenlock Abbey with Gaskell, the couple proceeded to the Mediterranean by way of several weeks' sightseeing in Bonn, Berlin, Dresden, Nurem-berg, Bern, and Geneva. Moving on to Italy they briefly decamped in Cadenabbia, a charming resort town on the west shore of Lake Como, before proceeding to Florence. In late November they sailed to Alexandria, commencing on the long-planned centerpiece of their trip: a Nile excursion aboard the comfortable *Isis,* a rented houseboat. While wending down the river Clover appears to have suffered some sort of ailment, perhaps even a brief collapse. The historiography is mixed, though most scholars believe that depression had set in. What we know is that she missed her father intensely and seemed nervous and slightly disoriented upon reach-ing Egypt after nearly five months abroad. Writing to Dr. Hooper in early December from Cairo, she offered a cryptic account of visiting a local mosque: "In one part of the immense building a dozen or more dervishes dressed in long stuff gowns and high white hats spun round and round for more than half an hour . . . the motion growing faster every minute; it was the most extraordinary spectacle and by no means a pleasant one. It gave one the feeling of being surrounded by maniacs."[8]

We know further that while on the Nile Clover remained unusually silent, going more than two weeks without attending to her cor-respondence. One biographer has conjectured that "she felt overwhelmed by all she was experiencing: the sights, smells, and sounds of the Nile, heightened by the heat, by confinement on the boat, and by the physical intimacy of married life." Accustomed to being in control of her actions, Clover, suddenly uprooted, may have grown distrustful and despondent. The easy affection she had for her father — who led a bachelor's existence after his wife's death — now found its tense complement in the careful politeness of a new husband. But Henry's attentiveness could not disguise the fact that most of their travels lacked the spontaneity of a shared experience. Their movements in Europe, rather, had retraced many of his previous transits, brought them into contact with his friends, and might even be said to have had the functional effect of enhancing his teaching of medieval history at Harvard. Clover could see nothing of herself aboard the *Isis.* Her experiences in Egypt seem to have been filtered through homesickness, fatigue, and the not yet negotiated circumstances of being a spousal adjunct to an Adams. Shortly before idling down the Nile she had described Alexandria, a city of some 220,000, as "the dirtiest and most hideous place I ever imagined."[9]

In March 1873, their Egyptian journey now over, Henry and Clover devoted some four months to a slow trek north, taking in Naples and Rome before brief stays in Paris and London prefaced the inevitable return home. Upon docking that summer back in America, Henry went straight to Quincy to visit his parents while Clover traveled alone to Beverly Farms to be with her father. United in Boston, they took as their residence a fashionable home at 91 Marlborough Street in the new Back Bay, just around the corner from Dr. Hooper's Beacon Street quarters. Though "very small," it held the couple's trove of books and the twenty-five packing crates filled with fashionable bric-à-brac brought back from Europe. Not long after, the Adamses purchased some twenty acres at Beverly Farms, erecting a summer retreat next to Hooper's. They prized this seasonal dwelling ("our log-hut in the woods" where Henry played the rustic), until Clover's death. For a few years, before Adams's 1877 resignation from Harvard, they fashioned a shared social life, part Brahmin, part Cambridge scholar, and, so they liked to think, part bohemian. Henry James, an acquaintance of Clover's since their childhood, captured the couple's particular bonhomie when he described them as "very pleasant, friendly, conversational, critical, [and] ironical." In another communication he allowed that the sharpness of their gossipy judgments threatened to become "rather too critical and invidious."[10]

The Adamses' choice of residences suggests the state of their respective obligations and emotional commitments. Clover clearly required the nearby presence of her father, while Henry sought a polite distance from his own people. His favorite relations, sister Loo and grandmother Louisa, had made similar escapes. And perhaps he saw elements of these women in Clover, recognizing in her "invidious" opinions of Boston a certain echo. Rarely did Henry suffer convention lightly and, in taking a wife, *this* wife, he reached for something both familiar and elusive.

Having returned, as he put it, to "the small Boston world" following his wedding year abroad, Henry introduced an advanced research seminar at Harvard on medieval institutions.[1] The course probed deeply into Anglo-Saxon law, a fresh area of interest for Adams stimulated during his recent stay in London, where his social circle included a scattering of legal scholars. The seminar proved to be the catalyst for Henry's initial effort in the emerging field of scientific history. Just as the old Puritans, to whom the past revealed God's divine plan, gave way to generations of patriotic writers, so the patriots, recorders of the nation's glorious Revolution, were now giving way to university-trained men. Among them, Adams did his share of training. Having received permission from President Eliot to go ahead with the section, he recruited a handful of doctoral students and together they produced an ambitious monograph that traced the roots of English Common Law — a welter of codes, customs, and legal practices — back to its purported Anglo-Saxon origins. Democracy, in other words, was but a matter of descent.

Henry's interest in comparative jurisprudence might seem ironic considering his disinclination to follow family protocol and study law. But as editor of the *North American Review* he ruminated with interest over the recent historiography in the field, developing a passion for, of all things, German legal studies, which he believed more scientific and less impressionistic than scholarship coming out of England. This notion convinced him that the German seminar method had much to offer students researching the past as well. "A scientific training is as necessary to the historian as to the mathematician," he wrote in an 1874 review of William Stubbs's *Constitutional History of England,* "and it is the misfortune of England that she has never yet had a scientific historical school."[2]

Henry's reading of the recent literature persuaded him that, contra the long-established view, Germanic rather than Roman law had spawned the constitutional rights enjoyed in the modern West. His interest conformed to a broader trend among a rising generation of American historians at this time who were taking terminal degrees in Germany. Albert Bushnell Hart, who commenced a four-decade tenure at Harvard in the early 1880s, completed a doctorate at the University of Freiburg; Herbert Baxter Adams (no relation) of Johns Hopkins took a Ph.D. at Heidelberg; and William E. Dodd, a distinguished University of Chicago scholar — and later U.S. ambassador to Germany — studied at the University of Leipzig. One could go on.[3]

From the German scientific perspective emerged in American seminars the germ theory of history. This hypothesis emphasized the Teutonic roots of democracy, claiming that the "germ" of representative government emerged from folk and shire "moots" (county courts) in the ancient Black Forest, whence it traveled in waves to England (following the fifth-century Roman withdrawal) and still later to New England (think Puritan town hall meetings). This clean, uncomplicated, and thoroughly Anglo-Saxon–centered history explained in its sweeping association of ideology and race everything from the Boston Tea Party to calls for immigration restriction. The germ theory further privileged a Wasp perspective of historical development that conveniently diminished the Latin Catholic world. First, it argued against the prevailing notion that antiquity — Greco-Roman culture — served as the primary impulse behind Western civilization's legal framework as embodied in the Code of Justinian. And second, in celebrating Anglo-Saxon law as a precursor to American law, it shone a reflective negative light on French civilization, now seen, after the German defeat of the French army at Sedan in 1870 (resulting in the collapse of the French Second Empire), as a deficient model for emulation. To American scholars, rather, modern French history appeared to be a chaotic and failed search for stability as monarchy gave way to republic, which gave way to empire, and so on. A unified Germany, by contrast, though in its bare infancy, presented an altogether different image as a conservative, prosperous nation. A consensus emerged that the source of this measured, mature development was the body of Anglo-Saxon laws that continued, presumably since the days of the shire moots, to inform the German legal code.[4]

Aside from abetting certain contemporary cultural and racial assumptions, the Teutonic school offered its American wing an additional advantage. Ever since 1776 a long train of European aristocrats, diplomats, and critics had prophesied the impending collapse of the United States. Apparently America, with its tradition-defying youth and conspicuously populist politics, lacked the stable ideological underpinnings to emulate the Continent's superior legal legislation. The theory of Anglo-Saxon law, however, suggested an altogether different narrative. Rather than regard the United States as an outlier, men like Henry Adams could see in their country's particular "racial" profile the most recent link in a long line of representative governments, predating by far the Enlightenment or even the Puritan origins of America. As an all-encompassing statement of civilizational development, the flexible germ theory neatly carried the considerable weight of Brahmin class conservatism.

Adams's handpicked seminar students consisted of Ph.D. candidates Henry Cabot Lodge, Ernest Young, and J. Laurence Laughlin. The last looked back upon their academic quartet with warm appreciation: "Those were busy but halcyon days when we dined at Adams's house on the Back Bay . . . and held our seminar meetings in his well-walled library with its open fire. We searched the early German codes . . . for the first glimmerings of the institutions which through the Normans and Anglo-Saxons formed the basis of English and, of course, of American legal development."[5] The papers they produced served as their degree-qualifying theses and, when joined by their instructor's separate piece, "The Anglo-Saxon Courts of Law," were collected in *Essays in Anglo-Saxon Law* (1876). The prominent Boston publishing house Little, Brown and Company released the book; Adams edited the essays and generously financed their printing to the tune of some $2,000 — a bit over $47,000 in current dollars.

Henry's lead essay, arguing for the continuity of Anglo-Saxon law throughout the Wasp world, established the tone for those that followed. Rather than a compilation of uneven opinions, they all carried in their titles the prefix "The Anglo-Saxon," followed by, in suffix succession, "Courts of Law," "Land-Law," "Family Law," and "Legal Procedure." The result is a tightly argued and thematically cohesive work, which, in the spirit of scientific history, is largely bereft of flowery prose or rhetorical flourishes. It equals the Romantic writers, however, in providing readers of American history with a usable past. Francis Parkman, for example, was at that time producing a colorful and richly acclaimed seven-volume study, *France and England in North America* (1865–92). It celebrated the removal of French Catholic power in the New World and with it the commensurate rise of Anglo influence, typified by congregationalism, constitutionalism, and capitalism. Assessing this immense project in 1969, one scholar wrote that Parkman uncritically accepted the notion of progress, "especially the progress of Protestant, Anglo-Saxon civilization."[6] The scientific historians, though armed with advanced degrees, arrived at more or less the same conclusion.

Adams's essay opens with a lengthy sentence trumpeting the virtues of Teutonic historiography: "The long and patient labors of German scholars seem to have now established beyond dispute the fundamental historical principle, that the entire Germanic family, in its earliest known stage of development, placed the administration of law, as it placed the political administration, in the hands of popular assemblies composed of the free, able-bodied members of the commonwealth." Moving from grand generalization to grander generalization, Henry insisted that as Americans enjoyed the power-sharing machinery of state and local governments, ancient Germans had lived in small districts that formed into larger states that might be said to constitute a kind of cohesive confederation. Assemblies fashioned by free men, he argued, made this "federal" system run.[7]

Adams's conflation of genetics and social development in *Anglo-Saxon Law* aligned comfortably with the dominant race thinking of his day. He presumed Germanic law to be more democratic and tenaciously entrenched than its Roman or Celtic coequals. How else could one explain its persistence through centuries of Viking raiders and Norman conquerors? He argued further that frequent separation from other groups allowed Teutonic jurisprudence to flourish, noting its

253

existence amid only the "purest Germanic stock." This type of racialist-isolationist rationale would find an institutional platform some years later (1894) in the formation of the Immigration Restriction League, established by three Harvard graduates. Responding to recent immigration from southern and eastern Europe, these men presumed the racial composition of the nation was under assault. Boston, already impacted by an earlier Irish diaspora, radiated an ethnic diversity that worried many of the city's older families. "By 1900," notes one writer, "more than 400,000 Bostonians out of a population of 560,000 had at least one foreign-born parent." John Murray Forbes, a wealthy Bostonian variously involved in railroads, industry, and the Chinese opium trade, offered financial assistance to the League, insisting, "The great struggle . . . centers on keeping our voting power and our reserves of public lands out of reach . . . of the horde of half-educated and wholly unreliable foreigners now bribed to migrate here, who under our present system can be dumped down on us annually."[8]

Believing that the problems of urban crime, poverty, and unrest could be traced in great part to recent immigration trends, the IRL sought to impose literacy standards for new arrivals and to cap the number of Catholic and Slavic immigrants coming from southern and eastern Europe. Lodge, Henry's former protégé and now a senator, supported a literacy bill — calling for the ability to read forty words in any language — that passed Congress in 1896 before succumbing to President Grover Cleveland's veto. Cleveland called the bill "a radical departure from our national policy relating to immigration."[9] Subsequent immigration acts did go into law in 1903, 1917, 1918, 1921, and 1924 that established various quotas and restrictions; the 1917 act, the most comprehensive immigration act passed to date, included a literacy exam.

Rather than a pioneering effort, *Anglo-Saxon Law* in fact conformed to a broader determination in certain intellectual circles to discern "difference" by constructing categories of human development based on variations in language, body size, environment, and so on. It was part, in other words, of the emerging social Darwinian worldview. This idea, popularized by the prominent English polymath Herbert Spencer, enjoyed a remarkable vogue in an America riven by racial division and industrial discontent. Accordingly, gross inequalities in income, education, and justice could be rationalized as a struggle for existence, a "survival of the fittest," as Spencer put it, dominated by the strong. Catching the cultural zeitgeist, *Anglo-Saxon Law* won favorable notices in a number of major publications on both sides of the Atlantic, including the Boston-based *American Law Review,* which called the essays "remarkable in the first place for their entire renunciation of English models and for their adoption not only of German methods, but of the authority and opinions of the now dominant German school." Herbert Baxter Adams, perhaps closer to the German bias than any scholar in the United States, reserved for Henry and his young dissertators a special distinction, calling their joint effort "the first original historical work ever accomplished by American university students working in a systematic and thoroughly scientific way under proper direction."[10]

Henry dedicated *Anglo-Saxon Law* to President Eliot with the short citation "This volume, fruit of his administration." He could have said as much of himself. Adams's tenure at Harvard lasted but a few years and he regarded this particular project with a special pleasure. "Nothing since I came to Cambridge," he wrote to Lodge late in his lecturing days, "has given me so much and so unalloyed satisfaction as the completion of our baking this batch of doctors of philosophy."[11] Of course for Henry one kind of satisfaction overshadowed all others, and it could scarcely be found in a Cambridge seminar room. As the project neared completion, another presidential election loomed, and in this coming canvass of 1876 he would try one final time to reform the "mess" of American politics.

20
POLITICAL ADIEU

In March 1874 the old abolitionist and senator Charles Sumner died in office. His passing reflected the weakening, in the public mind, of the race, rebellion, and Reconstruction triad that had for a generation confronted the country. It offered further the fleeting promise of rehabilitating the fortunes of the Adams family. For suddenly, at the age of sixty-six, Charles Francis emerged as the major statesman in Massachusetts. Edged out two years earlier by Horace Greeley for the Liberal Republican presidential nomination, the Governor, with his distinguished service in the country's diplomatic corps, brief congressional tenure, and indelible name, enjoyed a national reputation. As the next electoral cycle arrived, some reformers mechanically sought his candidacy — but not Henry. Perhaps reading his father's reluctance to revisit the political arena, or realizing the impossibility of his election, he laid to rest any fugitive dreams of a third Adams presidency. He remained determined, however, to see Grantism crumble.

An early shot from the Adams camp arrived that July in the form of Brooks's article "The Platform of the New Party," published, naturally, in Henry's *North American Review*. Taking his brother's line, Brooks criticized the rotation of office and caucus procedures that, he argued, led inevitably to the spoils system. "By offering places in the civil service as a prize for efficient party workers," he wrote, "a body of men were trained by degrees in all the methods by which . . . elections could be controlled." He further sought, as part of a more general reduction of radical Republican power, an end to what he called "Federal interference" in the South. Like Henry, he seemed unaware that the rights of African Americans in the former Confederacy were routinely ignored or that his complaint smacked of self-interest. In describing the enlargement of democracy in the Reconstruction era as little more than "an organized attack on ability, integrity, and education," Brooks offered the House of Adams's preferred opinion on the reasons behind its irrelevance.[1] Various and more penetrating attacks on Grantism followed in subsequent editions of the *North American Review,* including a lengthy exposé on the Tweed Ring, which had bilked New York City of many millions of dollars.

Aside from a few Adamses, the reform circle of "independents" included in its higher councils Schurz, Lodge, and *Springfield Republican* publisher Samuel Bowles. Looking to extend the independents' reach, Henry planned to purchase the *Boston Daily Advertiser* for $90,000 with shares going at $5,000, but that fell through. He later looked, futilely as things turned out, into the feasibility of having the reformers buy the *Boston Post* for $150,000 (some $3.5 million in current dollars); he hoped to entice Schurz to become its managing editor. A mixture of public-spiritedness and self-regard motivated the independents. Displaced by democracy and disgusted at the current governing class's evident nest feathering, the patricians resented their new political masters. In a caustic joint statement published during this period, Henry and Charles described the Republican Party as having been taken over by "as loud-mouthed and repulsive a set of political vagabonds as ever canted about principles or hungered after loaves and fishes."[2]

In letters to Gaskell, Henry tended to make light of the independents' efforts, joking of his own engagement in the cloak-and-dagger arena of "political intrigues" and in performing the "underhand work of pulling wires." In truth, however, he wanted badly for the independents to have a say in choosing the next president. But first they needed to create a "party of the centre," he supposed, and to offer support to the group "which accepts our influence most completely." In more convinced moments, Henry went so far as to linger over the possibility that "a new division of parties and a new assortment of party leaders will become inevitable." Oftener, he understood that the Republican-Democratic system, entering its third decade, was simply too entrenched to be toppled. He therefore looked to the impending election as an opportunity to revive the political influence of the old patrician elite by making it the balance of power in what promised to be an exceedingly tight national race.[3]

With his father's candidacy out of the question, Henry briefly played with the idea of trying to persuade Treasury Secretary Benjamin H. Bristow — prosecutor of the Whiskey Ring and champion of the gold standard — to accept a nomination from the independents. Such a move, he reasoned, might split Republicans and thus force the party to accept Bristow or face inevitable defeat. A little reflection, however, convinced him otherwise. "The public is not ready to support us," he wrote Schurz in February 1876, conceding further, "Mr. Bristow does not now share in our views" and in any event would never accept a third faction's nomination before

261

Republicans held their convention in June, at which time they might placate interparty critics by nominating a reform candidate of their own.[4] As spring approached, Henry and his candidate-less colleagues would soon have to make a decisive move or risk irrelevance.

Calling for a "conference of gentlemen independent of party ties," Adams played a weak hand out to a predictable end. In May some two hundred "leading academics and professional men" assembled for two days at New York's elegant Fifth Avenue Hotel in an effort to influence the coming canvassing. The invitations asked the gathering "to consider what may be done to prevent the National Election of the Centennial year from becoming a mere choice of evils." The attendees, crammed into a large conference room with inadequate seating, included the president of Williams College, the Yale political economist William Graham Sumner, Adams's brother Charles and his doctoral student Henry Cabot Lodge — but not the Beverly Farms–bound Henry, temperamentally disinclined to the sweat and speechifying of "real" politics. When trying to define shared principles, the body struggled to find common ground, though it did agree, as Schurz somewhat sharply noted, to support nominees who "deserved not only the confidence of honest men, but also the fear and hatred of the thieves."[5] Indeed, approached charitably, the meeting might be said to have succeeded merely by putting the major parties, their own conventions pending, on alert. By not choosing a progressive they risked alienating a potentially decisive voter bloc. In the end they bent just far enough. The Democrats, congregating in St. Louis's new Merchants Exchange Building, the first such convention held west of the Mississippi, nominated New York governor Samuel J. Tilden, known as a reformer. The Republicans, meeting in Cincinnati's vast wooden Exposition Hall, chose Ohio governor Rutherford B. Hayes, who had pledged to redeem the controversial greenbacks for gold. Thus both parties could be said to have appeased a number of independents.

Presuming that Hayes's nomination merely preserved the status quo, Henry remained independent. On a slow burn throughout the summer, he laid bare to Gaskell months of frustration:

After our utmost efforts we have only succeeded in barring the road to our opponents and forcing them to nominate as candidate for the Presidency one Hayes of Ohio, a third-rate nonentity whose only recommendation is that he is obnoxious to no one. I hope to enjoy the satisfaction of voting against him. The only good result of all the past eighteen months of work has been the

savage hunting-down of powerful scoundrels and the display of the awful corruption
of our system in root and branch. But our
people as yet seem quite callous.[6]

Several months later, in an unsigned article,
"The Independents in the Canvas," co-
authored with Charles and published in the
North American Review, Adams saw only
defeat in the insurgents' inability to maintain
a cohesive reform front:

No sooner were [the major parties' nomina-
tions] announced than those who had met
in the Fifth Avenue Hotel in May seemed in
an agony of impatience to declare their
adhesion to the one side or the other. In
this respect they displayed only that lack of
discipline and absence of leadership which
is almost invariably the fatal defect in such
attempted combinations. Could they have
held together, or acted upon the party
organizations with any degree of concentration, it can scarcely be doubted that before
the campaign was over they could have
forced their own issues to the front and
dictated their own terms of adhesion. As it
was, however, the instant the nominations
were made the members of the conference
resembled nothing so much as a group of
discreetly clad clergymen caught out in a
thunder-storm without any umbrellas. There

was something absurdly ludicrous in the haste with which they got themselves under cover.[7]

Nine days separated the Republican and Democratic conventions, and in that truncated period, with the reformers rapidly peeling away, a disappointed Adams raised a white flag. "Politics have ceased to interest me," he wrote Lodge. "I am satisfied that the machine can't be smashed this time. . . . The caucus and the machine will outlive me, and that being the case I prefer to leave this greatest of American problems to shrewder heads than mine."[8] Schurz's return to the Republican fold in particular wounded Henry, who finally decided on Tilden as the "best man." Aside from the question of character, Adams supposed the New York governor likely, if elected, to pull off tariff reform and perhaps find enough Republican support to replace paper money with hard money.

At bottom, however, Tilden's value for Henry was merely strategic. He claimed in correspondence that the Democratic candidate might conceivably "force the republicans to a higher level." Whether Henry actually believed this is debatable. The words were written in August to Lodge, his student, acolyte, and harried organizer of the inconclusive Fifth Avenue Conference. Adams further insisted in the communication that his "real object," the insertion of independent power in the electoral process, remained unchanged and suggested that the reformers' crusade was perhaps only beginning to hit its stride. But just a month later, in a more candid moment, he informed Gaskell that the independents showed little determination to carry on a long-term struggle. When the two parties made gestures in their conventions toward nominating "clean" candidates, he sighed, "We dissolved like a summer cloud."[9] Considering Adams's complete lack of political luck it should come as no surprise that in November Tilden, winner of the popular vote, lost to Hayes by a single electoral vote (185–184) in one of the most controversial national elections in American history.

Before retiring from the field of organized politics, Henry and Charles offered an angry parting shot: "Independents in the Canvas." This provocative piece served for Henry as something of a double adieu as it proved to be his final edition as editor of the *North American Review*. Ideological differences with the magazine's publishers — a small group of regular Republicans unamused at their editor's repeated attacks on regular Republicanism — disposed Adams to make the break. These leavings invariably led to yet another. Within months of the election, Henry resigned from Harvard and returned to Washington. Though painful, the failure of the independents served, in a larger sense, almost as a feint, offering Adams a solid reason for retreat.

What stands out to the contemporary reader of "Independents in the Canvas" is less its authors' by now de rigueur lament of Grantism than its crass unwillingness to recognize the rights of African Americans in the South. Aligning themselves firmly with "the white population in those States," Henry and Charles argued in the name of good government for the former Confederates "to throw off the odious rule of the enfranchised Africans." They did not elaborate on the methods for the throwing off, though more decisive men would resort to various shades of murder, torture, and terrorism. Seeking to leave "home rule" to a motley mix of Redeemers and paramilitary organizations, the brothers, both strong advocates of integrity in government, paradoxically challenged the constitutional rights guaranteed to former slaves by the Fourteenth and Fifteenth Amendments. In their haste to see America move beyond the southern "question," Charles and Henry radically underestimated the power of race and racism to shape the days and decades ahead. "So far . . . as the momentous political issues of twenty years ago are concerned," they wrote in a striking sample of short-sightedness, "little remains over which to struggle." If only, they suggested, Yankee reformers would let well enough alone. Calling the postwar South a "wreck," the brothers advised leaving the region in the hands of the Democratic Party (whose Dixie wing they had assailed as treasonous in 1861), presumably because its traditional Jeffersonian-Jacksonian allegiances would be familiar to the region's whites; Republicans, from this point on, were advised to stay out.[10]

In a manner of speaking, the brothers got their way. Shortly after assuming office, Hayes removed federal troops from the capitals of Louisiana and South Carolina, among the last states still undergoing Reconstruction. The appointment, moreover, of a Tennessee Democrat to the position of postmaster general and the promise of congressionally approved dollars for internal improvement projects in the South put the Republicans, eager to leave behind the "momentous political issues of twenty years ago," on a different path.

Before all this happened, however, one final November 1876 humiliation awaited Henry: the defeat of his father in Massachusetts's gubernatorial election. The state's Democrats nominated Charles Francis in the errant hope that his candidacy might turn out voters and help Tilden carry Massachusetts. A Thomas

Nast cartoon in the October 21 *Harper's Weekly* deliciously sported at the unlikely alliance between the Brahmin Adams and the Bay State's Irish constituency. Under the image of a dour, shamrock-chewing, cross-bearing, Celtic harp–wearing Charles Francis reads the improbable placard "Champion of the Fenians." Refusing to campaign (and decidedly short of Fenian support), Adams carried only 41 percent of the vote, losing decisively to former Boston mayor Alexander Hamilton Rice.[11]

For Henry, the tumultuous year's disappointments may have cut acutely, but they also provided a hard-earned clarity. Neither the Governor nor his sons counted in the capital city. There would be no more dreams of third-party heroism, no cabinet position, and no diplomatic mission. Near the end of that difficult summer Adams wrote soberly to Moorfield Storey, a young Boston reformer, "As it is, I must content myself by remaining outside any healthy political organisation."[12]

21
FILIAL PIETY

Four months after Tilden's narrow defeat, in the late winter of 1877, Henry approached Harvard president Charles W. Eliot with an unusual proposal. He suggested that Lodge, his newly plumed Ph.D., be hired "to establish a rival course to my own in United States History." For those who may lament the lack of ideological diversity in the twenty-first-century academy, Adams's reason for soliciting the additional section will strike a resonant chord. Lodge's "views being federalist and conservative," he explained to Eliot, "have as good a right to expression in the college as mine which tend to democracy and radicalism. The clash of opinions can hardly fail to stimulate inquiry among the students." Adams presumably measured his "radicalism" by the degree of political and intellectual independence he could claim as a member of a venerable but no longer electable dynastic family. Freedom, in this slender sense, could be equated with irrelevance. He scored Lodge

270

as conservative, by contrast, because the younger man gave already the appearance of coveting a political career — to Henry's thinking an utterly conventional decision that now, given the rising robber-baronocracy, lacked even its old honor.[1]

The entreaty to President Eliot (not taken up, as things turned out) anticipated a broader struggle between Adams and Lodge to set straight both family and national history. Their differences had to do with the controversial Hartford Convention of 1814, at which some two dozen New England Federalists condemned the unpopular War of 1812 for decimating their shipping economy, leaving their coastlines unprotected, and bolstering, in a burst of nationalism, the political fortunes of the pro-war Jeffersonians. Considering that the group met in secret while the war still raged, more than a few critics called their actions treasonous. And here, on the question of New England Federalism's loyalty and legacy, the two Henrys found themselves congenially but firmly at odds.

Lodge got the ball rolling in the summer of 1877, putting together a collection of his great-grandfather Cabot's correspondence with accompanying annotation. The finished product, *Life and Letters of George Cabot,* hued closely to the New England tradition of kin veneration, with Lodge quite clearly setting out to honor his ancestor — a U.S. senator, a devotee of the banker-and-businessman Federalism refined by Alexander Hamilton, and the presiding officer at the Hartford Convention.

This last item proved problematic. The motives and outcomes of the conventioneers remained in the 1870s a matter of opinion and perception. Friendly interpretations stressed their efforts — encapsulated in a released meeting report — to limit the ruling southern plantocracy's power by calling for an end to the Three-Fifths Compromise. Approached from this angle, Cabot might be said, in light of the Civil War (and Section 2 of the Fourteenth Amendment, which explicitly repealed the Compromise), to have served on the "right" side of history. If, however, as detractors would have it, he chaired a nascent secessionist movement in Hartford while the United States, its capital recently burned, battled Great Britain in "a second war for independence," then history was right to forget him. Lodge predictably sided with family and, by extension, those high Federalists whose views he happened to share.

Colloquially, Cabot and his allies — including former secretary of state Timothy Pickering, one-time congressman Fisher Ames, and the distinguished jurist Theophilus Parsons — were known as the Essex Junto, named after the Massachusetts county in which several of them resided. The moniker quickly hardened into an insult. It evoked a number of unfavorable impressions: peculiar, ill tempered, arrogant, and (later) secessionist. It signified further a patriotism perverted by insularity and eager, during the years of Virginia's political ascendancy, to abandon nationalism for a strictly northeastern conception of nationhood. Their New England critics included John Adams and John Quincy Adams, and thus Lodge inevitably reduced the reputations of these men in the *Life and Letters*. The senior Adams proved to be an ineffectual leader, he argued, hardly in Hamilton's class, while his son made rash and unproven accusations regarding the Essex Junto's alleged efforts to create a separate northern league. Actually, Lodge countered, Cabot had quashed any would-be revolutionaries at Hartford and thus performed a great national service. Recognizing the transparent partisanship of his venture, he acknowledged in *Life and Letters* the personal nature of the project: "I have not sought in treating New England Federalism to write a judicial and impartial history of the country. My object was to present one side, and that the Federalist, in the strongest and clearest light."[2]

Such an admission could only have raised a red flag for Adams, whose sharply negative appraisal of *Life and Letters* appeared that summer in the *Nation.* Shortly before its publication he had assured Lodge, with perhaps less than perfect candor, that he wished to stir up controversy only in order to prod sales. "[The review] is ingeniously calculated to make everyone, yourself included, furious with indignation," he wanly explained. "But I think it will excite interest in the book and sell the edition." Henry, so recently supportive of Lodge's contribution to *Essays in Anglo-Saxon Law,* now attacked his protégé's effort to rehabilitate the Essex Junto. Cabot, he argued in the review, "was Federalist to the core," and he refused to allow Lodge to wriggle his ancestor off the Hartford hook. The conventioneers were secessionists in waiting, he insisted, their shameful plans coming to naught largely because British and American envoys, then meeting in the Belgian city of Ghent, concluded a peace treaty that ended the War of 1812. As every *Nation* reader knew, John Quincy Adams served as chief negotiator for the American Commission.[3]

Not satisfied with a public critique of Lodge's *Life and Letters,* Henry spent the second half of 1877 editing a competing book of documents meant to vindicate John Quincy Adams's dim view of the Junto. Working quickly, he completed the study in December. The result, *Documents relating to New England Federalism, 1800–1815,* includes letters also appearing in Lodge's volume, though they read altogether differently with the addition of a long and spirited defense by John Quincy, "Reply to the Appeal of the Massachusetts Federalists," that consumes more than half of the book. Paired with the "Reply," which took the Junto deadly seriously as a secessionist force, the letters between Pickering, Cabot, and company assume a distinctly menacing tone. Packed in the book's appendix, they bear evidence of an unmistakable eagerness to create a new northern nation: "The principles of our Revolution point to the remedy, — a separation"; "Without a separation, can those States ever rid themselves of negro [Virginia] Presidents and negro Congresses, and regain their just weight in the political balance?"; "I have no hesitation myself in saying, that there can be no safety to the Northern States *without a separation from the confederacy.*"[4]

John Quincy drafted the "Reply" in the last weeks of 1828. Earlier in the year he had made certain provocative comments, published in the (Washington) *National Intelligencer,* regarding the Essex Junto and its disciples. He stated in part that the "object" of the ultras "was, and had been for several years, a dissolution of the Union, and the establishment of a separate confederation." In response to this damning charge old

275

Federalists and the sons of old Federalists demanded that the president prove his accusations. Declaring himself unwilling to engage in an "inquisition," in which their "avowed object [was] controversy," a defensive Adams, then in the midst of a tumultuous (and unsuccessful) presidential campaign against Andrew Jackson, gave no satisfaction.[5] Following the election, however, he penned the acidic "Reply." Perhaps thinking of the damage it might do him in conservative Massachusetts, he promptly buried the brief in his files, where it remained unpublished for nearly a half-century.

Eager to see it now exhumed, Henry believed the "Reply" a complete vindication of his grandfather. It included a letter from former New Hampshire senator William Plummer attesting that during Jefferson's presidency "several of the Federalists, Senators and Representatives, from the New England States, informed me that they thought it necessary to establish a separate government in New England." Playing the innocent — and perhaps as a private joke — Henry announced that students of history had Lodge, of all people, to thank for the resurrection of John Quincy's bracing "vindication." "The appearance of [*Life and Letters*], marking as it does the moment when party-spirit begins to yield to the broader spirit of impartial investigation," he puckishly

276

wrote, "has removed the last objection to publishing the paper entitled 'Reply.' "[6]

Lodge did not go down quietly. In his own *Nation* review, he snidely praised *Documents* as a "dramatic" collection, thus hinting at what he regarded as the theatrical — though in no sense secessionary — nature of New England Federalism's rhetorical attack on Jeffersonianism. And in doing so he called into question the judgment of John Quincy, implying that, in his dry literal-mindedness, the author of the "Reply" inflated the anxious if impotent writings of the Essex men into a full-blown conspiracy. Lodge further drew attention to Henry's tendency to embellish, kick, and bite to make a point more pungent. *He,* in other words, trafficked in drama as well: "When [Adams] launches out into invective the wealth of his vocabulary, the vigor of his sarcasm, the savage ferocity of his direct assaults, combine to make this paper an almost unequaled piece of political controversial writing, worthy to rank with the best efforts in this branch of literature."[7]

Perhaps in these words of polite dismissal Lodge recognized the difficulties he faced taking Adams on. And to be sure, in the battle of the books, in the contest pitting competing reviews, Henry came out ahead. His clipped opinion of the Hartford Convention, published a few years later in his magisterial history of the Jefferson and Madison administrations, long held the historiographical high ground:

> The delegates numbered only twenty-three persons, mostly cautious and elderly men, who detested democracy. . . . Possibly much was said which verged on treasonable conspiracy. . . . If any leading Federalist disapproved the convention's report, he left no record of the disapproval. In such a case, at such a moment, silence was acquiescence. As far as could be inferred from any speeches made or letters written at the time, the Federalist party was unanimous in acquiescing in the recommendations of the Hartford Convention.[8]

But was Henry's interpretation the right interpretation? Were New Englanders really on the edge of secession? More than a few Hartford delegates had major financial, shipping, and mercantile interests with the several states of the Union, while the region's vast classes of pensioners and investors were reliant on government securities. It was by no means certain, moreover, that the people of the Northeast would sustain a separation movement carried out in their name. Against such a stacked deck, secession seems a long shot.

Some years ago, in the 1960s, the scholar James M. Banner Jr. revisited the history of

278

the Hartford Convention and what he called "a decorous but always sharp historiographical war" between Adams and Lodge. The latter, he wrote, attempted

to distinguish Cabot from the radical and less gracious likes of Timothy Pickering, whose life and letters had been published five years earlier in a manner which inaccurately played down Pickering's secessionist schemes. Lodge tried both to exculpate Cabot and more fully to implicate Pickering. But the straightforward Lodge — himself a sort of later-day embodiment of Federalism: bluff, exclusivist, nativist, prejudiced, and all — was no match for Henry Adams, the master of the ironic style.[9]

Banner, I think, has identified an important temperamental difference between the two men that, beyond historiographical sword-crossing, goes some way in explaining their divergent occupational paths — Lodge into politics and Adams into a historical-literary career animated by a chilly, double-edged detachment.

Though "no match" for Henry as a scholar, Lodge knew his mentor well, respected his capacity for crafting an argument, and marveled at the older man's ability to make, as he put it, a compelling "drama" of the past. There would be more drama to come. For in addressing the Federalist feud, Adams put the intricacies of Anglo-Saxon law behind him and commenced a long engagement with the early American nation. His colorful portrayals in the *History* of interparty struggles among Republican chieftains Jefferson, Vice President Aaron Burr, and Virginia statesman John Randolph seem in retrospect a natural extension of the earlier project. As a précis on the young country's struggles with schisms, only the party labels had changed.

It seems fitting that Henry took up the *Documents* study in 1877, his last year teaching at Harvard and living in New England. The work thus serves as a eulogy of sorts, an effort to set the historical record straight while simultaneously honoring family. Bowing before both training and tradition, he left behind an immaculate offering, a mixed memorial to a city, a region, and a way of life long since gone.

22
EMANCIPATION

Musing over Adams's decision to vacate Boston, an observant niece once told a scholar, "Nothing has ever seemed strange to me in Uncle Henry's laying down his assistant professorship and seeking out Washington as a place at that time to live and work in. Writing, studying, using his imagination, creating was innate in him. He couldn't help himself. Teaching . . . and editorship couldn't hold him." It is less clear why Clover, particularly close to her father, consented to the move. Perhaps, like Henry, she found Boston uncomfortably constricting; possibly a fresh situation suggested the chance for better health; or she may have idled over the promise of presiding over a Washington salon. There are no definite answers, only conjectures. It is tempting to think that for both Clover and Henry the warm Upper South implied a subdual of certain family-centered stresses, a release from social monotony, and a chance to leaven the residual cultural puritanism rooted deeply in their shared ancestries. Clover may have hinted as much when she wrote hopefully to her father that Washington offered "new possibilities for us."[1]

We do know that Clover and her in-laws did not get along. As one scholar has noted, "Abby had very decided notions about a woman's role as wife which included cleaving to her husband's family, a proper devotion to the church, a discreet tongue, and the ability to bear children. Clover failed by all these measures." Abby called her "a queer woman" and mocked her invalidism: "She is always on the bed or sofa with *that* pillow." Relations between the two women eventually broke down, and Henry took to seeing his parents alone, on Sundays.[2]

For Henry, the move appears in hindsight merely a question of *when* rather than *why.* His recent efforts on behalf of the country's reform independents spoke, in a fuller than political sense, of a congenital resistance to the club, the swarm, the crowd. His equally timely editorial work on the *Documents* emphasized the rigid frame of reference that had warped the Essex Junto, twisting its perspective and poisoning its judgment. To retain self-mastery, in other words, meant carving out a judicious distance. This culti-vated aloofness aligned comfortably with Henry's emotional makeup; arch, reserved, and exclusive, he grew bored in the arid

Cambridge college-ocracy. Brooks, who as a first-year law student shared his brother's Wadsworth House residence, remembered that Harvard made an effort for Henry but inevitably fell short: "No man could have been more petted than he at Cambridge. . . . But he soon tired of Cambridge because Cambridge did not socially amuse him."[3]

Perhaps pining for London's bright variety, Adams, enframed in an academic calendar, began to realize himself as a caricature of all the unfortunate young men prematurely aged by the routine, the pose, and the empty ceremony. "I am going on to thirty eight years old, the yawning gulf of middle-age," he wrote Gaskell in the spring of 1875. "Another, the fifth, year of professordom is expiring this week. I am balder, duller and more pedantic, and more lazy than ever." As much as any sin, Henry condemned Harvard's depressing facility for producing a Brahmin type deficient in adventure or originality. The conversations and the social gatherings were to his mind numbingly repetitive — all depressingly "correct," all sober, solid, and settled. Unsurprisingly, he reserved his greatest scorn for the faculty, the purveyors of Anglo-Saxon certainty and spiritual insularity. He arraigned the professoriate for blunting enthusiasm, stifling critical engagement, and "forcing up a new set of simple-minded, honest, harmless intellectual prigs as like to

themselves as two dried peas in a bladder."
Giving students substance, he insisted to one
friend, meant teaching *against* the College.
He had no illusions that such a desperate
strategy could be sustained: "You can imagine
that my remarks to my students are gradually
growing somewhat sharp-pointed and calculated to get me into trouble some day."[4]

Henry's resistance to Cambridge signified,
in its closely overlapping currents, a bigger
rejection of Boston. The Brahmins were
undeniably narrowing in their social outlook
and turning ever inward; the Governor's editing of John Quincy's massive diaries (twelve
volumes appearing between 1874 and 1877),
Lodge's efforts to burnish ancient George
Cabot's reputation, and even Henry's response to Lodge in the *Documents* were
symptomatic of perhaps too filial an attachment to family. If the Civil War briefly restored New England's relevance as the epi-
center of a growing antislavery movement,
the postwar period saw power radiate outward
into the vast political and economic networks
now racing across the Continent. Between
1876 and 1890 seven new states entered the
union, midwestern presidents sat in the White
House, and the American Indian Wars entered their late stages; the Standard Oil
Company swelled into the Standard Oil Trust
during these years, while the opening of the
Brooklyn Bridge and arrival of several mil-

lion immigrants established a strikingly new urban sense of scale and mobility. Boston, once a Puritan entrepôt, knew not what to make of this flux and in its confusion somewhat defensively filled its churches with memorials, crammed its libraries with genealogies, and dotted its avenues with stone-faced statuary.

Finding the Brahmin milieu fiercely self-contained, Henry dreaded the prospect of remaining among its chosen. So he chose otherwise. The satisfied city, having made its peace with the old Christian strictures and the new Gilded Age, offended him as dismally smooth, sleepy, and lacking in higher purpose. "Boston is a curious place," he complained to Gaskell, "there is no society worth the name, no wit, no intellectual energy or competition, no clash of minds or of schools, no interests, no masculine self-assertion or ambition. Everything is respectable, and nothing amusing. There are no outlaws. There are not only no convictions but no strong wants. . . . I am allowed to sit in my chair at Harvard College and rail at everything which the College respects, and no one cares."[5]

It appears that in leaving New England, Henry strained to make of his emancipation a cultural critique or even, to borrow from Lodge, a "drama." His attacks on Boston's nepotistic social circles are well made, if one-sided. On the eve of his departure, rather, the city and its satellites contained a number of rising and setting intellectual suns that eclipsed perhaps any competing cohort to be found in America. These included Ralph Waldo Emerson, Henry Wadsworth Longfellow, George Bancroft, William Dean Howells, William James, and Oliver Wendell Holmes Jr. Boston housed important presses and magazines, including Little, Brown and Company, Houghton Mifflin, the *Atlantic Monthly,* and, of course, the *North American Review;* a number of distinguished colleges and museums, institutes and medical schools maintained their campuses and collections there as well. But where in this respectable galaxy of New World high culture did Henry fit? Despite his real achievements in both print and pedagogy, Boston remained the city of his ancestors, whose sundry political successes he could never match.

Adams resigned from Harvard in May 1877, and yet only two months earlier, as previously noted, he had petitioned Eliot to allow two sections of a "rival" U.S. history course — taught by himself and Lodge — to be offered "next year." His plans were altered in the interval by an unexpected invitation from Albert Rolaz Gallatin, the second and only surviving son of Albert Gallatin, to edit the latter's correspondence. Adams leaped at the offer. On April 14 he wrote to Gaskell, "I am . . . in New York devoting all my energies to the arrangement of a great mass of papers which have accidentally come under my hands, and which may give me some years work and exercise a good deal of influence on my future movements." Under the cover of an exciting scholarly project, Henry happily left the academic world, never to return. "I regard my university work as essentially done," he informed one correspondent, while notifying another of having "broken my connection with the University at Cambridge."[6]

It is possible that in removing to Washington, Adams, aside from engaging with "a great mass" of Gallatin papers, sought to play one final political card. Clearly his efforts as a reformer had proven ineffective, but in coming to the capital he might quietly advertise his availability. Under the auspices of historical research and writing, amid a salon setting in which he and Clover might shine, no one would question the place of an Adams in Washington. Precedent for second acts existed within the family. John Quincy returned to the capital at the age of sixty-four to serve in the House of Representatives; Charles Francis turned fifty-two the year he captured a congressional seat. Not that Henry would have suffered the "indignity" of campaigning for a public office, though again heredity suggested an alternative form of service: appointment. Three generations of Adamses had represented their country abroad, and Henry may have lingered ever so lightly over the idea of becoming the fourth of his line to serve as the U.S. minister to the Court of St. James's — or possibly claim a cabinet position on some distant day. His conspicuous encampment in Washington suggested to anyone willing to notice, or make an offer, a convenient availability. "I hob-nob with the leaders of both parties," he wrote shortly after taking up the Gallatin project, "and am very contented under my cloak of historian."[7]

To Charles Francis, however, Henry's resignation from Harvard signified a definite break with family. "I feel as if he was now taking a direction which will separate us from him gradually forever," he confessed to his diary. Clover's most recent biographer, Natalie Dykstra, contends that Henry's parents pinned much of the "blame" for their leaving on his wife, whom they seemed to resent. Dykstra quotes a cold journal entry written by the Governor two years after the couple absented Boston: "I have no feelings but those of affection and love for him. I pity rather than dislike his wife. But henceforth I must regard her as a marplot." What we know is that Charles Francis adored his son and doubted his prospects in Washington, a mere political town in which, so he moaned, "none of our name have ever prospered."[8]

The Governor's misgivings tell us something about what it meant to be an Adams — and the spouse of an Adams. And yet it is possible that Henry, still imbued by his boyhood trip to the capital to visit his grandmother Louisa, abandoned Boston as a Johnson. Anxious for a fresh start he turned south, eager to renew and deepen the life he had been living before the Harvard interruption. "Sooner or later," he wrote to a friend, "all the eccentric people in the world drift through Washington."[9]

■ ■ ■ ■

WASHINGTON

■ ■ ■ ■

As for me and my wife, we have made a great leap in the world; cut loose at once from all that has occupied us since our return from Europe, and caught new ties and occupations here. The fact is, I gravitate to a capital by a primary law of nature. This is the only place in America where society amuses me, or where life offers variety.

Henry Adams to Charles Milnes Gaskell, 1877

23
HEARTS PLAY

Settling in downtown Washington, Henry and Clover leased a large house on H Street belonging to William Corcoran, a banker, philanthropist, and founder of the Corcoran Gallery of Art. The structure, formerly occupied by Clover's recently deceased congressman uncle Sam Hooper, sat conveniently near Lafayette Square. "Possessed of large wealth," Hooper, so one eulogy stated, "attracted to his house and to his society men among the ablest and the best which our country furnishes."[1] The building's new occupants aimed to be equally hospitable. With a combined unearned annual income of $25,000, some $585,000 in current dollars, the Adamses were in a position to make their Washington homes — two successor residences followed the H Street experiment — exemplars of good taste. Numerous overseas trips yielded an impressive assortment of paintings and porcelains, bronzes and tapestries, along with a lesser collection of bibelots and bric-à-brac. Stylish and sophisticated, their Washington addresses offered an agreeable contrast to the congressional debates droning on a few blocks to the east. Taken in full, the Adamses had perhaps all they could reasonably want in these early capital years — all, that is, excepting a child.

If the move to Washington signified a host of breakings and beginnings, it also likely softened whatever strains came from the Adamses' growing awareness that they would never be parents. They were now five years into their marriage and, as the captives of distinguished New England genealogies, almost certainly cornered on the baby front by unspoken pressures and empty wishes. As if to draw unwanted attention to their childless situation, Henry's and Clover's brothers were, thanks to their fecund wives, fathers to fifteen children. Boston may have accordingly held difficult, even painful associations for the couple. Washington, on the other hand, moved to a different and decidedly less maternal beat. Its boardinghouses welcomed bachelor politicians and lobbyists, a small army of men whose invisible broods typically resided far beyond the capital's shadow. Society proved to be fluid and in its own way ephemeral; salons, gatherings, and parties filled the spaces that otherwise — and in much of America — might be occupied by the daily rituals of family life.[2]

It remains a mystery as to why Henry and Clover could not conceive. One possible clue is the appearance of a gynecological study in the couple's library, *Clinical Notes on Uterine Surgery with special reference to the management of sterile conditions,* written by J. Marion Sims, M.D., and published in 1873.[3] Though what particular ailment this may have pointed to, if any, is unclear. We do know that children were on Henry's mind during this time. In February 1876 he reflected upon the death of an acquaintance's great-uncle and the commensurate news of a birth within his own circle. "I wish — wish — wish — well, I wish various things," he wrote to one correspondent, "but among others that the mystery of Birth and the Grave were either less important to us, or more encouraging."[4] The following year he congratulated Gaskell, soon to be a father, in a labored letter advertising his presumed indifference to children:

I am glad you are going to have a family and I hope it will be at least as large as either of your sister's', for I find from experience that daily life becomes commonplace anyway, and perhaps its commonplatitude is less offensive among many daily commonplaces than among few. I have myself never cared enough about children to be unhappy either at having or not having them, and if it were not that half the world will never leave the other half at peace, I should never think about the subject.[5]

Determined to keep "half the world" away, the Adamses knew with whom to extend their social connections and when to close ranks. Henry acknowledged as much when he wrote to Gaskell just weeks into their new situation, "I have only room to add that we are quite well, very busy, and very happy. One consequence of having no children is that husband and wife become very dependent on each other and live very much together. This is our case."[6]

If Washington's cosmopolitanism diverted an unflattering focus on family life, the city more directly elevated Henry and Clover's status. In Boston they remained among any number of Adamses, Hoopers, Sturgises, Bigelows, and Cabots — and new "names" tied to fresh fortunes in banking, insurance, and industry were now pressing upon the old. But in the still green capital city, with a healthy private income, Henry and Clover could, as the latter put it, "strut around as if we were millionaires." A mutual friend, Henry James, recognized this facet of their marriage when he informed the British diplomat Sir John Clark, "[The Adamses] don't pretend to conceal . . . their preference of America to Europe, and they rather rub it into me, as they think it a wholesome discipline for my demoralized spirit. One excellent reason for their liking Washington better than London is that they are, vulgarly speaking, 'someone' here, and that they are nothing in your complicated kingdom."[7]

As if to demonstrate the veracity of James's statement, Adams wrote Gaskell in late 1878 of the special social amenities available to him and Clover in the American capital:

You see, in London I can't drop in of an evening to the palace to chat with the Queen. . . . Here society is primitive as the golden age. We run in at all hours to see everybody. I have a desk in our Foreign Office for my exclusive study, and unlimited access to all papers. We make informal evening calls on the President, the Cabinet and the Diplomates. Ten days ago I went uninvited to Yoshida's, the Japanese Minister's, and played whist with him and his Japanese wife till midnight.[8]

Evenings were crowded with entertaining, and though some of the anointed included "our eminent Boston constituents," as Henry put it, he seemed inclined to certain southern sympathies. He bragged to one correspondent that a "not unusual" H Street dinner included Mississippi senator (and future Supreme Court justice) Lucius Quintus Cincinnatus Lamar II ("the most genial and sympathetic of all Senators") and former Confederate general Richard Taylor, son of President Zachary Taylor and brother-in-law of Jefferson Davis.[9]

Henry and Clover's mornings, by contrast, were reserved for horseback riding about the capital and its environs. They typically departed — aboard the prosaically named Prince and Daisy — at about nine and returned for an eleven-thirty breakfast. The nearby Rock Creek Park, just a couple of miles north of the city, proved to be a favorite destination. "The riding is excellent hereabouts," Henry observed to Gaskell, though conceding the terrain's unfitness for fox hunting: "We are not so swell."[10]

The Adamses settled into a tight circle of friends who called themselves the Five of Hearts. Its roster included the pungent, dark-eyed, and smartly attired future secretary of state John Hay; his stout and pious wife, Clara (daughter of the Cleveland railroad tycoon Amasa Stone); and Clarence King, a prominent geologist and mountaineer known for a lively, playful manner. For Henry these were maturing acquaintances; he had first met Hay in Washington during the secessionist winter and King a few years later while hiking in Estes Park, Colorado. A conspicuous intimacy characterized the clique, who advertised their affection with heart-embossed stationery, a heart-shaped tea set, and enameled Five of Hearts pins ordered from Tiffany. Their closeness, however, remains a matter of question. Clara came aboard as a spousal appendage, while Clover's depression seemed a thing outside the group's gay orbit. Most striking, King led a secret life in which he passed (as "James Todd") for an African American and fathered five children with his common-law wife, Ada Copeland, thought to be a former slave.[11]

Just what united the Five of Hearts is a matter of speculation, though clearly a common snobbery put them at ease. Condescending toward the lower classes, they spoke as a group believing itself in possession of all the history, all the fine prizes their nation might bestow, and yet they were also restive in their recognition that this patrician proprietorship appeared to be nearing its end. As twin testimonials of class anxiety, Henry's 1880 novel *Democracy* admonished popular political power, while Hay's 1883 novel *The Bread-Winners: A Social Study* attacked organized labor; both books were published anonymously.

Though Henry and Hay were the most intellectually compatible and politically interested of the Hearts, Adams saw in King a romantic figure to whom he remained long devoted. Naturalist, author, and collector of fine arts, the geologist enjoyed an easy and extensive range of seemingly incompatible references that eluded the hyperintellectual Henry. While still in his twenties King wrote the classic *Mountaineering in the Sierra Nevada* (1872), a work that Adams enthusiastically praised in the *North American Review*. Calling its ruggedly handsome author "a kind of young hero of the American type," he valorized the Newport-born and Yale-educated rock hunter whose climbing expeditions suggested yet another episode in the centuries-long struggle pitting Puritan resolve against the "wild" North American continent. Comfortable on a mountain or in a museum, King represented a certain masculine ideal that would always elude Adams. Intrepid, brave, gallant, humorous, and above all unaffected, he was a "natural," a child of the open American scene in a way that Henry could never be. Without a trace of jealousy Adams wrote of his friend, "Whatever prize he wanted lay ready for him, — scientific, social, literary, political, — and he knew how to take them in turn."[12]

With a change in presidential administrations both King, first director of the U.S. Geological Survey, and Hay, assistant secretary of state, resigned their positions and left Washington in 1881. The Adamses kept in contact with their fellow Hearts, though King, increasingly engaged in risky mining ventures, moved stealthily around the country, allowing him the necessary freedom to keep secret his several relationships with nonwhite women. Henry remained closer to Hay, and their correspondence attests to a connection that only deepened over the years; theirs proved to be the strongest bond of the five, forming, in a sense, a separate clique.

Clover's salon operated efficiently, with a perpetual afternoon tea often prefacing a convivial dinner party. The Adamses, Henry James favorably observed, "have a very pretty little life."[13] Such sociable days would have been empty for Henry Adams, however, without a more vocational engagement. Still an Adams, still the offspring of letter collectors, diary keepers, and memoirists, he began during this period, having just turned forty, to justify his relocation to Washington by becoming the writer and historian he never was in Boston. In just five years (1879–84) he produced two "contemporary" novels and two biographies, all the while working steadily on a prolonged portrait of the Jeffersonian era. Moving easily between reportage and reflection, the projects announced their author's intention to write of democracy from within, to absorb the capital city's vast store of parties, archives, and rumors. Stimulated by the presence of power, Henry went to work.

24
GALLATIN

Among the late nineteenth-century Brahmin faithful, filial piety remained the dictum of the day. One wrote of ancestors with an eye toward edification, presenting cleaned-up versions of past and parent. This tradition continued deep into the next century, as evidenced in Harvard historian Samuel Eliot Morison's multiple memoirs (in 1913 and again in 1969) of the Boston Federalist Harrison Gray Otis, a "four generations removed" descendant, so Morison put it. In the 1913 edition he stated without apology, "Contrary to general opinion, I believe that a statesman's biography can best be written by a descendant."[1] Not all descendants deigned to agree. Aside from editing (without commentary) John Quincy's "Reply" in the *Documents* project, Henry showed little interest in publicly assaying the House of Adams. He did so only glancingly in his long study of the early republic, while the *Education*'s absorbing sketch of pre–Civil War Quincy is suggestive but teasingly incomplete. To a remarkable degree, his published work managed to avoid the trap of tribal worship. But in rendering Albert Gallatin, the subject of his first major study, into an ideal candidate for the independent cause of the 1870s, he stumbled into a different kind of snare.

The Geneva-born Gallatin (1761–1849) had arrived in America at the age of nineteen and within a generation, under the auspices of the Jeffersonians, became the country's longest serving Treasury secretary. He played a critical role in shaping the Democratic-Republican Party's agrarian political economy before discovering a second career as a diplomat, serving as U.S. minister to both France and (during John Quincy's presidency) Great Britain. Now, decades later, Albert Rolaz Gallatin invited Henry to edit his father's papers for publication and produce from them a definitive biography. The overture likely occurred after Rolaz read "The Legal Tender Act," in which, as noted, Adams commended the monetary acumen of Rolaz's brother James. Presiding over the Gallatin National Bank of New York, James had encouraged the U.S. government to finance the Civil War along the fiscally conservative lines followed by his father during the War of 1812.

Gallatin's invitation offered Henry an appealing alternative to journalism, organized politics, and classroom teaching. For though he gladly left Boston behind, he wished to have influence and thought a scholarly vocation — what he called "the historico-literary line" — to be the most plausible path.[2] Having concluded his Harvard run by offering a course on the history of the early republic from, as he had informed President Eliot, the Jeffersonian perspective, he seemed ideally positioned to write on one of Jefferson's chief lieutenants. Certainly Rolaz Gallatin thought so, offering to pay for Henry's research expenses and the cost of publication. Over several months Henry selected the Gallatin letters he wished to use and, now living in Washington, approached Secretary of State William Evarts, a personal friend, for certain accommodations. Evarts complied handsomely, lending Adams a third-floor office in the State Department Building and securing him access to the trove of Jefferson and Madison papers in the Department's extensive archives. These collections Henry supplemented the following year by visiting Jefferson's Monticello and Gallatin's Friendship Hill homestead in southwestern Pennsylvania. The trips provided Adams with impressions of their owners' living arrangements, architectural taste, and daily physical environment.

Upon completion the project came to four thick volumes. Two were packed with several hundred letters of correspondence (paired down from a formidable twenty thousand); a third contained Gallatin's public writings, speeches, and documents; and the fourth comprised Henry's biography, *The Life of Albert Gallatin* (1879). For such an immense undertaking — docking in at 2,700 pages — it jelled rather quickly. No longer attached to Harvard, the *North American Review,* or the independents, Adams worked without distraction, obviously stimulated by Washington, which proved an ideal location in which to conduct research. In just eighteen months he had finished. But rather than erecting a "scientific" or academic history à la *Essays in Anglo-Saxon Law,* he exercised the prerogatives of a gentleman scholar, relying heavily on narrative, irony, and pathos. *The Life,* after all, was an authorized text, bought and paid for. One scion of a distinguished clan came to the aid of another — and enlisted still other blue bloods to aid in the endeavor. Henry's acknowledgments in the biography to Secretary Evarts and to Sarah Randolph, "representative [i.e., granddaughter] of Mr. Jefferson," recognized the polite power of the nation's first families to extend certain courtesies to their own.[3] Who but a Brahmin, even a Brahmin in exile, could thank, as did Henry, "his friendly adviser," George Bancroft, then the doyen of American historical letters? And who but a moneyed gentleman could devote a year and a half to such a project on such terms as Gallatin had laid out? Rolaz kept his promise, of course, and paid Adams $237 (a little over $6,000 in current dollars) for his expenses.

Considering both the swiftness with which Henry completed *The Life* and the edifying light it shone on its subject, it is tempting to suppose that in writing on Gallatin's America he mused, in unspoken but evident contrast, a little invidiously on Jay Gould's America as well. The former comes out, of course, superior in nearly every way. Its pre–Tweed Ring era policies of government, diplomacy, and economic development, if imperfect and conducted on a comparatively small scale, are cast in a sentimental manner. Due to the efforts of men like Gallatin, Henry argued, the United States "had found a solution of its most serious political problems." No Gilded Age here. Interestingly, Adams made Gallatin's eighteenth-century Geneva something of a separate character in the biography, part of a Swiss canton (confederation) system that practiced the "proper" balance between deference and democracy. The dollars of industrialists, the francs of financiers, in other words, were largely kept at bay. And so no Gilded Age there either. "Aristocratic as her government was," Henry wrote, "it was still republican, and the parade of rank or wealth was not one of its chief characteristics." In

306

such partisan asides he presumed a golden era of Old World governance while simultaneously lamenting a lost American (or at least patrician) ideal of a nation led by the "best."[4]

Henry took care in the memoir to link Gallatin with John Quincy Adams ("his old associate"), thus suggesting a shared outlook and outcome. Though they often occupied different sides of public issues, he argued, "there was nevertheless a curious parallelism in the lives and characters of the two men, which, notwithstanding every jar, compelled them to move side by side and to agree in policy and opinion even while persuading themselves that their aims and methods were radically divergent." Notably, both men, residing above the Mason-Dixon Line, favored federal aid to internal improvements — roads, turnpikes, canals, and so on — and thus drew the suspicion of the more states' rights–minded. In time, the rise of Jacksonianism (a.k.a. common man democracy) is said to have secured their exiles from public service when men independent of party loyalties, as Henry insisted they were, were no longer tolerated. Reaching for a tragic ending, he wrote that they lived out their final years as "the last relics of the early statesmanship of the republic."[5] Grantism, he all but added, was just around the corner.

Despite its timely appeal, *The Life* failed to

win over reviewers put off by its intimidating size and demanding prose. The *North American Review* showed its former editor no favor, calling the project "too voluminous . . . to be attractive to the general reader," while the *New York Tribune* criticized the biography for showing "no extraordinary skill or practice in the arts of literary composition."[6] In a long and cutting two-part review published anonymously in the *Nation,* Henry's brother Charles attacked the tome for its lack of accessibility, going so far as to damn it for literally being *too heavy:*

In its superficial make-up this volume falls little short of being an outrage both on Albert Gallatin and on every one who wishes to know anything about him. . . . Mr. Adams . . . seems . . . to have . . . set to work in a spirit of defiance, and made every detail of publication as repelling to the general readers as he knew how. The book resembles in appearance a volume of a cyclopædia, — it measures ten inches by six, and weighs nearly four pounds. It is printed — narrative, extracts, and correspondence — all in one monotonous type, contrary to agreeable modern usage, and it bristles with letters in French which seem to say, as clearly as if in words, that the book is not for general readers.[7]

There is a good deal of truth in these remarks, and they do accurately convey Henry's shortcomings as a first-time biographer. Letters go on for too long, Gallatin's early life in the Pennsylvania backwoods is dispensed with superficially, and his last years receive little attention. Adams's unwillingness, as Charles noted, to translate Gallatin's French correspondence into English further compromised the work. The author's classic class-bound defense for this strategy — "It is always a little impertinent to suggest that one's readers are ignorant of French" — is pure Henry.[8]

So too is his insistence that Gallatin — once among the most respected and decorated statesmen of his day — was fundamentally ill-fated. No hero of Henry's, no (Swiss) prince among republicans could possibly have made peace with the country's erratic democracy. He saw Gallatin, rather, much as he saw himself. And when he confessed to Lodge, in reference to *The Life,* "The inevitable isolation and disillusionment of a really strong mind . . . is to me the romance and tragedy of statesmanship," he combined a deeply held personal philosophy with an equally embraced historical outlook.[9] This despairing sensibility, already evident in Henry's best *North American Review* pieces, would come increasingly to inform his scholarly work and to further give both shape and spirit to his experimentation as a novelist.

25
DEMOCRACY

The Gallatin project announced Henry's promise as a historian, even as it underlined the genre's inherent limitations. A document-based study, no matter how detailed, could only hint at the early republic's "spirit," mentality, and mood. His next book, by contrast, offered an unrestricted God's-eye-view of its subject — with Henry playing God. That is to say, he wrote a novel. Published anonymously on April Fools' Day 1880 while its author visited London, *Democracy* dissected a Washington political world that revealed itself in varying shades of ambition and vulgarity, ready for commentary and ripe for caricature. It proved to be one of Adams's most satisfying literary efforts, not least because its sharp and unsparing comments on the U.S. system of government found a wider and more appreciative audience than his earlier salvos in the *Nation* and the *North American Review*. There is an obvious effort in this small volume to pull off a social comedy, though it perhaps reads best as an attempt to update Tocqueville, the skeptical diagnostician of New World egalitarianism. Its strengths were obvious if uneven. "It is good enough," a half-impressed Henry James confided to a friend, "to make it a pity it isn't better."[1]

Democracy is a Washington-centered satire whose heroine, Mrs. Madeleine Lee, is a widowed New York "society girl" bored with New York society. Her old Virginia gentry husband recently buried, she comes to the capital eager to study the machinery of power; she has naïve designs on becoming a force for good government. In Washington she is promptly flattered, tempted, and proposed to by the ethically challenged Illinois senator Silas P. Ratcliffe, Henry's scornful send-up of the scandal-dogged Maine congressman James G. Blaine. A leading presidential candidate, Blaine saw his prospects sink in 1876 when a packet of correspondence — the Mulligan letters — implicated him in the corrupt granting of railroad charters. Shortly after the accused pol defended his actions before Congress, a tart Adams wrote to Lodge, "Poor Blaine squeals louder than all the other pigs. . . . Disgust has now filled my mind for the whole subject."[2]

The halting Ratcliffe-Lee courtship, cautious on her side, calculating on his, concludes unhappily, though Ratcliffe's naked designs on the presidency survive this minor turbulence of the heart. Lee is more impacted by the affair. Her plans to turn Ratcliffe into an "honest politician" humiliatingly rebuffed, she recognizes the folly of her undertaking and takes wing overseas. Any similarity in her efforts as a would-be reformer and Henry's are purely intentional.

One might profitably read *Democracy* as a savory parody of post–Civil War politics in all of its vote-buying, election-fixing, Gilded Age glory, though the book supports a still broader historical context. Published slightly more than a century after Jefferson penned the Declaration of Independence, it offers a negative progress report of sorts on the republic's ragged development. In one scene a select group undertakes the short pilgrimage from the capital to Mount Vernon. There, a stunned Lee, charmed by the graceful simplicity of Washington's Palladian-style home, is inspired by its pastoral surroundings to a somber recognition: "Why was it, she said bitterly to herself, that everything Washington touched, he purified, even down to the associations of his house? and why is it that everything we touch seems soiled? Why do I feel unclean when I look at Mount Vernon?" The passage clearly recalls Henry's own impressionable visit to Washington's house in 1850 and the sense that, though a mere boy, he "took to it instinctively."[3]

Other Lee-Adams overlaps are easy to spot, though unmistakable traces of him are evident in several characters. John Carrington, for one, is a Virginia-bred lawyer living in Washington and eager to keep Lee "pure" by blocking Ratcliffe's advances. Like Henry, he is resigned to witness the duplicity of the city's politicians. And Nathan Gore, a Massachusetts historian futilely angling for a ministerial post in Europe (modeled mainly on the altogether more successful historian and diplomat John Lothrop Motley), longs for the courtly cosmopolitan life that enticed Adams. There is also Baron Jacobi, a sarcastic old Bulgarian envoy who, if powerless to impede Ratcliffe's ascent, nevertheless sees through the senator's Machiavellian schemes. Jacobi's lyrical cynicism evokes in broad but certain terms Henry's defiant outlook.

But for all of these ancillary males, it is Madeleine Lee who carries the cross of Henry's concerns. Though denied the opportunity to vote or to hold office, women, as Adams knew, could attain influence as informal, unrecognized advisors. It was in this capacity, beyond the reach of elections and popularity contests, that he had once perceived a place for himself in the capital hierarchy. He thought the Adamses as politically chaste as any female in the country. Accordingly, he invests Lee with his own complicated mosaic of doubts, aspirations, and resignations. He writes of her being "tortured by *ennui,*" a frustrated reformer who discovered in polite philanthropy a "path [that] . . . seemed to lead nowhere."[4] Seeing clearly the limitations of a scholarly life spent attacking political corruption from the on-high pages of the *North American Review,* Henry preferred a front-row seat at the fight. His grudging understanding that he could only be a spectator in this particular blood sport is the late afternoon awareness that finally enlightens Lee.

But her discovery does little to still an inborn appetite for rallying around a perfectly lost cause. In a telling passage relating Lee's "eminently respectable" genealogy, Henry writes, "Was she not herself devoured by ambition, and was she not now eating her heart out because she could find no one object worth a sacrifice? . . . What did she want?" Like Henry, the already privileged Lee coveted neither wealth nor social status. She wished, rather, to observe "the action of primary forces" in Washington, to decipher the "massive machinery" of a politically corrupt society, and to measure "the capacity of the motive power" to shape an entire civilization.[5] Adams would later apply nearly identical terms in the *Education* when writing of the awesome dynamos.

And perhaps it is this evident concern with

"machinery" and "primary forces" that hampered Henry's efforts in *Democracy* to convincingly portray human drama. Its characters are stiff and drawn too closely to type; the book is overly intellectualized, with a crush of speeches, conversations, letters, and inner dialogues passing as action; and everything that transpires in the novel moves mechanically toward a predictable end: the disillusioning of Madeleine Lee. But just why readers should care about her is unclear, and thus the story's central theme, the quest for power, never cuts very deep. Lee piously wants to reform politics, while Ratcliffe unapologetically prefers politics as usual. There is little discussion of their motivations, and this is a crucial blemish, particularly in regard to Ratcliffe, whose moral poverty cries out for context. As he is a symbol of robber baron rule, readers want to understand his reasons, psychology, and justifications.

One further wonders if Henry realized that Ratcliffe could easily be read as the story's spry knight. No one else in the novel is as energetic, disciplined, charismatic, or capable. Yes, the senator facilitated voter fraud in the 1864 presidential election, but he did so in order to ensure Lincoln's Union-saving reelection. Carrington, by contrast, is an ineffectual southerner ineffectually courting Lee, and Lee, despite a host of *Nation*-approved arguments on the baleful effects of political corruption, is unable to refute Ratcliffe in their private parleys. One is inclined to see a bit of Henry in Ratcliffe, as when the latter counters Lee's lame case-making for reform with a wizened insistence that "no representative government can long be much better or much worse than the society it represents." There is also evidence in the novel that for all his Lee-like campaigning against corruption, Henry saw and perhaps even respected the efficacy of men such as Ratcliffe. In a tri-cornered conversation with Lee and Carrington, Gore is asked his opinion of the senator and whether the senator should not be expected to stump for clean government. "Mr. Ratcliffe has a practical piece of work to do," Gore evenly replies, "his business is to make laws and advise the President; he does it extremely well. We have no other equally good practical politician; it is unfair to require him to be a crusader besides."[6] Perhaps Henry is striking an ironic note here, but the reader's trust in Gore and doubts about Lee and Carrington carry the argument in Ratcliffe's favor. This impression is only reinforced when Lee and Carrington, their delicate sensibilities wounded, abandon America for travel and work abroad. It is Ratcliffe, now heading the Treasury Department, who remains in the country, doing its business and making not so distant plans to claim the presidency.

For contemporary readers, Carrington is of interest only to the extent that he tells us something about Henry's — and by extension, a number of patricians' — views of the Civil War. Carrington is the idealized southerner, a reluctant secessionist raised in "the old Washington school" and mourning the passing of his section's quasi-aristocratic traditions. On the issue of slavery, the cause of the secession movement that Carrington's Confederacy fought for, Adams is deafeningly silent. This is a highly selective history of the war and Reconstruction, essentially deferring to the white South's perspective. It is Carrington, the pardoned rebel, "whom life had treated hardly," and it is the "poor Lees" who were "driven away" from their Arlington home.[7]

In such blinkered scenes is *Democracy*'s grandee pedigree on display; its author commiserates with his "kind," and anyone hailing from, say, west of the Appalachians is in for rough treatment. The president is dismissed as "a small Indiana farmer" pushed forward by an aggressively unsophisticated wife and a brutish crew of "tobacco-chewing, newspaper-reading satellites"; Ratcliffe may run Washington, but this "Prairie Giant's" plebeian roots, summoned in the sterile atmosphere of "a horse-hair sofa before an air-tight iron stove in a small room with high, bare white walls," also invite satire.[8] The

318

unrelenting narrowness of these caricatures dilutes the novel's aspiration to be, as its subtitle insists, "an American tale." The many sins Henry exposes are no doubt worthy of reflection, though on balance the overall portrait is skewed. One finds in its pages nothing to suggest democracy's vitality and inspirational power, let alone why so many "prairie" Americans had just a generation earlier sacrificed their lives for the further-ance of popular government.

As a story of political intrigue, however, *Democracy* proved a surprising success. It sold well on both sides of the English-speaking Atlantic and received a French translation within a few months of publica-tion. Nearly three years after its appearance Henry James, ignorant of its author's identity but interested in the novel's surprising reach, wrote Clover, "[It] forms the favorite reading of [British Prime Minister] Mr. [William] Gladstone. Mrs. [Mary] Sands [an American expatriate] told me last summer that she had sat next to him at dinner, one day when he talked of it for an hour. 'He said it was writ-ten in such a *handy* style, you know!' "[9] Had James been intimate with the Adamses' Washington arrangement, he may have been able to guess *Democracy*'s author. Madeleine Lee furnished her Lafayette Square home with the variety of "Persian and Syrian rugs and embroideries, Japanese bronzes and

319

porcelain" prized by Henry and Clover; Carrington enjoyed horseback riding in Rock Creek, a favorite Adams haunt; and the novel ends with Lee planning an Egyptian retreat, this a defeat of sorts evoking for Henry, perhaps, the difficult period he and Clover experienced on the Nile.

Adams's authorship of *Democracy* remained more or less a secret for many years. This gave rise to a spirited guessing game among gossiping pols and literati to identify the writer. Blaine thought King the probable culprit but later came to suspect Clover; hedging his bets he cut both socially. Other likely candidates included Hay, the crusading Godkin, the journalist Manton Marble, and the lawyer and writer Arthur George Sedgwick. The Adamses enjoyed their mystery and actively protected it by deflection. Clover was much amused by her father's conjecture that she wrote *Democracy* and accompanied her letter of denial with an index of other candidates, which included two of her fellow Hearts but not her husband. Henry's English friend Sir Robert Cunliffe asked point blank if Adams knew who wrote the novel, prompting Adams to reply less than candidly, "I cannot enlighten you about the authorship of 'Democracy,' " before he too offered a "black list" of the usual suspects.[10]

Invariably some of the guesses hit the mark.

The British novelist Mary Augusta Ward detected an overlap in spleen venting between *Democracy* and an article Henry had published in the *North American Review*. Cecil Spring Rice, a young British diplomat who frequented the Adamses' Lafayette Square residence, had it half right when he wrote his brother in 1887, "Adams, son of the Minister and joint author of *Democracy,* is rather an interesting sort of cynic, and I had a real jolly evening with him last night talking over England and America. The feeling about politicians is very bitter, certainly." In the 1909 study *A Manual of American Literature,* Cornell scholar Clark Sutherland Northup wrote that *Democracy*'s "authorship . . . ha[d] hitherto baffled the critics," and then announced "definitely" that the work belonged to "the historian Henry Adams." Northup praised the novel as "keen and incisive" yet "all too pessimistic." Finally, in 1923, five years after Henry's death, Henry Holt, *Democracy*'s publisher, confirmed Adams's authorship.[11]

Upon reflection it is clear that the novel served a number of purposes for Adams. Most obviously it proved an ideal vehicle for dramatizing the catalog of complaints that he had piled piecemeal over the years in any number of small circulation journals. *Democracy* further afforded Henry a welcome

321

change of creative technique from his dense study of the Jefferson and Madison administrations, now well under way. And in terms of sharpening his instruments, he learned much from experimenting with fiction, thus enlarging his writer's repertoire. Certain stretches of the *History* — including the wonderfully written Burr affair, in which his antihero contemplates severing a piece of the republic for himself — contain pace, atmosphere, and irony the envy of any historian.

Finally, *Democracy* tells us something important about Adams's dimming view of America's prospects. The republic's assumed exceptionalism is treated in the novel as merely platitudinous. As Madeleine Lee discovers, getting "to the bottom of this business of democratic government" meant realizing "that it was nothing more than government of any other kind." This is the type of double-edged observation that can appear either solemnly wise or superficially clever. It pokes nicely at American arrogance while managing to underestimate the real power of its idealism. Theodore Roosevelt, no admirer of clever men, had little use for the book. "The other day," he wrote to Henry Cabot Lodge in 1905, "I was reading *Democracy,* that novel which made a great furor among the educated incompetents and the pessimists generally about twenty-five years ago. It was written by Godkin, perhaps with assistance from Mrs. Henry Adams. It had a superficial and rotten cleverness, but it was essentially mean and base, and it is amusing to read it now and see how completely events have given it the lie."[12] Roosevelt's dismissal of *Democracy* should come as no surprise. If Madeleine Lee retreated from the trials of her time, TR embraced those of his, eager to advance what he famously called "the strenuous life." Under the auspices of the Square Deal, Roosevelt piloted a series of regulatory reforms that furthered the cause of popular government and established something of a template for future progressive platforms. But did such initiatives really give *Democracy* "the lie"? Who would deny that when approached as a meditation on power, greed, and partisanship, Henry's "mean and base" send-up of Washington retains, nearly a century and a half on, every bit of its wit, bite, and relevance?

26

SECOND HEART

Henry's complicated marriage is never mentioned in the *Education*. That incomplete memoir moves from its author's impressionable boyhood to his meandering search for a vocation before abruptly and without explanation jumping a generation to a busy chapter titled simply "Twenty Years After." Despite this casual obliteration of the decades 1872–92, certain of its fragments and friendships invariably make their way into the narrative. Hay and King are warmly remembered, while the hapless politicos whom Henry — and Clover — espied from Lafayette Square are summarily dismissed. New players are also introduced, including Elizabeth Cameron and her husband, the Pennsylvania senator J. Donald Cameron. "Lizzie's" importance to Henry has long interested both scholars and readers, and yet it is her husband who receives more attention in the *Education*. A product of Pennsylvania's powerful Republican political machine, he interested Adams as a symbol of the country's "precipitous" political culture. Long contact with Senator Cameron, he wrote, "led to an intimacy which had the singular effect of educating [Adams] in knowledge of the very class of American politician who had done most to block his intended path in life."[1]

Despite their differing attitudes on party politics, Henry and Cameron shared one important bond: the burden of familial expectation. Cameron's father, Simon, dominated his son. After making a fortune in railroads and banking, the senior Cameron entered politics, became a senator, and served briefly as secretary of war in Lincoln's cabinet before resigning amid allegations of corruption. The House subsequently censured his handling of War Department purchases, though the pragmatic Lincoln, recognizing Pennsylvania's importance, sent him to head the U.S. ministry in Moscow. Henry, in London at the time, wrote to Charles that he hoped the "whited sepulchre," as he contemptuously called Simon, would "vanish into the steppes of Russia and wander there for eternity": "He is of all my countrymen, one of the class that I most conspicuously and sincerely despise and detest."[2]

If Simon Cameron is even dimly remembered today it is for the cynical quip "An honest politician is one who, when he is bought, will stay bought." Having "bought"

Pennsylvania's legislature, he returned to the Senate in 1867 and served ten years before passing the seat on to his son; critics derided the pliant state chamber as the "Cameron Transfer Company." The younger Cameron, a bushy walrus mustache drooping from his invisible upper lip, was forty-three at the time, having previously taken, under his father's efforts, the presidencies of a Pennsylvania bank and railroad. By this time, his eighteen-year marriage to Mary McCormick, mother to their six children, had ended with her death in 1874; four years later he married Lizzie, then only twenty. Cameron gave the distinct impression of treading water in the Senate, lacking completely his father's brute ambition and appetite for political infighting; his career seemed a thing wholly designed by Simon. One observer insisted that he suffered from a "queer self-distrust," while Emily Briggs, the Washington correspondent for the *Philadelphia Press,* caustically remarked of the Cameron dynasty's prominent drop-off, "The iron crown which Don Cameron inherited from his old Highland father seemed too heavy for his tender temples and weaker brain. He looks pale and extremely nervous."[3]

Cameron's inheritance of the kind of high placement that Henry sought for himself may have played a part in the latter's low regard for the senator. True, "the Don" (as Adams and others sometimes preferred) was a social bore and an alcoholic and spent much of his time talking politics and playing cards, but Henry knew many well-placed second prizes who merit no mention in the *Education*. It is "the Cameron type," however, more than a mere "Don" that is to be anatomized, for this particular *Homo politicus,* Henry swore, had "shipwrecked his career." And no better example of Cameronism existed, he presumed, than Pennsylvania. "The true Pennsylvanian," he nodded, was "as narrow as the kirk [the Church of Scotland]; as shy of other people's narrowness as a Yankee; as self-limited as a Puritan farmer. To him, none but Pennsylvanians were white." Conventional and conforming, the Pennsylvanian measured progress materially and rarely questioned the rights of the rising industrial gentry to do as it pleased. Where the dour Bostonian could be prickly, the earnest Pennsylvanian proved pliant. And this made him, Henry cracked, "the strongest American in America." For "as an ally he was worth all the rest. . . . If one wanted work done in Congress, one did wisely to avoid asking a New Englander to do it. A Pennsylvanian not only could do it, but did it willingly, practically and intelligently."[4]

The Adamses showed a social interest in the Don only because of their interest in his attractive wife. At five-feet-eight Lizzie Cameron looked down on most women and not a few men; strikingly slender at the waist, she had curly brunette hair, high cheekbones, and penetrating eyes. "On the whole," one of Henry's nieces later wrote, "[Mrs. Cameron was] the most socially competent woman that I had ever met. With perfect self-confidence she could tackle any situation and appear to enjoy it. She was perhaps not strictly beautiful, but she was such a mass of style and had such complete self-assurance that she always gave the appearance of beauty and she gave everyone a good time when she set out to please." Well-informed and unafraid to share her opinions, "Mrs. Don" could be a bit waspy, though men found her confident nature irresistible. "With perfection of grace and manner," a friend recalled, "she seemed to me a picture of accomplished seductiveness, of which her able and ambitious mind was in no way unconscious." Her marriage to Cameron provoked the press into calling their union a match of "Beauty and the Beast."[5]

Just why Lizzie married her Don remains elusive. She came from the powerful Sherman family in Ohio that traced its lineage back several generations to colonial Connecticut. Her father, Charles Taylor Sherman, was a prominent Cleveland judge, but her uncles, Gen. William Tecumseh Sherman and Treasury Secretary John Sherman, commanded national attention. Scholars agree that family fiat sent Lizzie to Washington in 1878 to live with her uncle John in order that she might be separated from an unsuitable suitor, one Joseph Russell, a young New York lawyer rumored to like his liquor a little too much. There is, however, some disagreement regarding why — and indeed if — she chose to marry Cameron. John Hay's latest biographer, John Taliaferro, contends that Lizzie made a calculated decision to become a senator's wife. Cameron's children (the oldest Lizzie's age) would not be under her care, and the senator's busy political affairs would presumably allow his wife time to cultivate her own interests and friendships. Should a contest of wills arise, Taliaferro ventures, Lizzie seemed confident that she could keep Cameron at bay; informing her mother of their engagement, she gaily wrote of the senator as though he were a poodle: "He is very nice about it all and keeps away from me except when I tell him he can come."[6]

The marriage's financial angle, however, is also worth considering. Arline Boucher Tehan conjectures that Cameron may have come to the aid of Lizzie's debt-burdened father and, with more certainty, notes that the Don signed a prenuptial agreement "by which the senator turned over to her the income from $160,000 worth of securities" — about $4 million in current dollars. The couple's wedding gifts, including an abundance of plates, figurines, and tea servers gilded in gold, silver, and bronze, were rumored to total some $100,000.[7]

Other biographers argue that Lizzie had little freedom in the affair. Natalie Dykstra believes that "the Sherman brothers stepped in to arrange" the marriage, while Patricia O'Toole, author of *The Five of Hearts: An Intimate Portrait of Henry Adams and His Friends,* goes even further. She writes that Lizzie, "bowing to the pressure of family members eager for a match with a powerful senator . . . finally agreed to marry Don Cameron. On her wedding day she begged that the ceremony be called off, but the Shermans held firm. . . . Lizzie and Don passed their wedding night aboard a luxury railroad car; years later she confided to a friend that his clumsy insistence had left her feeling like the victim of a rape." Whatever the circumstances leading up to her nuptials, Lizzie's marriage was clearly unhappy. She and Cameron, so different in interests, outlook, and age, never grew close; they often traveled and lived apart during their fraught forty-year union, which ended with the Don's 1918 death. Julia Stoddard Parsons, a young socialite who gained some intimacy with the Shermans and served as a bridesmaid at Lizzie's wedding, seemed to have put the relationship in perspective when, shortly after

Lizzie announced her engagement, she wrote in her diary, "I never saw Elisabeth look prettier, Mr. Cameron beamed. My Lady keeps him in order, but, an I mistake not, there is a canny Scotch will of his own hidden somewhere about this young-elderly lover, so have a care Elisabeth!"[8]

Lizzie became acquainted with the Adamses at a reception given by Clara Hay in January 1881. Shortly after that introduction she and her slightly older companion Emily Beale, the daughter of Gen. Edward F. Beale, a friend of Grant's who collected various appointments under several presidents, paid a call at the Adamses second H Street residence. A few months earlier, Henry and Clover had moved into another Corcoran property, assuming a six-year lease on a six-bedroom residence fronting Lafayette Square. The $200 a month rent (a little more than $5,000 in current dollars) included a stable with upstairs servants' quarters. The Camerons lived just a short walk away, on Madison Place along the Square's eastern border.[9]

Clover liked Lizzie, though she was quick to size up the younger woman's inexperience, writing, "[Mrs. Cameron] asked if she might come to tea and declined to wait till I called first. She is very young, pretty, and, I fear, bored, and her middle-aged Senator fighting a boss fight in Harrisburg; so she came on Friday, wailed about Harrisburg, and was quite frank in her remarks about men and things. Poor 'Don' will think she's fallen among thieves when he comes back."[10]

For Henry at least, attending to the Camerons meant proximity to Lizzie. In correspondence with Hay he often struck a note of domestic light comedy when relating the couple's interactions, though such remarks, as Hay surely knew, were meant to conceal heavier emotions. In a January 1883 letter Adams fell upon a sobriquet that would, much to his regret, too precisely characterize his relationship with the senator's wife: "Don is behaving himself again this winter and entertains. We were asked to a charming dinner there the other evening, and I am now *tame cat* around the house. Don and I stroll around with our arms around each other's necks. I should prefer to accompany Mrs Don in that attitude." More typically he made sport of Cameron's social inadequacies ("I . . . cannot saddle my friends with Don") and Harrisburg chauvinisms, which allowed him to linger over his "pity" for Lizzie. In discussing his feelings with Hay, he liked to play the role of sympathetic friend: "I adore her, and respect the way she has kept herself out of scandal and mud, and done her duty by the lump of clay she promised to love and respect." When the Camerons embarked for England in the summer of 1883 Henry urged Gaskell to make Lizzie's acquaintance but fairly apologized for her husband: "not my ideal companion for a cottage." Leaving little to Gaskell's imagination, he wrote, referring specifically to the Don and his young wife's rocky May-December romance, "As a rule, husbands and wives go best in single harness."[11]

Adams's connection to Lizzie never moved beyond "correct"; he remained throughout their nearly four-decade friendship a perpetual tame cat. It was the only role in which he could openly socialize with the Camerons, respect his wife (in life and in memory), and protect his name. A proper Victorian, Henry's impressive capacity for self-control contained both public and private dimensions. He lampooned in his correspondence, essays, and books those corporate and political figures that resorted to lies, corruption, and other sharp practices. It was his special pride to have "failed" for being too honest. In exile, he adopted the proud man's defense of self-denial, seeing renunciation as a sign of character and strength. But this questionable attitude contributed to a sense of isolation and despair when his high standards inevitably stiffened into a superior attitude. Forgoing became a habit. That he long remained a part of Lizzie's world, to the extent of making a meal upon his own heart, should come as no surprise — it revealed, rather, a certain and not always enviable consistency of character.

334

27
BACK TO BIZARRE

In the spring of 1881 John Torrey Morse, editor of Houghton Mifflin's prestigious American Statesmen Series, invited Henry to draft another political biography. Having read the *Gallatin* with pleasure, he now asked its author to take on the famously mercurial Virginia planter and congressman John Randolph of Roanoke (1773–1833). Eccentric, politically marginalized, and occasionally accused of being as mad as a March hare, Randolph proved too intriguing for Henry to pass up. From his Cumberland County plantation, "Bizarre," Randolph embraced an uncompromising states' rights philosophy that led to his break with fellow Virginians Jefferson and Madison. Reflecting on the conjoined questions of slavery and civil war, Adams saw Randolph as a precursor to the secession-minded "Fire-Eaters" of 1860, who cut the union in two. Thus, in approaching Randolph, he more generally sought to assay the "errant" South and somewhat reductively used his subject's flamboyant outbursts in Congress as a metaphor to explore what he took to be the plantocracy's unbalanced psychology.

Following a playful "Well! — I'll think about it," Henry accepted Morse's invitation and then completed the book in a remarkable three-months sprint. Well versed in American history, he returned to a wealth of materials carefully mined over the years in preparation for his large study of the early republic. He described the Randolph manuscript to Sir Robert Cunliffe as "a small volume which is really, like my life of Gallatin, only a preliminary essay," while reporting to Lodge that it constituted "but a feeler for my history." Confident in his grasp of the Jeffersonian era and eager to begin seeding the larger enterprise, Henry adopted the project with enthusiasm.[1] His participation requires little explanation, though perhaps Morse's invitation does.

Looking at the author roster of the American Statesmen Series, one notes a number of prominent figures — including Theodore Roosevelt, Carl Schurz, and Henry Cabot Lodge — remembered more for their political careers than for their literary talents. In securing Adams for the Randolph biography, however, Morse seized a real prize, bagging a rising scholar with a distinguished name. Even so, his decision to have Henry deliver the Randolph memoir might be sensibly questioned. The Virginian had opposed Adams's presidential ancestors (nationalists that they were), and a harsh judgment of his career by Henry might be dismissed in some quarters, particularly those south of the Mason-Dixon Line, as little more than score-settling. Presumably Morse expected a provocative, even controversial manuscript. Henry's description of Randolph in the *Gallatin* as a "bully" in Congress who enjoyed giving "speeches violent beyond all precedent, outrageously and vindictively slanderous," accurately communicates his fascinated if dim view of the man.[2] That biography followed Henry's earlier essay debunking another Virginia icon, Capt. John Smith, which first advertised its author's proficiency in the art of South-baiting.

Playing the iconoclast, Adams upended the traditional interpretation of Randolph. Rather than dismissing him as a rare curiosity isolated from the main trends of American governance, he made him into a representative figure, illustrative of the hard-core southern states' rights school. "Good" southerners certainly existed, Henry acknowledged, but Randolph embodied, so he contended, a "truer," more aggressive, and more emblematic strain of the plantocracy. This problematic line led, he had little doubt, straight to Fort Sumter. If Randolph idled, as

Adams wrote in the biography, on "perverse," it was a perversion that he shared with his people.[3]

This is a particularly revealing opinion considering that both author and subject, though products of different generations and geographies, came from a common "aristocratic" lineage impossible for either to elude. And thus while the *Randolph* obviously anticipates certain events and narratives embellished in the *History*, it more suggestively stands as a harbinger of the *Education*. The latter tells the story of a man overtaken by the speed, flux, and versatility of the modern world. As Randolph struggles to reconcile the Age of Enlightenment with a spreading cotton empire, Adams reflects on the decline of the old Massachusetts elite in a rising urban-ethnic nation. As Randolph is made to approximate the more provincial side of the squirearchy, Adams renders himself a child of rustic Quincy, ever in tension with metropolitan Boston. At root, both men are figures of a fading past. Henry observes of Randolph's "literary diet," a curriculum heavy on Shakespeare and Fielding, Burke and Gibbon, that it amounts to a splendid *eighteenth-century* initiation, hardly fitting for the coming day of frontier democracy. Adams similarly disparaged his own schooling in the *Education* as "colonial, revolutionary, almost Cromwellian."[4]

Still other links between Henry and Randolph include their mutual rejection of America's two-party system (both forged third factions), ineffectual efforts at reform politics (neither Randolph's Old Republicans nor Henry's independents enjoyed much influence), and sense of being "insiders" now relegated to the "outside." Adams's claim that in defeat Randolph adopted the persona of "a faultfinder, a common scold," might as easily be said of himself. And certainly over the years many did.[5]

It would be too much to say, however, that Henry sought an association with Randolph, whose theatrical temperament (he sometimes attended Congress accompanied by a slave valet and hunting dogs) and sectarian defense of planter power repelled him. And yet there is an underlying tone in the biography, beneath the sneers and jeers, that the loss of localism in America constitutes an unmistakable tragedy. Perhaps it is enough to note that in recording the collapse of Randolph's prewar southern aristocracy, Henry simultaneously wrote of the coming political and economic forces that later reduced the influence of the postwar Brahmins.

As a work of history, the *Randolph* tries to say and explain too much. In declaring that Randolph "discovered and mapped out from beginning to end a chart of the whole course on which the slave power was to sail to its

339

destruction," Adams indulges in the temptation to reduce the past to the actions of a single individual. Randolph's fingerprints were not on the Louisiana Purchase (1803) or the Missouri Compromise (1820), both of which enlarged slavery's domain, and he died before the Mexican War (1846–48), the Fugitive Slave Act (1850), and the territorial crisis in "Bleeding Kansas" (1854–61), which pitted Yankee settlers against southern sodbusters, broke up the conventional Democratic-Whig concert, and ushered in a far more divisive partisan culture. In making "that lunatic monkey," as Adams extravagantly referred to Randolph in his correspondence, the representative mind of the plantocracy he denied its calculation and foresight, its long-standing social and economic self-interest.[6]

Adams's biography, published in October 1882, earned favorable reviews in both the *Atlantic* ("one of the most effective books in the whole range of our historical literature") and the *Nation* ("an excellent piece of work"). Many southerners, however, dismissed the study's emphasis on the Randolph–states' rights side of Virginia, which slighted the bold nationalism embodied by Washington and the influential Supreme Court chief justice John Marshall. Henry's cherry-picking description of Randolph offering a corrosive 1795 dinner toast, "George Washington, — may he be damned!," seemed to some of these readers a low blow that said more about Randolph's muddled mind than the mentality of the Old Dominion.[7] Apart from such interpretive shortcomings, a more general question remains as to whether Randolph even belonged in the American Statesmen Series. Was he, in fact, an American statesman, or a statesman of Virginia? Henry's study clearly suggested the latter, and subsequent biographers have seldom argued otherwise.

Adams knew that he had written, as he put it, "an unpleasant book" and a month after its release said as much to Morse, pinning the blame on Randolph: "The tone was really decided by the subject, and the excess of acid is his." Morse supposed otherwise. Many years later he admitted to expecting a less piquant product from Adams. In referring to the recruitment of authors for the Series, he observed, "I think only one real blunder was made and that was in allotting Randolph to Henry Adams. I fancied that I should evoke something quite different from what I got." In 1930 James Truslow Adams (no relation) published a study of the Adams family that included an assessment of the *Randolph*. He too considered the biography problematic and faulted both editor and author. He interviewed Morse and wrote that the old man "counted, as he has told me, on Henry's

341

sense of humor, a sense in which the Adamses have always been largely lacking; and the choice was an unfortunate one. Henry should never have been asked to write the book, and, if asked, should have declined."[8] Biography requires a certain critical empathy or understanding of a subject's motives, but Adams stood too far outside of Randolph's "Bizarre" world to make anything more than surface observations. The writing is crisp and felicitous, but "the excess of acid is his."

One further episode of this period is worth relating, and that is Adams's efforts to place *two* books in the American Statesmen Series. In the same letter to Morse in which he agreed to write on Randolph, Henry indicated a strong interest in producing a biography of Aaron Burr, Jefferson's first vice president but better known for killing Alexander Hamilton in a duel. "If I find Randolph easy," he said, "I don't know but what I will volunteer for Burr. Randolph is the type of a political charlatan who had something in him. Burr is the type of a political charlatan pure and simple, a very Jim Crow of melodramatic wind-bags. I have something to say of both varieties." And wishing to say it, Henry, after completing the *Randolph,* moved just as quickly on the Burr biography. Houghton Mifflin, however, declined the finished manuscript on the grounds that the quick-triggered Burr was no statesman. Angered and perhaps a little embarrassed at the rebuff, Adams testily wrote to Morse that he cared nothing for Houghton Mifflin and had merely wished to do a friend a favor: "I want you to understand that my offer to write Burr was an offer to *you,* not to Houghton, to help you out in your editing. I should not choose Houghton for my publisher, and for many reasons prefer to publish in New York or Philadelphia. So long as it looked like going back on *you,* I would not back out of my offer, but I confess, if you will release me, I shall be glad of it; and you have only to tell Houghton that I have withdrawn my offer."[9]

Some months later, another emissary from Houghton Mifflin approached Henry with an offer to publish the Burr biography outside of the Statesmen Scrics. Adams's refusal prompted, several months after that, a similar appeal from Morse and this too was declined, though with an unmistakable finality: "I don't propose to be dictated to by any damned publisher."[10] Accordingly, the Burr biography never saw the light of day, per se. But given the lengthy treatment that Burr receives in the *History* (over 150 pages in volume 3) it is a reasonable guess that Henry massaged the material into his masterwork.

These early Washington years were wonderfully productive for Adams, rich in their results, though not without attendant difficulties. As he approached his next project, a second and final novel, personal rather than political concerns were to dominate its contents.

28

BETWEEN SCIENCE
AND SALVATION

The long contraction of Christian belief in the modern liberal West recast the place of faith in Henry Adams's America. Set in context, two centuries of deism, industrialization, and scientific discovery contributed to a ripening culture of religious doubt. Having only vicariously registered Puritanism's slow if certain New England retreat, Adams more directly faced the profound implications of his own secular age. This legacy of the Enlightenment reached confidently across generations, identified in a series of formerly heretical ideas. The Scottish philosopher David Hume and the English historian Edward Gibbon condemned, in their respective works, idolatry, ecclesiastical superstition, and the unsavory side of papal history; in their wake ranged thinkers as disparate as the political economist Karl Marx and the utilitarian theorist John Stuart Mill, who each argued powerfully for freedom from religion — "the opium," the former memorably

345

insisted, "of the people." The British novelist and poet Thomas Hardy (1840–1928), author of *Tess of the d'Urbervilles* and *Far from the Madding Crowd,* still later captured the cultural shift in his remarkable verse "God's Funeral":

And, tricked by our own early dream
And need of solace, we grew
   self-deceived,
Our making soon our maker did we deem,
And what we had imagined we believed.[1]

In Henry's day, the politician and orator Robert G. Ingersoll, known as "the Great Agnostic," proved to be the most arresting advocate of "freethinking" in the United States since Thomas Paine, author of the celebrated revolutionary pamphlet "Common Sense," though attacked a century later by Theodore Roosevelt as a "filthy little atheist" for his "impious" book *The Age of Reason.* As president of the American Secular Union in the 1880s and 1890s, Ingersoll often mocked religious belief, training, and cultural influence, thus making "Ingersollism" synonymous with "agnosticism." A Civil War veteran, speaker at the 1876 Republican National Convention, and attorney general of Illinois, he enjoyed, despite holding controversial opinions on religion (and women's rights), a prominent, even favorable profile.

For the nation's churches, the threat of Ingersollism paled beside the sundry miseries inflicted by the industrial process. In response, the Social Gospel movement (c. 1880–1920), strongest among Congregationalists, Unitarians, and Episcopalians, acknowledged the inadequacy of conventional Christianity to address the great inequalities of wealth and health in an America enamored of social Darwinism. Applying Christian ethics to community problems, reformers such as Hull House cofounder Jane Addams, the muckraking journalist Jacob Riis, and the theologian Walter Rauschenbusch sought to address, among other evils, the problems of poverty, alcoholism, child labor, crime, and urban slums. The movement's ability to rally large numbers around the cause of social justice offers some indication of the culture's desire to promote moral reform in an era otherwise dominated by technology and industry.

In his own way, Adams too, if principally interested in political morality, traced the transformation in thinking that led to a more secular society. In the summer of 1883 he took a brief break from the Jeffersonians to draft *Esther,* a short palate-cleansing novel of ideas. Selectively autobiographical, the book ruminated on the diminishing role of religion in a century filled with scientific discoveries.[2] There are few clues in his letters explaining the project's origins; aside from Clover, he kept his authorship a secret, telling only King and Hay and then only some years after publication. *Esther,* rather, is credited to "Frances Snow Compton," which almost sounds like an equivocal tribute to the Governor, whose name and chilly reserve are evoked in the nom de plume. The novel's tensions and emphases, however, are perfectly Henry. For to read Adams closely on nearly any subject is to encounter a restless mind lingering over those things lost, and *Esther* is no exception. Henry broods anxiously in its pages over the inevitable weakening of traditional forms of art, philosophy, and worship before the persistence of modern pressures. As in *Democracy,* this book too ends on an unmistakable note of quiet defeat.

Adams asserts the obsolescence theme quite obviously in naming his novel's heroine "Esther Dudley" after the title character of Nathaniel Hawthorne's story "Old Esther Dudley" (1839). Hawthorne's is a tale of an aged Revolutionary-era loyalist ("the daughter of an ancient and once eminent family") unable to grasp the fact that the defeated British are never returning to her native Massachusetts. She waits in vain for the restoration of the royal governor and the familiar way of life he represents. But the new republican governor bluntly informs Esther that America has moved on, abandoning convention to live as "a new race of men":

> Your life has been prolonged until the world has changed around you. You have treasured up all that time has rendered worthless — the principles, feelings, manners, modes of being and acting, which another generation has flung aside — and you are a symbol of the past. And I, and these men around me — we represent a new race of men — living no longer in the past, scarcely in the present — but projecting our lives forward into the future. Ceasing to model ourselves on ancestral superstitions, it is our faith and principle to press onward, onward![3]

Henry's *Esther* similarly scrutinizes a dying way of life, for the upheaval in thought, customs, and manners outlined by Hawthorne extended beyond the Revolutionary era, of course. Esther Dudley's fate could be said to have prefaced that of the Adams family, or even the waning high Brahminism of Henry's day.

Adams's *Esther* is a young woman, a gifted amateur painter and a nonbeliever. Her father, Dr. William Dudley, possesses an independent income that permits an early retirement; a nonpracticing physician, he is gravely ill and a skeptic like his daughter. The descriptions of Esther and William are so close to Clover (a gifted amateur photographer and a nonbeliever) and her father, Robert (a gravely ill physician with an independent income), as to beg for authorial anonymity. Adams, in fact, based several characters on acquaintances. George Strong, a professor of geology, a religious doubter, and a charming cut-up à la Clarence King, is Esther's cousin; Stephen Hazard, the reverend of New York's St. John's Church and Esther's would-be beau, is modeled on Henry's second cousin Phillips Brooks, the rector of Boston's Trinity Church; the artist Wharton paints murals for Hazard's chapel and approximates John La Farge, who produced Trinity's exquisite stained-glass windows; and finally Catherine Brooke, a fresh breeze from the unfenced West, is cast in the attractive image of Elizabeth Cameron.

In the interest of keeping *Esther*'s authorship a secret, Henry placed the novel in Manhattan. The principal actors are Esther and Hazard, who are in love, but her skepticism and his faith ultimately keep them apart. In having his heroine reject Hazard, Adams confirms his own journey through a godless universe. Esther's confession, "Is it not enough to know myself? . . . Some people are made with faith. I am made without it," is emblematic of a growing generation of agnostics and nonbelievers who have crossed the Darwinian Rubicon.[4]

350

While drafting *Democracy,* Henry targeted the graft and corruption culture that greased the skids of American politics. *Esther*'s probing discussion of religious doubt, by contrast, drew from its author a more internal reaction in which Adams mourned the passing of the old Emersonian universe of openness and possibility. *Esther* is a tragedy not because of Esther and Hazard's doomed romance (carried on in too rarified an air to interest warm-blooded readers), but because it sympathetically unpacks the exhaustion of traditional conceptions of community and spirituality. On this melancholy note, Henry wrote from the heart. His quest to leave behind a world of bankers, urban bosses, and evolutionists eventually led him far from industrial America and the quantitative nineteenth century. Though not a *believer,* he wished, nevertheless, to believe in something. In the final decades of his life he would fall under the spell of medieval French music, art, and architecture; his interests in chansons, cathedrals, and crusades no doubt met certain intellectual needs, and yet they struck also and perhaps primarily a resonant emotional chord.

Much commentary on *Esther* has focused, sometimes recklessly, on Henry's treatment of Clover in the novel. There is little doubt that he modeled Esther physically and somewhat emotionally on his wife — and perhaps on other women as well. Several decades after the book appeared, one of Adams's nieces related as much to a scholar: "I believe what H.A. told me — the only time he ever spoke to me about the book — that Esther, the character, was two or 3 people in one." A likely inspiration is Ann Palmer, a close friend and occasional traveling companion of Clover's whom Henry liked as well. But in writing of Esther's physical appearance, Adams seems to have had only his wife in mind. He once, as indicated, said of Clover, "She is certainly not handsome . . . [and] dresses badly"; Esther is described as having "a bad figure" and "dresses to suit her figure and sometimes overdoes it." A more intriguing connection between Clover and Esther involves the question of filial piety. Esther is devoted to an ill father and cannot make space for another man. In his 1979 biography *Clover,* Otto Friedrich speculates that Henry's resentment at standing second in his wife's affections found a vindictive voice in the novel. "Once it is read as a roman à clef," Friedrich argues, "it suddenly becomes a strange attack on Clover, an exasperated, middle-aged, long-suppressed outburst against her at almost every point on which she was vulnerable." Other scholars have noted that Henry's critical portrait of Esther is countered by a far more flattering representation of Elizabeth Cameron as a charming

352

expression of the ungoverned frontier.[5]

Some commentators have further maintained that Henry used *Esther* for the intensely personal objective of preparing his wife for Dr. Hooper's expected death, which followed in April 1885. This idea originated with Clarence King who, following Clover's suicide eight months after her father's passing, assumed that Henry must have felt "regret at having exposed" so much of Clover's private and religious views in the novel. There is inferential evidence for such an argument. Henry wrote to Hay several months after Clover's death, "I will not pretend that the book is not precious to me, but its value has nothing to do with the public who could never understand that such a book might be written in one's heart's blood."[6]

This gnomic admission should be balanced, however, by remembering that Adams wavered between shades of concealment and confession in the *Education* and may have done the same in *Esther.* Clover's suicide casts a retrospectively somber diagnosis on the novel, but Brooke's coltish enthusiasms and Strong's bonhomie give a vitality and occasional levity to the book that belies a merely funereal reading. Moreover, the philosophical back-and-forth between Esther and Hazard (which seconds as sexual tension) suggests that, above all, Henry aspired to write a study of ideas. Indeed, it is possible to see in the

353

questioning Esther even more of Henry than Clover. For like his protagonist, Adams never quite reconciled with the secularism that he absorbed as part of the general cultural drift. Esther, in some desperation, cries out to Strong, "I want to submit [to religion]. . . . Why can't some of you make me?"[7] Henry, a self-proclaimed martyr before the mechanical universe, would come to make of Chartres and Mont-Saint-Michel the foundations of a fresh faith, or at least a modern iteration of the Romantic ideal in which he might find meaning and inspiration. He too, in other words, sought submission to a higher power.

Having completed *Esther,* Adams again turned to the publisher Henry Holt. He recommended that the book be placed in Holt's American Novel Series but attached an unusual condition: it was to receive no publicity whatsoever. He wished to conduct, so he insisted, an "experiment" to see if the book might find a readership without the "vulgarity" of advertising. Recognizing the financial dangers for the publisher, he offered to pay Holt for the printing costs. There are several possible reasons for his extraordinary request. He may have sincerely wished to test the power of promotion, or, having revealed so much of himself, his wife, and their marriage, he perhaps self-consciously pulled back, or he may simply have doubted *Esther's* appeal, to which he could then hold his odd condition accountable. Later, when his lengthy *History* languished in small sales, Henry made disparaging comments on the fickle book-buying public, writing defensively to one correspondent, "I never expected that the book would produce anything for the author."[8]

A few months after publication, with fewer than six hundred copies sold, Henry conceded to Holt, "My experiment has failed. . . . So far as I know, not a man, woman or child has ever read or heard of *Esther.*" The novel's subsequent release in England proved equally humiliating to Adams, even as it received a slight marketing boost from publicists. Henry's acceptance of advertising in Britain calls into question the reason he had given for withholding it in America. "On the other side [England]," he improbably explained to Holt, "I wanted to try a different experiment: namely, to test the value of English criticism. For this reason, advertisement becomes necessary." But sales in England were tepid and the few reviews cold and unsympathetic. A notice in the *Saturday Review* said the book read "more like a theological treatise than a novel."[9] Henry eventually purchased the remaining stock from his publisher and had the books destroyed.

It is tempting to see *Esther* as an isolated, even peculiar project among Adams's writings. And yet when considered alongside certain of his other works a definite pattern appears. After clashing with John Torrey Morse over the inclusion of the Burr biography in the American Statesmen Series, Henry refused to release the manuscript. In a similar fashion he for years withheld completely from popular consumption his two late masterpieces, *Mont-Saint-Michel and Chartres* and the *Education,* which he had privately printed and distributed to a select few. Like *Esther,* these too were "personal" books. He seemed to take a grim satisfaction in ignoring the public and thereby denying it the opportunity to ignore him. He further and somewhat perversely insisted, in *Esther*'s case, that the novel was simply too intimate and audiences had no right to it. "I would not let anyone read the story," he explained several years after its stillborn birth, "for fear the reader should profane it."[10] He appeared, if anything, desperately determined to rise above mere sales and savor the pleasure of his superior secret. Whatever the case, the novel punctuated a period of Henry's domestic life. The year 1885 would bring deep and irreparable changes — and that relentless momentum began with a move.

Relegated in youth to a wintry Boston address, Henry delighted in long school-free summers spent in nearby Quincy, ambling about the ancestral Old House and its green garden. Purchased in the 1780s by his great-grandparents John and Abigail Adams, the property remained in the family until 1927.

Referred to by Henry and his siblings as "the President," John Quincy Adams communicated a standard of public service that both inspired and teased his heirs who were unable, in the post–Civil War "Robber Baron" republic, to emulate his political success.

Elizabeth Sherman Cameron, the great post-Clover love of Henry's life. Part of the famous Ohio Sherman family and unhappily married to a Pennsylvania senator, she maintained a kind of epistolary romance with Adams from the 1880s until his death in 1918. "If you should go back on me," he once wrote her, "I should wholly disappear."

John Hay, statesman, historian, and poet; he served as Lincoln's personal assistant in the White House and later headed the State Department in the McKinley and Theodore Roosevelt administrations. Hay and Adams were dear friends for decades; the relationship brought Henry as close to formal power as he ever got.

Henry kept within gossiping proximity of the writer Edith Wharton for years before striking up a closer friendship with her in Paris where the two kept apartments He thought her 1905 novel *The House of Mirth* splendid; she thought his practiced cynicism failed to improve her salon.

Henry James, an acquaintance of Clover, later became a valued friend of Henry's. As his generational circle thinned over the years, Adams came to see James as a connection not merely to his wife, but to the social and intellectual aspirations they shared as a young couple in Washington.

John La Farge, the painter and stained-glass window maker, accompanied Henry to Japan in 1886 and to the islands of the South Pacific in 1890–1891. Adams described these journeys as part of his "posthumous" life following the death of Clover; La Farge commemorated the trips with a great creative output of sketches, watercolors, and oil paintings.

The sculpture artist Augustus Saint-Gaudens created a number of iconic works, including the Robert Gould Shaw Memorial on Boston Common and the gilded William Tecumseh Sherman monument at the southeast corner of New York's Central Park. Following Clover's suicide, Henry contracted Saint-Gaudens to produce the Adams Memorial in her honor.

Mont-Saint-Michel, a tidal island off the Normandy coast in France, embodied for Henry a medieval civilization superior to the rush and anomie that distinguished the modern industrial world. Offering a print memorial to its memory, he privately published in 1904 *Mont-Saint-Michel and Chartres,* informally subtitled "A Study of Thirteenth-Century Unity."

The Adams Memorial, a silent sphinx meant to raise rather than answer questions, and the Rock Creek Cemetery (Washington, D.C.) resting place of Henry and Clover Adams. "The work," John Hay once said, "is full of poetry and suggestion."

29
THE NEW HOUSE

In the latter months of 1883 Henry and Clover grew concerned with their living arrangements at the Corcoran house. Just to the east of their rented property lay a large empty lot on the corner of H and 16th streets recently sold by Corcoran to Frederick Paine, a young Washington real estate promoter rumored to be interested in putting up a multistory apartment house. Such a dreary (and noisy) prospect, Clover complained, made the Adamses feel "very uneasy about our future life."[1] It was a life that Henry in particular enjoyed. Peopled with friends — the Camerons and the George Bancrofts — as well as the occasional scoundrel (Adams's bête noire, James G. Blaine), it offered the stimulating variety of social life that he could find nowhere else in America. Proximity to the State Department's treasures, moreover, aided greatly his literary labors, as did the "suggestiveness" of his neighborhood, the city's most exclusive. In Lafayette Square one could, following the example of every president since James Madison, attend St. John's Episcopal Church, stroll by homes once occupied by the Kentucky statesman Henry Clay and South Carolina senator John C. Calhoun, and see an equestrian statue of Andrew Jackson (another bête noire). Here, the antique world of the early republic liked to share its secrets.

Unable to quash Paine's apartment scheme on his own, Adams promptly enlisted John Hay as a financial guardian angel. Having inherited a fortune from his recently deceased father-in-law, Hay possessed the dollars to buy Paine out. Henry proposed that the two Hearts join forces and build houses on adjoining lots. Adams would be, monetarily speaking, the junior partner, though with the Hays currently living in Clara's native Cleveland on Euclid Avenue's "Millionaires Row," Henry negotiated directly with Paine throughout the autumn. Paine's investment had come to $64,000 and Adams agreed to offer a full refund of his outlay, plus interest on the amount for a year, plus an additional $5,000 — in all $73,500 (approximately $2 million in current dollars). After briefly holding out for $77,000, Paine accepted. Of this sum, Henry contributed $25,000, which entitled him to "a lot with a 44-foot front on H Street and extending 131 feet back to an alley that led into 16th Street."[2] He set aside

358

an extra $30,000 (inherited from Grand-father Peter Chardon Brooks's estate) to build the new home. Combined, his $55,000 investment comes to about $1.5 million in contemporary dollars.

Though reliant upon Hay's largesse to buy Paine out, Henry possessed considerable resources of his own. His several inheritances were supplemented by a number of investments that he believed brought in, about this time, a 10 percent rate of return. His common stocks portfolio included subscriptions in Calumet and Hecla, a major Michigan mining company that was at one time the leading copper producer in the world. In the nineteenth century it paid out some $72 million in shareholder dividends, something north of $1 billion in current dollars. Adams benefited from the acumen of two financial agents, Ward Thoron in Washington and his brother-in-law Edward Hooper, treasurer of Harvard College, who kept an eye on his assets in Boston. Figures are sketchy, though it's estimated that by the mid-1880s Henry's income may have exceeded $40,000 a year, much of which he tended to reinvest.[3]

The "junior" aspect of his partnership with Hay pleased Henry. He wrote to Gaskell of the purchase, "John Hay and I have bought a swell piece of land which looks across a little square. . . . Hay is the capitalist, and takes the corner." When the structures were completed some two years later they could be said to resemble the "uneven" situations of their owners. Hay's more elaborate home — as though he divined his future place in presidential cabinets — included a Syrian arched entrance, turrets, and gables. A showpiece, it served Hay well; his social life and public career mixed seamlessly, and building near the White House brought him to the doorstep of power. Henry's smaller house, by contrast, complemented the larger building. It sheltered the historian, the thinker upon whose council and wisdom Hay might conveniently consult. Their mutual purchase, employment of the same architect, and strong friendship implied such an association. In this sense, the homes might have typified for Henry the kind of vicarious relationship with politics that he had come to accept. No longer a Young Turk, he had all but given up his vagrant dreams of leading a coalition of reformers. He may have continued to hold out some attenuated hope, however, that his name and talents might yet yield access to president neighbors through informal counsel. Perhaps that had been part of Washington's appeal all along?[4]

The differences in size and adornment of the Adams and Hay homes might speak further to Henry's break from old New England. His family was still identified architecturally with the primitive colonial

Georgian-style box acquired by John and Abigail in 1787. He and Clover sought an entirely dissimilar design, creating a tasteful home of discriminating comfort embellished by a Neo-Romanesque façade. In the 1940s historian Harold Dean Cater offered a glimpse of the home by collecting the reflections of several visitors. They recalled an interior accented by eighteenth- and nineteenth-century English paintings and various objects of Japanese arts — the hand-picked treasures of Henry's global travels. "The furniture was English, low and comfortable," Cater wrote. "On the walls were Turners, De Wints, Constables, Blakes, and many other choice paintings." The main room featured a fireplace with cases on either side containing "jades, porcelains, and bronzes, several Kwannons and one statue of the Oriental god of happiness. Oriental design could be seen on screens, cushions, and a few lacquer pieces."[5]

A still more illuminating description of the house comes from Henry's niece Abigail, who first visited the four-story residence in 1895, the year she turned sixteen. "One entered a low hall," she recalled:

Above were the living rooms — a big one in the front looking out on Lafayette Square. . . . Also on the front of the house was Uncle Henry's study. In the rear was

361

the dining room which overlooked a pleasant tree-shaded yard enclosed by a stable
at the back. Two admirable colored servants
ran the house — William the butler and
Maggie the maid. There were others concealed downstairs, including a cook who
could make a particularly hearty gumbo
soup. . . . Uncle Henry's study was furnished
with a huge mahogany table which took up
most of the room. At this desk he could be
found every morning drinking his coffee and
ponderously making notes. . . . The living
room opened out of his study and was
larger and more formal. . . . It held two low
curved sofas and some equally low leather
armchairs, all chosen for his convenience,
while a few chairs of more standard size
catered to the comfort of his taller
friends. . . . There were shoulder-high
bookcases around his living room hung with
pieces of Chinese brocade, and above were
some of his collection of pictures which
were scattered everywhere all over the
house.[6]

Had Abigail inventoried her uncle's book-
shelves, she would have noted several gems,
including rare editions of a 1502 Dante illustrated by the Venetian printer Aldus
Manutius and, compliments of Gaskell, a
1762 copy of Jean de La Fontaine's anthol-
ogy of racy stories and novellas, *Contes et*

Henry and Hay contracted Henry Hobson Richardson to build their H Street homes. Presumably the overture came from the Adamses, who knew the architect and admired his work in the Romanesque Revival style. Born on a Louisiana plantation in St. James Parish, Richardson, a great-grandson to the English natural philosopher Joseph Priestly, attended Harvard with Henry and Edward Hooper. His most acclaimed work, Boston's Trinity Church, was erected while the Adamses lived on Marlborough Street and could observe its progress. Richardson resided nearby, maintaining his home and offices in a Brookline house that he had rented since 1874 from Clover's father. A handful of the Adamses' intimates, including the Ephraim Gurneys — Henry's former Harvard colleague and Clover's sister Ellen — and Henry's college friend Nicholas Anderson, lived in Richardson-built houses.

Expressive, impulsive, and the radiating center of all he surveyed, Richardson left a strong and affable impression. Clover wrote to her father of seeing him at a party: "He can say truly 'I am my own music,' for he carries off any dinner more or less gaily." The sculptor artist Augustus Saint-Gaudens once said of Richardson, "It would require a Rabelais to do justice to his unusual power and character." Hiding a handsome face behind a dark (and for the period) de rigueur full beard, he "wore a brilliant yellow waistcoat, had an enormous girth, and a halt in his speech, which made the words that followed come out like a series of explosions." Unknown to his admirers, Richardson suffered from Bright's disease, which causes swelling; the illness combined with a strong appetite for alcohol ballooned his weight to nearly 350 pounds and contributed to his death at the age of forty-seven in April 1886, just four months after the H Street homes became habitable.[8]

Perhaps Richardson intended his vivacity to put others at ease during the unavoidably delicate financial negotiations between builder and buyer. Known to put architectural temptations before his clients (the price of the Anderson house notoriously skyrocketed from start to finish), Richardson plied his patrons with attractive options. Clover looked down upon such easily influenced house hunters, dismissing Anderson as simply "not educated as to what is ultimate." Hoping to head off an escalating budget and punning on his architect's amplitude, Henry once described Richardson as "an ogre. He devours men crude, and shows the effects of inevitable indigestion in his size!"[9]

Aiming for the "ultimate," Richardson, who had promised to complete the Hearts' homes by the early summer of 1885, ran over by several months. The flat, heavy-looking façade, deep balcony, and large above-street-level windows that distinguished the Adamses' redbrick residence gave it a stern and unfriendly appearance. The art and architecture critic Montgomery Schuyler (1843–1914) once observed, "Richardson's dwelling houses were not defensible except in a military sense."[10] In the case of Henry's property, this martial evocation suggests something more than simply external appearance. For its owner carried with him a number of secrets as an anonymous novelist, as a member of a self-chosen circle of Hearts, and as a spouse increasingly anxious about his wife's delicate health. The exclusivity and privacy that defined Henry's new house defined the man as well.

30
EMPTY HEART

In the early afternoon of December 6, just weeks before the Adamses were to occupy their new home, Clover ingested a vial of potassium cyanide which she had kept in the house for developing photographs. The toxin deprives the brain of oxygen and almost certainly killed her within minutes. Her state of mind on that fatal day eludes the biographer as it apparently eluded her husband. During a typical Sunday noon breakfast a solicitous if not especially worried Henry inquired of her health. Apparently satisfied with the reply, he decided to care for his own — a bothersome toothache sent him, after dining, on foot to visit Dr. Edward Maynard, an F Street dentist.[1] Hardly had he left the house, however, when a caller for Clover approached Henry. In company now, he returned to see if his wife wished to receive a visitor. Entering her upstairs room, he discovered Clover unconscious on the floor before the fire. He immediately moved her onto a nearby couch and attempted to revive her; perhaps, though desperately demanding a physician, he now realized that she was dead.

Three torturous days later, Henry's 16th Street neighbor Nicholas Anderson noted with some concern that a grieving Adams preferred isolation to consolation: "I called as soon as I heard it, and offered to do all that I could, but Henry refused to see anyone. I appreciate his state of mind, but I am sorry he would not let me show my sympathy by my acts. Until his family arrived he saw, as far as I can learn, no one whatever, and I can imagine nothing more ghastly than that lonely vigil in the house with his dead wife. Poor fellow! I do not know what he can do."[2]

It is difficult to believe that Clover's suicide caught her intimates wholly unawares. Her intense devotion to Dr. Hooper and sporadic despondency were long matters of hushed observation. Her sister Ellen protested to one correspondent after the 6th, "We had been consumed with anxiety — and probably others think that if we had only done this or that and have shown feeling! We did the best we knew how — and we know no better now." From a greater remove, Clover's old friend Henry James took the suicide in stride, calling it a case of "hereditary melancholy" and writing somewhat impassively to E. L. Godkin, "Poor Mrs. Adams found, the other day, the solution of the knottiness of existence."

Not long after, James drew upon Clover's suicide for his story "The Modern Warning" (1888), in which Clover's "conflict" between father and husband is replayed in Agatha Grice's struggle to be loyal to both her beloved American brother and her new English spouse. The men's rivalry is framed on the cultural differences between the two countries, a favorite James theme and perhaps a topic of discussion whenever he and Clover convened. Distraught, Agatha swallows poison in her upstairs room; a loyal servant provides the official narrative: "She has taken something, but only by mistake."[3]

It seems certain that the death of Dr. Hooper earlier in the year initiated Clover's final slide. Theirs was a complicated and not altogether healthy relationship; with no practice to occupy his hours the doctor depended heavily on the attentions of his three children. The precise emotional demands this placed on Clover can only be conjectured, though it is worth recalling that her one previous breakdown, if that is what transpired, occurred shortly after her marriage. Her endearingly addressed letters to "My Angel Pa" and "Dearest Pater" typically prefaced equally endearing sentiments. In one message written during her wedding trip, she seemed almost to be asking a lover for his forgiveness and promising ongoing fidelity: "I miss you very, very much, and think so often of your love and tenderness to me all my life, and wish I had been nicer to you. But I'll try to make up my shortcomings when I come home, and you must keep my place open and let me come into it again."[4] Having never remarried after the 1848 death of his wife, Dr. Hooper seems to have come to depend on Clover, and she on him, in a loving but cloying, self-conscious, and ultimately exhausting bond.

Dr. Hooper's sinking health (a case of coronary heart disease) brought Clover to Cambridge in early March, and she came alone. Aside from a brief trip to Manhattan two years earlier, she had never been apart from Henry. Now, on this trip north, he accompanied her as far as New York before, as arranged, and following a "pleasant dinner" with Hay and King, turning back. Over the next few days he wrote her constantly. Compared to his later, longer, and more effusive communications to Elizabeth Cameron, these spousal missives are by turns careful and correct, though never less than loving. He described the ongoing progress of their new home, acquainted her with local gossip — including the engagement of New York socialite Edith Jones (soon to be Wharton) to a Bostonian — and detailed the exploits of their treasured Skye terriers, Boojum, Possum, and Marquis: "The dogs and I have just come in from picking some violets for you."

After a week, Clover requested Henry's company in Cambridge and he quickly made arrangements to join her. "My private relations have not run so happily," he informed a friend at the time, "for my poor father is a complete wreck, and my mother almost a cripple; while, only within a few weeks my wife's father has broken down, and my wife has gone to Boston to be with him in his last moments. I must follow her tomorrow."[5] But once there, Henry could realize no role. Presumably he sought to be solicitous and protective of Clover, while she perhaps felt his presence intrusive. She promptly sent him back to Washington.

Three days after he left, however, she suddenly asked him to return — only to telegraph the following day and just as suddenly request that he not. Clover's changeable behavior concerned Henry and he insisted on seeing the situation in Cambridge for himself. "After hesitating a moment, I have decided to obey your order; but tomorrow I mean to go, no matter what you say" — and he did. Following a few days in Cambridge, however, he was again turned out. By this time Clover had been gone a month and Henry allowed to a friend, "I bolt forward and back like a brown monkey." Understandably frustrated, he observed further, "Nobody wants me in either place. They won't take me for a nurse, and I can't live all alone in a big, solitary

370

house when it rains and I can't ride." A few days later, on April 12, he wrote with some annoyance to Clover, "So another day has passed. Uneasy as I am about you, and unable to do anything here, I go on from hour to hour and make no engagements at all." The following day, Dr. Hooper died; Henry then made his fourth trip north in five weeks, for the funeral. Nothing would ever be the same, he later wrote, "after that May in 1885."[6]

Taking into account the tragic ends of Clover's siblings, family illness must be considered the compelling factor in her death. Not quite two years after Clover's passing, the recently widowed Ellen walked along the tracks of the Fitchburg Railroad and into the path of an oncoming train. Several years later her brother, Edward, leaped from the third-floor window of his Beacon Street home. He died some weeks later in an asylum, having refused to take food; the press cooperatively described the cause of death as "a short illness." There is the additional possibility that Clover feared a disposition to mental breakdown and killed herself as a shield to institutionalization. Charles Francis's enfeebling dementia — the Governor went into a slow decline commencing at about the age of sixty-four (1871), gradually losing his memory — may have weighed on her mind. The evidence is slight, though she referred on at least one occasion to death being preferable to illness, remarking in 1879 of the apparent drowning suicide of a friend, the painter William Morris Hunt, that perhaps the act had "saved him years of insanity, which his temperament pointed to."[7]

Many decades later, in a private communication, the distinguished Adams scholar Ernest Samuels reflected on Clover's complicated mental health inheritance. "The gossip of the time," he wrote, "seems to have regarded the Hooper family as touched in some way with hereditary eccentricity. . . . They were one of the most distinguished families of Marblehead and, by the union with the Sturgises, an equally ancient family in New England history, formed one of the remarkable clans in Boston life. . . . There was a certain amount of inbreeding in this ruling society." Of course the Adamses also constituted an "ancient family in New England history" and it too struggled with mental health. Henry's great-uncle Charles Adams died of alcoholism at the age of thirty; his uncles George Washington Adams and John Adams II also died young of alcohol-related illnesses or, in George's case, of a suspected alcohol-related suicide. Their early deaths suggest something of the colossal expectations of being an Adams and perhaps contextualize as well Henry's efforts to retreat, both physically and emotionally, from the Boston pressure cooker. He could, of course, do only so much. "The Adamses themselves pose all sorts of interesting psychological problems," Samuels noted in the same letter containing his thoughts on Clover's health. "The almost hysterical pessimism of Henry Adams's later letters suggest[s] an almost abnormal state of mind. This is also true of the letters of his younger brother Brooks Adams."[8]

Other factors that may have caused Clover varying degrees of distress include her childless marriage (a niece recalled her once saying that all women wanted children), doubts about her abilities as a photographer, and an apparent dislike of her physical appearance. Few photographs of Clover exist and none that draw attention to her habitually screened face. She noted of an 1883 self-portrait (apparently destroyed), "Marian Adams in study — 15 sec— hideous but good photo." Given her symptoms, there is a possibility that she suffered from cyclothymia, a chronic mood disorder milder than bipolar disorder. Someone with cyclothymia might feel stable for a period of time before experiencing an emotional high that can then decelerate to an emotional low. A few weeks before Clover's death, Henry's brother Charles visited the couple and came away remarking on her despondency: "She sat there, pale and careworn, never smiling, hardly making an effort to answer me, the very picture of physical weakness and mental depression."[9]

There is further the suggestion that the impending move into a "permanent" home upset Clover. She once called the yet-to-be erected structure on H Street "a modest mausoleum" and seemed to see its completion as part of a larger and unwanted culmination: "we *can* have nothing to look forward to beyond the grave."[10] The house, which Henry moved into less than a month after her death, might have implied a commitment to the future that she refused to make.

Still another consideration, Henry's growing professional achievements may have negatively affected Clover's health. While he wrote several books during their years together, her chief means of artistic expression — photography — garnered little attention. Her images reveal the eye of a sensitive observer, and a few have become iconic representations of Boston's Brahmin gentry. But she sometimes denigrated her work and it is possible, perhaps even likely, that she believed it amateurish in comparison to her husband's. That Henry occasionally impugned his own efforts may have set some pernicious example.

It is equally conceivable that his often critical, ironic tone introduced or reinforced certain tensions and silences in their relationship. So much of his energy during this period found an outlet in his scholarship, and what remained in hours, empathy, and awareness can never be fully registered. As if to absolve her husband of blame, Clover, in a final (and never sent) letter to Ellen, assumed alone responsibility for her declining condition — "If I had one single point of character or goodness I would stand on that and grow back to life" — while praising her "patient and loving" spouse: "God might envy him — he bears and hopes and despairs hour after hour. . . . Henry is beyond all words tenderer and better than all of you even."[11]

Adams's anguish no doubt deepened when the press reported Clover's death as most likely intentional. The initial account, by the *Washington Critic,* vaguely suggested "Heart Paralysis," but two days later the paper bluntly raised the question "Was it a case of Suicide?," before accurately stating, "She came to her death through an overdose of potassium, administered by herself."[12] Now Henry's family and friends on both sides of the Atlantic knew the truth.

On December 12, Adams purchased lots 202 and 203 in a new section of Rock Creek Cemetery for $400. There, following a small funeral made up of family and friends and officiated by a Cambridge minister brought in by the Hoopers, Clover's body was interred. Henry subsequently arranged for a headstone, acquired for $411, to mark the grave. "She is laid on a sunny slope in a most

375

peaceful church yard," Ellen stated, "a place . . . where the spring comes early."[13]

Reluctant to indulge in shock, Adams determined to find some survivant meaning in the future. "You will understand as I do," he informed John Hay a few days after Clover's passing, "that my only chance of saving whatever is left of my life can consist only in going straight ahead without looking behind."[14]

Most immediately, "going straight ahead" meant moving into the new H Street residence on schedule. Concerned for her brother-in-law, Ellen wrote to Godkin on December 30, "I trust he will be in his new house tonight. The associations of the old were too intense to be safely borne." Theodore Dwight, a bachelor State Department clerk and Henry's loyal research assistant, moved in as well, telling one correspondent that he hoped to "help [Adams] by a sort of devoted doglike companionship to support his bereavement." Just how long that bereavement went on is uncertain. A surface inspection of Henry's long life after Clover — noting his ever-expanding intellectual interests, global travels, and deeply affectionate friendship with Elizabeth Cameron — might imply an inevitable peace. Yet Henry himself stated otherwise. In the summer of 1901 he wrote to a grieving Clara Stone Hay, whose twenty-four-year-old son Delbert had the previous month accidently dropped from a third-story window to his death. Straining to offer solace, Adams shared an unpleasant fact that promised little light for the community of sufferers: "When I was suddenly struck, sixteen years ago, I never did get up again, and never to this moment recovered the energy or interest to return into active life."[15]

■ ■ ■ ■

PART II
PERFORMING
HENRY ADAMS

■ ■ ■ ■

■ ■ ■ ■

FLIGHT

■ ■ ■ ■

As near as I could tell my feeling, I had not
one wish ever to see Washington or home
again. My only instinct was to run away.

Henry Adams, 1888

31
THE POSTHUMOUS LIFE

Clover's death initiated what Henry occasionally called his "posthumous" life. Hardly passive, he sought solace in his scholarship, in his uneven performance as an American Buddha enduring beyond desire and attachment, and in his regime of ambitious wanderings — trying on Asia and North Africa, Europe and Russia. These and other sojourns became a regular feature of Adams's "new" existence. He displayed a taste for the exotic, traveling throughout the South Seas, to select parts of Latin America, and to the sites of ancient civilizations. In such remote places the impeccably correct social face that he wore in Washington could for a season be relieved. Henry's ancestors too had traveled extensively if conventionally in Europe, though always in the service of their country and their careers. Adams seemed intent during his journeys, rather, to step aside, to temporarily elide the self-imposed strains of living his last decades saddled with the objectionable identities of the pitied widower and the chaste tame cat.

Other activities, of course, vied for Adams's posthumous time. He showed real affection for his numerous nieces, the five daughters of his older brothers and an equal number belonging to Edward Hooper. Over the years, as these girls matured, his relationships with them became increasingly important and, if their warm letters and affectionate memoirs are any indication, mutually valued. His friendship with Elizabeth Cameron also grew during this period. Locked in a loveless marriage, she appreciated (and may have felt flattered by) the passion that she so easily aroused in Adams. In time, the unrequited nature of the relationship — she seemed to find him physically unattractive — produced on Henry's side a long-standing frustration that only rarely rose to the surface. Most of their contact occurred within correspondence, and what stands out in these lengthy letters are the unsaid things, the sentiments that pass in brooding ambiguities. In the immediate months after Clover's suicide, however, Lizzie's presence provided Adams with a much-welcomed diversion from his grief. Days before settling into the new H Street house he sent Cameron a favorite piece of jewelry from his wife's collection. "Will you keep it," he wrote to her, "and sometimes wear it, to remind you of her."[1]

Henry juxtaposed the pleasures of female friendships — and those longer standing connections to Hay, Gaskell, Cunliffe, and King — with a defiant "afterlife" attitude of renunciation, by which he presumed that nothing in the world much mattered. He swore off neither money nor the pleasant things that money could buy — mere materialism, after all — but went out of his way to relinquish the false hopes of "improvement" and "progress" as proper Victorians properly understood these things. Accordingly, he would pursue a private path to nirvana, reflecting on Japanese brush-stroke art, medieval Rhenish cathedrals, and distant world's fairs. Clover's memory, by contrast, Henry kept at bay. For years he maintained an intense silence, ensuring, therefore, the silence of others.

This surface and selective reserve did little to mask his fundamentally restless nature. Aside from the perpetual routine of writing, Adams rode horses, experimented with photography, and indulged in watercolors. He rarely tired of gossip, read omnivorously, and conservatively managed (with assistance) a small investment portfolio that tended to pay decent dividends. Compulsive and skeptical, sometimes depressed, and often tiresomely mordant, he seemed in the wake of Clover's suicide to expect others to defer to the matter of his tragedy.

At times Adams's reclusive, world-weary attitude dropped into parody. Writing a niece from overseas in the early 1890s, he praised meteorologically inelegant England as a kind of Gothic paradise preferable to sunny Paris: "London is really tolerable when the fog is thick enough and it rains. At a pinch I can always return there and be fairly comfortable." Such deliberately cryptic enunciations produced mixed results among the initiated. Supreme Court Justice Oliver Wendell Holmes, for one, panned Henry's fondness for putting on dour airs: "I knew Henry Adams quite well. He had two sides. He had distinction, great ability, and great kindness. When I happened to fall in with him on the street he could be delightful, but when I called at his house and he was posing to himself as the old cardinal he would turn everything to dust and ashes. After a tiresome day's work one didn't care to have one's powers of resistance taxed by discourse of that sort, so I rarely called."[2]

Brooks Adams more generally remembered the catholicity of poses as a prominent feature of his brother's emotional makeup, particularly following the violent end of his marriage. He claimed, "Henry was never, I fear, quite frank with himself or with others. . . . [He] was always shy and oversensitive and disliked disagreeable subjects." As a result, Brooks continued, "he would surround himself with different defences, all of them calculated to repel tactless advances, and on these defences few of us cared to intrude. .... One of these was that, when his wife died, in 1884 [sic], he insisted that he also died to the world." The insightfulness of these words need not obscure the more positive facets of Henry's strategies for self-protection. His sensibility and tastes, as noted, leaned toward the less recognized Maryland side of his pedigree, and he found the Adamses' ingrained "rough play" off-putting. Their unwillingness to warm to his wife may have quietly erected additional barriers. Brooks's errant recording of Clover's death date in the quoted passage perhaps hints at this fundamental inconsideration, as does Charles's description of his sister-in-law as "an infernal bore."[3] And yet Brooks may be right in suggesting that Henry's "defences" were multidimensional and that in expressing a conspicuous, even excessive grief over his wife's death, he arranged matters so as to keep others at arm's length while simultaneously steering the self-conscious narrative of his posthumous life.

At the core of this performance lies an ironic, agitated, and complicated sensibility. The Cambridge don and the crusading editor now took a backseat to the sage-in-training who wandered a world he no longer loved. Having affected to quit politics he now pretended to quit life. "Do you not know," he once informed an acquaintance, "that I have been dead fifteen years?"[4] Such pronouncements, and there were others of this sort, drew attention to Adams's pattern of practicing an elegant ritual of grief. The striking Rock Creek memorial that he had installed to replace the simple stone formerly marking his wife's grave bore evidence of this tendency, as did his refusal to discuss Clover in the *Education.* The effect is a deafening silence that could only have teased even those readers who knew its desperate meaning.

Though Adams's "act" put some off, others, particularly younger acquaintances enticed by his conversational verve, were drawn in. The British diplomat Cecil Spring Rice developed a long and fruitful friendship with Henry, whose confident idiosyncrasies intrigued him. Sampling Rice's correspondence in the second half of 1887, the months that he first encountered Adams, one discovers a sympathetic observer:

I like the one here, who since his wife died has no friends and no absorbing interest and takes an amused view of life. . . . He found his wife dead on the floor one day. . . . Since then he has regarded life with a frivolity which rather shocks people who don't know him well. . . . He is queer to the last degree; cynical, vindictive, but with a con-

388

stant interest in people, faithful to his friends and passionately fond of his mother. . . . He has no cards and never goes out.

Others were similarly struck by Henry's unconventional orientation. The historian John Franklin Jameson once informed a younger colleague that Adams's eccentricities were all part of his singular way of negotiating the world: "You will find him a very interesting being — a small bird-like person, whose conversation is always brilliant and entertaining, but full of paradox and of whimsicalities. It seems impossible that he should believe most of the things he says; he has his dialect."[5]

The "paradoxes" and "whimsicalities" raised by Henry had positive connotations beyond the ken of either Rice or Jameson. For despite claims to the contrary, the compulsively restless Adams aimed to avoid turning into a living corpse. The move to the new house helped, as did Dwight's companionship. Still, the old resonances of life among the Hearts would beat against him daily unless he initiated some type of resistance or release. This he did in a grand gesture, chasing restoration abroad. Six months after Clover's death he left America, severing his immediate associations to Adamses and Hoopers, presidents and Congresses. Seeking a posthumous peace, he sailed to Japan.

32
JAPAN

Sometime in the empty months following
Clover's death, Henry decided to cancel his
annual summer retreat to Beverly. Neither
did he wish, however, to stew in a muggy
Washington while H Street's grandees whispered over his misery. The city, a historian's
oasis, seemed suddenly unable to stir, rally,
or waken him; the massive Jefferson and
Madison project, only half complete, now
languished in labored fits and starts. Clearly
its author required a respite — but Adams,
the obliging offspring of tireless Puritan
generations, lacked the capacity to "do"
leisure in any conventional sense. True, he
enjoyed the capital's salons and always
delighted in travel, though his inevitable
storming of assorted archives, cathedrals, and
museums suggested a certain laborious race
to chase down and corner culture. Above all,
he detested boredom. Determined to avoid
the grooved European circuit, he went instead
to Japan, in search of diversion, in search of

"death." Easing into a *post obitum* existence, he sought in Buddhism a philosophical system from which he might elevate his private grief to the status of spiritual enlightenment.

It would be wrong to imply, however, that distress alone or even principally drove Henry to Japan. Restive in Quincy, he had written to Gaskell in 1869, years before his marriage, "I shall go to the Pacific." A host of subsequent human contacts emboldened that pledge. Aside from corresponding with "Billy Big" — Clover's cousin William Sturgis Bigelow, a Buddhist convert living in Japan — Adams had befriended both the Chinese envoy Chen Lau-Piu and Yoshida Kiyonari, the Meiji government's minister to the United States. Yoshida, so Clover had informed her father in 1880, "has given Henry two water colours he brought him from Japan: one about four feet by two, by the best artist there, he says, Run Lin, a winter scene framed with brocade — it covers six feet of our bare wall in the front entry; the other is narrower and not so original, though very nice."[1]

Beyond these personal connections, the late nineteenth-century East became for Adams, as it did for many other Westerners, a vivid if largely imagined place. Only a generation removed from the Meiji Restoration (1868), which had inaugurated a period of industrialization and military reform along Western lines, Japan accommodated a growing tourist industry of elites who descended upon the country's main port cities. The prizes these visitors purchased — bronzes, kimonos, lacquerware, and *byōbu* (folding screens) — shaped the more refined tastes and fashion sense found in Europe and the United States.[2]

Victorian New England's infatuation with Asia in fact built off an existing tradition. Merchants, whalers, and China traders had for generations brought wealth to the region, making Salem, Boston, and New Bedford vibrant centers of commerce. A bit later, the Transcendentalists would invoke Eastern spiritual systems as a counter to Western materialism. "In the morning," Thoreau wrote in *Walden,* "I bathe my intellect in the stupendous and cosmogonal philosophy of the Bhagvat Geeta," while Emerson proposed in a journal, "These colossal conceptions of Buddhism and Vedantism . . . are always the necessary or structural action of the human mind." Following the Civil War, some among Henry's generation of alienated intellectuals, perhaps aching for Old Boston, looked to Old Japan as an antidote to the era's coarse political and industrial culture.[3] They hunted across the Pacific, that is to say, for a peace they could no longer find at home.

One of their number, Edward Sylvester

Morse, delivered the well-received Lowell Institute lectures in 1881, attended by several of Henry and Clover's friends. The son of a Portland, Maine, Congregationalist deacon, Morse, largely self-educated, had collected marine invertebrates in Japan and taught zoology at the Tokyo Imperial University. Taking an interest in Japanese arts and folklore, he was one of America's first orientalists — his collections of pottery, ceramics, and artifacts are currently held in Boston's Museum of Fine Arts and at Salem's Peabody Essex Museum. Not long after Morse's lectures, the Boston art collector Isabella Stewart Gardner, endowed by both birth and marriage with a tidy fortune, ventured to Japan for three months. A Beverly neighbor of the Adamses, she no doubt caught their attention as but the latest wayfarer in a Brahmin exodus east.[4]

As Henry sought Theodore Dwight's company following Clover's death, so he now prevailed upon the traveling companionship of John La Farge, paying for his friend's passage and various expenses. Of aristocratic French descent and raised Roman Catholic, the Manhattan-born La Farge, bald, bespectacled, and sporting a thick salt-and-pepper mustache, read widely and developed an interest in exotic cultures. A gifted muralist and maker of stained-glass windows, he had met Henry, three years his junior, in one of Boston's literary-artistic circles, perhaps at Harvard where he briefly taught art composition. He possessed, so Adams said, "the neatest humor, the nicest observation, and the evenest temper you can imagine." Though responsible for a wife and several children in Newport, Rhode Island, La Farge, committed to professional success, had lived independently in New York since the late 1870s. "He was going to lead his own life," remembered one relative. Talented, praised, and inundated with commissions, he established the La Farge Decorative Art Company in 1883, but the business soon dissolved following a bitter dispute with his partners over artistic control. Accused of taking designs belonging to the company, La Farge was arrested in May 1885. Though settled out of court with all charges dropped, the case made headlines; the *New York World* reported that the commotion caused "a decided scandal in both social and art circles and became the general topic of conversation whenever or wherever artists or connoisseurs met."[5] Now, a year later, with his name being gossiped about, a deeply embarrassed La Farge accepted Henry's invitation to seek his own season of peace.

In early June the two voyagers embarked from Albany and began a "brilliant run" aboard the Union Pacific Railroad, whose director, Adams's brother Charles, kindly lent them his private company car. La Farge spent much of the trip sketching the spacious western landscape, while a more academic Henry read up on Buddhism. "Our journey," he told one correspondent, "was a glorious success." Arriving in "dusty, wintry, and seedy" San Francisco on the 10th, they briefly put up at the Palace Hotel before setting off on the Pacific Mail Steamship Company line's *City of Sydney.* Suffering through his usual mal de mer, Henry complained to Dwight that "the Pacific Ocean is different from other oceans. . . . It contains nothing but head-winds, chopping seas, rains, cold and seasickness."[6] After three unpleasant weeks of fighting the elements and his stomach, Henry arrived in Yokohama on the second of July.

During the more than two centuries of national seclusion, in which foreigners were directed to Nagasaki (Japan's "window on the world"), Yokohama remained a sleepy fishing village. The 1853 arrival of Commodore Matthew Perry's small flotilla of U.S. Navy ships into Tokyo Bay, however, eventuated the opening of select Japanese ports to American vessels. This had the effect of turning Yokohama into a bustling metropolitan center of some seventy-five thousand, complete with gas-powered street lamps and a railway connection to Tokyo. Already an observer of "modernity's" progress on two continents, Henry would now measure its advance in Asia.

Many Westerners were first introduced to the city via Jules Verne's popular adventure novel *Around the World in Eighty Days* (1873). Though he had never visited Yokohama, Verne guessed to his readers' amusement at the beguiling mixture of Eastern exoticism and Western influence captured in a European section of elegant residences and beautiful peristyles neighboring a Japanese quarter filled with curio shops, restaurants, and teahouses. Predictably, rice plantations, saké, and scented camellias embellished the French novelist's spell. In a passage packed with clichés, one character walks through a district crammed with "sacred gates of singular architecture, bridges half hid in the midst of bamboos and reeds, temples shaded by immense cedar-trees, [and] holy retreats where were sheltered Buddhist priests and sectaries of Confucius."[7]

La Farge, by contrast, recorded his initial impression of Yokohama in language that left little doubt that he sought a journey of the senses: "Arrived yesterday. . . . We were in the great bay when I came up on deck in the early morning. The sea was smooth like the brilliant blank paper of the prints; a vast surface of water reflecting the light of the sky as if it were thicker air. Far-off streaks of blue light, like finest washes of the brush, determined distances." Moving about the bay were steamers and men-of-war; an occasional picturesque junk drew the attention of tourists. On land, Henry and La Farge noticed large numbers of Europeans in the port city; Western children were shepherded by Japanese nurses, while Western ladies cut through the oppressive summer humidity on horseback or in phaetons. The contrasting temperaments of the two men clashed after a few days, with Adams desiring a more structured routine than did La Farge. The latter wrote of their differences, "I enjoy, myself, this drifting [attending theaters, observing people, producing watercolors] though A is not so well pleased, and I try to feel as if the heat and the novelty of impressions justified me in idleness."[8]

Henry's spirits picked up when, concerned with a cholera outbreak and eager to escape the wilting temperatures ("The thermometer today is anywhere between 90° and 200°"), he and La Farge were taken to Nikko, a charming resort city in the cooler mountains, about eighty miles north of Tokyo. "Who has not seen Nikko," goes a familiar Japanese saying, "cannot say beautiful." There, they occupied a two-up two-down that Henry called his "baby-house" in wonder of its fragile "paper" interior.[9] Their Nikko neighbors included Bigelow and Ernest Fenollosa, a historian of American and Japanese art then teaching in Tokyo. Born in Massachusetts, Fenollosa studied at Harvard (like Henry), adopted Buddhism (like Bigelow), and placed a considerable portion of his collection at the Museum of Fine Arts in Boston (like Morse). All of these men withdrew into various fields of oriental aesthetics, seeking something more "authentic" than they could find in their native New England.

Henry approved of Nikko, writing to Dwight, "[It] lies high and is cool, with beautiful scenery." He once again dismissed their domicile, which he described as a "little Japanese toy-house" and "our doll-house with paper windows and matted floors." The efficacy of this and other such nimble structures erected to meet certain climatic practicalities and decorative preferences eluded Adams. In this, as in other respects, he refused to take Japan on its own terms. His escorted wanderings about its larger cities — including Tokyo, Kyoto, Osaka, and Kobe — were attended by an entourage of merchants eager to ply their wares, while visits to museums, temples, and traditional torii gates substituted for human contact; evenings often ended in expensive dinners. Henry spent lots of money, took lots of photographs, and, after ten days of giving the local teas their due, gratefully switched to an American brand that, expecting the worst, he had prudently packed in a trunk.[10]

Reading their various reflections of Japan in print and in private communications, one is left with the strong impression that La Farge made more of his time abroad than did Henry. Aside from producing dozens of watercolors, he published several incisive essays and a charming book, *An Artist's Letters from Japan* (1897). Adams, by contrast, frequently seemed at odds with his environment. Only when encountering the towering Kamakura Buddha, a fifty-foot-high outdoor bronze statue cast in 1252, did he quicken with recognition. The figure gave Henry a marvelously enigmatic example of the sublime anonymity that he now professed to seek for himself. "This remnant of the vanished splendor of Kamakura is about twenty miles from Yokohama," he wrote to a friend, ". . . and as La Farge says it is the most successful colossal figure in the world."[11] The statue's cultural significance struck Adams as transcendent and within a few years he would propose the soulless industrial dynamo as its symbolic heir — science's triumph over a waning spirituality.

When not contemplating the great Buddha's meaning, Henry remained otherwise unimpressed with Japan. He complained of its scent: "an oily, sickish, slightly fetid odor, — which underlies all things"; he snubbed its staple food: "Even Japanese rice is unappetizing"; and he made rather crude observations about its women: "They are all badly made, awkward in movement, and suggestive of monkeys." In this often untranslatable environment Henry struggled to find his footing: the presence of countless open Tokyo privies invaded his senses; a comely woman in a public bath demanded his shy Victorian eye. Unsettled, he ignored the Japanese people — "There is some society," he informed a friend, "but I have not sought it" — and reserved his praise for the country's edifying natural beauty. "In many ways nothing in Europe rivals it," he wrote. "I should class it very high among the sights of the world. If architecture falls short of perfection, nature steps in to give the perfection wanted; and the result is something quite by itself. Sky, mountains, and trees are exquisite."[12]

On October 2 Adams and La Farge boarded the iron-hulled steamship *City of Peking* and sailed for San Francisco. While stalking nirvana they had managed to spend some $7,500, or about $210,000 in current dollars, much of this advanced by Hay, who sought his share of oriental bric-à-brac. "I saw . . . two large six-leaved screens, painted by Chinanpin, a Chinese artist who came to Japan about 1680," Henry wrote his fellow Heart. "I thought you might fancy one."[13] A slightly different financial matter obliged La

Farge to recognize Adams's munificence by attaching his name to the dedication page of *An Artist's Letters from Japan.* The tribute is generous even as it recognizes, with a light touch, their private differences and fruitless pursuit of a state beyond suffering.

TO HENRY ADAMS, ESQ.

My Dear Adams: Without you I should not have seen the place, without you I should not have seen the things of which these notes are impressions. If anything worth repeating has been said by me in these letters, it has probably come from you, or has been suggested by being with you — perhaps even in the way of contradiction. And you may be amused by the lighter talk of the artist that merely describes appearances, or covers them with a tissue of dreams. And you alone will know how much has been withheld that might have been indiscreetly said.

If only we had found Nirvana.[14]

Adams reached San Francisco on October 20, greeted by Charles, who brought bad news: Henry's brother-in-law and former Harvard colleague Ephraim Gurney had died the previous month of anemia and the ailing Governor was soon to follow. The two quickly returned to Quincy and maintained a vigil until their father's death on November 21.

The difficult year, filled with loss, ended for Adams in yet another renunciation. On December 27 Harvard president Charles W. Eliot invited Henry to return to Cambridge as the McLean Professor, the endowed post vacated by Gurney's death. This may have constituted an act of kindness, even mercy on Eliot's part. From the outside, Adams's spouseless Washington situation looked uncertain and his father's passing might be supposed to have sparked thoughts of his coming "home." But not so. Calling the offer "very flattering," Henry nevertheless declined on the 30th, giving no reason for his decision. "I think," he enigmatically observed to Eliot, "there is a certain impertinence in offering reasons at all."[15]

Rather than return to Boston, he remained in Washington, determined to push on and complete the *History*. In abeyance for several months, it appeared to be a casualty of its author's posthumous approach. But Japan had proven a tonic of sorts, pulling Henry away from the cloistered Washington, London, and Paris worlds that contained so much of his grief. He now began, slowly, to move forward.

33
THE HISTORIAN'S TALE

Over a fifteen-month period beginning in October 1889 Henry's nine-volume *History*, some dozen years in the making, rolled off the presses. Mere length only hints at its singular achievement assaying the early American republic. A half-century after its appearance Columbia University's Henry Steele Commager called the project "the finest piece of historical writing, in our literature," and still another half-century later the noted Jefferson specialist Noble Cunningham Jr. agreed that it deserved "a high place among the great writings in American history." More recently Garry Wills wrote an entire book, *Henry Adams and the Making of America* (2005), revisiting the *History*'s origins, reviewing its contents, and arguing for its unbroken relevance. "It is," Wills insists, "the non-fiction prose masterpiece of the nineteenth century in America." Thinking even that encomium insufficient, Yale scholar Edmund S. Morgan raised the stakes still

403

higher: "Are the *Histories* the nonfiction masterpiece of the nineteenth century in America? Probably. Are they the masterpiece of historical writing in America in any century? Certainly."[1]

At its most basic level, the *History* tells the story of America's growth and development between 1800 and 1817, a period encompassing the presidential administrations of Jefferson and Madison, the War of 1812, and the rise of a new post-Appalachian West. Many of the details concerning this long drama Adams discovered in European archives. Extended stays in London, Paris, and Madrid yielded huge caches of hitherto inaccessible primary sources closed to less connected scholars. Though Henry himself labored in these repositories, notably identifying important materials and working in newspapers, the task might have proven impossible if not for the small teams of copyists he employed to transcribe documents. He further enlisted both friends and officials in America and Europe to aid in the search for sources. On some occasions, so Clover liked to jest, she, "being a woman, . . . could make requests for permissions which Henry was . . . too shy to make."[2]

In one signal case Adams successfully solicited Henry Vignaud, secretary of the American legation in Paris, for access to the French archives. "If your diplomacy . . . can succeed so far as to persuade the 'Sous-directeur' to let his copyist go to work, at my expense, at once," he wrote Vignaud in early 1880, "it may save me much delay at a later time." The secretary's tact did, in fact, prevail and Henry happily returned the favor with a gift that, in a sense, only an Adams could supply — printed editions of his ancestors' works and memoirs: "I have sent you through the State Department sets of the John Adams (10 vols.) and J. Q. Adams (12 vols.) so that you have now a tolerably fair beginning of the vast wilderness of Adams literature." Henry later hinted at his desire to do Vignaud a still more substantial service by extending his tenure in the American legation. The recent election had made James Garfield president and a chance existed that Vignaud, now working in James Blaine's State Department, might lose his post and Henry his important contact. Adams half-apologized for the unseemly scramble for offices about to transpire: "Garfield and Blaine are what are called popular men, that is to say, have hordes of needy politicians to feed." And he confessed the limits of his own personal influence: "[I] doubt whether any interference of mine would, in the long run, do you good." Still, as if asserting a kind of baronial privilege, or perhaps just offering a knowledge-able guess regarding Washington's prevailing political winds, he assured Vignaud, "It is not supposed that you will be disturbed."[3]

Other research courtesies were extended to Henry that emphasize the aristocratic nature of nineteenth-century historical writing. The National Archive at Madrid was opened for his use on a Sunday; copyists under his direction on two continents enjoyed unprecedented access to government documents; and Adams successfully prevailed upon Harvard librarian Justin Winsor to send to Beverly Farms various books and newspapers. These included *The Richmond Recorder* (1802), Albert James Pickett's *History of Alabama* (1859), the *New York Commercial Advertiser* (1801), William Henry Foote's studies of the Presbyterian Church in Virginia, and Benjamin Rush's unpublished autobiography. The last George Bancroft had tried unsuccessfully to consult in both 1849 and 1867. The security and preservation of the old materials need not be a concern, Adams assured Winsor, and he drew up a plan for packaging the precious items: "If the college carpenter will, under your orders, construct for me a strong box, with stout hinges, iron handles, and a double lock, into which the volumes may be put, I think there will be very little danger of loss or injury."[4]

This research paid off handsomely, and the treasures that Adams unearthed from the European archives in particular dramatically recast the project. At one time he anticipated needing no more than three volumes to tell the story of Jeffersonian America, but the richness of source materials and the lengthening shadows they shed across the Atlantic World forced Henry to reconsider the study's scope. Impatient with a mere national history, he drew, rather, a nuanced portrait of British diplomacy, documented the collapse of Spanish power in the New World, and traced Napoleon's policies in Europe and its colonies. By putting the names of two Virginia presidents in the prosaic titles — *History of the United States of America during the Administrations of Thomas Jefferson* and *History of the United States of America during the Administrations of James Madison* — Henry gave the appearance of a strictly American topic, and yet its transnational reach argued otherwise.

A further striking feature is the work's steep discounting of "great" men. While preparing the volumes Adams wrote to the philosopher William James, "With hero worship like [the Scottish historian Thomas] Carlyle's, I have little patience." Process rather than personality, so he stressed, catalyzed change. The Jeffersonians had come to power in 1801, Henry observed, as a "peace party" opposed, during the long French revolutionary and Napoleonic wars (1792–1815), to high taxes, a large national debt, and an expanding military. But this commitment ultimately collapsed. Near constant conflict between France and Britain enflamed the Atlantic and eventually drew the United States into the War in 1812. Such is the folly of men, parties, and platforms. In a letter to Samuel Tilden, written with the volumes well under way, Henry insisted that the celebrated Virginia triumvirate of Jefferson, Madison, and Monroe counted for very little in the larger scheme of things. "They appear like mere grass-hoppers, kicking and gesticulating, on the middle of the Mississippi river," he challenged decades of Founders' filial piety. "There is no possibility of reconciling their theories with their acts, or their extraordinary foreign policy with dignity. They were carried along on a stream which floated them after a fashion without much regard to themselves."[5]

Adams's dismissal of elite leadership had the salutary effect of commending non-elites. He lauds the doomed if resolute warriors fighting under the famous Shawnee chief Tecumseh for having "compelled the [U.S.] government to pay for once something like the value of the lands it took"; he asserts that "Burr's conspiracy" to carve out a rogue empire in the Southwest "had no deep roots in society, but was mostly confined to a circle of well-born, well-bred, and well-educated individuals"; and he further extols popular resistance to the great Bonaparte: "Napoleon's rule in politics, and one which cost him dear, was to disregard masses and reckon only on leaders."[6] There is a strong intimation in the volumes, moreover, that while American civil and military authority had stumbled badly during the War of 1812 — to wit, the burning of Washington and failure to conquer Canada — the people's resolve to rally and survive saw the young nation through. Not that any among them, Henry tutted, made "history" happen. Looking to identify a truly momentous event in the so-called Age of Jefferson, he designated the August 1807 maiden voyage of Robert Fulton's *North River Steamboat,* the first vessel to use steam propulsion for transport. Paddling *up* the southernmost part of the Hudson River at an average speed of five miles per hour, the experimental craft traveled from New York City to Albany and back, thus demonstrating technology's capacity to challenge nature.

Some readers have wondered over the years if the *History*'s downgrade of the Jeffersonians constituted a family vendetta. The evidence suggests otherwise. Yes, John Adams lost the 1800 presidential election to Jefferson, but John Quincy Adams, of whom Henry had a living memory, prospered under Virginia presidents, who secured him diplomatic posts and a cabinet seat. Rather than attack the southern plantocracy, Henry saw it as simply another ephemeral power structure invariably relegated to history's ash heap. His own people had stumbled along the same path to obsolescence. In an 1875 review of John Gorham Palfrey's *History of New England,* Adams had soberly described "the Puritan colonies . . . [as] an anachronism in the world. Virginia or Pennsylvania could flourish in such an atmosphere, but New England slowly perished. The descendants of Winthrop, Endicott, and Dudley found themselves in a new order of things. Their fathers' great experiment of a religious commonwealth had broken down. The past had to be abandoned."[7]

Perhaps recognizing the impossibility of attracting a significant audience for his tome, Henry presumed to be uninterested in sales, suggesting that the project constituted a gift to the nation. "If I were offering this book for sale," he wrote his publisher, Charles Scribner, a year before the first volumes appeared, "I should, on publishers' estimates, capitalise twelve years of unbroken labor, at (say) $5000 a year, and $20,000 in money spent in traveling, collecting materials, copying, printing, &c; in all $80,000, without charging that additional interest, insurance, or security percentage which every businessman has to exact. This book, therefore, costs me $80,000" (about $2.2 million in current dollars). But, far from begrudging the cost, Henry, the great scoffer of Great Man History, wanted only great men to write history, and he willingly paid for the pleasure. "History has always been, for this reason, the most aristocratic of all literary pursuits," he once observed, "because it obliges the historian to be rich as well as educated I should feel sure that whenever such a rate of profit could be realised on history, history would soon become as popular a pursuit as magazine-writing, and the luxury of its social distinction would vanish."[8]

Henry may have prized the aristocratic character of his craft, but it nevertheless rankled him when the *History* sold in small numbers. In the winter of 1892 he wrote irritably to Charles, "Literature has vanished from mankind. . . . My own works lurk in some dusty corner among other odd volumes." A few years later his former student Charles Franklin Thwing suggested that Adams continue his American story beyond the Jeffersonians. "His reply," Thwing later recalled, "was that the American people had never shown that appreciation of his history which would warrant him in further writing." And in 1916, long after the books appeared, Harvard historian Samuel Eliot Morison paid a social call on Adams and listened as the old man offered a last lament on the topic: "He said that the first volume of his *History of the*

United States . . . sold only to the extent of about 1,500 copies; and that by the time the ninth and last volume appeared in 1891, the sale of each new volume had fallen off to less than one thousand. That seemed to him proof that the American public did not care for his contributions to their history."[9]

Among associates on both sides of the Atlantic, however, the project received a more welcoming response. "You have made an invaluable contribution to American history," Francis Parkman wrote to Adams when the first volumes began to appear, and Hay singled out books 5 and 6 for, as he put it, "tak[ing] the cake. There is a gathering strength and interest in these later volumes that is nothing short of exciting." Several years later, shortly after Henry's death in 1918, the British political theorist Harold Laski praised the originality of Adams's scholarship to Oliver Wendell Holmes: "I think him on the whole the first of the Americans who wrote specifically American history. His book has the wrath and insight of a man who did not merely write from documents but had something of his own to say." Succeeding generations seem to have agreed. In 1955 Cornell University Press published the first volume's opening six chapters, which review the physical, intellectual, and economic conditions of the country at the moment the Jeffersonians assumed power. Titled *The United States in 1800,* it sold over 130,000 copies through the mid-1980s; in 2004 the University of Missouri Press put out a revised edition, and in 2007 yet another version appeared in the *New York Review of Books* Classics series. This latest iteration included not only the *History*'s first six chapters but also its four concluding chapters, "America in 1817," under the expansive title *The Jeffersonian Transformation: Passages from the "History."*[10] After being out of print for decades, the full work was reissued in a two-volume set by the Library of America in 1986.

One may still read with profit Adams's long meditation on the early republic, even as scholarly revision and shifting cultural priorities have naturally altered our view of the period. Today, for example, no such "definitive" study would downplay the impact of slavery, as did Henry. He regarded chattel servitude as a feature of the South, ignoring its still firmly rooted presence in the North; as one modern critic of the *History* has observed, Adams had nothing to say about the twenty thousand bondspeople living in New York in 1800 — the state having provided only the previous year for gradual manumission.[11] Women are similarly hidden in the work. The *History,* though an imposing

413

four thousand pages, contains fewer than a dozen references to women in its index. These exceptions, including Dolley Madison, a Spanish queen, and Theodosia Burr Alston (daughter of Aaron Burr), reflect the aristocratic tone of political society that interested Henry.

Adams betrays a similar chauvinism in treating states and sections. When handling the growing South, he leans too heavily on coastal Virginia; New England to him is Boston. His discussion of the expanding West, moreover, is both hurried and hypothetical. As an actual place with real cities, economies, and peoples, it receives little notice, and yet as an idea or concept of where America's democratic energies are moving, it is somewhat abstractly regarded as the nation's "future." Other absences and imprecisions — the lack of attention to religion outside of New England, the defining of culture as high culture, and a tendency by Henry to read his struggles with Grantism into the patronage battles carried on among the Jeffersonians — bear evidence of the *History*'s various partialities and limitations. And yet taken on its own terms the work offers a compelling (if perhaps too neat) interpretation of how the United States transformed itself from a backward-looking republic into a forward-looking democracy.

Written at the tail end of Romantic histori-

414

ography's heyday, Henry's *History,* though grounded in the new scientific rigor, is perhaps not quite as fashionably empirical as he presumed. For rather than drafting a narrow, footnote-heavy monograph, Adams adopted the then common practice of producing an "epic," distinguished as much for its literary merits as its sheer size. More important, he tacitly agreed with the Romantic view that a benevolent fatalism intervened in the New World's break from its old colonial masters. Bancroft's insistence that "the spirit of the colonies demanded freedom from the beginning" is echoed in Henry's claim that "every American, from Jefferson and Gallatin down to the poorest squatter, seemed to nourish an idea that he was doing what he could to overthrow the tyranny which the past had fastened on the human mind."[12] Between the two scholars we might define Adams as the more secular in that he avoided the apologias of manifest destiny and their attendant assumptions that other nations should emulate the democratic ideals of the United States. But in presuming the inevitable progress of America, Henry tells the familiar story of a rising people living in a blessed land and moving toward certain prosperity.

Edward Gibbon recounted in a memoir that directly after completing *The History of the*

Decline and Fall of the Roman Empire he strolled the grounds of his garden in reflection:

> It was on the day, or rather the night of the 27th of June 1787 . . . that I wrote the last lines of the last page, in a summerhouse in my garden. After laying down my pen, I took several turns in a . . . covered walk of acacias, which commands a prospect of the country, the lake, and the mountains. . . . I will not dissemble the first emotions of joy on the recovery of my freedom and, perhaps, the establishment of my fame. But my pride was soon humbled, and a sober melancholy was spread over my mind, by the idea that I had taken my everlasting leave of an old and agreeable companion, and that whatsoever might be the future date of my history, the life of the historian must be short and precarious.[13]

With Gibbon's sentimental model in mind, Henry sought a moment of equal gravitas. After composing the final lines of the *History* in Quincy while visiting his mother, the full import of the project, much of it researched and written with Clover's interest and aid, finally caught up with him. "The narrative was finished last Monday," he wrote on September 16, 1888. "In imitation of Gibbon I walked in the garden among the yellow and

416

red autumn flowers, blazing in sunshine, and meditated. My meditations were too painful to last. The contrast between my beginning and end is something Gibbon never conceived."[14]

In pursuit of yet another beginning, Henry made plans to go abroad. He may have desired a fresh setting to place Clover's absence into perspective; he may have grown self-conscious of his undeniable attraction to Elizabeth Cameron and sought to put oceans between them; or he may have simply repeated an old family cycle of writing and traveling. Among these possibilities resides a single certainty: Henry found peace in motion. Following college, he went to Germany; after teaching the sons of Harvard he haunted Europe's archives; and within months of Clover's suicide he had departed for Japan. And now, still teased by the search for an elusive and loosely defined nirvana, Adams looked once more to the Pacific, eager to sample Polynesia's "primitive" island societies.

34
BABES IN PARADISE

In August 1890 Henry and John La Farge, accompanied by the latter's Japanese valet, Rioza Awoki, embarked on a yearlong tour of the southern tropics. In setting out for Oceania, they broke from the traditional pathways of Brahmin tourism, and even of their earlier journey to Japan. "We wished to go very far," La Farge wrote. "Japan is too near. They have the telegraph there. The Pacific always means two months without news." Visiting, in a more or less leisurely succession, Hawaii, Samoa, Tahiti, Rarotonga, Fiji, Australia, Indonesia, and Singapore, they ventured into a host of puppet kingdoms whose barely century-old contacts with the West were largely confined to merchants, militaries, and missionaries. Herman Melville's popular Polynesian tales, *Typee* (1846) and *Omoo* (1847), sentimentalized the region, offering Americans what Nathaniel Hawthorne blithely called, in a review of the former, a "picture of barbarian life."

This is the life that Henry, the tame cat, now sought to sample and one that promised a much-needed rest following his intense labors wrapping up the *History*. That project averaged 416 pages per volume, though the final three volumes dock in at a comparatively svelte 344 pages per, possibly hinting at their author's fatigue. Adams now bid the Jeffersonians adieu by circling the globe and keeping an old promise. "I hope to finish the whole [*History*] on or about January 1889," he had told Gaskell several years earlier. "We [he and Clover, of course] mean then to go round the world."[1]

Henry's lengthy voyage might be read as a new twist on an old tradition: the Grand Tour. Reaching its peak in the eighteenth century, the Grand Tour promised its upper-class male clientele an advanced immersion in language, history, and the various arts (if not drinking, gambling, and the occasional sexual congress). A host of post-Oxbridge-ites might, on this educational rite of passage, spend several months or even years sampling a variety of European cultural cuisines, all the while making important contacts for future use. Some variation of cooks and coachmen, valets and guides would likely tag along. Henry enjoyed his own truncated version of the Grand Tour when tramping about Germany and Italy in his early twenties. By this time, anyway, the concept, in its classical sense, had lost its old meaning. The decline of aristocracy and commensurate rise of the middle class undermined the idea of the Tour as the traditional ruling caste's particular prerogative. Advancements in rail and ocean transportation further eroded the Tour's exclusiveness by making it affordable to a growing, if still quite slight, number.[2]

By trading the Atlantic Tour for a South Pacific swing, Henry joined a small number of European and American elites, intellectuals, and artists. Tahiti attracted Melville as well as the French novelist and naval officer Pierre Loti and the postimpressionist Paul Gauguin, while Samoa drew Robert Louis Stevenson, author of *The Strange Case of Dr Jekyll and Mr Hyde,* and the American landscape artist Joseph Dwight Strong Jr. The civilizations, cultures, and customs of Oceania challenged Henry's fastidious Yankee sensibilities, while La Farge's untidy intellect and bohemian tastes further complicated his more conventional manner. Adams chose wisely in bringing the artist along. "Of all of [my] friends," he later wrote, "La Farge alone owned a mind complex enough to contrast against the common-places of American uniformity."[3]

By distinguishing his island hopping as, in some sense, a response to the flat homogeneity of home, Henry could turn his travels into an implicit rebuke of Western modernization. The paramount forces pulling this colossal enterprise along — industry and empire — were to receive increasingly negative attention in his writings. One need not look deeply for parallels to notice that in exoticizing the South Seas, a place of "disappearing" peoples and practices, Adams anticipates the *Education*'s sentimentalization of Quincy as a pastoral holdout from metropolitan Boston's inescapable encroachments. That he extrapolated further while on his journey and felt some kinship with other peoples who were, like him, "endangered" by the restructuring of global economic, military, and political systems, is a credible guess. His extended stay, unexpected devotion to a dynastic Tahitian ruling family, and "adoption" into that family, intimate as much.

Certainly traveling in the lower Pacific gave Adams greater insight into imperialism's contemporary complexion. An earlier model of colonization (1492–1650), fueled by the Renaissance and the emergence of nation-states, saw a number of European countries move into the Western Hemisphere. A fresh round of expansionism (1880–1914), propelled by industrialization and technological advances, brought about the conquest of much of Africa and Asia. Europe again joined in this empire-making, though additional actors, including Japan and the United States, did so as well. In due time these new conquistadors — interested in accessing hitherto unexploited harbors and coaling stations — looked with interest to distant Oceania. France's 1880 annexation of Tahiti preceded an 1889 standoff between Britain, Germany, and the United States for control of the Samoan archipelago. Hawaii, Henry and La Farge's jumping-off point to the South Seas, was in its last years as a kingdom. The pressure of Western business interests — evident in Honolulu's simmering stew of antimonarchists, annexationists, and reformers, many of European and American citizenship — led to the January 1893 deposition of Queen Lili'uokalani and Hawaii's annexation by the United States in 1898. If Henry's search for paradise sometimes resulted in a romanticization of modernization's holdouts, his assumption that the weight of Westernization moved against these older Pacific civilizations nevertheless is accurate.

Despite an eagerness to flirt with the "simple" life of the South Seas, Adams and La Farge traveled in some decided luxury. Native (or French) chefs prepared their meals, local potentates smoothed their search for "managed adventure," and they remained in touch with the outside world through a web of complex shipping lines. In writing a family friend while in transit that the Greek poet Homer "is constantly before me," Adams signaled the limits of his willingness to go local. His interactions were typically with island elites, some of whom, with Western educations (and Western Grand Tours), may have hoped to meet the prominent American on a relatively comparable social or intellectual plane. Everyone else he tended to dismiss as "the simple savage" or "the simple native," dark faces that he found anthropologically interesting as "types" or "races" but not as individuals. While in Samoa Henry wrote to Hay, "We have associated only with the first society — the families of the powerful chiefs — and I know nothing of the common people except as I see them pass by."[4]

Despite such deliberate insulation, occasional leveling moments predictably arose. One occurred in Samoa when Adams, given with La Farge the run of a residence, discovered that they shared the space with several Samoans. "We could count ten men and women sleeping on the floor of our house," he reported. The nearly circular structure lacked interior walls, making privacy impossible. "There was room enough," Henry conceded, "but at first I felt rather awkward in putting on my clothes with at least six women, young and old, looking on, and very curious about the process." He perhaps understood the relative powerlessness of his situation best when, tiring of Tahiti, he discovered the difficulty in convincing the

423

few sea captains on the island to take him and La Farge to Fiji; his efforts to buy a boat were equally frustrating. This complication he sardonically commemorated in a letter to a fourteen-year-old nephew: "My dear Arthur. . . . If you ever come here, you had better bring your own boat, for you can't get away without it." Only when Adams agreed to pay $2,500 (some $70,000 in current dollars) did the *Richmond*'s captain agree to make the ten-day journey.[5]

Perhaps the thing that Henry least controlled in Polynesia was his awakening senses. Accustomed to a sartorial norm of stiff collars and three-piece suits, he now encountered an altogether different approach to both exhibiting and employing the human body. Observing traditional Samoan Siva dancers, in particular, coaxed from Adams long epistolary descriptions of their performances — the most vivid of which he recorded for the edification of Elizabeth Cameron. The extent to which he may have sublimated his feelings for Lizzie into such graphic recitations is an open question, but Henry James, privy to reports of the dance Adams wrote for Hay, found them illuminating and commented, "What a power of baring one's self hitherto unsuspected in H A!"[6] The subjects of sex and sensuality were rendered wooden in Adams's Victorian novels *Democracy* and *Esther,* but the indulgence of distance, the

424

implied permission to gaze on the "outrageous," and the temptation to communicate on an erotic level with Lizzie behind the screen of ethnographic interest may explain the suggestive accounts he forwarded to her. Approaching his fifty-third birthday and now widowed for five years, he never neared again this type of colorful carnal expression. The following passage from an October 1890 letter to Lizzie, in which Henry chastely plays the passive observer to La Farge's "excitement," is worth quoting at length:

The girls disappeared; and after some delay, while I was rather discouraged, thinking that the Siva was not to be, suddenly, out of the dark, five girls came into the light, with a dramatic effect that really I never felt before. Naked to the waist, their rich skins glistened with cocoanut oil. Around their heads and necks they wore garlands of green leaves in strips, like seaweeds, and these too glistened with oil, as though the girls had come out of the sea. . . . La Farge's spectacles quivered with emotion and gasped for sheer inability to note everything at once. To me the dominant idea was that the girls, with their dripping grasses and leaves, and their glistening breasts and arms, had actually come out of the sea a few steps away. . . . La Farge exploded with enthusiasm. . . . You can imagine the best female figure you ever saw, on about a six foot scale, neck, breast, back, arms and legs, all absolutely Greek in modelling and action, with such freedom of muscle and motion as the Greeks themselves hardly knew, and you can appreciate La Farge's excitement. . . . We were all sprawling over mats, smoking, laughing, trying to talk, with a sense of shoulders, arms, legs, cocoa-nut oil, and general nudeness most strangely mixed with a sense of propriety. Anyone would naturally suppose such a scene to be an orgy of savage license.[7]

Later that month Henry chronicled for Lizzie his interactions with Fa-auli, the young (he guessed seventeen — "may be") daughter of Lauti, a Samoan chief. Though he thought she lacked a fine face, her physical beauty and grace attracted him enormously: "I never tire of watching her, especially when she lies stretched at full length on the mats in the dusk, and rolls from one position to another." One afternoon he recorded the girl's proportions ("Taking her round the chest, including the arms, she measures fortyfive inches") and discovered that, at twenty-three inches, the circumference of her head matched his exactly.[8]

Adams cast Fa-auli as the healthy, innocent creation of a remarkably voluptuous world so different, so distant from anything in his proper Brahmin purview. The glistening bodies that charmed the evening Sivas hinted at a freedom and ease of female expression that impressed him deeply. Attracted to the inaccessible Cameron, he commented at length on the fine figures and perfect illustrations of "muscles and motion" he daily encountered.

Henry's interview with the convalescing Robert Louis Stevenson at the Scottish writer's Vailima estate proved less satisfying. Stevenson and his American wife, Fanny, were living in dire poverty and could entertain in only the most constrained fashion. "They, I believe, would come oftener to see me," Stevenson wrote of Adams and La Farge, "but for the horrid doubt that weighs upon our commissariat department; we have OFTEN almost nothing to eat; a guest would simply break the bank; my wife and I have dined on one avocado pear; I have several times dined on hard bread and onions. What would you do with a guest at such narrow seasons? — eat him? or serve up a labour boy fricasseed?" Henry, no doubt aware of his host's penury, apprised Cameron of Stevenson's obvious ill health ("Imagine a man so thin and emaciated that he looked like a bundle of sticks in a bag") and resort to pajamas. Throughout their travels Adams, the scion of an old and respected political family, typically enjoyed a certain notoriety over La

Farge. But his golden pedigree meant little to Stevenson. In a letter to James, the Scot referred to a recent visit by "La Farge the painter," but inattentively referred to the painter's appendage simply as "your friend Henry Adams."[9]

From Samoa Adams and La Farge journeyed to Tahiti, where Henry forged a lasting friendship with Arii Taimai, the seventy-year-old matriarch of the Teva clan. A widowed chiefess, she spoke no English but discovered in Adams a chronic scholar eager to document her history as the titular head of a dead island aristocracy. Henry befriended as well a few of her nine "half-caste" sons and daughters whose father was a Jewish London-born banker named Alexander Salmon. "Hebrew and Polynesian mix rather well," he patronizingly observed of Arii's forty-year-old son, Tati, "when the Hebrew does not get the better."[10] Tati and most of his siblings were educated in England and Australia and thus facilitated communication between their mother and Adams.

Henry learned that the Teva had once dominated southern Tahiti's Papara district. There, a full generation before John Adams became president, Amo of Papara and his wife Purea, the great-great-grandparents of Arii Taimai, greeted the arrival of Capt. Samuel Wallis, the British "discoverer" of Tahiti.

Wallis's 1767 voyage inspired Capt. James Cook, who journeyed there two years later. Arii Taimai's dynastic pretensions were furthered when, in youth, the widow of King Pomare II adopted her. She later advised Queen Pomare IV while maintaining her separate role as chiefess of the Papara district. These aristocratic connections heightened her cosmopolitan outlook, apparent in her children's international education and marriages. Her daughter Marau became the wife of Pomare V, the last Pomare king of Tahiti, while others wed British and Americans typically involved in diplomacy or finance. Impressed with this contemporary island nobility, Henry called Arii Taimai "the last pure native princess of Tahitian blood."[11]

If Henry valued the Teva clan's high rank, the Teva clan appreciated his possible use to them as a member of a famous American family. Here were two fading houses finding various kinds of support in the other. For Arii Taimai and her children, a close association with Adams would bring yet another distinguished Westerner into their orbit. Accordingly, in April 1891 both Henry and La Farge were ceremoniously adopted into the Salmon clan. Adams, already in possession of an acclaimed name, took on, in a manner, yet another: Tauraatua I Amo, "Bird Perch of God." Aside from a tiny plot of land that accompanied the investiture, he received various gifts and curios, including a stone "brainer," a nearly ten-inch poi grinder probably used to prepare food but that could be passed off to credulous Westerners as an ancient instrument of human sacrifice. That Henry identified strongly with the dimming grandeur of his new family is evident in a sentimental note written to a niece: "Tahiti is melancholy even when the sun is brightest and the sea blue as glass. . . . [It] has retired a long way out of the world, and sees only her particular friends, like me, with the highest introductions; but she dresses well, and her jewels are superb."[12] As the years passed Adams remained close to the Salmons, occasionally servicing the clan's debt and introducing his "brother" Tati to several powerful Americans, among them Theodore Roosevelt.

During the final weeks of his four-month stay in Tahiti, Henry, obviously growing bored, undertook to write the history of the Teva clan with Queen Marau at the story's center. The project, he informed one correspondent, came about "by way of excitement or something to talk about." He proceeded to interview Arii Taimai with Marau and several of her siblings serving as translators. With too much history to pack into a few sessions, the project remained unfinished until 1893, when Adams privately published a small edition of *Memoirs of Marau Taaoro*

Last Queen of Tahiti. Working on the manuscript, he assured Hay, deepened his respect for Tahitian civilization: "It shows me . . . why I loathe American history. Tahiti is all literary. America has not a literary conception. One is all artistic. The other is all commercial."[13]

Henry's history told the old and familiar story of a once great family's and people's decline before modern pressures — the same saga he later recited in *Mont-Saint-Michel and Chartres* and the *Education.* All of these works utilize to some degree art, history, tradition, and ritual to assess exhausted if culturally rich civilizations. And all are filtered through Adams's tragic historical sensibility. Consequently, some have argued that Henry imposed too much of himself in the tropics, surrendering too little to his surroundings. The distinguished New Zealand anthropologist Derek Freeman, for one, had no patience for Adams's Polynesian fantasies. In a 1967 communication to J. W. Davidson, author of *Samoa Mo Samoa,* Freeman remarked, "I know the Samoans . . . a shade too well to stomach the effusions of Adams and [the English poet Rupert] Brooke. What was it that they wrote of? Themselves, surely, themselves, and the ill-understood tumult of their own emotions — and *not* the Samoans."[14]

431

After the intensities of the Samoan Siva and the quick dip into Tahitian dynastic history, Fiji, Adams and La Farge's next destination, proved to be an altogether different, briefer, and less satisfying stay. A British colony since 1874, the archipelago operated in a more race-conscious way, with distinct social barriers separating whites and blacks. Imported Indian contract laborers worked on sugar plantations and heightened racial and caste divisions. Henry, though he interacted little with the locals, took a dim view of this conspicuous colonialism. After a three-weeks' journey through Viti Levu, Fiji's largest island, he sarcastically reported to Hay that even the remotest tribes were now peopled by "good churchmen." He more favorably observed that such conversions were superficial and praised the tribes for their "heathen practices," which included "pray[ing] to their grandfathers to come back" from the grave, a Lazarus-like wish for resurrection that brought down the governor's enlightened wrath.[15]

In Fiji, as on his other stops, Adams habitually complained of monotony. One can chart in his letters a litany of references to dead and dragging time: "The boredom has not been small"; "The Polynesians are a singularly superficial people"; "Taïti . . . is lovely and comfortable enough, but easily exhausted"; "Up and down the Pacific for many grey weeks, my friend La Farge and I have paraded our ennui"; and so on.[16] One might read into such sighs the false quality of Henry's posthumous pose. The immense energy, expense, and planning that went into his extended journey suggest a man still eager for fresh experiences and open to new relationships. Clearly he wanted more rather than less.

And what he wanted now was to be near Elizabeth Cameron, his attraction for her having failed to burn off in the tropical sun. Leaving Fiji in late July, Adams and La Farge dropped anchor in Sydney, Indonesia, Singapore, and Ceylon along their return voyage home. At the last location Henry sat under the sacred fig tree in Anuradhapura, planted some two thousand years earlier and said to be a branch from the Bodhi tree under which Siddhartha Gautama attained enlightenment and became the spiritual teacher known as Gautama Buddha. But Adams had now his fill of "managed adventure." As his ship neared Europe in September he made arrangements to visit Lizzie in Paris. Their meeting would constitute the real ending of his journey. When it had begun over a year earlier he had written to her from Honolulu, "I enjoy myself, and the sense of living, more than I had done in five years."[17] That calendrically attuned line evoked the transit of lost time since Clover's fatal act and may have inferred Henry's emotional availability. He returned to Lizzie slightly older and a bit grayer, but certainly redolent of "exotic" and "romantic" exploits. He returned with a younger man's song in his heart.

THE FIRST LAW OF TAME CATS

Following Clover's death, Henry's correspondence with Elizabeth Cameron grew slowly in both volume and intimacy. *The Letters of Henry Adams* cite nearly one hundred printed and omitted notes from Adams to Lizzie prior to his Polynesian travels — only four of which were written while his wife was alive. Several of these communications convey the attitude of a fretting, disappointed lover. In one August 1888 letter dispatched from Quincy he fairly moaned, "I hardly know which is worse, — to hear, or not to hear, from you; for when I do not hear, I am uneasy, and when I do hear, I am homesick." The following month he wrote directly to Lizzie's two-year-old daughter, Martha, in words that must have had a very different meaning for Martha's mother: "I love you very much, and think of you a great deal, and want you all the time. I should have run away from here, and looked for you all over the world, long ago." Shortly thereafter he ended a note to

Lizzie with an aching transparency: "Give Martha my tenderest love. Propriety forbids me to send as much to her mamma, so I remain only conventionally hers."[1]

In pushing against convention, however, Henry's letters threatened to become conspicuous and thus problematic. An overt declaration of love on his part would wreck the unstated arrangement that existed between them. Neither seemed to want this. Lizzie appreciated Henry's attentiveness, though she enjoyed the interest of other men as well. She considered him a close friend and confidant, but never, even after years of discord and separation, did she seek a divorce from the Don. And even if she had, Henry was temperamentally disinclined to ensnare himself in scandal, particularly of the messy marital kind. Such an affront would have compromised several of his friendships and possibly resulted in permanent exile from Lafayette Square. He could well guess the caustic gossip forever to follow if he made a public spectacle of his stray affections. At some point someone might even meanly opine that a broken heart had prompted Clover's suicide. Clarence King maintained a secret wife for many years, but Henry, hemmed in by family, self, and circumstances, could never have managed such a deception; he had struggled merely to keep correct his letters to Lizzie.

These missives grew only more elaborate once Adams embarked for Polynesia, a sojourn that allowed him to play the gallant gadabout. He battled seasickness and braved the blue Pacific, watched La Farge "quiver" before half-clad women, and indulged in a series of harmless flirtations. He could be said to have proven himself a man in full; having just come off the triumph of the *History,* a display of discipline and intellect, he now blazed an unexpected trail to the South Seas in a show of valor and adventure. Perhaps emboldened by distance, Henry drafted lengthy serial communications to Lizzie — filling over two hundred pages of the *Letters* — that reveal an almost desperate longing. While in Hawaii, his journey just beginning, he all but confessed to a bottled-up love: "Then I must say — what you must understand without saying — that I am something more than dependent on your writing. Now that I am here I find what I expected to find when I came away — that you are my only strong tie to what I suppose I ought to call home. If you should go back on me, I should wholly disappear."[2]

The words "wholly disappear" suggest various shades. Perhaps Henry alluded to the posthumous life's limitations, spending his days in monastic dedication to archives and writing, losing touch along the way with the carnal side of his self. His subsequent and

437

detailed accounts of the sensual Samoan Siva lifted a certain veil of innocence on what must have been, for him, a decidedly erotic experience. His participation in the ceremony — and determination that Lizzie should know about it — could only have advertised the urgency of his romantic readiness. He writes in one letter:

Towards the end, when the dancers got up and began their last figure, which grows more and more vivacious to the end, Fanua, who had mischief in her eyes, pranced up before me, and bending over, put her arms around my neck and kissed me. The kissing felt quite natural and was loudly applauded with much laughter, but I have been redolent of cocoa-nut oil ever since, and the more because Fanua afterwards gave me her wreaths, and put one over my neck, the other around my waist, dripping with cocoa-nut oil.[3]

Perhaps relatedly, Henry sent photographs of unclothed Samoan girls to Hay, who had developed strong and apparently reciprocal feelings for Nannie Lodge, the wife (and cousin) of Henry's former student Henry Cabot Lodge. The quietness of Adams's pursuit of Lizzie found a match in Hay's proper behavior to Nannie, whom he politely escorted to any number of museums, lun-

438

cheons, and concerts. In passing the images on to his fellow Heart, Henry recommended that they be circulated to a very select group, not to include Mrs. Hay: "Please show or send the photographs to Mrs Lodge and Mrs Cameron, as I refer to them in my letters. To your civilised eye they may appear a little nude; but here nudity is a dress."[4]

More generally, Henry offered in his South Seas correspondence to Lizzie a subtle if unmistakably sincere form of "love making." The expansive length of these letters, their knight errant quality and self-consciously attentive tone revealed the surprising depth of his distress. There were moments when pretenses were lightly lifted and Adams, still striving for control, offered brief, frank glimpses of his emotions. Ostensibly remarking on the natural beauty of Tahiti, he ventured the following compliment: "I do not think that, outside of London and Paris, I could find a spot even in Europe where I should want to pass more than three days at a time, — unless you were there." Each fresh setting offered Henry an opportunity to remark on Cameron's particular importance to him. Naturally Ceylon's venerable Bodhi tree paled beside a stronger passion: "I sat for half an hour, hoping to attain Nirwana. . . . Even under Buddha's most sacred tree, I thought less of him than of you."[5]

Lizzie, however, *was* thinking of others,

including John Hay, yet another tame cat candidate. In April 1891, while Adams ambled about Tahiti, Hay, his brief and almost certainly platonic romance with Nannie Lodge now ended, traveled alone to London for an extended period seeking out old friends. A few weeks later Lizzie arrived in England with a small party. Over the next several months she and Hay grew close, though he wanted more. In a January 1892 letter, he wrote to her in some frustration at the courteous but reserved way she now greeted him in society: "Perhaps the fault is all in me: the resentment may be purely personal, because I have lost the place I have held dear. You know you appointed me No. 3. I can remember the day and the hour, opposite the Knightsbridge Barracks."[6] Presumably numbers 1 and 2 were reserved for the Don and Henry. But even at a distant 3 Hay remained over the years devoted to Lizzie. In 1897, while again in London, he walked along Duke Street's shops and upscale flats thinking forlornly back to their time there together. The remembered neighborhood, swollen with memories, caused him to write her a lovesick letter:

My heart ached with the vision of the beautiful small feet that caressed the pavement on an errand of mercy so long ago. You are a sweet, sweet woman. There is no other word. You are beautiful, and clever, and splendid, and charming and fascinating and lovely. But you are, more than all, sweet. It is a keen, living sweetness that lifts you up above all others in charm; that makes the sight of you, the sound of your voice, the touch of you, so full of delight. One can never have enough of you, never. . . . You sweet Lizzie; the words are forbidden but I say them over and over.[7]

There is evidence that Henry guessed or at least sensed Hay's feelings. In 1900 he wrote knowingly to Lizzie, "Hay got your letter yesterday, and told me your news. I rarely mention your letters to me, because it makes people jealous of me. Too many men still love you."[8]

In late September 1891 Henry, with Polynesia now a memory, left Ceylon and slowly made his way to Europe to see Lizzie. His ship, the French steamer *Djemneh,* crossed the Indian Ocean to the Gulf of Aden and into the Red Sea before negotiating the Suez Canal and entering the Mediterranean. From there it passed between Corsica and Sardinia en route to Marseilles, which it reached on October 9. Henry left immediately for Paris and put up at the luxurious Second Empire–style Hôtel du Louvre, opposite the Louvre Museum. At ten o'clock on the morning of the 11th he sent Cameron a message: "Arrived at midnight, and wait only to know at what hour one may convenablement pay one's respects to you. The bearer waits an answer."[9]

That "answer" left him cold. With La Farge having gone to Brittany to visit cousins, Henry spent an annoying two weeks in Paris being politely put off by Lizzie. Accompanied by her daughter, Martha, a governess, and one of the Don's daughters from his first marriage, she maintained an ambitious social calendar and perhaps inferred a little nervously Adams's desire to introduce a more intimate condition to their relationship. From Paris the two parties moved on to London, where Henry stayed at the family-style Bristol Hotel and Lizzie, with her small entourage, lodged in Piccadilly until leaving for America on November 4.[10] Hours before her departure they said their awkward, unsatisfying goodbyes in a parked hansom cab on Half Moon Street. The following day Henry, remaining in Europe for most of the winter, composed a long letter confessing to Lizzie all that he had held in over the preceding weeks. He began by allowing that, sensing the rawness of his feelings, she might already suspect the contents of the note: "You, being a woman and quick to see everything that men hide, probably know my thoughts better than I do myself." He then confessed his

442

desire for what he called "the experiment" of a more amatory relationship, before acknowledging the futility of "running so fatal a risk":

No matter how much I may efface myself or how little I may ask, I must always make more demand on you than you can gratify, and you must always have the consciousness that, whatever I may profess, I want more than I can have. Sooner or later the end of such a situation is estrangement, with more or less disappointment and bitterness. I am not old enough to be a tame cat; you are too old to accept me in any other character. You were right last year in sending me away, and if I had the strength of mind of an average monkey, and valued your regard at anything near its true price, I should guard myself well from running so fatal a risk as that of losing it by returning to take a position which cannot fail to tire out your patience and end in your sending me off again, either in kindness or in irritation.[11]

He then proceeded to speculate on her feelings, all the while exposing the cold stone that sank inside his heart:

I lie for hours wondering whether you, out on the dark ocean, in surroundings which are certainly less cheerful than mine, sometimes think of me, and divine or suspect that

443

you have undertaken a task too hard for you; whether you feel that the last month has proved to be — not wholly a success, and that the fault is mine for wanting more than I had a right to expect; whether you are almost on the verge of regretting a little that you tried the experiment; whether you are puzzled to know how an indefinite future of such months is to be managed; whether you are fretting, as I am, over what you can and what you cannot do; whether you are not already a little impatient with me for not being satisfied, and for not accepting in secret, as I do accept in pretence, whatever is given me, as more than enough for any deserts or claims of mine; and whether in your most serious thoughts, you have an idea what to do with me when I am again on your hands.[12]

In closing, he insisted equally upon the strength of his devotion and its capacity to injure Lizzie: "One may be innocent as the angels, yet as unhappy as the wicked; and I, who would lie down and die rather than give you a day's pain, am going to pain you the more, the more I love."[13]

Over the next several months Adams sulked. He wrote to one correspondent in December of his disappointment at not seeing more of Lizzie in London: "Mrs Cameron is no good.

She has too much to do, and lets everybody make use of her, which pleases no one because of course each person objects to other persons having any rights that deserve respect. As long as she lives, it will always be so." Seeking safe ground, Adams's letters to Lizzie balanced self-pity (he described to her a "dreary" Paris Christmas alone) with varying degrees of gossip and chat. "She is very intelligent," he reported of an encounter with Edith Wharton, "and of course looks as fragile as a dandelion in seed." Still, the ache of his situation persisted into the following summer. That June Lizzie scolded Henry for his long silences, only to receive a sarcastic reply: "How should I write? The first law of tame cats is that under no circumstances must they run the risk of boring their owners by writing more than once a month or so. You never consider that a tame cat's business is to lie still and purr. I am trying to learn to purr satisfactorily." In a follow-up letter he blamed Lizzie for his unhappiness, accusing her of "talking so invitingly about my coming to you. Why do you say such things?" Just what things he had in mind are unclear, though she had once written him, while he roamed about the Pacific, "I feel sure now that you will come to Europe. . . . Of course you understand that if you come here you come home. I'll use force, if necessary, but home you must come." Investing unspent emotions in flirtatious exchanges must have offered Lizzie, struggling in a loveless marriage, a respite from her own disappointments. Presumably she counted on Henry's understanding of that. When he felt too much, pursued too openly, she backed away, protective of her social position and that of her daughter. He understood all of this, ridiculed time and again his impossible romantic ambitions, and once apologized to Lizzie for being "a nuisance to you and myself."[14] Such sharp self-awareness made him a reflective diagnostician of his bruised feelings, but it did not bring him peace.

Henry remained close to Lizzie for the rest of his life. Whatever resentments he may have harbored from being number 2 — and Martha's dutiful "dear uncle Dordy" — he kept to himself. He received for his friendship physical proximity to Lizzie, the pleasure of her correspondence, and her genuine appreciation of his presence, wisdom, and devotion. "The everlasting truth prevails that you are of your sex a specimen apart, and that you are as true as the north star," she wrote, one might say lovingly, to him in 1894. "I have been doing such a lot of thinking lately about you and what you have been to me. I was in the darkness of death till you led me with your gentle guidance into broad fields and pastures green. Even sorrow and trouble lessen under your light — a light so calm and still. I wonder if any man was ever so *big* as you."[15]

That Henry's empty pursuit of Lizzie may have altered his interest in other relationships is a matter of conjecture. He never felt strongly for another woman and certainly never considered remarriage. A flock of young nieces provided female companionship over the years, toward whom Adams adopted a politely attentive if politely withdrawn posture. The long season in Samoa, the fugitive passions rehearsed over many months at sea, were now allowed to recede — but this brought to Henry only a limited ease. The safe, chaste letters to Lizzie resumed, though so did the still deeper need to reconcile, question, and account for Clover.

36
WHAT THE SPHINX SAID

Throughout his thirteen-year marriage, Henry had obligingly if not always happily shared Clover with her father. And in deciding for her burial at Washington's Rock Creek Church Cemetery rather than the Sturgis family plot back in Boston, he perhaps struck a belated note of possession. This suspicion is compounded when one considers the prominent memorial he placed at his wife's grave: Augustus Saint-Gaudens's brilliant cast-bronze sculpture of a shrouded androgynous figure resting on a granite block. Listed in 1972 on the National Register of Historic Places, the Adams Memorial is an iconic, enigmatic work of art, willfully suggestive in its deep silence. What the statue "meant" Henry refused to say, just as he kept his authorship of *Democracy* a secret and permitted only a limited print edition of the *Education* to circulate in his lifetime. In each of these instances he sought to withhold, but did so in ways certain to seed conversation.

448

Despite its surface calm, his mute statue, its cold eyes closed to the world, begged for attention. Far from realizing a solemn, inscrutable anonymity, it endures as an Adams memorial in the fullest sense, as much a part of its patron's complex legacy as the Old House in Quincy or the voluminous collection of his letters at the Massachusetts Historical Society.

Henry met Saint-Gaudens while the artist, employed by Henry Richardson and serving as something of a draftsman under La Farge, worked on the Trinity Church frescoes. Born in Dublin to an Irish mother and a French father, Saint-Gaudens (1848–1907) was raised in New York. After taking courses at the Cooper Union and the National Academy of Design, he studied at the École des Beaux-Arts in Paris before embarking on a celebrated career. His major works include the Robert Gould Shaw Memorial frieze in Boston Common, the gilded William Tecumseh Sherman equestrian statue placed at the Grand Army Plaza (in the southeast corner of Central Park) in Manhattan, and the bronze gilt *Diana* sculpture once raised, as a glittering window vane, high above New York's old Madison Square Garden and now presiding in the Philadelphia Museum of Art.

The inspiration for what became the Adams Memorial took root while Henry and La Farge toured Japan. Buddhism's promise to temper suffering through the purging of desire attracted Adams as philosophically analogous to the posthumous life he now affected. As with most matters, he approached his "afterlife" intellectually, eager to absorb through study and travel the history, art, and culture of this new diversion. While in Japan, he discussed Buddha figures with Ernest Fenollosa's colleague Okakura Kakuzō, a young art historian later to be a curator of oriental art at the Museum of Fine Arts, Boston, and, as noted earlier, stood in some wonder before the immense bronze Buddha statue in Kamakura.

Upon returning to America, Henry went to Saint-Gaudens's West 36th Street studio, where, in vague terms, he expressed his conception of Clover's marker — with the majestic Kamakura figure providing inspiration. La Farge attended this meeting and, in a 1910 interview with the *Washington Evening Star,* related the exchange between patron and artist:

Mr. Adams described to him in a general way what he wanted, going, however, into no details, and really giving him no distinct clue, save the explanation that he wished the figure to symbolize "the acceptance, intellectually of the inevitable." Saint-Gaudens immediately became interested, and made a gesture indicating the pose which Mr. Adams's words had suggested in his mind. "No," said Mr. Adams, "the way that you're, that is a Penseroso" [melancholic — from John Milton's lyric poem *Il Penseroso*]. Thereupon the sculptor made several other gestures until one of them struck Mr. Adams as corresponding with the idea. As good luck would have it, he would not wait for a woman model to be brought in and posed in accordance with the gesture indicated by the sculptor, so Saint-Gaudens grabbed the Italian boy who was mixing clay, put him into the pose, and draped a blanket over him. . . . "Now that's done," said Mr. Adams, "the pose is settled. Go to La Farge about any original ideas of Kwannon [known also as Guan Yin, the Bodhisattva of mercy]."[1]

After Henry and La Farge left his studio, Saint-Gaudens scribbled in a notebook, "Adams — Buhda — Mental Repose — Calm reflection in contrast with the violence or force in nature." Two years passed before Henry returned and, following a discussion of the memorial's scale, announced to Saint-Gaudens that he would offer no further guidance: "I did not think it wise."[2] Over yet another two-year period a restless Adams put the finishing touches on his *History,* grew increasingly close to Elizabeth Cameron, and methodically sampled the South Seas with

La Farge. He also paid Saint-Gaudens some $20,000 (about $560,000 in current dollars) to bring his Buddha to life.

Henry's decision to ignore the statue's progress forced Saint-Gaudens to fall back upon his own ideas. In finished form the piece resembles an earlier work by the artist, *Silence,* an 1874 marble figure of a woman with closed eyes wearing a seamless garment with shrouded hood. She has a raised forefinger to her lips, gesturing for quiet. Commissioned by Levi H. Willard for the New York City Lodge of the Masonic Order, it evokes the deep sense of contemplation and even isolation later found in the Adams Memorial. Both works are bereft of inscription and lack elaborate decoration. Their faces are classical and any resemblance to Buddha is largely imputed, prevailing upon viewers to glean their meaning. A much earlier antecedent might be glimpsed in Michelangelo's Ancestors of Christ series in the Sistine Chapel. In one fresco a woman sits as though immersed in meditation, and the back of her hand caresses her shaded cheek. A similar resting pose, along with folded eyes and hand-to-cheek graze, distinguishes the Adams Memorial.

In defying easy description, Henry's Buddha attracted considerable attention, and Saint-Gaudens was often asked over the years to reveal its essence. His various responses —

"Perhaps 'The Peace that Passeth Understanding' "; "I call it the Mystery of the Hereafter"; and "It is beyond pain, and beyond joy" — are generic and unilluminating. But the statue's capacity to inspire hinged, as he knew, upon its unfixed premise. "I am certain that my father never of his own volition stamped the monument with that absolute definition so often demanded," Homer Saint-Gaudens wrote in 1913. "He meant to ask a question, not to give an answer."[3]

Others, however, sought to explain the Sphinx's riddle, and this included pinning down its indeterminate gender. In early 1909, during the final weeks of his presidency, Theodore Roosevelt had described the statue as female on at least two occasions, one of them a public address. Henry enjoyed needling Roosevelt (whose boyish, bullying demeanor irritated him), and he took this opportunity, with a winking self-regard, to set him straight: "Whatever the President says goes! . . . But!!! After March 4, [TR's last day in office] should you allude to my bronze figure, will you try to do St Gaudens the justice to remark that his expression was a little higher than sex can give. As he meant it, he wanted to exclude sex, and sink it in the idea of humanity. The fixture is sexless." The shrine's neutral gender is consistent with Adams's urging that it radiate a universal

453

quality, and thus he resisted efforts to tease out its "true meaning." Like Saint-Gaudens, he replied opaquely to the inquisitive, telling one correspondent, "My own name for it is 'The Peace of God.' "[4] To have actually defined the figure would have allowed anyone to claim familiarity. He went out of his way, rather, to keep the memorial allusive and beyond reach — even of presidents. In this way, protecting his secret, guarding his ground, and knocking down errant (that is to say all) assumptions, Henry proved to be the true Sphinx.

One critic of the marker, Julia Stoddard Parsons, a friend of Lizzie Cameron's, thought Adams had cruelly denied his wife an identity in death. She condemned the nameless shrine as a selfish tribute to his peculiar taste and somber sensibility — less a commemoration of Clover than a paean to her husband's self-pride. "But to *me*," she wrote in a 1938 memoir,

if the sculptor intended everyone to read from it their own impressions — were I lying under such an image of pagan hopeless-ness — shut in, as it is, by chill cypresses in gloom and dampness, with no letter to mark that it was I, or no inspired or human word to promise for the future, then indeed Nirvana might engulf

"The deep dark vault,
The darkness and the worm."[5]

Years earlier Adams had prepared in the *Education* a powerful and perhaps self-serving response to such critics. He maintained that the statue embodied a dying ideal that puzzled only because contemporary society lacked the patience, empathy, and understanding to grasp its defiant rebuke of the modern world. The curious could not see it because they could not *feel* it. He seemed in the memoir almost to be baiting those blinkered seekers who dared to look dumbly upon the monument:

As Adams sat there, numbers of people came, for the figure seemed to have become a tourist fashion, and all wanted to know its meaning. Most took it for a portrait-statue, and the remnant were vacant-minded in the absence of a personal guide. None felt what would have been a nursery-instinct to a Hindu baby or a Japanese jinrickshaw-runner. The only exceptions were the clergy, who taught a lesson even deeper. One after another brought companions there, and, apparently fascinated by their own reflection, broke out passionately against the expression they felt in the figure of despair, of atheism, of denial. Like the others, the priest saw only what he brought.

455

Like all great artists, St. Gaudens held up the mirror and no more.[6]

The monument's long gestation caused Henry to sometimes doubt its eventual unveiling. Five years elapsed between contract and completion, leaving him to wonder if he had erred in refusing to approve a formal design. "I am not certain," he once complained to Dwight, "that [the] work will ever be delivered." Perhaps Saint-Gaudens, taxed with a prominent, complex, and hard-to-read client, awaited a convenient moment to finish the figure before bracing for that client's uncertain reaction. Only when Henry withdrew to the South Seas did the monument escape the studio. Among early appraisers, Lizzie wrote to assure Adams, "The bronze is most beautiful in color. . . . The whole pose is strong and calm, full of repose"; John Hay also endorsed the statue, calling it "indescribably noble and imposing. It is to my mind St.-Gaudens' masterpiece." Henry's first glimpse of the figure occurred while overseas, Dwight having sent him several photographs to consider. Unwilling to offer a strong commitment, he laconically informed Saint-Gaudens from Fiji that he thought the pictures "satisfactory" — and that slight nod proved to be high praise compared to his brother Charles's petulant opinion. Perhaps still nursing his disdain for the "crazy"

456

Hoopers, he tactlessly called the statue "awful," insisting that it resembled a "mendicant, wrapped in a horse-blanket."[7]

Henry's coy reaction to the monument continued upon his return home. He arrived in Washington in February 1892, but it was not until weeks later that he could write to Dwight of having visited the memorial. He diffidently called the statue "the Rock Creek work" and seemed to regard it as nothing more than a completed task: "I made a formal, and, so to speak, official examination . . . and gave it final approval." In later years his remembrance of the day warmed. He claimed in the *Education* that "every detail interested him; every line; every touch of the artist." More telling, he began to visit the cemetery regularly, thinking of the memorial as a fitting effigy of his posthumous life. In the most insightful remark he ever made of the marker he wrote, "The interest of the figure was not in its meaning, but in the response of the observer."[8] There were to be many responses.

And in reply to these various conjectures and commentaries, Adams predictably bristled, complaining, "Every magazine writer wants to label it as some American patent medicine for popular consumption — *Grief, Despair, Pear's Soup,* or *Macy's Mens' Suits Made to Measure.*"[9] But for one regular visi-

457

tor, the statue presented no mystery at all. In 1918, the year of Adams's death, Eleanor Roosevelt discovered that her husband Franklin, then assistant secretary of the navy, was involved in an affair with Eleanor's social secretary, Lucy Mercer. She offered Franklin a divorce and, searching for guidance, went often to Rock Creek Cemetery, brooding before the Adams monument which, like her uncle Theodore, she took to be a female figure. Fifteen years later, in March 1933, the day before Franklin's first inaugural, Eleanor and her close friend Lorena Hickok walked through the cemetery and approached the Saint-Gaudens figure. There, according to Hickok, Roosevelt said, "In the old days when we lived here, I was much younger and not so very wise. Sometimes I'd be very unhappy and sorry for myself. When I was feeling that way, if I could manage, I'd come here alone, and sit and look at that woman. And I'd always come away somehow feeling better. And stronger. I've been here many, many times."[10]

The English novelist and Nobel laureate John Galsworthy, author of *The Forsyte Saga* (1906–21), a penetrating social satire of Britain's fading high bourgeoisie, also responded thoughtfully to the statue. Galsworthy's protagonist, the conservative Victorian man of property, Soames Forsyte, wanders about Rock Creek Cemetery with his daughter Fleur and her husband while on a trip to the United States. The following day he returns by himself, drawn to Saint-Gaudens's striking creation. Galsworthy writes of Soames's reaction to the statue:

> Some called it "Grief," some "The Adams Memorial." He didn't know, but in any case there it was, the best thing he had come across in America, the one that gave him the most pleasure, in spite of all the water he had seen at Niagara and those skyscrapers in New York. Three times he had changed his position on that crescent marble seat, varying his sensations every time. . . . Easy to sit still in front of that thing! They ought to make America sit there once a week![11]

Adams might have enjoyed Galsworthy's attentive remarks, for the novelist appears to have understood the blue note in the Sphinx's silence. His Soames is a relic from a bygone era whose aristocratic pretensions — obvious in his impressive collection of paintings and tasteful Georgian mansions — cannot keep a congested, noisy London at bay. If lacking Adams's distinguished patrimony, he nevertheless shares his sense of being at the end of something — perhaps himself. The 1901 death of Queen Victoria brings to Soames's mind an awareness of shifting centuries, technologies, and sensibilities. His evocation of a female monarch perishing as the industrial process gained ground recalls Henry's devotion to Marau Taaroa, the last Tahitian queen, suddenly outdated in the emergent, liberal, scientific, capitalist configuration: "Well-nigh two generations had slipped by — of steamboats, railways, telegraphs, bicycles, electric light, telephones, and now these motorcars. . . . Morals had changed, manners had changed, men had become monkeys twice-removed, God had become Mammon."[12] Perhaps it is enough to say that for both Soames and Adams, Saint-Gaudens's splendidly grieving statue is nothing less than a defiantly idealized monument to the history and traditions of a vanishing preindustrial people.

■ ■ ■ ■

FURY

■ ■ ■ ■

I am deeply interested in the furious rapidity of change I find here. Another fifty years, at this rate, will fetch us to the end.

Henry Adams, 1902

Fury

I am deeply interested in the furious rapidity
of change I find here. Another fifty years, at
this rate, will fetch us to the end.
Henry Adams, 1902

37

CHICAGO

In 1893 Adams traveled twice to Chicago, eager to absorb the World's Columbian Exposition, a six-month celebration commemorating the four-hundred-year anniversary of Columbus's arrival in the New World. Extolling America's power and progress barely a generation removed from the Civil War, the fair featured a hastily built plaster "White City" of exhibits that spilled over Jackson Park and into the adjoining Midway Plaisance. An incredible twenty-seven million visitors from around the world passed through its ornate gates. Henry had come to Chicago believing that the city, the industrial capital of the ascendant Midwest, the country's dominant political region following the collapse of the old southern plantocracy, represented a definite turn in American if not global civilization. It combined the country's liberal, democratic qualities with an unprecedented technological prowess that pointed toward a new chapter in human history.

Meditating some years later on the Exposition's importance, he wrote, "Chicago asked in 1893 for the first time whether the American people knew where they were driving. . . . Chicago was the first expression of American thought as unity; one must start there."[1]

By "unity" Adams supposed Chicago to be the epitome of the dynamic urban-immigrant-industrial process coming to define the nation's surging metropolitan areas. The country's fourth-largest city in 1880, it more than doubled in population to some one million by 1890, second only to New York; fully three-quarters of its residents were the offspring of foreign-born parents. Chicago's rapid rise, its questionable distinction as the roiling center of newly erected mills and machine shops littered about a thick brick forest of foundries, received a boost when the city, following a fierce competition with New York and St. Louis, won the right to host the Exposition. Ostensibly a quadricentennial of America's accomplishments, one could easily have interpreted the fair more narrowly as a tribute to nineteenth-century industrial development, or still more precisely as a coming-out party for its host. Barely two decades earlier (1871) the Chicago Fire had ravaged over three square miles of the city, left more than 100,000 homeless, and gutted much of the central business district; some three hundred perished. The

October blaze, its exact cause unknown, followed a summer drought and originated near a barn belonging to Catherine and Patrick O'Leary in an area choked with wooden buildings. An enterprising reporter for the *Chicago Republican* claimed the O'Leary's cow had kicked over a lantern and started the inferno, though he later owned up to the fib. In the fire's aftermath arrived the new Chicago, a banking, commerce, and manufacturing phoenix; its buildings, insinuating the architectural imagination of Louis Sullivan, were scaffolded by iron and steel and soared high above whatever indifferent infrastructure had survived the flames. This birth of the skyscraper, a mechanical civilization's reply to the pyramids of Giza and the medieval Towers of Bologna, announced the city as an avatar of a coming age.

Not everyone, of course, appreciated the extraordinary energy emanating from Chicago. The British writer Rudyard Kipling, like Henry an inveterate global traveler, condemned the city's emphasis on dollar-chasing in a teasing piece, "How I Struck Chicago, and How Chicago Struck Me: Of Religion, Politics, and Pig-Sticking, and the Incarnation of the City among Shambles," written shortly after the Exposition ended. "This place is the first American city I have encountered," he confessed, before hastily adding, "I urgently desire never to see it again. It is inhabited by savages. . . . They told me to go to the Palmer House [hotel] which is a gilded and mirrored rabbit-warren, and there I found a huge hall of tessellate marble, crammed with people talking about money and spitting about everywhere." The Italian poet and playwright Giuseppe Giacosa also toured America and, much like Adams, saw in Chicago the incarnation of a fresh civilization: "I think that whoever ignores it is not entirely acquainted with our century and of what it is the ultimate expression." The nature of that expression caused Giacosa to think that "the dominant characteristic of the exterior life of Chicago is violence."[2]

Contra such critics as Kipling and Giacosa, the chimeric White City accentuated the efforts of Chicago's elite to promote its roseate vision of contemporary urban living. The amenities stressed at the Exposition, including incandescent lamps, paved streets, and sewage lines, advertised the kind of urban courtesies enjoyed by the denizens of the city's North Shore, also known as the Gold Coast. Chicago's central and southern neighborhoods, by contrast, swelled with industry, butchering yards, and immigrants — these were the "pig-sticking" places referred to by Kipling. But more than putting a shiny gloss on the city, the Exposition overlooked entirely the crucial issue facing Americans in 1893, the year of the crippling financial Panic, which prefaced a great economic depression in all but name. The fallout came following a series of bank failures connected to the overbuilding and overfinancing of railroads. Millions were left unemployed in a four-year slide that merged with an ongoing agricultural recession in the West and South. The fair conspicuously ignored this general unpleasantness, projecting, rather, a vigorous show of confidence, stability, and expansion even as the Panic pointed to a more ambiguous and less secure path. Henry had hoped to see the "future" in Chicago, and perhaps he did in entering this restless city of uncertainties.

Accompanied by the Camerons, Adams first attended the Exposition in May (he called it "my flying visit," staying only two days) before summering with Lizzie and the Don in England and Switzerland. He returned to Chicago for two weeks in October. Along with a rotating cast of brothers, in-laws, and nieces, Adams and his housekeeper, Maggy Wade, stayed at the swank Hotel Windermere at 56th Street and Cornell Avenue, fronting south on Jackson Park. From that posh trailhead Henry experienced the fair as a series of disassociations and clashing perspectives, with older cultural expressions rapidly giving way to new. "The first astonishment became greater every day," he later wrote.

That the Exposition should be a natural growth and product of the Northwest offered a step in evolution to startle Darwin; but that it should be anything else seemed an idea more startling still; and even granting it were not, — admitting it to be a sort of industrial, speculative growth and product of the Beaux Arts artistically induced to pass the summer on the shore of Lake Michigan, could it be made to seem at home there? Was the American made to seem at home in it?

One could not hope to find continuity in Chicago, he continued, for the city represented nothing so much as a pronounced "rupture in historical sequence!"[3] Eager to identify the forces behind this upending of the old cosmic order, Adams designated the Exposition a celebration of the "watt," the "ampère," and the "erg," units of energy that symbolized, both literally and metaphorically, the harnessing of hitherto untapped physical and chemical resources.

Though Henry favored rural Quincy over Boston, marveled at the coherence of medieval civilization, and eagerly sampled the South Seas' "primitive" island societies, he nevertheless thrilled at the fragmented modern urban experience evident in Chicago. He described the Midway Plaisance to Hay as a "sweet repose," an enigma or puzzle that showed off so much of America, if Americans were willing to notice. "I revelled in all its fakes and frauds," he admitted to his fellow Heart, "all its wickedness that seemed not to be understood by our innocent natives, and all its genuineness which was understood still less."[4] Presumably the fair's authentic nature could be found in the dynamos and steam engines that Henry had discovered in one of its vast exhibition halls. These impressive machines, as inscrutable in their clean, monotonous routine as the Adams Memorial, pointed to an American future far removed from the simple agrarian republic, now in its death throes. The "fakes" and "frauds," by contrast, included scale-size productions of Columbus's three ships, the (impeccably scrubbed) *Niña, Pinta,* and *Santa María,* which docked at Jackson Park's south lagoon while an actor playing Columbus, standing before kneeling monks and San Salvador natives, reenacted the moment of European contact with the New World. They were, to use Adams's category, "phonies" in that they venerated a buried past characterized by the kind of pioneer individualism and small-scale economies that no longer enlivened America's robber baron republic. He thought the greater emphasis in Chicago on new forms of material power, by contrast, to be "honest."

In a letter to Lucy Baxter, an old acquaintance, Henry sounded like the perfect modernist, taking in with equanimity the White City's tangle of sights and impressions, equal to the task of digesting the education it had to offer. "Chicago delighted me," he wrote, "because it was just as chaotic as my own mind, and I found my own preposterous state of consciousness reflected and exaggerated at every turn. A pure white temple, on the pure blue sea, with an Italian sky, all vast and beautiful as the world never saw it before, and in it the most astounding, confused, bewildering mass of art and industry, without a sign that there was any connection, relation or harmony or understanding of the relations of anything anywhere." One can catch several sides of irony in Henry's embrace of Chicago's "delights," but what stands out in this sumptuous evocation is his awareness of the city's creatively disruptive nature reflecting his own sense of displacement as a colonial figure in a modern framework. Having survived the Adams family's irrelevance by inventing for himself a new career as a cosmopolitan, and conjoining that cosmopolitanism with the fabrication of a posthumous life, Henry had already released certain inherited cultural views, aspirations, and anchors. He could appreciate Chicago's flux because he felt it in himself. "I have long recognized the same chaos in my own mind," he told Baxter, "and know it when I see it, while [the Exposition's visitors] probably feel it for the first time."[5]

Favorably observing the fair's disordered "mind," Henry discovered in it multiple meanings, though he took from his wanderings along the Midway Plaisance a firm conviction of what it ultimately *meant*. Chicago was no aberration, no commotion of disconnected exhibits. An underlying harmony gave reason and purpose to the ceaseless energy that escaped from its exhibition halls. These displays proclaimed the intensity and chaos of Chicago — and of America, a socially, economically, and spiritually mobile nation of constant unrest and inevitable fracture. In writing his great *History*, Adams had stressed the country's unending evolution beyond its primitive colonial roots. The narrative concluded with a review of the War of 1812, a far more decisive conflict than customarily understood, so he argued, as it ushered in "a new episode in American history." That fresh chapter, registering the decisive break from European "church, traditions, and prejudices," led to an unprecedented phase in human history — it led to Chicago.[6]

38
THE GOLD-BUGS

If the Columbian Exposition revealed to Henry the instruments of industrial "anarchy," the year's devastating financial Panic involved him in more immediate and personal ways. Prompted by the January bankruptcy of the Philadelphia and Reading Railroad and followed over the next few months by the insolvencies of several other key lines, the economy shed nearly six hundred banks and fifteen thousand businesses while unemployment exceeded 40 percent in some areas. President Grover Cleveland, uneasy with the Treasury's thinning gold reserves, successfully pushed for a repeal of the Sherman Silver Purchase Act (1890), which had committed the government to procuring (with said gold) 4.5 million ounces of silver each month. The action pitted the country's eastern pro-gold financial establishment against western "Silverites," who called for an inflationary monetary policy to help the region's heavily mortgaged farmers. The repeal and its consequences, Henry had little doubt, made a small class of finance capitalists — the men controlling the gold — the country's true masters. The old struggle in the 1790s between the agrarian-minded Jefferson and the monetary-minded Hamilton over the constitutionality of a national bank, revisited in Jackson's neo-agrarian "Bank War" in the 1830s, now appeared to have culminated in a complete victory for the plutocrats. Like Chicago, the nation's money clique moved at the rapid rate of a dynamo.

Unlike the staged exhibits of the White City, however, the financial Panic had touched Henry and his siblings directly. Following the Governor's death in 1886, the Adams Trust was established for the benefit of his five surviving children. A family business combine, it featured a small real estate empire valued at over $900,000, about $26 million in today's dollars. But in the Panic spring of 1893 it appeared to be teetering on the edge of oblivion. Mainly looked after by Henry's brothers John and Charles, the Trust had incautiously invested substantial sums in now busted Kansas City banks. "The storm broke!" Charles later remembered. "There was the misadventure of my life. . . . The fury of the gale was weathered; but its results were felt continuously through five long, precious years. They were for me years of simple Hell." Unaware of the downturn's severity, Henry boarded the British passenger liner *Paris* in New York on June 3, sailing with the Camerons to England. After visiting the usual cluster of friends — including Gaskell, Cunliffe, and Henry James — he crossed over to the Continent. On July 23, while in Switzerland, he received an anxious communication from Charles stating that the recent collapse put the Trust in "serious financial trouble" and requesting his immediate return home.[1]

It is difficult to gauge Henry's initial thoughts on the Panic. He seemed almost to go out of his way, while preparing to sail from Liverpool, to accentuate his affluence. "I have been to the steamer office and committed what I trust may not be my last extravagance," he wrote Elizabeth Cameron, and then confessed to having secured a smart £60 stateroom on the *Umbria,* a large Glasgow-built Cunard that carried nearly two thousand passengers and crew. Before leaving, he tried on coats at his tailor's and stopped by a shirt maker to collect a bill. These may have been concern-defying gestures, for at the same time he described himself in multiple communications as "scared," confessing to one friend, "The times look more stormy than I have known them for thirty years."[2]

Settled somewhat uncomfortably among his siblings for several weeks in Quincy, Henry bunked at the Old House, now in Brooks's possession. Tolerably bored, he toured the area visiting old friends, including Sturgis Bigelow (Billy Big) at Tuckernuck Island and the Lodges at Nahant; he also played lots of solitaire. On the financial front Henry, his brothers, and their sister Mary jointly decided to sell some of the Adams Trust's landholdings in the East in order to retain their properties in the West, which they would otherwise have been forced to relinquish at ruinous prices. Charles described the meeting, at which he suffered Brooks's shrill second-guessing, as a "very unpleasant two hours."[3]

Other investment decisions were made that summer that once again put the Trust on solid footing, which presumably meant more for Henry's siblings than himself. Though critical of America's new capitalist order, Henry proved to be a prudent speculator and came out of the Panic with his own portfolio largely intact. "Personally I cannot see that I am affected," he wrote Lizzie. "I owe nothing either on my own account or as trustee; and all my property seems to me excellent in every respect." He held shares in copper, mortgages, and railroads, among other commodities. He studied the market carefully and felt comfortable enough in his judgment to offer Gaskell asset advice in August, when the cash-starved American economy opened opportunities for those with capital to spend. He wrote to his friend, "I think I can

475

safely . . . guaranty you six per cent for one year for any amount you can supply, up to one hundred thousand pounds. Mortgages and notes with the solidest collateral are going begging at that rate, and I think I should be willing to take ten or even twenty thousand pounds myself at those terms."[4]

As the summer of 1893 wore on, a discernable anger crept into Adams's correspondence. He detected England's hand in the crisis (under considerable economic strain, Britain called in numerous American loans) and thus revisited an ancient family animus against an old foe. "England," he wrote to Hay, "has tried her best to save herself by squeezing us." More typically he took to abusing finance capitalists, both in and outside of London, as "gold-bugs" for their opposition to monetizing silver and thus alleviating the money shortage. Perhaps a little surprised to find himself on the same side of the free coinage debate as the Peoples' Party (1892–1908), a largely left-of-center agrarian and working-class coalition that thrived in the Plains states and Southwest, Henry sardonically embraced the Silverites: "The amiable but quite lunatic gold-bug has ended by making me a flat-footed Populist and an advocate of fiat money." With considerably more seriousness he commenced a stubborn rhetorical attack on Jewish financiers. "In a society of Jews and brokers, a world made up of maniacs wild for gold," he complained to Cameron, "I have no place."[5] In such remarks — and there were many — did Henry resurrect the economic anti-Semitism that, at least since the medieval era, had connected the Jewish people to greed, moneylending, and the accumulation of power through finance. Adams, in fact, trafficked in two types of late nineteenth-century anti-Semitism, one that shared the Populists' disdain for the gold-bug and another reflecting the Brahmin's sense of cultural displacement before rising ethnic groups.

To be clear, Adams never presumed that all gold-bugs were Jews; the term signified to him, rather, a larger censure of the sharp financial practices afflicting the industrial West. As editor of the *North American Review* he had first attacked traders, profiteers, and speculators in "The New York Gold Conspiracy" and "The Legal Tender Act." Now, twenty years on, he renewed the struggle, believing himself personally victimized by the recent economic smash. It must have embarrassed him when a well-meaning Gaskell wrote in the guise of a financial white knight, "I have a largish balance at my bank quite at your service." Perhaps this explains Henry's somewhat clumsy counteroffer to advantageously invest Gaskell in the depressed American mortgages and notes markets. Adams did, in fact, lend a sizable sum to his

Tahitian "brother" Tati, which allowed the displaced island aristocrat to escape bankruptcy. Other casualties included the old Heart Clarence King, who had organized and held stock in the National Bank of El Paso. After losing everything in the crash, King spent two months at Bloomingdale Asylum for the insane in White Plains, New York. In November Henry wrote to Hay, "I would pardon [the gold-bugs] their rascality on the stock-exchange and their imbecility in politics, but I can't forgive them their massacre of my friends who are being cleaned out and broken down by dozens. King is only one."[6] Possibly Henry's brother John was yet another; while burdened with managing the Adams Trust in difficult times, John suffered a stroke and died at the age of sixty in August of the following year.

One unintentional consequence of Henry's brief return to Quincy is that it strengthened his relationship with Brooks. In youth Henry preferred Charles's company, but different temperaments and perspectives quietly drew them apart. Several months after his elder brother's 1915 death, Henry wrote to Lodge, "As you know, I loved Charles, and in early life our paths lay together, but he was a man of action, with strong love of power, while I, for that reason was almost compelled to become a man of contemplation, a critic and a writer." It took Henry many years, by

478

contrast, to discover that he could be friends, or at least intellectual companions, with his youngest brother. He never connected emotionally with the bald and thickly mustached Brooks, finding him too insistent, dogmatic, and perhaps, as Theodore Roosevelt once put it, "a little unhinged." Accordingly, he kept his brother at bay, sometimes, and much to Brooks's frustration, going years between visits.[7] But in the summer of 1893, the brothers were brought together by their shared belief that the recent market meltdown constituted an epochal moment in world history.

Described by one biographer as a "philosopher manqué," the pessimistic Brooks, eager to draft a kind of universal history consistent with many a high Brahmin's sense of eclipse by newer families and fortunes, turned his attention in the period of the Panic to a curious study of cultural degeneracy that appeared in 1895 under the title *The Law of Civilization and Decay.* This work encapsulated its author's appetite for combining science and politics, economics and geography into sweeping and provocative historical generalizations.

By no means a singular exercise, Brooks's book variously corresponded with numerous scholarly (and pseudo-scholarly) social Darwinian exercises exploring the degeneracy theme. These include Cesare Lombroso's

Criminal Man (1876), Richard von Krafft-Ebing's *Psychopathia Sexualis* (1886), and Max Nordau's *Degeneration* (1892). The last, among other criticisms, dismissed the convention-flouting Oscar Wilde for dressing in "queer costumes" and "do[ing] more by his personal eccentricities than by his works."[8] In common, these studies shared the century's anxious awareness that sharp social and cultural change defied easy control.

During his Quincy stop, Adams had read and commented favorably on Brooks's manuscript in draft. It surveyed three distinct periods, the Roman, medieval, and modern; in each, Brooks argued, struggles to control finance and debt were the catalysts for change. The Roman world developed around the standard of economic centralization, which created a small class of money holders; this led to debt among the many and opened the way to both slavery and the search for external sources of revenue, attained through a problematic empire-building. Catastrophe — à la decline and fall — awaited. In claiming that rapacious "capitalists" weakened classical Roman civilization and attended to its disintegration, Brooks almost certainly paid tribute to the gold-versus-silver debates of his own day.

Moving on to the medieval era, Brooks argued that post-antiquity Europe mercifully developed in a less consolidated fashion with a quilt of fiefdoms and feudal grants guided by religion and superstition. "The ancient stock of scientific knowledge was gradually forgotten," he insisted, striking a romantic note, "and the imagination had full play." The Crusades began to unite the Continent once more, however, and, under the auspices of an emerging bourgeoisie, moved it toward a money-centric system. The Reformation augmented this process by taking wealth and political influence away from the Catholic Church. Under this momentum, the modern era saw increasing concentration as spreading financial markets, industrial development, and colonial expansion facilitated capitalism's triumph. And now, in still more recent times, the old New World mercantilism practiced by the Spanish, Portuguese, Dutch, and French was sinking rapidly before a rising regime of transnational bankers.[9]

Over a few summer weeks, Henry studied *Civilization and Decay* in draft and thought it marvelous. "All I can say," he wrote Brooks shortly after the manuscript's publication, "is that, if I wanted to write any book, it would be the one you have written." He subsequently described the study to Elizabeth Cameron as "astonishing" and extolled its author for discovering intuitively what no amount of careful combing of dusty archives (hitherto Henry's medium) could yield:

Indeed it is the first time that serious history has been written. He has done for it what only the greatest men do; he has created a startling generalisation which reduces all history to a scientific formula, and which is yet so simple and obvious that one cannot believe it to be new. My admiration for it is much too great to be told. I have sought all my life those truths which this mighty infant, this seer unblest, has struck with the agony and bloody sweat of genius. I stand in awe of him.

Henry's (mostly sincere) admiration must have been palpable, for years later Brooks, the "mighty infant" himself, recalled with an acute clarity those few important weeks in Quincy with his brother: "If I live forever, I shall never forget that summer. Henry and I sat in the hot August evenings and talked endlessly of the panic and of our hopes and fears, and of my historical and economic theories, and so the season wore away amidst an excitement verging on revolution."[10]

Henry in particular seemed eager to test this new unrest. From that August on, his work turned increasingly toward the idea of civilizational decay, in which religious, chivalric, and decentralized habits were arrayed against more powerful scientific, professional, and consolidated practices. Along with Brooks, he began to defend the anachronistic

482

warrior and priest against the ascendant capitalist and his congeries of attorneys; both men resisted the idea of historical progress, both harkened back to the jeremiad tradition of the Calvinism they no longer believed in, and both interpreted the Adams family's political collapse as characteristic of greater economic and cultural change within the United States. "Brooks and I," Henry smiled to a friend in the early autumn of 1893, "are radical silver men."[11]

39
"My Cuba"

Prior to his free silver turn, while meandering about the South Seas, Henry had reveled in the histories, pedigrees, and social customs of other cultures. But for the now fifty-something sojourner, such arduous travels were a thing of the past. Closer vistas, however, beckoned. Encouraged by his fellow Heart Clarence King, Adams had canvassed Cuba in 1888 while on a brief break from writing the *History*. Accompanied by his secretary and sometime housemate Theodore Dwight, he joyfully soaked in the picaresque, counting himself among the island's ruling class — "we . . . Spaniards" — and moved from diversion to diversion. Occupying a front-row seat for an afternoon bullfight, he seemed more taken by the "ladies in . . . soul-moving costumes" of red dresses and white mantillas than on the bull-baiting, which, he admitted, "I was too unwell to watch long." Later, he attended a masquerade carnival — "I had much amusement watching the costumes and people" — and enjoyed three successive evenings of opera. Returning to H Street with trinkets and a cache of cigars, he found the excursion on the whole highly agreeable. "Havana," he wrote Hay, "is just my affair."[1]

Struck by the convenience of a tropical entrepôt just off the American coast, Adams returned to Cuba in 1893 with William Hallett Phillips, a young State Department lawyer, and with King in 1894, and again the following year with Chandler Hale, son of a U.S. senator from Maine. Never one to let paradise just be paradise, Henry romanticized Cuba as a rebuke to the relentless course of modernization clamping down on the West. With the Cuban independence movement — a long-building nationalist uprising against Spanish rule beginning in the late 1860s — gaining momentum, he sympathetically opened his Washington home to its revolutionaries, thus offering support to yet another island Eden endangered.

Of his several Cuban tours, Henry seemed most content when collaborating with King. His correspondence during this period is unusually light, expansive, and playful. "I love the tropics," he confessed to Gaskell, "and feel really at ease nowhere else." He began his winter journey in January by staying at the Camerons' Coffin Point plantation on St. Helena Island in South Carolina, roughly equidistant to Charleston and Savannah. He explained his southerly removal to one correspondent as a necessary response to the recent economic Panic and its ruinous aftermath on those near to him: "The collapse has been, and still is, very sad to me. Among my friends and family, the strain has told terribly. . . . My brothers and their contemporaries are old men. I am myself more than ever at odds with my time."[2] Once committed to the quaint, "sound" money certainties that had informed the Governor, Adams felt himself cast out into a brave new economic world, cut adrift on a turbulent sea of speculation.

From Coffin Point, Henry traveled to Tampa, where he met King. Recently discharged from Bloomingdale Asylum following his own crash crisis, King sought to refurbish his finances by conducting a geological survey in the West Indies. For Henry, the temperate Gulf Coast proved an unexpectedly welcome diversion from "history," "economics," and "politics." Sensitive to the change in color, he complimented Florida's "lovely blue skies" and took pleasure in the constant cooling motion of the tropical sea breeze.[3]

By early February Adams and King were in Cuba. An evening pattern soon developed, King catting about while Adams attended to his letters. Considering that his principal correspondent was Elizabeth Cameron, however, one might say that, in his own cerebral and celibate way, he too courted while abroad. After a brief stay in "noisy, dirty, and fascinating" Havana the two adventurers rented a fine residence just outside of Santiago de Cuba (population forty thousand) on the island's southeastern shore and once Spain's colonial capital. While there, lounging, so he said, "in an ideal country-house in an ideal valley," Henry sketched, painted watercolors of the landscape, and practiced his Spanish. "You would appreciate me at last," he wrote Cameron, "if you could hear me hablar." The sun-splashed setting and smooth rhythm of unbroken balmy days — "The climate is divine" — invited ease, and he went weeks without picking up either an American or a Cuban newspaper.[4] He occasionally joked of buying a coffee plantation.

A pleasantly surprised King reported to Hay that time in Cuba had marvelously lifted Henry's spirits. "He was simply delightful, genial and tropical in his warmth," King wrote. "If he could only live in a capital in Cuba, I think the world-hate would perspire out of him and he might take hold of life and even of letters again."[5]

From Cuba, Adams and King went to Nassau, though Henry ordained it a "bore" and the Bahamas left little positive impress on him. Presumably out of disapproval he described the Bahamians, darker-skinned than the Cubans, as "a peculiar type" among whose female population King predictably "managed to amuse himself." On issues such as skin color and sensuality, however, Henry liked to have it both ways. While he primly shied from some of the franker exhibitions of sexuality he encountered in his various tropical travels, preferring to be an observer (and recorder) rather than a participant, he nevertheless liked to imagine that these "uncomplicated" civilizations were in their own ways superior to the overcivilized, industrialized, gold-bug-driven economies of London and New York. He embraced Cuba, in other words, as he had once embraced Quincy. "Society here, as well as in Europe, is shaking," he wrote to Gaskell soon after returning from the West Indies. "I prefer my Cuba, which is frankly subsiding into savagery. At least the problems there are simple."[6]

Siding with the world's Cubas and Quincys, Henry adopted in 1894 the ironic honorific "conservative Christian anarchist." Rejecting the rising scientific-mechanical world, he assumed the role of dissenter and held up various examples of island innocence as the sane man's antidote to the rush and crush of so many Chicagos. The alias suggests both a looking back and a bold (if only rhetorical) resistance to the main lines of contemporary industrial development. Increasingly he

488

sought to honor past traditions in his written work while assailing the energy, vulgarity, and avarice that so brutally pushed, so he swore, commercial civilization forward.

And that civilization, he little doubted, stood poised to own the next century outright. Tramping about the Caribbean, Adams enjoyed his "ideal valley" just prior to the brief Spanish-American War (1898) in which the victorious United States ended up directing Cuba's economic and political development. This involvement, which included occupying the country between 1906 and 1909, prefaced a number of other incursions over the next several years. During the final two decades of Adams's life the United States, to take but a few instances, intervened in Columbia's Panama province; landed marines in Honduras, Nicaragua, Haiti, and the Dominican Republic; and occupied the Mexican city of Veracruz. President William Howard Taft's Dollar Diplomacy policy (1909–13) — a belief that American financial power could promote stability throughout the Western Hemisphere and East Asia — seemed premised on the kind of gold-bug principle that Adams loathed. As in his earlier South Pacific travels, he again found favor in a tropical peoples' distance from Washington and London.

While in Santiago de Cuba, Henry became

fascinated with the Cuban independence movement. King had made contact with a few rebel leaders during their stay, and Adams lived a little vicariously through his friend's assignations. The uprising began decades earlier with the unsuccessful Ten Years' War (1868–78) and was now reaching its final phase in what would come to be known as the Cuban War of Independence (1895–98). Henry took great interest in this revolt against the fading Spanish Empire, though in late 1895 his attention turned temporarily to another hemispheric concern: the Venezuelan boundary crisis. Briefly, a long-standing dispute existed between the United Kingdom and Venezuela over territory that Britain insisted belonged to British Guiana. President Grover Cleveland claimed for the United States an interest in the outcome and, rather than see the British define the boundary by dragooning a weaker nation, argued for arbitration. Britain dragged its feet but ultimately complied; in 1899 a Tribunal of Arbitration meeting in Paris decided that the bulk of the disputed territory belonged to British Guiana.

During the crisis Henry had been on the side of arbitration, meaning, despite the eventual outcome, that he favored the Venezuelan cause. In the summer of 1895 Secretary of State Richard Olney, citing the Monroe Doctrine (1823), which had warned Europe

490

away from future political interference in the Americas, prepared a statement vigorously defending the U.S. position of hemispheric dominance; it was subsequently passed on to the British government. "The United States is practically sovereign on this continent," Olney argued, "and its fiat is law upon the subjects to which it confines its interposition." Henry, with his detestation of Lombard Street's money lords and a residual family animosity inherited from his Patriot forefathers, thoroughly enjoyed this twisting of the British lion's tale. He wrote enthusiastically to Olney, "As a rule of delicacy and good taste, I never volunteer remarks of any sort, on public affairs, to public officials. I do not mean to do so now; but if the opinion of a class of private persons is in any degree worth having, and if mine is any clue to that of others, I pray you to be assured that your message of this day commands my strongest possible approval and support."[7] A few days later, his blood up, Henry facetiously wrote to a niece that he expected war between the United States and Great Britain.

In January Britain agreed to accept arbitration in principle, after which a pleased (and somewhat smug) Adams apprised his old friend Sir Robert Cunliffe, "We have never had the smallest intention of fighting you. . . . All we wanted was to wake you up in time to prevent trouble" — by which he meant turning England's attention away from profit squeezing at the expense of other nations. This effort to connect the boundary dispute and the Panic of 1893 is labored at best and gives some sense of Henry's hostility to British financial power as well as to his simmering anti-Semitism. "What with your Jew crusade for gold, and your hopeless subservience to the speculative interests of the city of London," he lectured Cunliffe, "we were drifting very far apart."[8] For a few months in the winter of 1895–96 the Venezuelan situation concentrated Adams, and he celebrated Britain's acceptance of arbitration. This meant that the Monroe Doctrine — conceived by Monroe's secretary of state John Quincy Adams — had "won out" over the presumed wishes of the bankers and the goldbugs; the great John Bull, though master of much of the world, could not do as he pleased in America's backyard. With a satisfying victory on the home front, Henry eagerly took up the Cuba question.

The 1895 outbreak of rebellion on the island put Adams into motion. He encouraged his political friends to simultaneously aid the rebels while applying pressure on Spain to abandon Cuba. "My share in it," he assured Brooks, "is wholly behind the scenes."[9] Lizzie's husband, the Don, and her uncle John Sherman of Ohio sat on the Senate Foreign Relations Committee and gravitated to Henry's arguments. At their behest he drafted a committee report, subsequently informing the nonbinding Morgan-Cameron Resolution of April 1896, calling for America's endorsement of Cuban independence. Adams further involved himself in the affair by welcoming into his home Gonzalo de Quesada and Horatio Rubens, two important Cuban rebels seeking American support.

Henry now counted Grover Cleveland among the major impediments to the independence movement. The president had signed a proclamation of neutrality in June and remained throughout the final twenty-one months of his tenure in office committed, despite considerable congressional pressure, to staying out of Cuba. Cleveland's position, coupled with his earlier decision to repeal the Silver Purchase Act, disappointed Adams, who had voted for the president in 1892 as a protest to high-tariff Republicanism, which he regarded as the gold-bug party. "The Democrats," he defended his ballot, "represented to [me] the last remnants of the eighteenth century."[10] Forgetting the plantocracy's former influence on the old Jeffersonian coalition, Henry embraced the Democrats' quaint agrarian vision, critical of both centralized banking and industrialization. Had he his way, the Cuban future would apparently have looked a lot like the American past.

In less assured moments, however, Adams thought the long-term prospects of Cuban independence doubtful. Certainly Spain's withdrawal appeared imminent, but to what end? A "free" Cuba saddled with a large postcolonial debt merely meant a different kind of colonialism, and Henry could see the commercial needs of its people then becoming, as he evocatively put it, "only one more link in our servitude."[11] They would, in other words, be as dominated by dollars as any Kansas populist. Perhaps needing to place in perspective both the Panic and the Cuban debate, Adams, his mind fixated on the rapidly shifting geopolitical scene, returned to historical writing. These new offerings often abandoned the narrative approach favored in the *History,* featuring instead a more theoretical and openly pessimistic style. Their author, detesting the strong bond between industry and empire, seemed almost desperately eager in these acerbic exercises to discover the gilded path to Armageddon.

40
THE TYRANNY OF SCIENCE

As a young professor, Henry had eagerly preached the science of history to a rising generation of green Harvard scholars. In later years, however, he seemed to think that he had done his young a great disservice, playing the role of a modern Socrates. In 1901 he wrote to Henry Osborn Taylor, a former student, complaining of "my dreary *Anglo-Saxon Law* which was a *tour-de-force* possible only to youth. Never did any man go blind on a career more virtuously than I did, when I threw myself so obediently into the arms of the Anglo-Saxons in history, and the Germans in art."[1] Growing older, Adams came to regard his inherited Boston worldview as witlessly positivistic, capitalistic, and imperialistic. It reflexively worshiped science and technology, making the heartless dynamo the center of contemporary civilization. *Essays in Anglo-Saxon Law,* Henry now sheepishly acknowledged, had uncritically stressed the prevailing centuries-long march toward democracy by the German *Volk* and their Anglo offshoots — a neat pattern of historical progress he no longer believed. The opportunity to raise a heretical voice presented itself in response to a professional honor he had tried desperately to avoid.

At their July 1893 meeting in Chicago, members of the American Historical Association voted Adams president of the organization. His ties to the AHA were largely social and superficial, and he struggled in its early days to remember even its name, referring to it variously in correspondence as the "National Society of History," the "History Congress," and the "Historical Congress." He had attended a few of its earlier gatherings — "Our sessions were long, mostly dull, and often ludicrous" — but had missed the past several.[2] Travel in Europe and the South Seas offered ready excuses for his repeated absences, but Henry, fully into the chilly freedom of a posthumous life, had moved beyond professional societies and their professional prizes. This did not stop the AHA from electing him vice president in 1890 (while he obliviously sunned and Siva-ed in Samoa) and reelecting him in 1891 and 1892. Now, as presiding officer, he was expected to actually stand before his fellow scholars and deliver a presidential address; thus ensued a delicate cat-and-mouse game between a reticent Henry and the man poised to lead him to the podium, AHA secretary and Johns Hopkins historian Herbert Baxter Adams.

The spirit of renunciation had long been a prominent feature in Henry's emotional equipment. Had the Association's secretary understood this — or simply have conferred with Harvard president Charles William Eliot on the unusual difficulties of insisting an honor on Henry Adams — he would have saved himself a great deal of frustration. The year prior to Henry's receiving the AHA's presidency, Harvard had attempted to award the author of the *History* an honorary degree; naturally he would be expected to participate in the commencement exercise. Considering his distaste for such occasions, along with an aversion to nepotism — Charles and John sat, respectively, on the University's Board of Overseers and the Harvard Corporation — it is unsurprising that Henry resisted the overture. He stated in a long lecture-letter to President Eliot that the recognition tacitly presumed the honoree "to be the first in his profession," a notion he absolutely resisted. Rather, he artfully swore, the ten-volume *Lincoln: A History* (1890) written by John Nicolay and Hay, personal secretaries to the sixteenth president during the Civil War, exceeded in every respect his own modest *History:* "Nothing that I have ever done, or ever shall do, will hold its own beside portions of the Lincoln. . . . I could not without positive shame put myself in a position where I should seem to countenance the idea that any work of mine compared in importance either of purpose, of moral value, or of public interest to the singularly noble and American character of this monument to the greatest man of our time."[3]

Not to be put off, Eliot politely pressed his case, noting that Harvard wished to recognize Henry's good scholarship *and* teaching, which had "greatly enlarged and improved," so he insisted, historical training at the school. He further observed that the *Lincoln* constituted a contemporary study, "literary," he called it, as opposed to historical. And in any case, he reminded Adams, "the question of the propriety of this degree may better be settled by the judgment of your elders and contemporaries than by your own. You are not conferring this degree on yourself — it is the act of the University. To decline it would require a thousand explanations — to accept it is natural and modest." Sensing himself boxed in ("Your very kind letter of the 14th leaves little opening for a reply"), Henry proceeded to reply — twice. In the first communication, labeled "Private," he declared himself too young for such a recognition — "Wait till I am sixty" — and noted further and with some embarrassment that those wishing the degree upon him were "old friends, relations or connections" at the university.[4] Again he declined. In the second "official" note, he expressed regret that a sudden health crisis — a sprained ankle — precluded his appearance at the commencement.

Had his presence been pardoned there is reason to believe that he may have accepted Harvard's dollops in absentia. Only two weeks after spurning Eliot, Henry consented to receive the degree *honoris causa* from Western Reserve University in Cleveland, on condition that he be excused from attending the ceremony. Yes, the Harvard invitation may have bothered him because it bore the fingerprints of so many friends and family, though his connections to Western Reserve were only slightly less conspicuous. John Hay sat on its board of trustees while Adams's former student Charles Thwing served as its president. Attendance appears to have been the sticking point. In a wonderfully cryptic letter to Thwing ("My dear Scholar"), Henry replied that Western Reserve's lack of conditions for the award were agreeable: "For that, I am in no way responsible, and can accept it without rousing internal questions of any ignorance or error. For that, I feel no self-reproach."[5]

The AHA honor, by contrast, presumed a present and address-giving Adams to perform before the historians. A few months after the

499

Association election Henry tried to beg off, telling Herbert Baxter Adams that while "the compliment [was] flattering" he would, due to travel plans, be unable to attend the September 1894 meeting in Saratoga, New York. Perhaps troweling it on a little thick, he told the secretary that he expected "to be absent from the United States during the next twelve-month." Henry did spend part of the late summer of 1894 with Hay and a group of geologists tracing the Yellowstone River's headwaters. There, he fished, tracked "big elk" and bear, and fought off swarms of mosquitoes. Riding for several weeks over hundreds of miles, he thought the Teton Mountains "really fine," enjoyed, so he told Lizzie Cameron, a "delicious" early morning "bath of hot geyser-water" compliments of Old Faithful, and seemed to think the "empty" landscape sympathetic to the parameters of a posthumous existence: "I rather like this rambling all alone, from day to day, with no purpose, no reason, and no thoughts! . . . It is a queer Nirvana, but it seems to work."[6]

Attentive to courtesies, Henry had sent his presidential address to Herbert Baxter Adams before leaving for the West, assuming the matter laid to rest. How wrong he was. The industrious secretary, now referred to by Henry in his correspondence as "my bêtenoire," had postponed the meeting till late

December and relocated it to Washington — Henry's backyard. "Really," Henry complained to Hay, "he has put me in a tight place." Searching for a suitable pretext to avoid the gathering, he tried without success to corral King into joining him on a trip to Mexico before finding a travel partner in Chandler Hale. Redating his presidential address "December 12" and identifying his whereabouts as "GUADA'-C-JARA," Adams extricated himself cleanly from the secretary's "trap," delivering but not reading his paper. The bête noire knew when he was beaten. "We ought never," he complained to AHA treasurer Clarence Bowen, "have elected Henry Adams president."[7]

Henry's address, "The Tendency of History," opened with an ironic apology that slyly scored his colleagues for making him the object of their dubious tribute: "At the moment I am believed to be somewhere beyond the Isthmus of Panama. Perhaps this absence runs in some of the mysterious ways of nature's law, for you will not forget that when you did me the honor to make me your president I was still farther away — in Tahiti or Fiji, I believe — and never even had an opportunity to thank you." Subtle jibes aside, he then moved on to the topic of his talk, noting that ever since Darwin's *Origin of Species* (1859) historians had worked furiously to modernize their profession by constructing a "science of history." Producing dissertation after dissertation, monograph after monograph, the historical community sought to slip the grip of the gentleman scholar by creating a rigorous peer review process dominated by academics trained in the latest techniques and practices. This in itself he thought fine. Both Henry and his brother Brooks were, by degrees, committed to the use of statistics and scientific models in their own works. But whereas many Ph.Ds. predicted an upward evolutionary ascent for society, the pessimistic Adamses believed civilizational chaos and decay equally if not more likely outcomes. In one of the address's (several) sardonic passages, Henry a little unfairly described his fellow historians as high-minded innocents, true believers in a neat and quasi-divine scholasticism of order, organization, and arrangement: "Not one of them can have failed to feel an instant's hope that he might find the secret which would transform these odds and ends of philosophy into one self-evident, harmonious, and complete system."[8] Yet if history had any "secrets" to share, Adams countered, might they not tell the less than edifying story of the great and divisive clashes between capital and labor, Silverites and gold-bugs, or colonizers and colonized — did not the social Darwinists posit an *ongoing* struggle for the survival of the fittest?

But polite society quite obviously wished to dismiss such unpleasantries, Henry observed. It tolerated historians only because they belonged to "a safe and harmless branch of inquiry." What would happen if they posited "laws" that challenged the interests of powerful organizations or that doubted the virtues of popular democracy? Would property holders accept the idea of a "historical tendency" that claimed the errancy of property rights? Could Christians tolerate the notion that an unfathomable and perhaps amoral force determined events? Might socialism turn out to be on the right side of history after all? And if so, would the universities ignore their banker benefactors and allow their professors to preach such heresies? Tracing this argument to its logical and assuredly knotty conclusion, Adams maintained that far from offering historians the tools to better perform their duties, the still untested scientific history might make them vulnerable to public condemnation. "If," he observed, "the new science required us to announce that the present evils of the world — its huge armaments, its vast accumulations of capital, its advancing materialism, and declining arts — were to be continued, exaggerated, over another thousand years, no one would listen to us with satisfaction." Should that be the case, he impishly shrugged, historians would certainly be ignored, left to wander the scholastic wilderness writing for a tiny audience of "artists and socialists."[9]

Henry's "Tendency" takes obvious pleasure in predicting for the world a coming crisis. Addicted to unbridled industrialization, the major global economies, he argued, would ultimately fall into the hands of either the workers (that is, communism) or the factory owners (plutocracy); in either case, he warned his colleagues, "we must preach despair." Above all he wished his audience to feel every oppressive ounce of its professional responsibilities — and relished telling these satisfied scholars that the price of objectivity might be higher than any of them suspected: "A science can not be played with. If an hypothesis is advanced that obviously brings into a direct sequence of cause and effect all the phenomena of human history, we must accept it, and if we accept we must teach it. The mere fact that it overthrows social organizations can not affect our attitude. The rest of society can reject or ignore, but we must follow the new light no matter where it leads."[10] These half-serious, half-spoofing remarks reflect Adams's thoughts on the historian's dilemma, as delivered from the temperate December climes of a distant "GUADA'-C-JARA." He devilishly cornered his colleagues, challenging them to repudiate their distinguished if eccentric president. Should Association members take seriously his more satiric claims, he could snicker with cold satisfaction at their foolishness, and should they ignore him, he could assail their failure to recognize the bold prophet among them.

Conventional men, they ignored him.

41
THE FELT EXPERIENCE

Nearing sixty and increasingly interested in
what statistics and the hard sciences might
make of modern industry and empire, Henry
could be excused for assuming the expiration
of his carnal education. Widowed now for a
decade and stoically reconciled to his tame
cat status in the Cameron court, he thought
himself perhaps beyond the point of passion,
surprise, or hunger. He often performed as a
kind of wizened H Street Buddhist, oblivious
to the appetites and ambitions that excited
the less enlightened. But in truth, he wished
very much to be moved again, to be "rescued,
as often before," he wrote, "by a woman" who
might calm the engines of cultural disorder
and bring form to his world. Such unlikely
salvation came about through an unexpected
invitation in the summer of 1895 to accompany the Lodges to London and from
there to Normandy, Touraine, and Paris on a
journey of several sites — many of which he
had seen but never before felt.[1]

It was Henry Cabot Lodge's wife, Anna ("Sister Anne" to Henry), who asked Adams to spend several weeks abroad with them and their two sons, George and John. The small party toured the northern cathedral towns of France: Amiens, Rouen, Bayeux, Mont-Saint-Michel, Le Mans, and Chartres. And in these active Gothic haunts Henry suddenly discovered a medieval counterpoint to the turmoil of the modern condition.

In Normandy, a "paradise," he called it, "of outward austerity and inward refinement," Adams realized a world that had completely escaped his eye on earlier excursions. He had visited Amiens twice, taught an advanced course at Harvard on medieval institutions, and intellectualized the period in years of glancing study and reflection. He now realized, however, that the feudal theme constituted "a chapter [he] never opened before." Once again Brooks seems to have stolen a march on his older brother. As Henry had massaged *Law of Civilization and Decay*'s twilight mood into his own work, so he appears to have emulated Brooks's reaction to Europe's ancient cathedral culture. Six years earlier Henry and Brooks's mother, Abigail, died and a then forty-one-year-old Brooks, following Abigail's deathbed concern, determined to marry. Working quickly, he asked Anna Cabot Mills Lodge to suggest a partner, preferably someone like herself, and she

507

sensibly recommended her spinster sister, Evelyn (Daisy) Davis, whom Brooks then wed in September. A few months later the couple embarked for Normandy. There, in the vast scaffolded silences of naves, bays, and transepts, Brooks experienced an intense pleasure in his surroundings. "Everything pales before my discovery of the meaning of Gothic," he subsequently wrote to Henry, "which was to me a revelation. My intense excitement when I first began to read Chartres, and Le Mans, and all the rest, could never be equaled again by anything."[2]

Brooks communicated his infatuation with the Gothic into *Law of Civilization and Decay,* arguing that after the year 1300 the pace of history quickened as the development of European economies, militaries, and manufacturing became more pronounced. Henry readily absorbed Brooks's perspective while reading the manuscript and it began to shape his own writing and historical outlook. In time and with only the slightest emendation of his brother's calendar analysis, he too came to regard the end of high medievalism as the critical break that demarcated the premodern from the modern. "Behind the year 1400," he later noted, "the process certainly went on, but the progress became so slight as to be hardly measurable."[3]

Brooks's influence goes only so far, however, in explaining Henry's sudden and strong response to Normandy's architectural treasures. Something internal, rather, a deepening of perspective and an enlargement of experiences, perhaps, prepared him for such an epiphany. Travel in Asia, the South Seas, and Latin America had introduced him to other cultures, references, and practices. Situated, so he insisted, on "the edges of life," these civilizations lacked the progressive underpinnings and the capitalist economies of the liberal Atlantic world.[4] Drilled in youth to live within Boston's constricted emotional scope, Henry began his mature education abroad.

Rejecting the rational, Enlightenment side of the recent European past, Adams once more picked a persona that met certain psychical needs. As he had "become" Tauraatua in Tahiti, a silent Buddha in Japan, and a wishful seigniorial lord of a Cuban coffee plantation, he now identified as a Norman — or at least a Norman-of-the-heart. He reported to Hay of rediscovering "my respectable ... ancestors" amid the proud cool stone structures "I helped to build, when I lived in a world I liked." Taken particularly by Coutances, he exalted, "My soul is still built into it." Other countries could, of course, also point to a medieval heritage, but Henry never liked any so well as he liked France, which embodied for him a valiant resistance to the commercial-mechanical complex that was the pride and joy of the Anglo-Saxon peoples. "In spite of all its drawbacks," he wrote to one niece during this time, "France has, still, more to give one than any other country has, that I know. Outside of Paris and the manufacturing cities, life seems still quite possible. The French . . . do not get on my nerves as the Germans and English do."[5]

Eager to set aside the industrial regime, Adams came to the great artifacts of Gothic civilization eager for a sensory experience. The word "felt" suddenly and conspicuously entered his correspondence. In a letter to Elizabeth Cameron he wrote, "Though it is the third time I have seen Amiens, I never thoroughly felt it before," and two weeks later he informed her that Coutances's "innate nobility and grace and infinite tenderness . . . can only be felt by a finished life." To Brooks he confessed, "I have rarely felt New England at its highest ideal power as it appeared to me, beatified and glorified, in the Cathedral of Coutances." He considered the American Puritan personality type conspicuously deficient of imagination, artistry, and religious inspiration. Banks and insurance houses, rather, held the high ground and reduced "success" to a mad scramble for material comfort. "Our ancestors have steadily declined," he wrote in Coutances's golden glow, "so we get Boston."[6]

Detesting the eternal Anglo-Saxon gave

510

Henry license to lament his dear Normandy's penetration by the latest wave of invaders. He spurned the "wretched plats du jour" prepared in restaurants for the hordes of tourists, claiming that "where the American, Englishman, or German, goes, there life has no longer an interest except for market-values." The Norman pose permitted Adams to couch his acidic observations as valid cultural criticism. As usual, his lettered reflections were pungent and provoking, though not a little boorish. His fellow Cathedral seekers constituted a "mob," the streets throbbed with "harmless and feeble" American art students, and "odious Frenchwomen, gross, shapeless, bare-armed, eating and drinking with demonstrative satisfaction," annoyed him. He was intrigued, however, by "ladies in bicycle costumes."[7]

In correspondence Henry explained his own appearance among the tourist trade as that of a simple seeker. An incessant scholar, he had read, thought, and written of feudalism but not really appreciated it. He observed to one niece that experiencing the cathedrals "was something quite new to me, and humbled my proud spirit a good bit. I had not thought myself so ignorant or so stupid as to have remained blind to such things, being more or less within sight of them now for nearly forty years. I thought I knew Gothic."[8] The grace Adams discovered, however, did little to increase his fund of compassion, sympathy, or liberality. Instead it amplified the process of distancing him from the main trends of democratic-industrial development. Henry's "humility," it seems, extended only to those private Gothic preferences that drew Brooks in as well. To make his stand with the feudal past meant refusing to support the "plat du jour" world that had settled in its place; this Norman-of-the-heart sought seclusion rather than inclusion, solemnizing thirteenth-century poetry, sculpture, and stained glass as aesthetic instruments to elevate his divine alienation.

Despite finding a "felt" peace in the summer of 1895, Henry soon turned cerebral. Newly initiated in the Gothic, he collected books, music, and photographs, explored every nave in Normandy, and commenced the long process of making the things he read, saw, and admired a part of his intellectual purview. Four years later, while in Paris, he wrote *Mont-Saint-Michel and Chartres,* an imaginative journey into the heart of the medieval mind. There is evidence that Henry regarded this project as a kind of cognitive palate-cleansing, a final throwing off of the Teutonic historical model that had so impressed him as a young scholar. Following his impressionable cathedral journey, he later wrote in the *Education,* "Adams drifted back to Washington with a new sense of history."[9]

One might also say that he returned with yet another anti-Anglo identity — and with it this presumptive child of Norman glory wandered still a bit deeper into the archaic.

42
BLAME

Adams's freedom to play with identity owed
something to his measured removal from
ancestral obligation. He had no spouse,
fathered no heirs, and maintained sibling
relations from a polite distance. An independent income and lack of professional portfolio
accentuated his autonomy of time. Presumably he once anticipated an altogether different life, a long marriage, daughters rather
than nieces, and government or diplomatic
work to shape his days. None of these possibilities came to pass, of course, though
precisely when the weight of unspoken expectations finally, if ever, lifted is difficult to
gauge. The old family instinct for public
service remained strong, and under its demands Henry donned still another mask, that
of the modern intellectual. Packed with
opinions and beholden to no president,
plutocrat, or party boss, the ostensibly detached Adams could yet spar for his share as
a cultural critic.

Accordingly, Henry copiously, perhaps even obsessively documented his exile from American politics. His novels, histories, correspondence, and *Education* coolly considered the practice of "clean" government impossible, a fool's errand in a spoilsmen's paradise. In defense of this terrible truism, Adams affected to deeply, purely, and righteously loathe the contemporary world along with its congressional movers and Wall Street shakers. He invariably identified bankers and robber barons as the enemies of tradition, attacking Jews, Germans, and English alike for turning calm into chaos and chaos into profit. Left unchallenged and thus unedited by the prerogatives of privilege, these views and antipathies, which seemed to peak in the 1890s, long remained a residual condition of his thinking. His frantic insistence to Hay that "the whole carcass" of the Anglo-Continental civilization was "rotten with worms, — socialist worms, anarchist worms, Jew worms, clerical worms," is one that he variably repeated over the years.[1]

So untethered was Henry from social constraints that he seemed oblivious to the unmistakable narrowing of his perceptions and judgments. One yearns to read in his late letters the deft social criticism without the anti-Semitism, the sharp cultural commentary minus the gratuitous acid. A deficit of sympathy seems to have strongly informed

515

his attitude, which made caricatures of the tourists and shopkeepers, the politicians and investors his correspondence singed. Oliver Wendell Holmes thought Henry lacked the graceful levity to laugh — joyfully, forgivingly — at his own shortcomings as a prelude to accepting the shortcomings of others.

Adams gave no indication, however, that he wished to alter his situation. He never showed interest in a second marriage, and his ceaseless travels were often pressed into the questionable service of supporting a bleak historical perspective. True, he could appreciate on their own sublime terms Ravenna's brilliant mosaics, Chartres's striking cobalt-blue windows, or a stunning display of Persian embroideries that, so he sighed, "made one's heart bleed," but these artifacts were also invoked to damn by comparison modern economies and sensibilities.[2] "Freedom," in other words, had paradoxically penned Adams in. Responsible only for himself, he too often tangled with abstractions, unable to take life on more immediate, multiple, and generous terms. He once presumed to compensate for his intellectual isolation by sending copies of the *Education* to various colleagues and acquaintances for criticism, but almost none of the manuscripts was returned. Who, after all, would dare to dispute the dismal truths arranged in this forbidding tome? And who could hope to disabuse its erudite author of the enemies he had so lovingly assembled?

According to one niece, Henry's wavering between "great kindness [and] sudden brusqueness" got to the core of the man, touching a quality both "temperamental and involuntary."[3] Sensitive to these contrary elements in his friend's character, an inspired John Hay commissioned Saint-Gaudens in 1904 to create a medallion of Adams in portfolio with a porcupine body and cherub wings; its inscription reads "PORCVPINVS ANGELICVS HENRICVS ADAMENSO." The medal captures its subject's emotional complexity with a fine satirical touch, an evocation both gentle and gruff in the fanciful semblance of a sharply quilled angel.

Any extensive biographical treatment of Henry Adams must at some point consider his conspicuous anti-Semitism. By the 1880s his letters were littered with awkward and ugly references to Jews considered rough even by the day's standards. Such remarks do Adams no credit, though they tell us much about his relationship to his times, his conception of history, and his complicated sense of irrelevance in a republic no longer dominated by the old patrician clans. For Henry, Jew-baiting served a purpose. It gave flesh to the gold-bug and bone to the dynamo, much as his impactful travels through France's cathedral towns had more benevolently suggested a world of medieval grace and gallantry. Certainly the urban-industrial-immigrant synthesis effected, as Adams predicted, a dramatic change in American life, though his often acrid references to the Jewish people as the indispensable instruments of modernism reveal an underlying historical confusion. He had stood on firmer ground in the long *History* when describing a nascent process of development in America that belonged to no "race" or group. In that study he observed an inexorable transformation beyond the dictates of mere politicians, bankers, or bureaucrats — but in later years he began pointing fingers.

In his final, important works, *Mont-Saint-Michel and Chartres* and the *Education,* Henry successively adopted the attitudes of a Norman Goth and an old republican, each identity soundly, defiantly out of step with the industrializing trend of the modern West. His anti-Semitism found room for expression in each of these voices, constituting a private reply to tumultuous times. Late nineteenth-century America witnessed a slew of mass strikes, the arrival of millions of southern and eastern European immigrants, and a severe depression that sparked unprecedented economic hardships. A number of otherwise disparate constituencies responded to this predicament with various degrees of race

518

hostility. As the historian John Higham wrote some years ago:

Three groups in late nineteenth-century America harbored anti-Jewish feelings that went beyond mere social discrimination: some of the agrarian radicals caught up in the Populist movement; certain patrician intellectuals in the East, such as Henry and Brooks Adams and Henry Cabot Lodge; and many of the poorest classes in urban centers. Different as they were, each of these groups found itself at a special disadvantage in the turmoil of an industrial age — the poor because it exploited them, the patricians because it displaced them.[4]

One can observe the patrician reaction in its tenacious efforts to remain a people apart. The nation's old cultural elite began in the 1880s to establish country clubs and create patriotic societies with membership dependent on pedigrees reaching deep into the American past. Groton (1884) and a number of other private schools — including Westminster (1888), Woodberry Forest (1889), Choate (1890), Taft (1890), and Hotchkiss (1891) — were founded in part to provide a class-based education. As Leonard Dinnerstein has noted, "the appearance of the first *Social Register*" in 1887 furnished "people who counted in society [with] a book to inform them of who belonged to their most exclusive circles."[5] More aggressive efforts on behalf of race snobbery followed, such as the founding of the Immigration Restriction League (1884), whose membership included the influential historian John Fiske, future Harvard University president A. Lawrence Lowell, and Senator Lodge. The growth of the League outside of its New England stronghold — into New York, Philadelphia, Chicago, and San Francisco, among other cities — gives some indication of its appeal beyond the Brahmins. At the progressive University of Wisconsin, a number of talented social scientists, including the economist Richard Ely, labor historian John R. Commons, and sociologist Edward A. Ross, were sympathetic to the League's concerns with the "coarsening" of the American population via the rapid introduction of Mediterraneans, Slavs, and Jews. Ross, particularly alarmed by the prospect of "race suicide," became an advocate of eugenics. Lending his scholarly reputation to a number of organizations seeking to "enhance" genetic quality in America, he provided testimony to the Wisconsin legislature when it considered a law to authorize sterilization. He called critics of the bill "essentially sentimental."[6]

In Great Britain and its dominions during this period, support also built for limiting immigration. The Aliens Act of 1905 slashed the number of Jewish arrivals in the United Kingdom dramatically, while Canada, Australia, and New Zealand all moved, through literacy tests and other means, to promote a form of white nativism. Concerned with the declining British birth rate, the socialist Sidney Webb feared for a "national deterioration" as the country "gradually [succumbed] to the Irish and the Jews."[7] It is within this heightened racial context, one informed by widespread movements of peoples and cultures, that Adams's views should be assessed and understood.

Prior to the 1880s Henry had exhibited no particular grievances toward Jews; indeed he counted among his kin a Jewish brother-in-law, Charles Kuhn, married to his beloved sister Louisa. A few years after Loo and Charles's 1854 marriage Henry, then studying law in Germany, witnessed perhaps his first overt episode of anti-Semitism. Bertha and Fanny Gans, American friends of his older brothers, were snubbed at a Court Ball in Dresden and then became the subjects of town gossip. The experience disgusted Henry, who wrote to Brooks of the attacks on the Misses Gans, "The Germans are still a semibarbarous people and the ideas of the middle-ages are alive and kicking in the nineteenth century." Years later, Henry and Clover enjoyed cordial acquaintances in London

521

with the Goldsmids and the Montefiores, "Jews," one Adams scholar tells us, "of their own class and complexion."[8]

Interestingly, considering his views, Adams took some mixed pride in pointing out that a certain "Hebraic" tradition linked the "chosen people" of Israel to the Puritan plantationeers occupying their own hallowed "city upon a hill." He played upon this idea on the opening page of the *Education* when comparing his "branded" birth into a founding family of the American nation to that of a Jewish babe belonging to a "holy nation." Perhaps he was also making a comment on the dangers of insularity. "Had he been born in Jerusalem under the shadow of the Temple," he wrote of himself, "and circumcised in the Synagogue by his uncle the high priest, under the name of Israel Cohen, he would scarcely have been more distinctly branded, and not much more heavily handicapped in the races of the coming century, in running for such stakes as the century was to offer." This putative connection of Brahmins and Jews may sound self-serving in Henry's hands, though it is one that Thomas Jefferson had made many years earlier while attacking the Federalist Party. In a 1798 letter to a Virginia politician, Jefferson had insisted, "Our New England associates . . . are marked, like the Jews, with such perversity of character, as to constitute, from that circumstance, the

522

natural division of our parties." Adams quoted this line in the *History,* poking fun at the intolerance to which Jefferson, a champion of Enlightenment liberalism, so innocently advertised. The quip, he assured readers, was humorous largely "because no humor was intended."[9]

It is further worth remembering that Henry drew a respectful portrait of a Jewish character in the novel *Democracy.* His description of the old diplomat Baron Jacobi, a "witty" and "cynical" Washington transplant who rues America's cultural backwardness and "seemed to have met every noted or notorious personage of the century," sounds almost like an authorial self-description. Jacobi saw through the thin tissue of corrupt capital politics but chose to be an amiable guest who "accepted the prejudices of Anglo-Saxon society, and was too clever to obtrude his opinions upon others." He would not, however, accept humiliation. We last see the resourceful baron getting much the better in a physical altercation with an offensive senator who, on a public sidewalk, attempts to block his path; the proud diplomat staggers the dull pol with the full force of his walking cane. Jacobi, Henry approvingly wrote, lacked not for "high temper and personal courage."[10]

Some years after *Democracy* appeared, Adams became acquainted (through La Farge) with the young American art historian Bernard Berenson. Despite their differences in age and ethnicity, the two struck up a sociable correspondence. Adams could never forget, however, Berenson's Jewish Lithuanian roots. In the winter of 1904 Berenson and his wife joined a small breakfast party at Adams's house. Their host, admitting to being in a "dark purple gloom," proceeded, so he relayed to one correspondent, to make the Berensons uncomfortable:

[A]t last — Barenson and his wife! Well, you know, you see, you know I *can't* beat it. There is, in the Jew deprecation, something that no weary sinner ought to stand. I rarely murder. By nature I am humane. Life, to such people, is perhaps dear, or at least worth living, and I hate to take it. Yet I did murder Barenson. I cut his throat first, and chopped him into small bits afterwards and rolled the fragments into the fire. In my own house I ought not to have done so. I tried to do it gently, without apparent temper or violence of manner. Alas! murder will out.

In her diary afterward, Mary Berenson described Adams as "pretty rude."[11]

This insolence arose principally from Henry's association of Jews with the historical process of liberal capitalist development. It is a race prejudice he held in common with

524

some of America's most significant writers of the late nineteenth and early twentieth centuries. Edith Wharton's social-climbing Simon Rosedale plays to type in *The House of Mirth;* Theodore Dreiser once called New York "a Kyke's dream of a Ghetto"; and the journalist and satirist H. L. Mencken described "the Jews . . . as the most unpleasant race ever heard of." Ezra Pound and T. S. Eliot, the latter calling it "undesirable" to live amid "any large number of free-thinking Jews," have elicited in scholarly circles cottage industries on this theme. And yet other notable Progressive-era personalities, such as William Dean Howells, William James, and the essayist Randolph Bourne, were unsparing critics of American parochialism; Oliver Wendell Holmes, himself among the highest of Brahmins, maintained strong friendships over many years with Louis Brandeis, Felix Frankfurter, and Harold Laski. In Adams's case a number of circumstances converged to stiffen his anti-Semitism: disappointment at the development of Victorian civilization, a congenital mental rigidity (liberally evident as one peeked up the family tree), and the quiet complicity of friends. Hay, Gaskell, and Lizzie Cameron at the very least tolerated his remarks. Adams felt comfortable enough with Gaskell to write of his 1895 return to London, "I plunge into a horde of Jews, the most terrible since the middle-ages. They are secret and banded together; they lie; they cheat the Christian; they are gutter-Jews at that, the new lot; and they own us all."[12] He is obviously speaking for effect, but there is more than a soupçon of real scorn in such ugly words.

With Brooks, Henry found a willing ally in his indictment against the Jewish people. The *Law of Civilization and Decay* offered statistical "proof" for the claims made earlier by the European clerical press that international (that is, Jewish) bankers advantageously manipulated global finance. In the storm of trade wars and expanding economic empires, older spiritual expressions, along with regional markets and low-intensity capitalism, presumably succumbed to a parasitic finance capitalism bereft of honor, paternalism, and social responsibility. Brooks describes this process in his book, indicating the recent and to him regrettable decline of Anglo-Saxon leadership before a new moneyed aristocracy:

The ideal statesman had been one who, like Cromwell, Frederic the Great, Henry IV., William III., and Washington, could lead his followers in battle. . . . In France and Germany the old tradition lasted to within a generation. Only after 1871 came the new era, an era marked by many social changes. For the first time in their history the ruler of the French people passed admittedly from the martial to the monied type, and everywhere the same phenomenon appeared; the whole administration of society fell into the hands of the economic man.

And the embodiment of the economic man, Brooks warned readers, was "the Jew in London."[13]

Henry's spiteful references to Jews have generally overshadowed his equally crude, if not equally abundant, Irish-taunting. Both ethnic groups were in a sense inheritors of traditional Anglo power and thus ripe for Adams's derision. He crassly wrote to Elizabeth Cameron in 1910 of Boston's new mayor John "Honey Fitz" Fitzgerald (grandfather of John F. Kennedy), "Poor Boston has fairly run up against it in the form of its particular Irish maggot, rather lower than the Jew, but more or less the same in appetite for cheese."[14] Together the Irish and Jewish peoples in America challenged the already fading genteel tradition. More, they contributed to the indispensable labor power that made the United States an industrial giant. Their energy, outlook, and ambition matched the dynamic needs of the nation, and Adams, who thought of himself as "eighteenth century" in outlook, was not wrong in claiming that he felt a stranger in his own land.

Filled with a sense of displacement, he

527

drifted around the globe in search of an antidote to Anglo-Saxon materialism. As noted, France attracted him greatly and he began to spend summers there. "On the whole France impressed me favorably," he wrote to Brooks in 1895. "The signs of decay are less conspicuous than in any other country I have visited. Capitalistic processes are less evident. The small man has a better chance. The people understand the age better, and still make a fight. Of course the Jew is great, but he is not yet absolute, as he is [in England]." Perhaps not surprisingly Henry read with interest the French anti-Semite Édouard Drumont and the former Boulangiste Henri Rochefort. Both men were sharp critics of bourgeois civilization and zealous anti-Dreyfusards.[15]

The Dreyfus Affair — Alfred Dreyfus, a Jewish French artillery officer, was wrongly convicted in 1895 on charges of treason — rocked France for several years. Touching upon questions of justice, citizenship, and anti-Semitism, it exposed a deep and searing rift between traditionalists (the church and army) and modernists (republican and anti-clerical sentiment) over the nation's future. Henry unhesitatingly favored the former. The difficulty hovering over the affair, he believed, concerned Western civilization's tenuous commitment to its conservative military and religious traditions. He insisted to Hay that the Dreyfus case constituted nothing less than "a moral collapse that involves soldiers and civilians alike, and the capacity of the French to maintain a character of any sort in a world like Europe."[16]

Yet as early as 1898, a year before Dreyfus was pardoned, Adams recognized the injustice of the situation. "I grant the innocence of Dreifus," he wrote. The artillery officer's fate interested him less, however, than the fate of France. "What I am curious about is the thing that comes next," he wrote to Elizabeth Cameron. "Dreifuss is to be set free — that has been foreseen . . . but what is to become of France? They can't acquit Dreifuss without condemning France." Henry took the position that come what may, the integrity of the French Army must at all costs be preserved. As late as 1899, several years into the affair and after it was known that high-ranking military officials had suppressed evidence demonstrating Dreyfus's innocence, he swore to being "rather impressed by the good appearance of the army." In a strained analogy, he claimed that the American Civil War had taught him "to back the Army and Navy against everything everywhere on every occasion," and he now presumed to support the French military to the same degree, even if it resided, as he put it, on the side of "injustice." No doubt he saw in the coming victory of the Dreyfusards the imminent collapse of the comparatively pre-industrial culture that drew him to Paris each year. For an old Norman, this depressing eventuality provoked an outpouring of unseemly sentiments. In one letter acknowledging his belief in Dreyfus's innocence, he could not contain himself from adding, "Dreifus himself is a howling Jew."[17]

It is easy to regard Henry's Judeophobia as remote and private, a personality tic largely confined to his correspondence. The historian Albert S. Lindemann has noted that Adams "did not try to bring his anti-Semitic ideas into the political arena or to transform them into action; his was not the crusading or populist anti-Semitism." And yet the wide and influential circle of his friends and acquaintances was such that his race snobbery became a point of open conversation. Some of those near to him remembered well his fierce language and corrosive tone. After listening to Henry once too often despair of the Dreyfus "convulsion," Hay drolly declared to Elizabeth Cameron that Adams "now believes the earthquake at Krakatoa was the work of [the pro-Dreyfusard novelist Émile] Zola and when he saw Vesuvius reddening the midnight air he searched the horizon to find a Jew stoking the fire."[18] Hay no doubt knew just how far to take his old friend's views, though the writer Owen Wister suggested that Adams's sardonic tongue perhaps negatively influenced the younger and less intellectually secure who shared his society:

> His talk was informed and pointed, he knew an extraordinary number of things very well — better than almost anybody you were likely to see in America — to be with him, dine with him, was a luxury and an excitement. He fascinated not only beautiful and particular ladies, but clever and aspiring young men as well. For some of these his influence was not quite wholesome; not only your patriotism, but your faith in life, had to be pretty well grown up to withstand the doses of distilled and vitriolic mockery which Henry Adams could administer.[19]

Not long after his death, Adams began to appear in many of his acquaintances' memoirs. These accounts tended to ignore his inelegant remarks on Jewry, a topic in any event not typically discussed in polite circles. As Professor J. C. Levenson has noted, "The question of Adams's anti-Semitism really was not raised until the post-Auschwitz era, and when it finally did come up beginning in the 1950s, it was brought into discussion principally by Jewish scholars."[20] Two of these men, Richard Hofstadter (actually half-Jewish) and Alfred Kazin, were good friends who, in their respective fields, sought to recast, in light of the Great Depression and Second World War, the political and literary history of America. Both formed early, lasting, and conflicting opinions of Adams. While preparing a study on social Darwinism in the United States, a twenty-something Hofstadter wrote Kazin, "Been skimming through Henry Adams' letters for my book. I never realized before what a . . . real pig of a genteel Anglo-Saxon Jews-are-commercial-and-have-no-manners anti-Semite . . . he was." Kazin, as Hofstadter knew, admired Adams and "liked," so Kazin noted, "to mock my fascination . . . by quoting Adams's insane hatred of Jews, especially immigrant Jews." They agreed, however, that American industrial power was a uniquely unsettling force. "We were both," Kazin later reflected, "in the spell of what had caught and frightened Adams."[21] In these two prominent public intellectuals of the twentieth century do we see on a slight scale the broader struggle among critics and readers alike to make sense of Adams's anti-Semitism. No doubt it accompanied certain class chauvinisms shared by many Brahmins, but even some of these highly educated Bostonians casually wondered at Henry's intolerance. He seemed since youth a crusader in search of a distant cause. And what offended him — Grantism, gold-bugs, dynamos — he interpreted as the instruments of a coming apocalypse. This contemplative Buddha, presumably surviving quietly on the "edges of life," sheltered a scattering of spoken and silent resentments, a few of which proved in their glistening appeal too rooted and too strong to overcome.

■ ■ ■ ■

DYNAMO

■ ■ ■ ■

But to Adams the dynamo became a symbol
of infinity.

Henry Adams, 1907

Dynamo

But to Adams the dynamo became a symbol
of infinity
Henry Adams, 1907

43
THE JINGO

After returning from his long South Seas withdrawal, Henry largely confined his overseas sojourns for the next several years to England and the Continent. But late in the winter of 1898 he returned to Egypt for the first time since navigating the Nile on his honeymoon. He appeared to be chasing ghosts. Just a few weeks earlier he had written pointedly to Clover's old friend Rebecca Dodge Rae, explaining his weary widower's existence: "When one has eaten one's dinner, one is bored at having to sit at the table. Do you know that I am sixty in six weeks, and that I was only fortyseven when I finished my dinner?" Shortly thereafter he told Elizabeth Cameron that his "old instinct of running away" had suddenly resurfaced. He felt unable to remain any longer in Washington, "still less . . . Boston."[1]

Perhaps his impending birthday produced a pause, or maybe the posthumous life no longer struck the same symbolic chords, or possibly he needed to more definitively reconcile with Clover's memory, to confront whatever long-held resentments remained from her depression and suicide, to finally, so to speak, walk away from the darkening dinner table. Egypt, the site of Clover's initial "breakdown," offered, even in the traveling company of the Hays, the opportunity for a kind of private communion. As a particularly delicate memory, it preceded the couple's hopeful removal to Washington, the invention of the Five of Hearts, and the shared secret of *Democracy*'s authorship. In describing to Cameron his sudden need for Egypt, Adams noted somewhat vaguely and without elaboration that his desire for decamping ran "strong just now" and must be attended to "so that I can settle down to a new situation."[2]

Not long after writing these words Henry experienced a powerful sense of recall while cruising on a steam *dahabieh* off Memphis. The emotional release he perhaps longed for had at last arrived. "I knew it would be a risky thing," he later reported to Cameron, "but it came so suddenly that before I could catch myself, I was unconsciously wringing my hands and the tears rolled down in the old way. . . . A few hours wore off the nervous effect, and now I can stand anything, although of course there is hardly a moment when some memory of twentyfive years ago is not brought to mind. The Nile does not change."[3]

Hardly had his stirred emotions settled when Adams, now docked at Aswan in the Upper Nile Valley, learned that the American battleship *Maine* had blown up in Havana Harbor on February 15. Half a world away, "hiding in a hole," he suddenly redirected his energies toward the Cuban crisis and the growing possibility of a Spanish-American War endgame. Within two months Congress, claiming an external mine destroyed the *Maine* and eager to see Spain out of Cuba, pushed through a joint resolution calling for Cuban independence — and American military assistance if necessary. President William McKinley signed the measure on April 20, and America's "splendid little war," as Hay called the campaign, had begun. Utterly absorbed watching this unexpected conflict slowly take shape, Adams wrote to Cameron, "Step to step, [I] was dragged back to the life I fled."[4]

That spring Henry remained on the move. In early May, while in Belgrade, he learned that the American Asiatic Squadron under Commodore George Dewey had destroyed Spain's Pacific fleet at the Battle of Manila Bay — thus ending nearly four hundred years of that nation's rule over the Philippines. "It is time to look ahead once more," he wrote to a niece, "and to see where things are drifting." By the middle of the month Adams had taken rooms at the Hotel Brighton in the heart of Paris. While there he played at heading the State Department, musing in correspondence that he hoped to see Spanish recognition of Cuban independence and some measure of self-government in Puerto Rico; the United States, he ventured, might do well to annex Hawaii and recall its forces from the Philippines in return for maintaining a harbor outfitted with a coaling station. With America's victory in sight, he now feared that Spain's defeat might destabilize half of Europe. Journeying on to London, he confided to Brooks, "In my eyes, Spain is too rotten to hold together, and I fear her total extinction. Western Europe is in a parlous state. If we do not take care, we shall drag the whole rotten fabric down on our heads. I want peace."[5]

Shortly thereafter Adams joined the Hays and Camerons at Surrenden Dering, a grand ivy-covered Kent house constructed during the reign of Charles I and later rebuilt. "The country around Surrenden was lovely," remembered one of their party, "and we were blessed all through the summer with the most divine weather in which to enjoy it." Comfortably situated, the Americans followed the papers; with several of their acquaintances or the offspring thereof fighting in Cuba, they collectively felt, so Henry reported to Brooks, "anxious about the casualties." These tensions, however, more generally gave way to

540

sociable days of ambling and exploration. "Uncle Henry" dutifully conveyed his companions about the region, reciting for their consideration the history and human drama lying as quiet as crypts about the surrounding villages, farms, and fields. Adams, so a niece recalled of their busy itinerary, exhibited a remarkable "bird-dog instinct" for sniffing about "a number of old parish churches in the immediate neighborhood" as well as a couple of crumbling castles "sacred to the stormy memory of Anne Boleyn."[6]

When not wandering around the countryside, Adams spent much of his time at Surrenden Dering in discussion with Hay, then serving as U.S. ambassador to the United Kingdom. Their conversations were interrupted in late August, however, when Hay returned to Washington, heeding McKinley's invitation to serve as secretary of state. This, of course, left Hay's ambassadorial post vacant. With a powerful friend heading the State Department and an unimpeachable pedigree, Henry had reason to hope that he might finally duplicate at least one of his celebrated antecedents' achievements. Beyond the advantage of a venerable family tree, he could be said to have cultivated, as one of the country's most distinguished historians, an appropriate profession for diplomatic work. George Bancroft (naval secretary in the Polk administration), Henry Cabot Lodge,

541

Theodore Roosevelt, and Hay all wrote American history, and Adams's acclaimed interpretation of the early republic, with its careful combing of the British and European archives, served as something of an advertisement for his ability to broadly conceptualize statecraft.

As usual, Henry qualified his ambitions even as he privately disclosed a desire that others might at last recognize his fitness for a major diplomatic role. "All my life I have lived in the closest possible personal relations with men in high office," he wrote Gaskell. "Hay is the first one of them who has ever expressed a wish to have me for an associate in his responsibilities." He claimed to have no serious designs on leading the American embassy in London, as, he said, "nothing short of a cataclysm" would induce the GOP's power brokers to elevate an independent bereft of party backing. Still, he assured Gaskell that "poor Hay" would certainly need assistance, and "if he called on me, I should no doubt be obliged to do whatever he wished."[7]

In such careful communications Henry offered evidence as to why he never found his footing in the American political system. He clearly longed to emulate his ancestors' successes, though even these anti-party men had occasionally been aided by parties. His unwillingness to bow to ambition contains a certain attractiveness, and yet there were some around him who wished that he might have exerted at least some small effort to claim his share of prizes — as Hay, a giver of time, advice, and money to the party of Lincoln, had strained to claim his. Instead Adams seemed eager to deny the republic his talents, as he thought the republic had so often denied him. "If the country had put him on a pedestal," Justice Holmes once said, "I think Henry Adams with his gifts could have rendered distinguished public service. He wanted it handed to him on a silver platter."[8]

And so, for a moment, the ambassadorship appeared to be. In late September a Philadelphia dispatch to that effect made its way into both the London *Times* and the Paris *Herald:* "Mr. Henry Adams, of Massachusetts, son of Charles Francis Adams, and a friend of Mr. Hay, is reported to have been suggested for Ambassador in London. He is a prominent author and historian. His father, grandfather, and great-grand-father have all been on missions to London." But the call never came. Instead Henry left London and returned to the United States in November. He subsequently wrote to Elizabeth Cameron that Hay had casually met him on the doorstep of his house. The two went inside, chatted for an hour about a number of matters, but conspicuously avoided "political" talk. "We did not," he pointedly observed, "even mention the embassy." He closed his note by adding that James McMillan, a Detroit industrialist and Michigan senator, would receive the London post. This news, he assured Cameron, came as a "vast relief."[9] The ambassadorship actually went to the distinguished New York lawyer Joseph Hodges Choate, a venerable GOP warhorse who had campaigned for every Republican presidential nominee since 1856. Confirmed by the Senate, Choate held the London post for six years (1899–1905), longer than any minister since Charles Francis Adams.

On the questions of war and empire Henry took conflicting positions. One can find in his correspondence many and sincere comments sharply critical of American expansion. In one communication, written during the debate over whether the United States should remain in the Philippines, he denounced the mounting pressure to pocket colonies, condemning "our present state of Washington. We are disgustingly fat, oily, greasy and contented." In other moments, however, the emergence of American power made him proud. Thus, while he wished for nothing more from the Philippines than a coaling station, he had little patience for the American Anti-Imperialist League (1898–1920), which opposed annexation of the islands as a violation of the United States' founding principles of self-government and nonintervention. The League's eclectic membership included Grover Cleveland, Andrew Carnegie, Mark Twain, and William James. James furiously scolded his country's Pacific push: "God Damn the U.S. for its vile conduct in the Philippine Isles." How, he queried, could the United States, a nation born in a great anticolonial struggle, so casually "puke up its ancient soul . . . in five minutes without a wink of squeamishness." The League also counted Charles Francis Adams Jr., among its numbers, and Henry privately dismissed his older brother as making "a fool of himself by talking . . . idiotically." He thought younger brother Brooks's realpolitik more sensible, observing, "The anti-imperialists are perfectly right in what they see and fear, but one can't grow young again by merely refusing to walk."[10]

Henry's desire to punish Wall Street, however, strongly compromised his foreign policy realism. Taking note of the bankers' aversion to ending Spanish rule in Cuba, he presumed that American and British financiers wanted to see the old colonial system survive for their own selfish ends. Accordingly, he moved into the opposing camp, joining the bulk of American public opinion — and the yellow journalism of Joseph Pulitzer and William Randolph Hearst — in shouting for war. But

Adams's underlying ambivalence — wanting freedom for Cuba, a presence in the Philippines, and a protectorate in Puerto Rico — spoke of broader ambiguities. His family had made its good name contesting the world's largest empire; what would history now make of his own generation's actions overseas? Even for a master ironist, the question seemed fraught with peril.

44
SILENT AND INFINITE FORCE

Beginning in the summer of 1899, a few months after Spain relinquished its colonial possessions in the Americas, Henry made Paris his half-time home, summering on the Continent and wintering in Washington. Though he continued to travel until the First World War, his journeys were now strictly American and European affairs. Even these, however, were not without their attendant pedagogical possibilities. The brief but effectual junket through Normandy in 1895 had reawakened his old academic and aesthetic interest in medieval civilization while offering an attractive counterpoise to the modern capitalist condition. As the century came to a close he continued to revisit the feudal theme and, under the influence of both Coutances's beauty and Brooks's doctrine of modern-day decay, made an idol of its obsolescence.

Exhibiting his usual weakness for sweeping cultural statements, Adams kept an eye on the Exposition Universelle held in Paris from mid-April through early November 1900. Attracting an astounding fifty million visitors the Exposition, so one historian has written, "probably was the largest and most ambitious international gathering for any purpose ever." Eager to be near the action, Henry stayed through the summer in an apartment at 20 Rue de Longchamps near the Trocadéro in the 16th arrondissement, from which he steered guests — including Lizzie and fourteen-year-old Martha Cameron and his former brother-in-law Edward Hooper — through the grand fair. Happily playing the attentive uncle, Adams escorted Martha and two of her companions to luncheon in the Asiatic Russian Pavilion, where they enjoyed a simulated ride along the Trans-Siberian Railway; afterward a brightly lit "Street of Cairo," complete with a fashionable bazaar and lithesome belly dancers, drew their attention. Adding to the variety, he later shepherded the girls to see the French stage actress Gabrielle Réjane perform in *Madame Sans-Gêne,* a historical comedy-drama of a plain-spoken laundress who becomes a duchess. Other outings yielded only limited temptations. A knowledgeable collector of art, Adams found surprisingly few objects at the Exhibition to garnish his Washington home. "There are no pictures for sale," he wrote to Gaskell, "no bronzes; no marbles, of a quality worth getting." To this tart disclaimer Henry made but a single exception, adoring the exquisite tapestries in the Spanish pavilion which he called "by many times the finest ever brought together."[1] Perhaps while enjoying such handsome textiles, he meditated on the stark contrast between Spain's still vivid artistic sensibility and its recent collapse as a global power.

Surrounded by a sampling of the world's aesthetic, mechanical, and architectural treasures, Adams lingered about the exhibition halls over weeks and months trying to read their meaning for the modern condition. One wonders if he watched a flickering film, negotiated a newly issued escalator, or took note as Campbell's Soup received a gold medal (the icon still present on a number of its products and evident in Andy Warhol's famous artistic appropriation). If he is to be believed, enlightenment suddenly arrived for Henry in the great Gallery of Machines, a large iron, steel, and glass structure built for the earlier 1889 Exposition Universelle. Illuminated by electrical light and housing a variety of engines, dynamos, and transformers, the gallery blazoned the rapid evolution of energy from horsepower to machine power. Entering the hall, Adams immediately sensed that traditional measures of social and economic development were now defunct: "I . . . go down to the Champ de Mars and sit by the hour over the great dynamos, watching them run as noiselessly and as smoothly as the planets, and asking them — with infinite courtesy — where in Hell they are going. They are marvelous." Reflecting on the relatively small span of time that distanced the Chicago and Paris expositions, he believed, "In these seven years man had translated himself into a new universe which had no common scale of measurement with the old."[2]

Seeking the eye of an expert, Adams recruited the distinguished physicist and founder of the Smithsonian Astrophysical Observatory, Samuel Pierpont Langley, to serve as his guide in the Gallery. Langley offered a practical assessment of the apparatuses on display and Henry used this information to extrapolate a deeper cultural significance. His observation of the steam-driven dynamo in the *Education* remains to this day a profound, disquieting, and elegiac articulation of humanity's Faustian bargain with technology: "As he grew accustomed to the great gallery of machines, he began to feel the forty-foot dynamos as a moral force, much as the early Christians felt the Cross. . . . Before the end, one began to pray to it; inherited instinct taught the natural expression of man before silent and infinite force." The human desire for communion with the "infinite" endured, Adams noted, even as traditional faith receded before the onslaught of contemporary science. Placed in historical context, the Gallery of Machines, a vast monument to the world's most advanced technology, represented an old, indestructible idea housed now in a new electric church.[3]

As the summer of 1900 progressed, Henry navigated emotionally and intellectually between two worlds. His meditative journey among the dynamos was paired with an intensive study of the influential thirteenth-century theologian Thomas Aquinas, some of this material soon to make its way into *Mont-Saint-Michel and Chartres*. Adams's adventures in Thomism shaped his thinking on the contrast between the medieval and modern worlds, the divergence, as he put it, between the dynamo, the "male," capital-centric sphere of scientific reason and flux, and the Virgin, the "female," church-centric field of imagination and tradition. Leaving philosophy (and theology) aside, he took from Aquinas an aesthetic sensitivity evident, he argued, in church architecture, music, and iconography. Compared to St. Thomas's sublime scholastic authority, "all modern systems," Adams insisted, "are complex and chaotic, crowded with self-contradictions, anomalies, impracticable functions, and outworn inheritances."[4] All resembled the apparently confused man reflexively offering a silent invocation before a brute, mute machine.

The Paris Exposition, combined with his Normandy travels and still earlier excursion to Chicago's World's Fair, provided Henry with the creative tensions and materials to embark upon his last great writings. These offerings, many scholars have argued, constitute his most lasting literary achievements. Both the *Chartres,* a selective consideration of feudal France, and the iconic *Education* advanced their author's fullest statements on the duality — faith versus reason, temple versus motor — of Western civilization and the supposed long decline of creative inspiration. But before committing the Virgin, "the greatest and most mysterious of all energies," to paper, he discovered that still more immediate and earthly matters required his attention.[5] With America suddenly a growing power and Hay, as secretary of state, nominally at its helm, Adams might well have wondered of his own role as a Washington wise man in a republic leaning precariously toward empire.

552

45
LAMB AMONG LIONS

As Henry entered his sexagenarian decade, evidence of aging began to press upon him. During a visit to a Parisian antique dealer, so he told Elizabeth Cameron, "I happened to . . . ask a question, and, to my consternation, my French tumbled out all in a heap. The words came out without connection." His correspondence shows that he complained of rheumatism and dyspepsia and put himself under the knife of a London surgeon to have a wen (protruding cyst) removed from a shoulder: "I feared [I] might . . . look like a camel if I left it alone." Ailing teeth drove him to a Paris dentist because, he said, "Even at my age I am unwilling to have false teeth or to go toothless." He began to take increased notice of the obituaries (and rumors of impending deaths) in the several papers he perused, observing as well the published details of probated wills. He enjoyed knowing who got what. He remained a tireless reader, a chronic gossip, and an

553

almost desperate traveler, but the pace began to slow. "My machine," he wrote to a niece about this time, "is quite worn."[1]

But worn, torn, or otherwise, the sudden occupational ascendancy of men in Henry's immediate orbit failed not to kindle his interest. Hay's State Department appointment coincided with Lodge's emergence as a force in the U.S. Senate and Roosevelt's improbable presidency, assumed after the September 1901 assassination of William McKinley at the Pan-American Exposition in Buffalo. Knowing these men — one a close friend, the other a former student, and the third an occasional dining companion — brought Adams, weaned on memories of presidential relatives, as close to actual power as he would ever come. "In a small society, such ties between houses become political and social force," he remarked in the *Education* on this unusual period. "Without intention or consciousness, they fix one's status in the world. Whatever one's preferences in politics might be, one's house was bound to the Republican interest when sandwiched between . . . John Hay and Cabot Lodge, with Theodore Roosevelt equally at home in them all."[2] Despite this image of a cozy Lafayette Square quartet, generational and temperamental differences kept Adams and Hay at a certain remove from Lodge and Roosevelt. There would be no Hearts Redux. The graying, gimlet-eyed

Cabot, so Henry insisted, had grown pompous and imperious, a secure Senate seat only exacerbating his already pronounced sense of privilege. Adams's relationship with Roosevelt, rarely warm, often idled near mutual contempt.

Twenty years Henry's junior, TR, a caricaturist's dream of chubby cheeks, flagrant teeth, and granny glasses, sized up the older man as a chronic cynic, too shrewd, detached, and cerebral for his own good. Adams returned this aspersion with relish, never quite shaking the suspicion that Roosevelt resembled in his dapper Rough Riders ensemble an overly excited eight-year-old. The two men invariably grated on each other; the president's typically buoyant, often artless, and inevitably insistent nature made for a poor complement to Henry's ironic disposition. During a casual dinner with Adams, the Cabots, and the Hays in January 1902, the new president, all of four months in office, presumed to instruct Henry before the others. "He lectures me on history as though he were a high-school pedagogue," Henry complained to Lizzie. "Of course I fall back instantly on my protective pose of ignorance, which aggravates his assertions, and so we drift steadily apart." Two months later he fumed to Gaskell that America was being "run by a school-boy barely out of college."[3]

For both TR and Cabot, intimacy with Adams and Hay meant a certain vicarious connection to American history, both made and written. Henry's people were enshrined in the nation's textbooks as revolutionaries, while Hay had served as Lincoln's assistant and private secretary. Each of the four could claim to be historians, though Adams and Hay were clearly a cut above their younger colleagues. Henry's *History* and Hay and Nicolay's *Lincoln* were considered masterworks, while Lodge's filiopietistic profiles of early republic conservatives — Washington, Hamilton, and Daniel Webster — and Roosevelt's drama-filled studies, *The Naval War of 1812* and *The Winning of the West,* occupy distinctly lower rungs.

For a number of reasons these men never engaged in outright competition. Adams and Hay refused to vie for elective office and enjoyed reputations as cultured gentlemen who traveled, collected art, and, in Hay's case, wrote poetry. They appreciated satire, could be sharp-tonged, and savored Washington society; they were in love with the same inaccessible woman. And having served the Union during the Civil War (if not in the field), they could be said to have had little to prove. Lodge, by contrast, was eager to make his mark on American diplomacy. An unapologetic imperialist, he thought McKinley and Hay had lingered indecisively on the question of annexing the Philippines. Resentful of such criticism, Hay once complained to Adams that Lodge caused him more difficulty "than all the governments of Europe, Asia and the Sulu Islands, and all the Senators from the wild West and the Congressmen from the rebel confederacy."[4]

As virtual H Street housemates, Adams and Hay fell into a pattern of daily late afternoon walks, on which the secretary unburdened himself of various State Department pressures. In a note to Lizzie Cameron, Henry briefly discussed the nature of these excursions:

> Of course my chief visitor is John Hay who comes to take me to walk at four o'clock, and . . . occasionally dines here. John . . . is singularly detached. His attitude towards Theodore is that of a benevolent and amused uncle. He has usually some story to tell, or some outburst to repeat, partly with fun and occasionally with surprise or even astonishment, but never as though he felt any responsibility.[5]

In his own letters to Lizzie, Hay portrayed Adams as a welcome fund of comic relief from the rigors of office: "I go to the Department at nine and work till five and then carry home a little portfolio of annoyances. . . . If it were not for the blessed Dor [a nickname for Adams] my lot would be most pitiable. He takes me for a walk in the gloaming and predicts catastrophes and ruin till my own cares fade away in the light of the coming cataclysm."[6]

As a loyal companion, Adams nodded sympathetically at Hay's concerns, knew his place, and generally agreed with his friend's judgments. In February 1904, the month the Russo-Japanese War began, he wrote to Lizzie, "Hay came at four to walk, and talked an hour straight, about Russia and the situation. We fought over the whole field, as you may imagine, and differed only as to the measurements of our own dangers."[7] Hay's first biographer, William Roscoe Thayer, came to the conclusion that Adams exerted an "indirect, almost subconscious influence" on the secretary. His *Life and Letters of John Hay* appeared in 1915, a decade after his subject's death, though Thayer had access to Cameron's and Adams's impressions. In a 1916 letter to Cameron, Thayer maintained that he could see no explicit connection between Adams and State Department decisions:

As to Henry Adams: I undertook the work without any preconceived notions; but many persons told me, as you intimate, that Mr. Adams really guided Hay's policy as Secretary of State. There is nothing to indicate this in the record. The great pilot after 1901

558

was Roosevelt, who put through several of the chief measures which were commonly attributed to Hay. . . . Mr. Adams himself assures me that Hay rarely consulted him, or any other friend, on State Department matters.[8]

It is unlikely, of course, that had Henry strongly impacted Hay's thinking, he would have told Thayer. Among closer companions, however, he occasionally suggested a kind of informal working relationship with the president and his leading men. He wrote Gaskell late in the fall of 1901, "I am afraid to go home and get kicked by my triumvirate friends — Roosevelt, Hay and Lodge — who are now running our foreign affairs and have a way of running them in my house at the cost of my comfort." This wry report proved prophetic. In early 1905 Adams, at the instigation of the White House, welcomed to his home the British diplomat Cecil Spring Rice, on leave from St. Petersburg, where he served as chargé d'affaires. While parking his toothbrush on H Street, Spring Rice carried on private discussions with Roosevelt regarding the Russo-Japanese War. The conflict interested Henry, for it seemed to confirm Brooks's geopolitical outline of rising (Japan) and declining (Russia) powers while lending itself to the kind of statistical sampling of raw materials and energy then much on Adams's mind. He believed, so he told Spring Rice, that Russia's defeat in the war prefaced America's own eventual downturn. "We can not run our machine another thirty years," he remembered the dynamos of Chicago and Paris, "without some similar convulsion."[9]

Whether or not Henry actually believed a looming crack-up threatened the United States (his "thirty years" guess works out to 1935 — the depths of the Great Depression), he certainly worried over America's strategic role in the world. In 1901 he condemned several examples of what he considered Western overreach, panning British efforts to subdue the Dutch Boers in South Africa, questioning a mainly European alliance's response to the anticolonial Boxer Rebellion in China (1899–1901), and scolding America's brutal ongoing war (1899–1902) against the Philippine Republic. He saw in these counterrevolutionary efforts on the part of the major powers a self-defeating strategy. "I hold our Philippine excursion to be a false start in a wrong direction," he wrote Brooks, "and one that is more likely to blunt our energies than to guide them. It is a mere repetition of the errors of Spain and England." Having little faith in the efficacy of old empires, he proposed a new structure of statecraft, later, under Woodrow Wilson, to take the name "liberal internationalism." Reflecting on the futures of various emancipated or soon to be emancipated peoples, Adams believed that only the United States could lead the world forward. European colonialism, he contended, "creates, nourishes and preserves more dangers than it eliminates." He suggested to Brooks that the New World's defining historical moment was now at hand: "We all agree that the old, uneconomical races, Boers, Chinese, Irish, Russians, Turks, and negroes, must somehow be brought to work into our system. The whole question is how to do it. Europe has always said: Buy or Fight! So the Irish, the Boers and the Chinese are likely to remain unassimilated. We Americans ought to invent a new method."[10]

But even when calling for Washington to take the reins, Henry still demurred, still sometimes posed as a Populist or a Silverite on the sinking side of history's beautiful losers. He occasionally mocked Hay's pretentions to American hegemony in Asia — "Your open door is already off its hinges," he wrote his fellow Heart during the Boxer Rebellion — and claimed to be making his stand with modernity's malcontents. As if it were not enough to be a twelfth-century Norman or brother to a Tahitian prince, he took on still more identities in his quest to resist the colonizers: "I who am a worm — and trodden upon, at that — am quite Chinese, Asiatic, Boer, and anarchist."[11]

Parsing Adams's views on the emergent American Empire can be an exercise in ambiguity. He seemed to grudgingly accept the necessity of U.S. global leadership while at the same time supposing that this path led straight to the kind of consolidated capitalist West that he so loathed. This conundrum nettled Henry, who, as usual, sought insight through travel. Certain of Britain's eclipse and doubtful of Germany's global reach, he identified Russia, with its sprawling population, immense territory, and vast resources, as America's likely future adversary. As the old imperialism wound down, he was determined to see for himself what fresh menace might follow in its place.

46

IN THE LAND OF THE CZARS

Over three crowded weeks in August and
September 1901, Henry journeyed with the
Lodges to Russia, eager to survey the Ro-
manovs' "century behind" civilization.[1] The
trip afforded Adams the opportunity to
reflect on the accuracy of Brooks's *Law of
Civilization and Decay,* which questioned the
lazy assumption among the Anglo-American
elite that liberal democracies were soon to
encircle the globe. Like his brother, Henry
rejected what he considered to be a glib
ideological argument for one frankly materialistic. He deemed population, industrial
capacity, and land resources as far more telling triggers of power than polling booths. Two
countries in particular impressed Adams as
having the inside track in the race to build,
exploit, and extract. The United States' bour-
geoning size and strength left him little doubt
of its sunny place in the Darwinian order,
presumably putting Europe in shadow. But
Russia intrigued Henry; if currently running

behind America, its undeniable potential to win the evolutionary sweepstakes and dictate terms in both Asia and the Continent could not be ignored. As the new international structure began to take shape in the wake of German unification, Britain's gradual decline, and Spain's expulsion from the Western Hemisphere, America and Russia — one a democracy, the other an autocracy — struck him as the likely beneficiaries.

Henry's Russian sojourn followed a desultory German holiday in late July. He traveled with the Lodges to Rothenburg ob der Tauber, a town in the Franconia region of Bavaria famed for its medieval architecture. Following a rainy day (a perfect excuse to luxuriate over "good fourteenth century glass") the party continued east to Bayreuth for the city's annual music festival performing the operas of Richard Wagner. The scores were enormous and presented just as written, with no intermission, no concessions made for the patience or comfort of the audience. After sitting through hours of *Das Rheingold,* a less than impressed Henry wrote to Lizzie, "I was nearly asphyxiated, and thought the performance rather mediocre. . . . I am quite clear that for a delicate digestion like mine, with a tendency to insomnia, the Wagnerian beer-and-sausage should be taken in short gulps, and at concerts."[2]

Presumably to cleanse their Wagner-sodden

palates, Adams and the Lodges went next to Salzburg, where they attended a Mozart festival. But the city, Henry discovered to his disappointment, was "a fashionable summer haunt . . . filled with Americans." The ubiquity of U.S. English grated on his ears, and a tourist collective — "Everybody looks like everybody else" — applauded the "very pretty, and easy, and familiar" music meant to content them.[3] A little bored, he noted that a certain royal personage in one performance hall resembled a prominent New York banker. As the festival wound down, Lodge unexpectedly, and perhaps citing his seat on the Senate Foreign Relations Committee as a pretext, expressed an interest in observing conditions in Russia firsthand. Enjoying as always "Sister Anne's" company, Henry decided to go along, and in a succession of dreary night trains they headed east to Moscow.

Adams had thought often of Russia that year. In February he had written to Brooks that America (in which he included Central and South America) should turn isolationist and "stand on our internal resources alone." He believed it likely that with the United States tending to more local concerns and the older western European powers in eclipse, "Germany and Russia [would] try to run the machine." Should that be the case, he assured Brooks, "they cannot be shut out." He then

565

wrote Cecil Spring Rice that Russia presented to the thoughtful observer a true enigma. Espying a largely peasant-ridden country through maps, atlases, and statistical tables, Adams nurtured the suspicion that it lurched into the new century a "colossal dwarf," equipped with tremendous potential for growth. The course of Eastern development confused him, for it represented such a strong rebuke to the liberal lines of social and economic progress embraced by the West. "Behind that oriental curtain of Russo-Germanism," he confessed to Lizzie six months before setting foot in Russia, "I can divine nothing."[4] Raising his gaze beyond the familiar London-Paris–New York axis, he hoped now to appraise the dynamo's prospects in the land of the czars.

Passing through Warsaw ("a big, bustling city"), Adams took notice of its large Jewish population, which he called "a startling revelation." He looked upon British and American Jews as the couriers of modernism and found this formerly unrealized "backwards vs. forwards" distinction among Semitic peoples fascinating. Simultaneously repelled by the archaic material culture of this Polish population yet attracted to its "edge" rather than "center" existence, he warmed to it, as he had earlier embraced aspects of Polynesian and Latin American "primitivism." Undoubtedly he saw a bit of

566

himself in the occupants of this rustic city. Here lay another kind of Quincy, an eighteenth- or even sixteenth-century holdout to the mass of organizing energy then rippling through western Europe. "The Jews and I are the only curious antiquities in it," he wrote to Lizzie. "My only merit as a curio is antiquity, but the Jew is also a curiosity."[5]

Entering into the Russian heartland aboard a bobbing Moscow-bound train, Henry meditated in the thick August heat on the living peasant past. The vast landscape, filled with drifting peoples in seemingly random passage, fully occupied his imagination. Years later he wrote sublimely of this thirty-hour journey, "From the car-window one seemed to float past undulations of nomad life, — herders deserted by their leaders and herds, — wandering waves stopped in their wanderings, — waiting for their winds or warriors to return and lead them westward; tribes that had camped, like Khirgis, for the season, and had lost the means of motion without acquiring the habit of permanence. They waited and suffered." During the trip Adams experienced the vicarious sensation of entering a younger America. The size of the country overpowered him and he wondered at its latent capacity for economic development. "Small things do not seem at home in it," he assured Lizzie. The route to Moscow confirmed his notion that Russia lay at least three generations behind the United States. Massive forests dotted with log cabins dominated the landscape, and widely dispersed industryless cities offered the only signs of modern amenities. "Her scale is greater, but her energy less" than Europe's, Adams informed Hay. "She is still metaphysical, religious, military, Byzantine; a sort of Mongol tribe, almost absolutely unable to think in western lines."[6]

In Poland and Russia, Adams happily reported, the alliance of religion and government, economy and thought remained firmly tied to older conditions and traditions. "From the first glimpse . . . of the Polish Jew at the accidental railway-station," he later observed, "to the last vision of the Russian peasant, lighting his candle and kissing his Ikon before the railway Virgin in the station at St. Petersburg, all was logical, conservative, christian and anarchic." Not even the rhapsodized virtues of medieval Normandy could match the Virgin's vital, living presence in Moscow. Attending high mass at the immense Cathedral of the Redeemer (destroyed by Stalin in 1931 and rebuilt and reconsecrated in 2000), he felt a spiritual connection that had long eluded him in the secular West. "At Chartres I have only the empty shell, and have to imagine the life," he explained the difference to a niece. "Here I find the life absolutely unchanged; just what it was all over Europe in 1100."[7]

From Moscow, Henry and the Lodges traveled to St. Petersburg, which, Henry reported, felt "cold like October." There, Lodge had a number of conversations with government officials, including Sergei Witte, the influential policymaker and champion of Russian industrialization. With the aid of Anna Cabot Lodge's first cousin, Herbert Peirce, third assistant secretary of state, Adams enjoyed a private evening tour of the Hermitage. Nearly a century earlier his grandparents John Quincy and Louisa Catherine Adams had lived for several years in St. Petersburg as the American minister to Russia and his wife. On occasion they attended plays and operas at the handsome Hermitage Theater. Henry now roamed this same complex of connected buildings with real interest. And despite the prevalence of Dutch paintings — a matter of personal distaste — he delighted in the vast gallery, visiting it twice during his short stay. "The Hermitage pictures are next to the Madrid for condition," he wrote Lizzie. "I am not disappointed."[8]

In early September Adams and the Lodges split up, the latter deciding to return to western Europe by way of Berlin. Having no interest in revisiting the city whose language and lecture system had long ago defeated him — "forty years of varied emotions had not deadened [my] memories of Berlin" — Henry went alone to Stockholm and then Trond-heim, Norway, the old Viking capital, and still farther north to Hammerfest.[9] There, in the land of the Lapps and the reindeer, near the silent Arctic Circle, he witnessed the brilliant Northern Lights, whose dominant visual presence and striking colors eclipsed Trond-heim's functional urban electric illumination that never varied, never broke, and never provoked among the sleepy Trondheimians a sense of wonder, awe, or adoration.

Adams's opinion of Slavic supremacy in the East varied over the years, particularly fol-lowing the Russo-Japanese War (1904–5). He thereafter worried about the health of the czar's empire, seeing in its potential collapse a fracturing of states and peoples from Europe to the Pacific. In Russia he thus observed a possible template for the process of civilizational entropy that he fully expected to one day break down the modern industrial, imperial order. Peasants and gold-bugs alike, he surmised, were equally compromised in the cold science of decline.

■ ■ ■ ■

RESONANCE

■ ■ ■ ■

The only record I care to leave is St Gaudens' figure at Rock Creek. . . . We shall tell
no lies.

Henry Adams, 1915

47
NONE BUT THE SAINTS

In early 1903 Adams put the finishing touches
on *Mont-Saint-Michel and Chartres,* his idiosyncratic homage to high medievalism. A
candidly subjective reckoning of the past, the
book materialized from a number of its
author's private concerns and interests.
Doubtful of booming America's ability to
match the cultured achievements of feudal
Europe, Henry framed the Western mind in
the contrasting "racial" categories of Norman
mysticism and Anglo-Saxon empiricism. He
further employed gendered categories when
thinking architecturally about the era, inter-
preting Mont-Saint-Michel, the island fortress a half-mile off France's Normandy coast
near Avranches, as a "masculine" statement
of the Middle Ages; looking for a "feminine"
counterpoint, he adopted the Virgin, palpably
residing, so he swore, in the stunning Chartres Cathedral, earthly seat of the Virgin Mary
and indicative of the poetic mind in a pre-
scientific age.[1]

Aside from passing as an ancient Norman narrator, Henry drew upon a host of more contemporary concerns while drafting the *Chartres*. Perhaps most obviously, the financial Panic of 1893 and recent scramble for colonies called the country's republican identity into question. More broadly the long post–Civil War "incorporation of America" encapsulated decades of labor unrest, westward expansion, and urban-industrial development that cohered in a new regime of manufacturing monopolies and middle-class consumers.[2] Adams, we know, remained a restless critic of this ascendant order. His resistance came largely through irony and deflection and in his satiric preference for more traditional civilizations, be they in Asia, in Hispanic America's Latin diaspora, or in the religio-cultural setting of feudal Europe. Accordingly, his spacious conception of the Virgin exceeds by far its presumptive Franco-medieval roots.

The same might just as easily be said of Adams's tender impression of Chartres Cathedral, which also emerged from multiple origins. As a young man Henry discovered James Russell Lowell's poem "A Day at Chartres," later published in the *Atlantic Monthly* as "The Cathedral." While a Harvard undergraduate, he gravitated to Lowell's opinions and preferences, describing him affectionately as "a new element in the boy's

574

life." Embracing what he took to be a kindred spirit, Adams claimed in the *Education* that Lowell had "revolted against the yoke of coming capitalism, its money-lenders, its bank directors, and its railway magnates."[3]

Several of the themes addressed by Adams in his own work on Chartres — communion with a higher power, architecture as a cultural language, and preference for an ordered civilization innocent of the erratic gyrations embedded in democratic capitalism — are anticipated in Lowell's verse. "The Cathedral" describes the pre-Renaissance world as "so strangely beautiful," and Lowell, as if to prod Henry into adopting his Norse mien, describes himself as "a happy Goth." He distrusts the technical-mechanical age with its predisposition for the rational, the secular, and the controlled:

> This age that blots out life with
>   question-marks,
> This nineteenth century with its knife and
>   glass
> That make thought physical, and thrust far
>   off
> The Heaven, so neighborly with man of
>   old,
> To voids sparse-sown with alienated stars.
> . . . .
> Science was Faith once; Faith were
>   Science now.

Lowell concludes that the nineteenth century lacks something vital, moral, and aesthetic. Its scientific achievements may dazzle the mind, but these can scarcely conceal the era's evident deficit of higher insight and spiritual faith. "This is no age to get cathedrals built," he quailed in a ringing line that finds new life in the *Education:* "All the steam in the world could not, like the Virgin, build Chartres."[4]

Other men in Henry's milieu almost certainly influenced his thinking on the Virgin. Brooks's provocative *Law of Civilization and Decay* undoubtedly drew his brother's attention to Chartres's splendid stained glass:

In France the churches long were miracles; the chronicles are filled with the revelations vouchsafed the monks; and none can cross the threshold of one of these noble monuments and fail to grasp its meaning. They are the most vigorous of all expressions of fear of the unseen. The Gothic architect heeded no living potentate; he held kings in contempt, and oftener represented them thrust down into hell than seated on their thrones. With the enemy who lurked in darkness none but the saint could cope, and them he idealized. No sculpture is more terrible than the demons on the walls of Rheims, none more majestic and pathetic than that over the door of the Virgin at Paris,

576

while no colour ever equalled the windows of Saint Denis and Chartres.[5]

And beyond Brooks's romantic reflections it is further possible that Clarence King, to Henry a "natural" man unencumbered by overcivilization, suggested the Dionysian virtues of a sensual, spontaneous existence. "It was not the modern woman that interested him," Adams wrote of King, a year after completing the first draft of the *Chartres*, "it was the archaic female, with instincts and without intellect. At best King had but a poor opinion of intellect, chiefly because he found it so defective an instrument, but he admitted that it was all the male had to live upon; while the female was rich in the inheritance of every animated energy back to the polyps and the crystals."[6] The separate spheres of male intellect and female instinct, as enlisted by King, are replete in the *Chartres.* If unoriginal to Adams, he nevertheless amplifies and extends their categorical possibilities in the interest of reducing empiricism to a decidedly lesser virtue.

The appearance of the *Chartres* began a new phase in Adams's writing. Much of his previous work had borne the unmistakable imprint of the era's self-conscious scientific training. But the *Chartres* is by turns literary, suggestive, and subjective — it is the work of an author unapologetically imposing his personality on his material. Unlike the orthodox *History*, with its political personalities and implied masculine audience, the *Chartres* assumes an avuncular voice gently instructing a sociable circle of interested females. In its preface Adams promises readers an imaginative journey: "The following pages, then, are written for nieces, or for those who are willing, for the time, to be nieces in wish. . . . The party, then, with such variations of detail as may suit its tastes, has sailed from New York, let us say, early in June for an entire summer in France." Docking at Cherbourg, or perhaps Le Havre, the troupe will travel by rail and motorcar to Mont-Saint-Michel and there take rooms at La Mère Poulard, a hotel and restaurant founded in 1888 by Victor and Annette Poulard. Frequented by Adams as well as many notable guests over the years, including Ernest Hemingway, Yves Saint Laurent, and Leopold II, king of the Belgians, the establishment continues in operation to this day.[7]

The *Chartres* differs further from the *History* in its near avoidance of conventional chronology. Henry interpreted the American story as a relentless progression of markets, migrations, and popular politics. His study of the Gothic period, by contrast, is a thematic enterprise emphasizing continuity over uncertainty, craft over economy. In 1911, while preparing a revised printing of the volume, he wrote to Ward Thoron, his sometime research assistant and later nephew-in-law, acknowledging the book's limitations: "In reprinting my volume, I am struck with its inadequacy. When I think that it leaves out the Crusades, and the whole of politics, I wonder how to make it stand up."[8]

Another and perhaps more serious short-coming of the book is its French-centric view of the Middle Ages. Aside from briefly assaying a smattering of Italian saints and making a reference to Robin Hood, Adams offers readers a geographically and thus artistically and religiously constrained Gothic era. There are no discussions of English monasteries, German cathedrals, the Old Norse sagas, or the long Iberian Reconquista (711–1492) from its Islamic rulers. One finds, rather, wonderfully descriptive reflections on sparkling high rose windows, an informative disquisition on the conceptualist ideas of Abelard, and a concise sermon cum seminar on the epic poem *La Chanson de Roland.* All are important to understanding medieval civilization, but they tell only a truncated tale. Feudalism's impact is neither the story of a country nor even that of a continent; its dimensions are international, as Adams, a Goth of the heart by way of Boston, surely knew.

One might, therefore, justly criticize Henry's stress on the putative unity of medieval civilization. The period suffered through an abundance of panics, plagues, and papal disputes, including the Great Famine (1315–17), the devastating Black Death that soon followed, and the Investiture Controversy, a church-state conflict that led to decades of civil war in Germany. His discussion of church affairs, cursorily presented as a harmonious history, concludes before the Western Schism (1378–1417) paired off multiple popes vying for parishioner loyalty. Adams erred further in presuming a kind of solid Catholic phalanx in Europe. Pockets of paganism were a vital feature of Gothic peasant civilization and influenced the early medieval church.

To be fair, however, Adams sought not to write a definitive study but rather to produce a selective interpretation of a sensibility. Accordingly, he wrote against prevailing opinion. America's most popular treatment of feudalism was perhaps at that time Mark Twain's satiric *A Connecticut Yankee in King Arthur's Court* (1889), which, among its many targets, poked fun at both priestcraft and divine-right kingdoms. The novel's protagonist, Hank Morgan, a time-traveling Yankee, winds up in sixth-century England, where he manages to briefly modernize and democratize the people. Morgan is a symbol of reason (his science is greater than Merlin's mysticism), a booster of industrialization (his loyalists wipe out the old knight class with dynamite and a few Gatling guns), and a champion of republicanism (he aims to turn England against aristocracy). But for all of his advanced ideas, Twain's Yankee is defeated in the end. True, "slavery was dead and gone; all men were equal before the law; taxation had been equalized," though the very peasants he wished to elevate missed their old worship, rites, and rituals. Morgan's astute lieutenant informs him that the weight of the past works assuredly against his success: "Did you think you had educated the superstition out of those people?" Twain and Adams agree on the potency of a medieval mentality, but on little else. Twain disdains the peasants' devotion and has little doubt that remnants of feudalism continue to (negatively) impact modern life; Adams, of course, mourns feudalism as a spent historical force. He writes wistfully of the Virgin's cessation as a source of authority, to be replaced by the rising Puritan, the thrifty merchant, and the dynamic industrialist — in a word, by Twain's inevitable, indestructible Yankee.[9]

But Henry knew that even the Yankee's latest deity, the scientist, appealed to faith, producing reports, experiments, and data unintelligible to most people. In struggling over the arcane language of physicists and

581

chemists, lay audiences reprised the experience of sitting through a Latin mass. "The atomic theory; the correlation and conservation of energy; the mechanical theory of the universe; the kinetic theory of gases, and Darwin's law of Natural Selection, were examples of what a young man had to take on trust," Adams wrote. "Neither he nor anyone else knew enough to verify them."[10] Henry's trust ran only surface deep, however, and he doubted science's confident promises to reveal the universe's secrets. Like the most myopically written history, he argued, it simply posited a false sense of order and structure that ignored humanity's long and bloody record of violence, ignorance, and upheaval. Preferring to invent his own myths, he rallied to the Virgin.

In December 1904 Adams had privately printed one hundred copies of the *Chartres,* what he called his book of "Miracles." Inevitably some of the copies found their way into the hands of readers beyond Henry's elect, many of whom pressed its author for a wider distribution. In 1912 he revised the study and authorized a second edition of five hundred, which he again quietly dispersed. The following year Ralph Adams Cram (no relation), a leading figure in Gothic revival architecture, convinced Adams to let the American Institute of Architects sponsor the sale of the manuscript by the Boston publisher Hough-ton Mifflin. "Ever since I first became ac-quainted with this book," he wrote Henry, "I have talked about it without cessation. There are hundreds of people who want it, and who should have it." Henry played coy — "No one wants to read the book, don't be foolish" — before happily giving way: "Oh, very well, be it on your own head; I give you the book. You may do what you like with it."[11]

The new edition of the *Chartres* appeared in November 1913, much to Henry's amuse-ment. "Here am I, telling everyone that I am quite dotty and bed-ridden," he laughed to Gaskell, "and the papers reviewing me as a youthful beginner."[12] The book's polite reception seemed a validation of its author's distinctive historical outlook. Mere presidents and gold-bugs invariably came and went, but the Virgin offered something more vital to the human condition. Her maternal touch grew increasingly important to Henry as he faced in the new century the inexorable cycle of diminishing years, waning strength, and the irreplaceable loss of old friends.

48
STRANDED

On July 1, 1905, John Hay died of a lingering heart ailment at his Lake Sunapee country house near Newbury, New Hampshire. Adams, an ocean away in Paris, took the news personally. "Hay's death strands me," he wrote to Lizzie Cameron on the 2nd. "I am now left quite alone." Agreeably acquainted for over forty years, Adams and Hay had drawn close on the Lafayette Square social circuit, were occasional travel companions, and, as the years passed and the men in power grew younger, recognized each other as relic survivors of an older republic. On any number of subjects their correspondence slipped easily into a familiar and often farcical inflection — more controlled on Hay's side, more unbuttoned on Henry's. Of late they had warmly disdained the self-important Lodge and believed Roosevelt a fatuous bully; on a cure, they had spent much of April touring the Italian Riviera before moving on to Germany. Now bereft of Hay's familiar presence, Adams felt isolated: "My last hold on the world is lost with him. I am too old to make new efforts or care for new interest. . . . I have clung on to his activities till now, because they were his, but except as his they have no concern for me, and I have no more strength for them. He and I began life together. We will stop together."[1]

For years Adams had quietly predicted Hay's broken health. "I think [him] very far from strong," he wrote to Brooks in 1901, "and doubt his ability to remain in office." In the winter of 1904 he warned Lizzie, "Hay . . . is still too weak to walk around the square. At the same time, he is regularly besieged and overrun by diplomates and colleagues." The following year Hay himself pled infirmity. "I have great doubts whether this tenement of clay which I inhabit will hold together," he informed the British historian George Trevelyan. "Walking with Henry Adams the other day, I expressed my regret that by the time I got out of office, I should have lost the faculty of enjoyment. As you know Adams, you can understand the dry malice with which he replied: 'Make your mind easy on that score, sonny! You've lost it now!' "[2] Henry noticed that his friend tired easily, had visibly aged in the State Department, and suffered from recurring bouts of bronchitis. He may have known too that Hay now kept a journal, had made out a will, and, as if passing a gift on to

585

posterity, recently sat for John Singer Sargent, the leading portrait painter of the Edwardian era. When his friend died, Adams took little time apportioning blame.

"Politics poisoned him," he flatly told Hay's widow, Clara. "The Senate and the Diplomates killed him." He wrote much the same to Lizzie, though adding in a score-settling kind of way that "political bravos like Cabot and Theodore" were equally accountable.[3] More generally Henry supposed that Hay, a poet, novelist, and historian, stood no chance of surviving in the contemporary climate; his demise seemed to offer proof that the "best" of his generation, those sensitive, literary, and intellectual, were being summarily ground down in the process of empire-building and fortune-making. Naturally Henry, himself sensitive, literary, and intellectual, assumed that Hay's passing pointed to his own.

No one understood better than Adams the obligation to commemorate a loved one. Decade after decade, generation after generation, his family had long honored its fallen with carefully crafted editions of letters, biographies, and diary extracts. Naturally, Clara Hay asked Henry to write her husband's biography. A "print memorial" from a dear friend, a man recognized as one of the nation's most distinguished historians, seemed an altogether natural and fitting tribute. "No one else," William James told

Adams, "will ever be so qualified." And Henry, it is true, knew how to salute a fallen colleague. He had recently acknowledged the death of yet another Heart, Clarence King, with a brilliant essay that appeared in *Clarence King Memoirs: The Helmet of Mambrino* (1904). Published for the Century Association in homage to "their distinguished fellow-member," the memorial stressed King's remarkable capacity for friendship, his infectious humor, and his several Cuban adventures. "He was the ideal companion of our lives," Adams mused.[4]

But Henry had no interest in writing Hay's biography. A light, short piece on King, to be circulated among a select circle, allowed its author to emphasize what he wished, suppress the rest, and put friendship above the historical record. A study of Hay, on the other hand, would require an altogether different effort and set of expectations. Hay's life was in many respects public property. He had served in Lincoln's White House, represented the United States overseas, and headed the State Department for nearly seven years. No mere confection of warm remembrances would do. And Henry knew that any biography he set his hand to would be taken as a scholarly work, certain to be measured against the *Gallatin* and the *Randolph* as well as the *History*'s finely honed profiles.

In March 1907 he wrote to Anna Cabot

Lodge of his reticence to dissect Hay's life: "I never knew a mere biography that did not hurt its subject. One must dodge it as one can." At the same time he observed to the historian James Ford Rhodes, "Unless a man of [Hay's] importance takes the precaution to write his own life, no one else should risk it for him, in the character of a friend."[5] Seeking to prevent such "a friend" — or an independent scholar — from digging into his own affairs, Adams had only a few months earlier completed a draft of the *Education.* To now produce an exhaustive "Life of Hay," or some such construction, would defy the logic of that protective exercise and perhaps suggest a "Life of Adams" to any number of intrepid researchers.

Clara Hay eventually backed away from recruiting Henry — or anyone else — to sketch her husband's biography. But she remained determined that some type of print tribute be undertaken and successfully enlisted Adams's editorial aid in a project to be published in three volumes under the title *Letters of John Hay and Extracts from Diary.* She wrote to her husband's chief correspondents, including John Nicolay, Theodore Roosevelt, and the former *New York Tribune* editor Whitelaw Reid, asking that they forward their collections of Hay's letters to Adams. With delicacy in mind, Henry, who contributed correspondence from his own private file, never asked Lizzie to share her store. He had considered it fair in the King memorial to draw attention to his subject's attraction to non-Anglo peoples — "He loved the Spaniard as he loved the negro and the Indian and all the primitives, because they were not academic" — as his clubby readership already knew of King's autonomous tastes. But Hay had forged a prominent public career while accommodating the Victorian standards of his day. Clara, perhaps realizing as much, did well in securing Henry's assistance with her husband's correspondence; he took seriously the sensitive issues of privacy, reputation, and the impending judgment of history.[6]

The best collection of letters belonged to Reid, a longtime power broker in Republican circles. After receiving Henry's request for correspondence, he replied asking for guidance. Hay, he reported, had habitually closed his communications with such instructions as "burn when read," *"delenda,"* and "destroy." Obviously Reid, thinking his friend merely overcautious, had kept the letters. But should they now be more generally circulated? Henry responded curiously: "As editor I have always strained liberality of assent. No editor ever spared any one of my family that I know of, and, in return, we have commonly printed all that concerned other people. Whether this state of war ever injured anyone I do not know; but it lasts to this day, and makes me rather indifferent to conventional restraints."[7]

Considering Henry's proficiency in the art of evasion, this remark is either innocent in the extreme or, more likely, self-serving. The exclusion of Hay's flirtatious letters to Cameron from the memorial is one example; Adams's highly selective *Education,* for which he had just read the proof sheets, is yet another. To say that "no editor ever spared" the family, moreover, is a polite fiction, for the Adamses themselves decided what would and would not go into their many homemade memorials. To give but a single illustration, Henry convinced Brooks about this time to suppress his biography of John Quincy Adams, their grandfather's labors for slaveholder presidents cited as the unpardonable offense. "The sum of it," he wrote Brooks, is "that he had no business to serve Jefferson or Jackson; that he knew better; that he did it for personal ambition quite as much as for patriotism."[8] The manuscript has sat quietly since then in the Massachusetts Historical Society.

Henry took no joy in editing Hay's letters, though he counted himself lucky when Clara backed away from the biography. "I am far from willing to publish," he assured Lizzie, as the letters and permissions began to arrive, "and am driven to it only as a defence against the pressure to write a memoir of Hay."[9]

Even in the more limited capacity of an editor, however, Henry took care to conceal his connection to the project. "My part is quite mechanical," he told Gaskell, "and Mrs Hay's name will alone appear." He did agree to draft the (unsigned) introduction to *Letters of John Hay,* and that itself served as something of an abridged life story. Though an appreciative account, it notes with some small envy Hay's "easy" climb up the political mountain. "He went to Springfield to study law," Adams telescoped years of obscure apprenticeship, and "the rest was simple"; Hay's important relationships with Nicolay and Lincoln are described as springing merely from "chance" and "accident." A dismissive tone also inched into Henry's remarks on Hay's early writings, which included the travelogue *Castilian Days* and a collection of poems, *Pike County Ballads* — these, he noted offhandedly, had won "a sudden popularity," but he offered no account as to why. Of the masterwork *Lincoln,* Henry said almost nothing, except to glancingly note that it was "laboriously edited in the *Century* [*Magazine*] and afterwards published in ten volumes." Writing of Hay's elevation to the Court of Saint James's, by contrast, Henry put down words that he longed to have attached to his own name: "The choice was personal rather than political, and showed regard for the fitness of the public service rather than reward for service in the party."[10]

Whether intended or not, the introduction can also be read as an awkward juxtaposition of Hay's rising fortunes in the new West with his memoirist's diminishing returns in the old East. Adams devotes more than four pages of a relatively brief prelude to his subject's genealogy. Of Scottish origin, the original John Hay (grandfather to the future Heart) was born in Berkeley County, Virginia, in 1775. Before reaching adulthood he migrated to Lexington, Kentucky, and, critical of slavery, moved again, in 1830, to Sangamon County, Illinois. Adams notes that Lincoln, nineteenth-century America's symbol of social mobility, made a similar pilgrimage, leaving Kentucky in 1816 for Indiana, and later sojourning to New Salem, a small village in Sangamon County. These overlapping migrations, from southern peasantry to northern opportunity, suggested that the Lincolns and the Hays mirrored the emerging Midwest's restless spirit. Henry, by inference, could excuse his own failure to emulate his ancestors' distinguished careers as a question of geography.

During the winter of 1908 Clara Hay put her heavy editing hand to the memorial manuscript with unfortunate results. She forwarded a copy to Adams along with an ominous explanatory note: "You see I have suppressed all names. I thought it best, as it seems less personal."[11] In her well-meaning but artless way, Clara had made the memorial practically unreadable. An 1888 letter from Hay to Adams, sent from the posh Tuxedo Club in the Ramapo Mountains of Tuxedo Park, New York, is an all too typical entry: "This is a beautiful place and it makes one happy to think how much money it has cost P— — L— —, who being a Democrat and a free-trader is the predestined prey of the righteous. We pass our Sunday here, and Monday go back to the Hotel B— — and then, if K— — is ready, we will go to S— —. Give our fondest love to S— — R— —"[12]

Remarkably, Clara edited herself out of the memoir as well, making it, as she wished, a "less personal" project. One perfectly innocuous entry reads, "We went up Pike's Peak today. The kids were amused. Mrs. H— — and I found something to be desired. We start for home the day after to-morrow." Adams quietly dismissed the memorial as "a chaos of initials."[13]

Privately printed, *Letters of John Hay,* even with its protective suppression of identities, generated considerable conversation in the capital. Not all of it appreciative. Clara Hay's careful editing to the contrary, her husband's critical view of Roosevelt came through. TR took note. In a 1909 letter the president responded, indicating to Lodge his attitudinal distance from Hay — and Adams as well.

His negative verdict stands as a condemnation of Lafayette Square snobbery in favor of the strenuous life:

> [Hay's] temptation was to associate as far as possible only with men of refined and cultivated tastes, who lived apart from the world of affairs, and who, if Americans, were wholly lacking in robustness of fiber. His close intimacy with Henry James and Henry Adams — charming men, but exceedingly undesirable companions for any man not of strong nature — and the tone of satirical cynicism which they admired, and which he always affected in writing them, marked that phase of his character which so impaired his usefulness as a public man.[14]

Pairing Hay and Adams is fitting in more ways than Roosevelt perhaps knew. For the *Letters* project overlapped with Henry's own autobiography, the *Education,* thus extending the "close intimacy" of the old Hearts beyond the grave. A complex man, overly impressed by paradox and more moved by his emotions than he guessed, Henry sought in this work to tell a universal story of inevitable fragmentation and breakdown. Naturally he counted himself among its many casualties. While applying the manuscript's finishing touches he wrote to Lizzie Cameron, mocking it as an exercise in authorial immolation: "All memoirs lower the man in estimation."[15]

49
BOOK OF ILLUSIONS

A juried poll initiated by the Modern Library
(Random House) in 1999 ranked *The Education of Henry Adams* the best English-language
non-fiction book to appear in the twentieth
century. *The Varieties of Religious Experience,*
written by Adams's friend William James,
came in second, with Booker T. Washington's
Up from Slavery and Virginia Woolf's *A Room
of One's Own* close behind. One *New York
Times* story surveying the list described the
Education correctly enough as "weighty but
evasive." It is autobiographical in the sense
that Henry contextualized certain episodes of
his life into a broader narrative demonstrating the movement of the modern West away
from, as he put it, "Thirteenth-Century
Unity" and toward the uncertainties of
"Twentieth-Century Multiplicity." The book
should thus not be approached, excepting in
set and often brilliantly descriptive pieces, as
an accurate memoir. Too much of Adams's
inner life is suppressed, too little of his private

emotions, folded beneath blankets of beautifully arranged irony, are on display. Concerned with what he called "the strangely blighting shadow of *The Education,*" the biographer Ernest Samuels informed readers of his 1948 study, *The Young Henry Adams,* that it played only a very small role in his research. "For the most part," he cited its propensity for distortion, "I have put [it] aside . . . as a primary source."[1]

The *Education* might, for the sake of clarity, be divided into two sections; the first, briefer, and more satisfying segment details Henry's singular adolescence. These passages include fine material on his initial encounter with Washington, D.C., his callow enthusiasm for Sumner, and his well-aimed jabs at Harvard College. Holding it all together is the irrepressible spirit of remembered youth that lights up many of the pages in a celebration of simple, impressionable pleasures. "But as far as happiness went," he writes in one such extract, "the happiest hours of the boy's education were passed in summer lying on a musty heap of Congressional documents in the old farm-house at Quincy, reading [the Sir Walter Scott historical novels] *Quentin Durward, Ivanhoe* and *The Talisman,* and raiding the garden at intervals for peaches and pears. On the whole he learned most then."[2]

The second and longer portion of the *Edu-*

cation contains often exceptional and still quite relevant commentary on the cultural impact of industrial capitalism. At their best, such clauses combine history, art, science, economics, and literature to selectively tell the profound story of modernization. They formally introduce readers to the iconic dynamo that lessened the importance of reproduction and the family, pulled Russia away from Eastern mysticism to Western empiricism, and elevated technocrats into a kind of high priesthood. Too many of these latter chapters, however, bog down in Adams's idiosyncratic rendering of historical "laws" that implacably prophesy social breakdown. The deterministic tone often strikes the reader as a forced if not a false strategy that detracts from the play of possibilities and personal discovery informing the earlier material. In leaving a twenty-year gap in the chronology (1871–92), moreover, Henry omits not only his marriage (and long-simmering attachment to Lizzie Cameron) but also the *History,* his most successful scholarly achievement. Without their inclusions, both his complicated inner life and intellectual progress remain remote, even shielded from the reader.

In full, the *Education* is a work of multiple attitudes and identities. Henry obsesses in the book over his "failure" to have been properly trained for the modern age, but this

598

is a charade. He is himself an example of multiplicity taking turns as an aristocrat, a philosopher, a scientist, a patriot, a historian, a voyager in the South Seas, and so on. In pleading deficient he plays a rhetorical trick on the reader, who, impressed with the study's casually intimidating roster of great names (Alexander I, Aquinas, Archimedes . . .), historical phenomena (Italian unification, the American Civil War, Darwin's deep shadow . . .), and often abstruse thoughts, suspects that Adams is probably a sage repeating in his own way the Socratic paradox "I know that I know nothing." Indeed the *Education*'s greatest irony is its claim to telling the story of its author's ignorance, confusion, and misdirection, all the while assailing in vigorous prose and confident assertions the West after 1400. With an attitude of awe, Henry enumerates the technical advances made by mathematicians, physicists, and industrialists, only to reveal their complicity in fashioning a culture of anomie. Setting aside the failure motif, his more plausible role is that of the "wise fool," the intuitive talent unburdened by the book knowledge ushered in during the Renaissance. He played neither part perfectly, and close observers could tell that he occasionally read from a script. Shortly after Henry's death Brooks wrote, "I think in his 'Education' he has carried his joke, at times, perhaps a little too far."[3]

Viewed more positively, the "joke" that Adams tells is painfully on target and thus goes some way in explaining why he resorted to satire. The *Education,* after all, is an exercise in counterintuitiveness that questions the liberal nineteenth century's hasty endorsement of science, order, progress, property rights, rationality, and self-improvement. All, he suspected, were superlatives, rationalizations for the violent overturning of an older economy of scale for something ultimately unsettling. The cultural historian Clive Bush finds Henry's skepticism completely appropriate:

In terms of liberal economics the age of the entrepreneurial individual was, for the mass of the population, over. America itself changed startlingly, from a largely self-employed and family-business economy in 1870 to one where in 1900 12 per cent of the population owned 99 per cent of the wealth. The sciences passed out of range of common-sense knowledge, or, perhaps more accurately, the early, long and expensive training needed to grasp the fundamentals of science placed them out of range of the mass of the people. It is little wonder that the "Henry Adams" of Adams's *Education of Henry Adams* wondered who, where, and what he was.[4]

600

Other commentators would come along in the 1920s who too puzzled over their identities in a radically reconfigured world. Adams's memorable division of chronology, contrasting thirteenth-century consensus in tension with twentieth-century clash, is echoed in Hermann Hesse's popular 1927 novel *Steppenwolf:* "Now there are times when a whole generation is caught . . . between two ages, two modes of life, with the consequence that it loses all power to understand itself and has no standard, no security, no simple acquiescence."[5] A generation before Hesse — and James Joyce, T. S. Eliot, and Ernest Hemingway, among other modernists — so unequivocally questioned the Victorian legacy, Adams had already, and without the prod of a global conflict, laid such a foundation.

But if Henry anticipated an emerging school of writers critical of contemporary life, he also retained a place in the older practice of literary Bostonians whose influence he could never completely escape. Like the Puritan jeremiads, Nathaniel Hawthorne's deliberations on ancestral guilt, and well-bred Beacon Hill's condemnations of a sinful slave republic, his *Education* came freighted with predictions of gloom and doom for a country all too corruptible. There is in the book a fairly strong connection to New England's lapsarian tradition that makes it perhaps less

601

sui generis than one might suspect. As a child, Henry learned early of Boston's annoying superiority and Quincy became for him a kind of paradise lost. It is a parable that formed the core of his mature thinking and one he often revisited.

Committed to the Quincy perspective, he attacked those organizing principles (Darwinism, imperialism) and rising classes (manufacturers, financiers) that he associated with the dynamo. Its unpredictable energy belied restraint, he asserted, and gave humanity a false sense of its power. He wrote in the *Education* that those technocrats and their patrons who pursued "force" were only hunting down their own deaths: "Every day nature violently revolted, causing so-called accidents with enormous destruction of property and life, while plainly laughing at man, who helplessly groaned and shrieked and shuddered, but never for a single instant could stop. The railways alone approached the carnage of war; automobiles and fire-arms ravaged society, until an earthquake became almost a nervous relaxation."[6] One is reminded in this striking passage of the twentieth — and twenty-first — century's problematic relationships with chemical gases, environmental destruction, and, of late, mass shootings. Adams's concerned references to "nervous relaxation" and the universal man who "shrieked" in futility might be paired with the Norwegian painter Edvard Munch's contemporaneous *Scream* (1893), whose sudden inspiration, the artist recalled, came on a walk with two friends as the setting sun turned the sky a vivid red: "I stopped — leaned against the fence — deathly tired. . . . I heard a huge extraordinary scream pass through nature."[7]

The unease that Adams captures in the *Education* is partly a result of his own shifting identity. The Irish gardener's quip at the Old House questioning a young Henry's right to be president — a gibe recorded in the memoir — accentuates the confident assumptions of the antebellum ruling class. But between that moment and Henry's putting it down on paper, the white liberal New England nation, despite its momentary Civil War–era recovery, lost its vitality as a sovereign people. No more would an Emerson — or an Adams — be seen as a representative man of the republic.

In February 1907 Henry sent copies of the *Education* to friends and family under the pretext that they strike out objectionable material, correct inaccuracies, and rework imprecise language. He asked that after making such emendations, the individual return the volume. Many of these chosen first readers were mentioned in the book, and Adams may have wished for a rigorous editing process by those in the best position to comment. But one wonders if he really intended to be inundated with several dozen marked-up manuscripts calling for revision. He must have known that the likelihood of any being returned were slim. Who would venture to correct the history of one of America's most respected historians? Who would know what to make of his curious detour into the hard sciences (evident in such befogged passages as "At the calculated acceleration, the head of the meteor-stream must very soon pass perihelion"), and how many would dare him to introduce the details of that two-decade open sore that he so loudly refused to discuss?[8] Perhaps in asking for corrections Henry stayed true to the spirit of the work. He adopted yet another identity, that of the humble searcher who had only questions but no answers.

By May he had dropped the pretense of expecting his readers to polish the *Education.* "You need not bother yourself about returning the volume," he wrote to Gaskell. "I had meant to call them all back, expecting large changes or omissions; but thus far, no changes of any consequence have been asked, and no omissions." He could not hide from Gaskell his pride in the work's popularity. "The President [Roosevelt] tells me that he means to keep the volume, whatever I say; and the various ladies not only refuse to return it, but clamor for more copies." He later reported that only Charles Eliot, the man who recruited him to teach medieval history at Harvard nearly forty years earlier, had actually relinquished his manuscript. Several readers wrote to Adams, however, and their responses varied widely. Clara Hay frankly counseled Henry to drop the dynamo and return to Jesus: "But it seemed to me that you have studied too much to find that *'Force'* you are still seeking. Why, instead of all those other books, you have gone to, to find it — did you not go back to your Bible? . . . I have wanted, for so long to tell you this, but have not had the courage." William James, being William James, utterly rejected the deterministic universe constructed in the *Education,* telling Adams, "I don't follow or share your way of conceiving the historical problem. . . . Unless the future contains genuine novelties, unless the present is really creative of them, *I don't see the use of time at all."* And a few years after Henry's death, the British statesman John Morely read the *Education* and sniggered to a colleague, "If A. had ever looked at himself naked in a glass he would have rated other men a little more gently."[9]

With Henry's privately printed copies of the *Education* circulating over the years, interest built in seeing the manuscript more widely distributed. In January 1916 Ferris

Greenslet, literary editor at Houghton Mifflin, under whose colophon the *Chartres* appeared, asked about publishing the *Education.* Replying the following month, Adams said "no" — and "yes." "Please bear in mind that, for reasons personal to myself, I do not want publication. I prefer the situation as it stands. Under no circumstances will I bind myself to publish or to help publication. If you drop the matter altogether I shall be best satisfied." But in the same note Adams, then two days beyond his seventy-eighth birthday, all but drew a path to the *Education*'s publication: "After my death I should leave my corrected copy to the Massachusetts Historical Society to do what they pleased with. You could make what arrangements you liked with them."[10] Adams died in 1918, in which year the book appeared; it captured the 1919 Pulitzer Prize for biography.

The First World War undoubtedly played an important role in making the *Education* appear a prescient, even a prophetic text. The conflict produced a vast civilizational shock, resulting in a bifurcation of historical time already, in some sense, outlined by Adams. Just as he had lingered doubtfully over the prospects of the postwar West, very many Americans in the 1920s, feeling taken in by President Woodrow Wilson's naïve appeal to make the world "safe for democracy" and uninspired by the decade's withdrawal into Wall Street exuberance, were equally skeptical. The market crash of 1929, the resulting Depression, and the great ideological struggle between fascism, capitalism, and communism that followed further initiated a strong mood of disillusionment. Readers of that period discovered in the *Education* an expression of mounting anxiety that had rolled through Adams's life and, surprisingly, into theirs — its dry, mordant wit made to capture the tone of difficult times. Succeeding generations have ever since returned to this unusual book for its oracular chapters. To engage deeply with the *Education* is to look beyond both its memoirish surface and its pseudo-scientific sheen and to accept it as something of a disquieting statement on humanity's imperilment in a civilization it has created but cannot control. Contentiously organized around the theme of failure, it has managed since its issuance to interest readers skeptical of the materialism, militarism, and technological progress that has so definitively come to define both the promise and the sorrow of the American Century.

607

50
THERE WAS A BOY

In late August 1909, with the *Education* idling in select and small circulation, George Cabot Lodge, son of Henry Cabot Lodge, died of ptomaine poisoning at the age of thirty-five in a friend's summer house at Tuckernuck Island off Nantucket. The fatality both pained and interested Adams as a portent of sorts. He had liked George, called "Bay," immensely, counted him among his nephews "in wish," and, perhaps straining to support a point, saw in the young man's unexpected passing a herald of ill tidings for the rising generation of Americans to which the strong-jawed, dark-haired, and bright-eyed Bay belonged. With no children of his own, Henry enjoyed, if that is the right word, the freedom to speculate without restraint on the dystopic days ahead. The death of a young friend could only have heightened the temptation to indulge in a store of somber premonitions.

Bored at the idea of a legal, political, or business career, Bay had briefly broken from

608

family pressure to pursue poetry. He mastered several languages before entering Harvard, where he adopted the attitude of an alienated artist. Little known today, he is sometimes linked by specialists with Joseph Trumbull Stickney, Philip Savage, and Hugh McCullough among a minor set of writers known collectively as the Harvard pessimists. The Spanish American philosopher George Santayana, their companion and friend, later insisted that these men, none of whom saw the age of thirty-six, were destroyed by their country's commitment to the conventional: "All those friends of mine . . . were visibly killed by the lack of air to breathe. People individually were kind and appreciative to them, as they were to me; but the [emerging industrial] system was deadly, and they hadn't any alternative tradition (as I had) to fall back upon."[1]

After graduation Bay embarked for Europe to study medieval literature and modern languages. Perhaps feeling, as had Henry following his own collegiate turn, the grave weight of familial expectation, Bay struggled to reconcile with his future. He wrote from Paris in January 1896:

The thing which tore me worst in all this mental struggle I have been going through was the continual thought of money and my crying inability to adapt myself to my time

609

and to become a money-maker. I felt as if it was almost cowardly of me not to turn in and leave all the things I love and the world doesn't behind, and to adjust myself to my age, and try to take its ideals and live strongly and wholly in its spirit.[2]

Upon returning to the United States, Bay dutifully served as his father's secretary while making do as a nocturnal poet. Dissatisfied, he sought adventure as a naval cadet on board the USS *Dixie* during the Spanish-American War, after which he married and settled into a low-intensity life, writing in between domestic obligations. "Bay is growing rapidly conventional and urbane," Henry observed in 1901, and family friend Edith Wharton believed that the young man's artistic skills — greater in aspiration than outcome — were smothered in good intentions: "He grew up in a hothouse of intensive culture, and was one of the most complete examples I have ever known of the young genius before whom an adoring family unites in smoothing the way. This kept him out of the struggle of life, and consequently out of its experiences, and to the end his intellectual precocity was combined with a boyishness of spirit at once delightful and pathetic."[3]

In counting up Bay's hurdles, Wharton, an adopted Bostonian by virtue of her difficult marriage to Edward Wharton, included what she considered Adams's negative impact on the "boy," chiefly his snobbery and transparently scornful attitude. Bay was ill-served, she wrote, by "the slightly rarefied atmosphere of mutual admiration and disdain of the rest of the world, that prevailed in his immediate surroundings . . . [whose] dominating spirits were Henry Adams and Cabot Lodge. . . . The influences there kept Bay in a state of brilliant immaturity." Living alone in Paris after her divorce, Wharton knew Adams's cynicism well as she enjoyed gathering in her elegant Rue de Varenne apartment various American and French friends. In such a seemingly agreeable salon, a stubborn Henry, so one scholar has noted, with his "world-weary raillery . . . neglected to improve the occasion."[4]

Bay, in any case, displayed little evidence that he might mature into an important poet. His clichéd use of classic man-versus–the elements settings, his inborn Victorianism and narrow search for self-divinity embodied much of the emotionally constricting genteel tradition that Henry had rejected in his long-ago flight from Boston.

Adams's interest in Bay rested, rather, on something other than artistic grounds. He may have seen in Bay a more than faintly recognizable version of his younger self. Both knew the pressures of belonging to aristocratic Brahmin families, had served as secre-

611

taries for famous political fathers, and had pined for foreign service positions. Bay too rejected American capitalism and, influenced by William Sturgis Bigelow, went through a Buddhist "phase" reminiscent of Henry's. Some, including Wharton, thought him a minor-key Adams acolyte.

Drawn to Bay's "boyishness of spirit," Henry impulsively liked the young man and felt his death keenly. Years earlier, while touring Normandy with the Lodges in August 1895, he had written to Hay, "Bay . . . and I go about together a good deal; so do Cabot and I; but I prefer Bay who is a nice fellow, with only one failing, which is the kind of ambition and aspirations which you and I had forty years ago. I have tried to teach him better. . . . I find him sympathetic, intelligent, well-educated and unselfish. Of the three — father and two sons [including Bay's brother John] — I like him best." Over the years Henry had remained in touch with Bay, who visited both his Washington and Paris residences. During one noon breakfast in the former, an uncharacteristically effusive Adams pulled out the thirteenth chapter of his then unfinished *Chartres* ("Le Miracles de Notre Dame") and gave Bay a rare private reading. Henry seems to have been very near to sincere when, learning of his young friend's sudden death, he wrote, "Bay was my last tie to active sympathy with men. He was the best

612

and finest product of my time and hopes."[5]

Aware of Adams's feelings for Bay, a grieving Henry Cabot Lodge asked Henry to take on yet another commemorative work. Adams could find no way to say no, and so, despite the pretense of a posthumous life, he became yet again an indispensable man.

Houghton Mifflin published *The Life of George Cabot Lodge* in 1911; despite requesting anonymity, Henry discovered his name on the book's flyleaf. The biography, much of it potted around Bay's poems and correspondence, served as a companion publication to a two-volume edition of his collected verse and drama, also released by Houghton Mifflin. Though generous to its subject, the *Life* is quietly dominated by its author. Adams's omnipresent dynamo, his concern for artistic expression in America, and mistrust of philistine Boston are all packed into a single dense sentence detailing Bay's formative environment: "The twenty-five years between 1873 and 1898 — years of astonishing scientific and mechanical activity — were marked by a steady decline of literary and artistic intensity, and especially of the feeling for poetry, which, at best, had never been the favorite form of Boston expression."[6] Henry's diminishing human connections further inform the *Life*, hinting at his fear of isolation. King and Hay had been dead for several years, Elizabeth

Cameron — her Don now gone from the Senate — no longer lived on Lafayette Square, and few historians any longer sought his opinions. Adams wrote in the *Life,* ostensibly of Bay, "However much he tried, and the more he tried, to lessen the gap between himself . . . and the public, the gap grew steadily wider. . . . The suffocating sense of talking and singing in a vacuum that allowed no echo to return, grew more and more oppressive with each effort to overcome it."[7] These desperate words bear the ring of an earlier inspiration. Only five months before Bay's death, Henry had written to a colleague, "I have just had a long discussion with Bay Lodge on our more or less common difficulties, and our less-than-more successful efforts to deal with them. . . . We are obliged to compose our music for ourselves alone, and of course this sort of composition means that we go on repeating our faults. No echo whatever comes back."[8]

If Adams's concerns did shape the manuscript, he could perhaps be excused on the grounds that his subject's short and sheltered life left him little to say. His goal, in any case, was neither to produce a definitive biography nor to please himself, but rather to appease Bay's family. "I've arranged Bay's letters, &c, down as far as the Spanish War (1898), with a thread of narrative and explanation," he had written to Cameron while preparing the volume. "I can make nothing very good out of it, but perhaps it will do to satisfy Nanny [Bay's mother] and Bessy [Bay's widow]."[9]

The book more than mollified the grieving family's patriarch. Looking over the *Life,* Henry Cabot Lodge praised its insightfulness and understanding. "I cannot find words to tell you how much I like it — how delighted I am with it," he wrote Adams. "No one else could have done it or given such an analysis of his character & his thought. It is the monument of all others which I should wish to see raised to his memory." But Henry, despite Lodge's gratitude, had no illusions about the biography. It told half-truths, demanded a diplomatic tone, and forced its author to traffic in the dubious art of hagiography. In a private communication Adams reported to Lizzie, "So Cabot came to dinner last night to talk about Bay's publication, and of course I was beautiful and approved everything, and said that I agreed with everybody, which I always do because nobody cares."[10]

Nearly a year to the day after Bay's passing, Henry's old friend William James died. His absence touched Adams deeply, further thinning a once brilliant cohort of contemporaries. "I did not write to you about your brother William, because I fancied that letters were a burden to you," he addressed Henry James in the winter of 1911. "The other reason is that I felt the loss myself rather too closely to talk about it. We all began together, and our lives have made more or less of a unity, which is, as far as I can see, about the only unity that American society in our time had to show. Nearly all gone. Richardson and St. Gaudens, La Farge, Alex Agassiz, Clarence King, John Hay, and at the last, your brother, William; and with each, a limb of our own lives cut off."[11]

51
To Finish the Game

In January 1912, having just completed a revised edition of the *Chartres,* Henry, a month shy of seventy-four and in increasingly frail health, informed Elizabeth Cameron that he could now die. "At last I've finished!" he opened on a mock-triumphant note. "My final proof-sheets are sent off; my final occupation is ended; since Monday I wake up every morning with the happy thought that I've nothing more to do in the world, and that it doesn't matter now whether I go blind or deaf or senile, or have aphasia in public, or forget my name." Age, he well understood, was attacking him from all sides. For perhaps three or four years he had experienced memory and vision loss, worried about his nervous system, and occasionally found it difficult to form words. The distressing memory of the Governor's slide into dementia frankly scared him. "Between ourselves," he had written to Cameron in the fall of 1908, "I am quite aware that I am done for already. Any fati[g]ue or digestive derangement upsets my head at once, and some fine day I shall wander off and get lost, like my father."[1]

Instead the months and years continued to pass without significant change in his health. Brooks, used to Henry's hypochondria, mildly scolded his brother for screening an iron constitution behind a raft of complaints: "Seriously the trouble with you is that you are so uniformly well and active that you do not know what it is to be hurt. . . . You can write longer, remember better, and read double the number of hours that I can." But time invariably caught up with Henry. In February 1912 he confided to one correspondent of plans for another Paris summer, excited particularly at the idea of cruising aboard the new British passenger liner *Titanic* on its maiden return voyage. Its tragic sinking in the early-morning hours of April 15 with appalling loss of life distressed him deeply. "The foundering of the Titanic is serious, and strikes at confidence in our mechanical success," he wrote Cameron. "Bessy Lodge and Margaretta [Cameron MacVeagh] dined here last night and drove me insane by repeating the stories of the wreck. . . . Very little more, and we should all be as hysterical as the newspapers." On the 21st he complained of his "poor old memory," and three days later, dining alone at his Washington residence, he suffered a stroke.[2]

Henry's manservant William Gray, having heard a thud, found Adams on the floor calling for assistance — "I can't get up, you will have to help me" — and he and the female cook carried Adams to his upstairs bedroom. There was no telephone at 1603 H Street, so Gray rushed next door to the Hay residence and called for a physician. Henry woke up the next morning with limited use of his right hand, but other than feeling lethargic, he appeared to be in good shape. His brother Charles soon arrived on the scene and took charge. Anticipating a home convalescence for Henry, he ordered a telephone installed. Several days went by with no apparent change in the patient's condition, but on the evening of May 2 Henry's health dramatically declined. He became incoherent and two days later was described as "vague." On the 8th he expressed a wish to write to his mother (dead nearly twenty-three years), though he also maintained that she went down on the *Titanic.* On the 10th Henry Cabot Lodge reported that Adams "had another bad night; was very violent and striving to get out of the window. They were obliged to . . . give him a sedative."[3]

Biographer Ernest Samuels speculated that Henry, with a rational mind, sought to end his life, fearing a descent into "mindless senility." But this presumes that Adams had control over his faculties at a time when, as the report of May 8 indicates, he may not. We know with more certainty that Henry's personal physician, Dr. Harry Crecy Yarrow, believed his patient's prospects for a full recovery dim. "I see very little hope for the future," he wrote the London-situated Elizabeth Cameron on the 25th. "He may recover in part his . . . mental faculties, but I believe they will never be the same as before."[4] Nine days later, on June 3, Charles sent a similarly bleak note to her:

He seems quite indifferent to visitors. . . . I think it not improbable he may recover so far as that he can be wheeled through an open window on to a balcony, or even perhaps, carried on to the grass and sit in the shade under a tree. That, however, he will recover so far as to be capable of consecutive thought or continued articulate utterance and judgment I hardly think probable. Dr. Worcester, in whose experience and judgment I have the utmost confidence, holds out little hope of either.[5]

Dr. Alfred Worcester maintained a general practice outside of Boston. Many years later Worcester drafted a self-serving twenty-two-page memoir, "Reminiscences of a Country Doctor," describing the situation, as he remembered it, at Adams's house:

I found Henry Adams cooped in a crib-cot with slat sides, from which he said he wanted to get out. There were several doctors there, one of them a permanent resident, and as many nurses. They said their patient had had a shock several weeks previously, that he was deranged, partially paralized and difficult to manage. I found little in his condition to warrant either their objections to his removal or the generous amount of soporific drugs which the records showed he was having. As we were going down stairs for our consultation the colored butler whispered to me "They are all living here on terrapin and drinking up his champagne." Perhaps it was this revelation that stiffened my insistence that it would be perfectly safe to move the patient North. When the disagreement of the doctors was reported to his brothers they accepted my advice in spite of the Washingtonians.[6]

Along with a physician and two nurses, Henry boarded a private rail car (arranged by Henry Cabot Lodge) and headed toward Boston. From there, on June 16, the small convalescent party arrived in Lincoln, where Henry stayed at Birnam Woods, close to Charles's home. Making a marvelous recovery, he walked the grounds (including strolls to nearby Walden Pond), lifted light weights, took open-air drives, and endured massages.

He reported to his friend Cecil Spring Rice with a flash of the old acid, "[They] have proceeded to rub me, and pound me, and make me generally exceedingly uncomfortable, with the idea that I was going to be quite well again."[7]

On June 26 Elizabeth Cameron, under the cover of returning to America to attend the marriage of Colgate Hoyt, her widowed brother-in-law, arrived in Lincoln. Her attention, and that of several nieces and a host of ancient Quincy and Boston connections, seemed to lighten Henry's outlook. Though Charles reported that his brother's tongue remained sharp throughout the summer, Henry's correspondence suggested, at least on occasion, a mellower mood. In a late August communication to Gaskell, he fairly basked in his surprising situation:

> I've really passed quite a happy summer, — rather better than in a rainy Paris, for the weather has been good. Nothing has happened. A few very old friends have been with me. Mrs Cameron is in America. My niece Louly Hooper has stuck to me. My niece Elsie Adams . . . has not deserted me. Various Lodges, Endicott's, &c, have lighted near my perch. My brother Charles comes here every day to growl about politics and the nature of newspapers.[8]

Having resumed his correspondence in June, Henry dispensed with dictation in August. His health steadily returning, he predictably turned his eye toward the coming presidential canvas, a perfect smash-up for the Republicans as Theodore Roosevelt, eager after a fitful four-year retirement to reclaim the White House but unable to wrest the GOP's nomination from his former protégé William Howard Taft, formed the Progressive ("Bull Moose") Party, a vote-splitting insurgency that ensured the November victory of New Jersey's Democratic governor, Woodrow Wilson. Adams thought it a beautiful disaster. He wrote to Anna Cabot Lodge while in Lincoln:

Do not be alarmed about the election. Whatever way it goes it is sure to go against us, so we might as well look on it with perfectly philosophical eyes. . . . I am somewhat more puzzled to know what satisfaction Theodore gets out of it, or will be likely to get out of it, and I have only one hope in regard to him, and that is that he will be firm on the point not to spend any of his own or of Edith's money on it. It is bad enough to ruin oneself and one's party too, without absolutely throwing away one's fortune.[9]

His attitude, in any event, seemed to have

made a rather complete recovery.

That fall Henry arranged to return to Washington, though he would now need a permanent secretary-companion to care for him. On the recommendation of Mabel Hooper La Farge and Louisa Hooper Ward, he invited their friend Aileen Tone to join his household. Tone, then living in New York, was thirty-four, unmarried, a Roman Catholic, and an adept musician; her connection to the Hoopers only strengthened her appeal to Adams. Flashing the old blend of charm and exaggeration that he typically reserved for Elizabeth Cameron and any number of nieces, he courted the tall, attractive Tone like an avid suitor: "Truly come, and bring me life in some form, for I perish."[10] In need of a situation to support herself, Tone agreed to become an H Street niece-nurse in residence. On the last day of October, slightly more than six months after his stroke, Henry left Lincoln and returned to Washington. There, on November 7, he wrote to Charles thanking him for his many kindnesses and care. He also reported that he was at peace, expected to live but a few months longer, and wished only to finish the "game" strong:

I have no illusions. I accepted my notice to quit in full consciousness of its bearing, and, between ourselves, with a breath of relief. My return here, and the changes ahead, smooth the way. My general decline in vigor and endurance notifies me that a few months at most are all I have or want. But I've got to go on as though I could see ahead, and everyone will have to lend themselves to the game. It will not be easy, but I will be as docile as I can.[11]

52
THE REST IN SILENCE

Despite fretting over a "general decline," a surprisingly robust Henry returned to Paris in 1913 and again in 1914, a welcome resumption of his seasonal regime. There he enjoyed the amenities of an impeccably cultured capital, putting into sharp relief his youthful, errant hopes that Washington, D.C., might one day achieve its own outstanding artistic glory. Much to his frustration the Federal City remained a predominantly political city, inevitably attuned to the rhythms of congressional sessions and national elections. It attracted no bohemian district, sheltered no expatriate enclaves, and went without a distinguished university, symphony, or opera. Paris, by contrast, never disappointed him. For several years he had kept a well-appointed apartment favoring the French Rococo style at 23 Avenue du Bois de Boulogne. Adams scholar Harold Dean Cater once described its furnishings as "chiefly French, tied in with Chinese pieces that he bought from two shops which he loved to haunt: Chines's and Mme. Langweil's. His library was long and narrow, between a big salon and his bedroom. There were books in eighteenth-century lacquered cabinets. His desk was a Louis XV table, with drawers, and on it he kept alternately a pair of Yung Cheng ginger jars or an exquisite Greek figure in a glass case. There was usually a slight look of disorder about the room."[1]

In France Henry enjoyed the pleasing dichotomy of blending, so he liked to imagine, a medieval patina with modern conveniences. He may have despised the growing prestige of machines, but in more personal and immediate settings he embraced the fruits of industrial development. This contradiction is grandly captured in his enthusiastic report to a niece on the pleasures of a "perfect automobile": "My idea of paradise is . . . going thirty miles an hour on a smooth road to a twelfth-century cathedral."[2]

For about a decade Adams had been an auto enthusiast. Karl Benz's 1885 gasoline-powered contraption, complete with single-cylinder engine, helped to inaugurate the mobile age; a generation later the mass production of Henry Ford's basic black Model T forged a global industry. In between, Henry took to the motorcar while it was still something of a rich man's pleasure. "As I grow older," he wrote to Gaskell in 1900, "I loath pigging in troughs with . . . tourists, and the only alternative is the automobile." He purchased "a very pretty" eighteen-horsepower Mercedes in France four years later and, resisting a top, procured as well a pair of "water-proofs." Under the steady hand of a chauffer ("my man"), Adams relished the open road. "To be private secretary or professor is nothing," he informed an acquaintance, "compared with being a slave to an automobile. . . . I will show you miracles."[3]

Aside from cathedral-hopping, Henry, in his final Paris seasons, became a passionate student of medieval songs. Several visitors remarked on his devotion, including a young Harvard historian, Samuel Eliot Morison, who wished to engage Adams on the internecine battles that had long ago consumed the Federalist Party. But upon breaching Henry's doorstep, he found the septuagenarian unwilling to pick over the American past: "I called at his Paris residence . . . and tried to get him to discuss New England Federalism. He then expressed a great disinterest in that subject, but a lively interest in French medieval music. . . . Mr. Adams then gave me the impression that he no longer cared about American history."[4] Perhaps unsurprisingly, Morison never entered the select association of favored nephews.

The summer of 1914 proved to be Henry's

last in Paris. The June 28 assassination of Archduke Franz Ferdinand of Austria and his wife, Sophie, by the Bosnian Serb Gavrilo Princip started in motion a series of diplomatic and military maneuverers that culminated in a general European war. By the first week of August German armies were moving through Belgium and into northern France, beginning the Battle of the Frontiers. Feeling the war daily creep closer and showing signs of mental confusion (he failed to remember his mother's name at a registration point), Henry evenly referred to his situation as that of "a trapped . . . octogenarian rat"; as late as August 13 he was determined to remain in Paris: "In every respect I am better off, than I could be elsewhere." But the Belgian city of Liège fell on the 16th and Brussels followed on the 20th. Between the 21st and the 23rd the German 2nd and 3rd armies defeated the French at the Battle of Charleroi, sending French and British armies south on a fighting retreat to Paris. From his apartment Henry watched nervously as conscripts passed by on the streets below. Knowing his situation to be untenable and feeling responsible for the two companions in his care — Aileen Tone and his brother Charles's daughter Elsie — he finally resolved to go to England. His party moved north to Dieppe, where they witnessed trainloads of wounded — some of whom occupied the corridors of their hotel — and from there, on August 26, crossed the Channel on a crowded boat to Folkestone. Bedding down in rustic Dorset after "a week of heat and dirt in London," Henry declared himself a "refugee."[5]

During his improvised time in England, Adams dined with Henry James, who offered to Edith Wharton his impressions of their old mutual acquaintance:

Yesterday I saw Henry Adams and his two young nieces, the natural and the artificial. . . . Henry, alas, struck me as more changed and gone than he had been reported, though still with certain flickers and *gestes* of participation, and a surviving capacity to be very well taken care of; but his way of life, in such a condition, I mean his world-wandering, is all incomprehensible to me — it is so quite other than any I should select in his state.[6]

Briefly settled in a country house with his companions, Adams consumed the papers for war news while Tone entertained at the piano. Finding Jane Austen on a shelf, he reported to Gaskell of "read[ing] *Persuasion* aloud" in the evenings. After six weeks of rest and simple rural pleasures, the "refugees" secured passage on the ocean liner *Cedric* and headed home in late October.[7]

Henry never returned to Europe, though

from the safety of the American shore he championed the Anglo-French powers and favored U.S. intervention against Germany. Living in Washington, he observed with pride the sight of young men in uniform, a memory that took him back more than a half-century to the Secession Winter of 1860–61. In a world, so he often stated, of multiplicity, he could see in the Allied cause a unity across nations, generations, and societies. He had no doubt that the United States and Britain — historically at odds — now fought for a common civilization, and he nourished this notion, seeing in it the completion of a long progression in the relations of the two powers. Their shared struggle made him feel as though a great future lay ahead, uncompromised by the deterministic historical "laws" that dominated his late work. He wrote with pride to Gaskell in June 1917, "Here we are, for the first time in our lives fighting side by side and to my bewilderment I find the great object of my life thus accomplished in the building up of the great Community of Atlantic Powers which I hope will at least make a precedent that can never be forgotten."[8]

Back on H Street, Adams maintained a quiet home, peopled by his servants, Tone, and the inevitable drift of nieces and nephews. More eclectic callers, however, occasionally landed on his doorstep, including Father Sigourney Fay, a convert and conversational magpie knowledgeable of medieval art, music, and philosophy. Henry found Fay's "Irish love for the 12th century" amusing. Mentor, while affiliated with the Newman School in Hackensack, New Jersey, to a young F. Scott Fitzgerald, Fay appears to have brought the budding writer to meet Adams. Fitzgerald later "dropped" him into *This Side of Paradise* (1920), his celebrated Jazz Age novel, as Thornton Hancock, "author of an erudite history of the Middle Ages and the last of a distinguished patriotic, and brilliant family." Scott told his editor Maxwell Perkins, "I didn't do him thoroughly of course — but I knew him when I was a boy."[9]

Among Henry's company, Charles's daughter Elsie proved particularly loyal. Though living for some years in Boston, she descended upon Washington on the first of each month to discharge a host of household duties. Such chores, including the payment of bills and settling of domestic accounts, helped to keep a rather urbane space in order.[10] Margaret Chanler offers a portrait of that apartment in Adams's final years:

The library, where he and his friends passed so many pleasant hours, was of course overflowing with books, but there were choice bibelots, Chinese bronzes, and flowers on his big table; the best of the water colors were hung there — the lovely Turner landscape, the curious Nebuchadnezzar crawling on all fours and eating grass, painted by William Blake — and all the rarest Italian drawings were disposed by the mantelpiece.[11]

Tone provides a more personal recollection of the home she shared with Adams:

Uncle Henry always made [dinner] into a festive occasion. We dressed, even when alone — he insisted that I should have good clothes and look well — and there was always champagne, which he would drink in such rapid gulps that I was sometimes afraid he would choke. "It's the only way to taste good champagne," he would retort if I protested.

He never dined out, even when asked to the White House — "I'm in bed with a nurse" was his invariable excuse — and he never asked people in, but he expected them to propose themselves. Young people were shy about this, but I soon learned to tell when he wanted company and would suggest to friends of my own . . . that they come in on a given night. In this way we had many pleasant parties.[12]

Perhaps Henry guessed at the polite nature

of these social gatherings; he seemed to understand that he had become an object of some well-intentioned pity. "A few people come still to see me," he wrote Elizabeth Cameron, "with that curious air which we used always to wear when we went to make duty-calls on the George Bancrofts."[13]

Aside from the occasional guest Adams passed his time perusing a much-diminished correspondence, being read to (in French and Italian as well as English), and listening to his beloved twelfth-century chansons. Falling back on a familiar refrain, he called his days "innocent! no one cares." If Tone wished to attend a party she needed permission — "I had to beg" — and suffered a gentle interrogation before it was granted. At the inevitable after-breakfast debriefings that followed, Adams expected to know all the details of the dinner. Reflecting on his own once rich social calendar and his current situation, he wrote to Gaskell, "It is quite astonishing how the circle narrows."[14]

Though his energy flagged and his vision dimmed, Henry nonetheless exhibited a desire to remain active and engaged. Despite years of gravely carping about stock manipulators and gold-bugs, he maintained a robust investment portfolio. In effect, he banked on the dynamo and cashed in accordingly. A December 1915 letter to Ward Thoron demonstrated a solid knowledge of various markets. He liked coppers ("I hear great things of them"), thought smelters worth a look ("They ought to be excellent if well managed"), insisted that telephone stocks were "about the best of all," and pondered America's looming car culture: "Apparently there is no limit to the future of these."[15]

With war-torn Europe unavailable, Adams spent the summers of 1915 and 1916, respectively, in Dublin, New Hampshire, and on an estate in Tyringham in the rural Berkshire Mountains of western Massachusetts. In 1917, for reasons known only to himself, he returned to Beverly Farms, to the summer house built for him and Clover in 1876 and which he had not seen since her death in 1885. He surprised himself with the act, writing to Gaskell, "And now, I have returned here . . . thinking that nothing on earth would ever bring me back." Perhaps he sensed that it might be his final summer and wanted to retrace the still remembered moments of his marital past. Henry James's death the previous year had stirred in him unexpectedly strong emotions. "Not only was he a friend of mine for more than forty years," he wrote Lizzie, "but he also belonged to the circle of my wife's set long before I knew him or her, and you know how I have clung to all that belonged to my wife. I have been living all day in the seventies. Swallow, sister! sweet sister swallow! indeed and indeed, we really were happy then."[16] His human connections to those who knew Clover all but extinguished, Adams may, in the months following James's death, have slowly come to the sudden decision to embark for Beverly.

He arrived in May to find the familiar mansard roof, the wooded acres, and the ocean that many Americans, he laughed, thought infested with German U-boats. In a letter to Lizzie, Henry brought forward a number of associations that, in a lighthearted way, suggested why he had escaped from Harvard and Marlborough Street all those years ago: "The weather is usually freezing which helps to make me feel at home. The family is very good about coming to see us, and of course help to disapprove everything we do, after the manner of Boston."[17] Adams spent his summer months with a shifting cadre of family, friends, and the curious; he took morning walks in the woods and often wondered in some small amazement at his extraordinary return to Beverly. The half-remembered environment, bereft of fresh associations, deepened his sense of displacement. "There are just three of my contemporaries living on this Shore," he wrote Gaskell, one of his last living friends from youth:

but we have all lost our minds or our senses and no one thinks it worthwhile to tell us so.

636

No books come out. I am not aware that there are any writers left, certainly none in my branch which was extinct five and twenty years ago or more. No one even remembers the name of Lord Macaulay. I once wrote some books myself, but no one has even mentioned the fact to me for nearly a generation; I have a vague recollection that once some young person *did* mention an anecdote to me that came from one of my books and that he attributed to someone else.[18]

He returned to Washington that fall.

How ironic that Henry should die in the last year of the Great War, the year the long nineteenth century (1789–1918) finally ended, a period encompassing nearly the entirety of U.S. history. Though he complained of having to step aside for Gilded Age potentates — the dull Ohio presidents, the Wall Street scoundrels — Adams has taken a lasting place in cultural memory. His observations on the perils of modernity and the Faustian price paid for technological wizardry appear all too timeless and strike at the heart of our contemporary concerns. So much of what we are was built upon what he saw being made. One wonders if this self-described "failure" ever realized the fullness of his legacy or his perfect good fortune avoiding a White House tenancy paid for in tariff disputes, treaty fights, and patronage scrums.

During the winter of 1918 the house on H Street played host to the usual comings and goings of nieces and nephews. All were dependably polite to the grand man, who now moved with a deliberate slowness. One of Adams's guests, Alice Longworth, the eldest child of Theodore Roosevelt, thought he "looked sadly little and old."[19]

On the evening of March 26, Henry wished Elsie a good evening and retired to his room. The next morning, a bit after eight o'clock, Aileen Tone went upstairs and found him in bed, his lifeless body still warm. She thought his face looked "marvelously beautiful," its closed eyes locked indelibly in an "expression of *consciousness* and *will* and intellect." He had died of a massive stroke.[20]

The following day the rector of St. John's Episcopal Church, standing near vases of forsythia and lilacs, performed a brief service in the house before a small gathering of mourners; a shawl belonging to Clover, kept for years in a reliquary trunk in a top-floor storage closet, was placed in the casket.[21] Adams's remains were then taken to Rock Creek Cemetery and laid in an unmarked grave, beside and below spouse and sphinx, emblems each of grief, of peace, in passage to journey's end.

ACKNOWLEDGMENTS

Supposing myself in something of an extended conversation, my deepest debt goes to a host of Adams scholars who have developed a rich and varied historiography of both the man and his stormy times. Their names and publications can be found throughout the notes section of this study, though I should particularly like to acknowledge here Edward Chalfant, William Merrill Decker, Natalie Dykstra, the late J. C. Levenson, Patricia O'Toole, the late Ernest Samuels, Brooks D. Simpson, John Taliaferro, the late Charles Vandersee, and Richard White.

My agent, Chris Calhoun, believed immediately in the manuscript and to my good fortune placed it at Scribner, where Colin Harrison both edited the work and furthered my education as a writer. Colin's fine-drawn promptings and observations broadened my thinking on a subject I thought I knew well. Sarah Goldberg, also at Scribner, piloted the late stages of this project, keeping it — files, illustrations, and all — on track and on time. Mark LaFlaur and Judith Hoover delivered a copy impressively clean and clear.

The staff at the Massachusetts Historical Society made amenable a number of Adams-related items, while archivists at the Deering Library at Northwestern University eased access to the Ernest Samuels papers. I'm grateful as well to the curators of the Berg Collection at the New York Public Library and to colleagues at Elizabethtown College's High Library.

640

NOTES

Abbreviations

Education: Henry Adams, *The Education of Henry Adams,* ed. Edward Chalfant and Conrad Edick Wright (Boston: Massachusetts Historical Society, 2007).

Letters: Henry Adams, *The Letters of Henry Adams,* vols. 1–6, ed. J. C. Levenson, Ernest Samuels, Charles Vandersee, and Viola Hopkins Winner (Cambridge, MA: Belknap Press of Harvard University Press, 1982–88).

ESP: Ernest Samuels Papers, Archival and Manuscript Collections, Deering Library, Northwestern University.

Introduction

1. *Education,* 3; *Letters,* 5:322.
2. Ernest Samuels, *Henry Adams* (Cambridge, MA: Belknap Press of Harvard University Press, 1989), 372.
3. *Letters,* 1:290.

641

4. *Education,* 176; Harold Dean Cater, ed., *Henry Adams and His Friends: A Collection of Unpublished Letters* (Boston: Houghton Mifflin, 1947), xciv; *Letters,* 5:277, 4:206, 207.

5. Elizabeth Donnan and Leo F. Stock, eds., *An Historian's World: Selections from the Correspondence of John Franklin Jameson* (Philadelphia: American Philosophical Society, 1956), 138; Cater, *Henry Adams and His Friends,* lxxx.

6. Richard Hofstadter to Alfred Kazin, internal evidence suggests 1943, Alfred Kazin Papers, the Berg Collection, New York Public Library; Alfred Kazin, *Alfred Kazin's America: Critical and Personal Writings,* ed. Ted Solotaroff (New York: HarperCollins, 2003), 501. Kazin engaged with Adams over several decades. For something of a summation, see his chapter "A Postponed Power: Henry Adams," in Alfred Kazin, *An American Procession: The Major American Writers from 1830–1930, The Crucial Century* (New York: Vintage Books, 1984), 277–309.

7. Though some might lean toward Francis Parkman as the nineteenth century's greatest American historian, I agree with Edmund S. Morgan's observation that "for anyone with an ear for style, for words and ways of using them, Adams is unmatched. To the modern ear Parkman's prose is so

florid as to be embarrassing. The rolling periods and wordy pen-pictures that entranced his contemporaries no longer seem like high style, particularly in comparison with Adams. Adams's wit, insight, and economy give his writing a resonance that reaches us as freshly today as when the words were written." Edmund S. Morgan, "The Unread Masterpiece," *New York Review of Books,* November 17, 2005, 19.

Prelude: Back to Beverly

1. *Letters,* 6:747.
2. Ibid., 6:754.
3. Ibid., 6:762.

PART I: BECOMING HENRY ADAMS

Chapter 1: Quincy

1. *Education,* 4, 3. Reading Adams's evocation of Boston in the first paragraph of the *Education,* with its familiar references to "Boston State House," "Beacon Street," and "the third house below Mount Vernon Street" (the house of Henry's birth), one is reminded of George Santayana's later elicitation of the old Puritan city in the opening paragraph of his 1936 novel, *The Last Puritan:* "A little below the State House in Boston, where Beacon Street consents to

bend slightly and begins to run down hill, and where across the Mall the grassy shoulder of the Common slopes most steeply down to the Frog Pond, there stood . . . a pair of old brick houses, flatter and plainer than the rest." Perhaps Santayana, himself a fascinated observer of the fading genteel tradition, purposely paid tribute to Adams's memories of Boston, which may have enlivened his own. The art historian Bernard Berenson, a friend to Adams and a Harvard classmate of Santayana's, insisted that *Last Puritan*'s Caleb Wetherbee — "a warm patriot in his odd prophetic way" — was Adams. George Santayana, *The Last Puritan: A Memoir in the Form of a Novel* (New York: Charles Scribner's Sons, 1936), 15, 184; Hanna Kiel, ed., *The Bernard Berenson Treasury: A Selection from the Works, Unpublished Writings, Letters, Diaries, and Journals of the Most Celebrated Humanist and Art Historian of Our Times: 1887–1958* (New York: Simon and Schuster, 1962), 186.

2. *Education,* 9; Edward Chase Kirkland, *Charles Francis Adams, Jr., 1835–1915: The Patrician at Bay* (Cambridge, MA: Harvard University Press, 1965), 2; Freeman Hunt, ed., *Lives of American Merchants,* vol. 1 (New York: Office of Hunt's Merchants' Magazine, 1856), 134, 151.

3. *Education,* 18.

4. Charles Francis Adams, *Charles Francis Adams, 1835–1915: An Autobiography* (Boston: Houghton Mifflin, 1916), 107; Martin B. Duberman, *Charles Francis Adams, 1807–1886* (Boston: Houghton Mifflin, 1961), 27.

5. Duberman, *Charles Francis Adams,* 38; Adams, *Charles Francis Adams, 1835–1915,* 11.

6. Edward Chalfant, *Both Sides of the Ocean: A Biography of Henry Adams, His First Life, 1838–1862* (Hamden, CT: Archon Books, 1994), 31; Adams, *Charles Francis Adams, 1835–1915,* 9.

7. *Education,* 12, 13.

8. Ibid., 5, 6. Henry resented the inference that he was unable to lead a robust life. "You seem to think that I'm adapted to nothing but the sugar-plums of intellect," he once accused his brother Charles, "and had better not try to digest anything stronger" (*Letters,* 1:22). His many and sometimes arduous international travels may have responded in some sense to this complaint.

9. *Education,* 7; Adams, *Charles Francis Adams, 1835–1915,* 7.

10. George Santayana, *Persons and Places: The Background of My Life* (New York: Charles Scribner's Sons, 1944), 68.

11. *Education,* 17. In the winter of 1907 Henry sent copies of the *Education* to a

select audience for what he called "correction." His brother Charles delighted in reading of their shared youth: "Lord! — how you do bring it all back! — How we did hate Boston! — How we loved Quincy! — The aroma of the Spring, — 'Henry greedy, cherry-eater' — and you and I alone of all living, recalling it all!" (*Letters*, 6:48, n1).

Chapter 2: Party of One

1. Duberman, *Charles Francis Adams*, 111, 63.
2. *Education*, 20.
3. Duberman, *Charles Francis Adams*, 148; Frederick J. Blue, *The Free Soilers: Third Party Politics, 1848–54* (Urbana: University of Illinois Press, 1973), 70; David S. Reynolds, *Walt Whitman's America: A Cultural Biography* (New York: Alfred A. Knopf, 1995), 122.
4. "1848 Free Soil Party Platform," Our Campaigns, http://www.angelfire.com/indie/ourcampaigns/1848.html; *Education*, 19.
5. *Education*, 22–23.

Chapter 3: The Madam

1. Margery M. Heffron, *Louisa Catherine: The Other Mrs. Adams* (New Haven, CT: Yale University Press, 2014), 10; Meade Minni-

gerode, *Some American Ladies: Seven Informal Biographies* (New York: G. P. Putnam's Sons, 1926), 290.

2. *Education,* 15, 13.

3. Ibid., 33.

4. Wilhelmus Bogart Bryan, *A History of the National Capital: From Its Foundation through the Period of the Adoption of the Organic Act,* vol. 2 (New York: Macmillan, 1916), 23, 32; Harriet Martineau, *Retrospect of Western Travel,* vol. 1 (London: Saunders and Otley, 1838), 144.

5. *Education,* 35, 34.

6. Ibid., 36, 35.

7. Duberman, *Charles Francis Adams,* 167; Paul C. Nagel, *John Quincy Adams: A Public Life, a Private Life* (New York: Alfred A. Knopf, 1997), 346.

8. David Donald, *Charles Sumner and the Coming of the Civil War* (New York: Alfred A. Knopf, 1960), 203; *Education,* 35.

9. *Education,* 36.

10. Ibid., 37.

Chapter 4: Heroes

1. *Education,* 21; *Letters,* 4:269.

2. *Education,* 26.

3. Ibid., 27.

4. Adams, *Charles Francis Adams, 1835–1915,* 14.

5. *Education,* 27. Perhaps Henry's rejection

of Emerson owed something to his grand-father Adams's dismissive attitude, evident in one of the old man's diary entries from 1840: "A young man, named Ralph Waldo Emerson, a son of my once-loved friend William Emerson, and a class-mate of my lamented son George, after failing in the every-day avocations of a Unitarian preacher and school-master, starts a new doctrine of transcendentalism, declares all the old revelations superannuated and worn out, and announces the approach of new revelations and prophecies. Garrison and the non-resistant abolitionists, Brownson and the Marat democrats, phrenology and animal magnetism, all come in, furnishing each some plausible rascality as an ingredient for the bubbling cauldron of religion and politics." John Quincy Adams, *Memoirs of John Quincy Adams: Comprising Portions of His Diary from 1795 to 1848,* vol. 10, ed. Charles Francis Adams (Philadelphia: J. B. Lippincott, 1874–77), 345. For Henry Adams's tepid impression of Transcendentalism, in which he finds the Concord philosophy "unutterably funny" and full of "airy metaphysical pinnacles," see his review of O. B. Frothingham's *Transcendentalism in New England: A History* in the *North American Review* (October 1876), 471, 469.
6. *Education,* 23, 24.

7. Ibid., 39.
8. Ibid.

Chapter 5: Harvard

1. *Education,* 42.
2. *A Catalogue of the Officers and Students of Harvard University, for the Academic Year 1854–55* (Cambridge, MA: John Bartlett, Bookseller to the University, 1854), 34, 87.
3. Ernest Samuels, *The Young Henry Adams* (Cambridge, MA: Harvard University Press, 1948), 13.
4. Chalfant, *Both Sides of the Ocean,* 61; Isabel Anderson, ed., *The Letters and Journals of General Nicholas Longworth Anderson: Harvard, Civil War, Washington, 1854–1892* (New York: Fleming H. Revell, 1942), 106.
5. Samuels, *Young Henry Adams,* 15; Cater, *Henry Adams and His Friends,* xviii.
6. Samuels, *Young Henry Adams,* 44–45.
7. *Education,* 47.
8. Ibid., 46.
9. Ibid.
10. Ibid., 43.
11. Ibid., 51.
12. Cater, *Henry Adams and His Friends,* xxii; Samuels, *Young Henry Adams,* 50.
13. Samuels, *Young Henry Adams,* 49.
14. William Merrill Decker, *The Literary Vocation of Henry Adams* (Chapel Hill: University of North Carolina Press, 1990), 103.

Chapter 6: Germany

1. Chalfant, *Both Sides of the Ocean,* 98.
2. *Letters,* 1:xvii.
3. Chalfant, *Both Sides of the Ocean,* 102; *Education,* 65. E. M. Forster's 1910 novel *Howards End* also sides with pre–great power Germany. Forster writes that the Schlegel sisters' father "was not the aggressive German. . . . If one classed him at all, it would be as the countryman of Hegel and Kant, as the idealist, inclined to be dreamy, whose Imperialism was the Imperialism of the air." E. M. Forster, *Howards End* (New York: Everyman's Library, 1991), 29.
4. *Letters,* 1:87–8.
5. Ibid., 1:2.
6. Samuels, *Young Henry Adams,* 56; *Letters,* 1:7–8, 25.
7. *Letters,* 1:21.
8. Harold Dean Cater, "Henry Adams Reports on a German Gymnasium," *American Historical Review* (October 1947), 68; Cater, *Henry Adams and His Friends,* xxv.
9. *Letters,* 1:28; *Education,* 64.
10. Cater, *Henry Adams and His Friends,* xxviii; *Letters,* 1:46, 47, 44, 53.
11. *Letters,* 1:55, 58, 78.

Chapter 7: Italy

1. *Letters,* 1:100.
2. David S. Reynolds, *John Brown, Abolition-*

650

ist: The Man Who Killed Slavery, Sparked the Civil War, and Seeded Civil Rights (New York: Vintage Books, 2005), 393.

3. *Letters,* 1:105, 100.

4. Ibid., 1:106.

5. Ibid., 1:110.

6. Ibid., 1:115.

7. Ibid., 1:119, 122.

8. Ibid., 1:129, 130.

9. Robert J. Robertson, "Louisa Catherine Adams Kuhn: Florentine Adventures, 1859–1860," *Massachusetts Historical Review* (October 2009), 127; *Letters,* 1:77, 181.

10. *Letters,* 1:128; *Education,* 66–67. "Lou," wrote one of Henry's nieces, "must have been a remarkable woman, for all her brothers were devotedly attached to her — one of the few subjects on which they could all wholeheartedly agree. She was not beautiful but she had style, self-confidence and wit and was evidently very charming, for she was invariably spoken of as a *femme fatale.*" Abigail Adams Homans, *Education by Uncles* (Boston: Houghton Mifflin, 1966), 17.

11. *Letters,* 1:143; *Education,* 70.

12. *Education,* 71; *Letters,* 1:149.

13. *Education,* 73.

14. *Letters,* 1:167–68.

15. Ibid., 1:168.

16. Ibid., 1:177.
17. Ibid., 1:186.

Chapter 8: Washington

1. Adams, *Charles Francis Adams, 1835–1915,* 90–91.
2. Donald, *Charles Sumner,* 368; David R. Contosta, *Henry Adams and the American Experiment* (Boston: Little, Brown, 1980), 23.
3. Samuels, *Young Henry Adams,* 81.
4. Donald, *Charles Sumner,* 374.
5. *Letters,* 1:91, 217.
6. James Truslow Adams, *The Adams Family* (New York: Blue Ribbon Books, 1930), 247; Adams, *Charles Francis Adams, 1835–1915,* 90.
7. *Education,* 79, 84.
8. *Letters,* 1:67.
9. Ibid., 1:204; Mark J. Stegmaier, ed., *Henry Adams in the Secession Crisis: Dispatches to the* Boston Daily Advertiser, *December 1860–March 1861* (Baton Rouge: Louisiana State University Press, 2012), xiv.
10. Stegmaier, *Henry Adams in the Secession Crisis,* 9, 25, 146.
11. Charles Francis Adams, *Charles Francis Adams, by His Son Charles Francis Adams* (Boston: Houghton, Mifflin, 1900), 145–46.
12. Stegmaier, *Henry Adams in the Secession*

Crisis, 146; Education, 83.

Chapter 9: London

1. Chalfant, *Both Sides of the Ocean*, 225.
2. *Education*, 100.
3. *Letters*, 1:237–38.
4. *Education*, 159.
5. *Letters*, 1:248.
6. Ibid., 1:247, 249.
7. Sarah Agnes Wallace and Frances Elma Gillespie, eds., *The Journal of Benjamin Moran*, vol. 2 (Chicago: University of Chicago Press, 1948), 1120, 1166, 1269, 1167.
8. *Letters*, 1:282.
9. Ibid., 1:351, 354.
10. Ibid., 1:357, 363, 361, 383, 548.
11. Ibid., 1:xix.
12. Ibid., 1:450.
13. Samuels, *Henry Adams*, 55.
14. *Letters*, 1:369.
15. Ibid., 1:371.
16. Cater, *Henry Adams and His Friends*, xxxvi–xxxvii.

Chapter 10: The Correspondent

1. Samuels, *Young Henry Adams*, 107.
2. Ibid., 113, 115.
3. Ibid., 116–17; *Letters*, 1:269.
4. Wallace and Gillespie, *Journal of Benjamin Moran*, 940; *Letters*, 1:278.

5. *Letters,* 1:257, 294, 295, 299.
6. Ibid., 1:299.
7. Ibid., 1:258, 287; Henry Adams, *The Great Secession Winter of 1860–61: And Other Essays,* ed. George Hochfield (New York: Sagamore Press, 1958), 34. For reviews of the Smith controversy, including Adams's role, see Edwin C. Rozwenc's "Captain John Smith's Image of America," *William and Mary Quarterly* (January 1959), 27–36, and more recently, J. A. Leo Lemay, *Did Pocahontas Save Captain John Smith?* (Athens: University of Georgia Press, 1992). Lemay points out weaknesses in Adams's argument and conjectures, though not completely convincingly, that Smith's account is reliable.
8. Adams, *Great Secession Winter,* 35, 58, 50, 45.
9. *Letters,* 1:330, 350; Tocqueville quoted in Brooks D. Simpson, *The Political Education of Henry Adams* (Columbia: University of South Carolina Press, 1996), 21.
10. *Letters,* 1:315. Judith N. Shklar has written, "Harvard changed no one. It failed to create a new American elite or to teach the old one how to survive. That is why, in memory . . . [Henry] Adams came to hate old schools, especially his own. They had failed to educate his generation in the art of survival." Judith N. Shklar, *Redeeming*

American Political Thought, ed. Stanley Hoffmann and Dennis F. Thompson (Chicago: University of Chicago Press, 1998), 84.

11. "Men and Things in Washington," *The Nation,* November 25, 1869, 454–56.

12. Tom Lewis, *Washington: A History of Our National City* (New York: Basic Books, 2015), 162.

13. *Letters,* 2:58.

Chapter 11: Going South, Coming Home

1. *Letters,* 2:24.

2. Paul C. Nagel, *Descent from Glory: Four Generations of the John Adams Family* (New York: Oxford University Press, 1983), 241; Adams Homans, *Education by Uncles,* 30. Henry proudly cheered on John's unsuccessful candidacy: "John alone has acted the part of a man. I care mighty little who gets the offices or the popular applause, but I admire John all the more for what he has done, in proportion as I feel how in his place I should have fallen" (*Letters,* 1:528).

3. *Education,* 188.

4. Ibid., 165.

5. *Letters,* 2:2.

6. Ibid., 2:5.

7. Ibid., 2:7, 5.

Chapter 12: The Race Question

1. W. E. B. Du Bois, "Reconstruction and Its Benefits," *American Historical Review* (July 1910), 784.
2. "Lynching Statistics," *Journal of the American Institute of Criminal Law and Criminology* (May 1918), 144–46, http://www.jstor.org/stable/1133750.
3. Charles Francis Adams, *Richard Henry Dana: A Biography,* vol. 2 (Boston: Houghton, Mifflin, 1890), 331.
4. *Letters,* 1:528, 2:6.
5. William E. Gienapp, ed., *This Fiery Trail: The Speeches and Writings of Abraham Lincoln* (New York: Oxford University Press, 2002), 221.
6. *Letters,* 1:498.
7. *Letters,* 2:16. On Adams's skepticism of the Fifteenth Amendment, see Charles Vandersee, "Henry Adams and the Invisible Negro," *South Atlantic Quarterly* (Winter 1967), 16.
8. James P. Young, *Henry Adams: The Historian as Political Theorist* (Lawrence: University Press of Kansas, 2001), 118; Leslie Butler, *Critical Americans: Victorian Intellectuals and Transatlantic Liberal Reform* (Chapel Hill: University of North Carolina Press, 2007), 177.

Chapter 13: Waiting on Another Washington

1. Decker, *Literary Vocation of Henry Adams,* 132.
2. E. Digby Baltzell, *Puritan Boston and Quaker Philadelphia* (New Brunswick, NJ: Transaction, 2007), 378.
3. *Education,* 203. Though Adams claimed that "at least four-fifths of the American people" supported Grant in the 1868 election, the general received less than 53 percent of the popular vote.
4. Ibid., 207. In twelve presidential polls conducted between 1948 and 2000 by a number of organizations and media outlets, including the Siena Research Institute, the *Wall Street Journal,* and C-SPAN, Grant received an average ranking of 33.9 — putting him in such company as Millard Fillmore, Franklin Pierce, James Buchanan, and Warren G. Harding. In seven polls since, his average ranking has risen to 25.4, and thus in the same neighborhood as Martin Van Buren, William Howard Taft, Gerald Ford, and Jimmy Carter. For contemporary assessments of the eighteenth president, in what is proving to be a booming cottage industry, see Jean Edward Smith, *Grant* (New York: Simon and Schuster, 2001); Joan Waugh, *U.S. Grant: American Hero, American Myth* (Chapel Hill: University of North Carolina Press, 2009);

H. W. Brand, *The Man Who Saved the Union: Ulysses Grant in War and Peace* (New York: Doubleday, 2012); Ronald C. White, *American Ulysses: A Life of Ulysses S. Grant* (New York: Random House, 2016); Ron Chernow, *Grant* (New York: Penguin, 2017).

5. *Letters,* 2:22; Adams, *Great Secession Winter,* 65.

6. *Letters,* 2:15.

7. Adams, *Great Secession Winter,* 68, 71.

8. *Letters,* 2:31–32.

9. Samuels, *Young Henry Adams,* 181–82.

10. *Letters,* 2:25. Senator Charles Sumner used the term "Grantism" in a May 1872 speech to emphasize the difference between the Republican Party ("Republicanism") and Grant, with whom he had broken.

11. Butler, *Critical Americans,* 247.

12. *Letters,* 2:37.

Chapter 14: The High Road to Reform

1. *Letters,* 2:41.

2. *Education,* 202; *Letters* 2:42–43, 47.

3. Adams, *Great Secession Winter,* 98, 102, 104.

4. James G. Sproat, *"The Best Men": Liberal Reformers in the Gilded Age* (New York: Oxford University Press, 1968), 249; David Emory Shi and George Brown Tindall, *America: A Narrative History,* vol. 2, brief 10th edition (New York: W. W. Norton,

2016), 715; Adams, *Great Secession Winter,* 104.

5. Adams, *Great Secession Winter,* 111, 112; Richard Hofstadter, *The American Political Tradition: And the Men Who Made It* (New York: Alfred A. Knopf, 1948), 163.

Chapter 15: Following the Money

1. *Education,* 193; *Letters,* 5:199.
2. Mark Van Doren, ed., *The Portable Walt Whitman* (New York: Viking, 1945), 400; Henry George, *Progress and Poverty: An Inquiry into the Cause of Industrial Depressions, and of Increase of Want with Increase of Wealth* (New York: D. Appleton, 1886), 6.
3. David M. Tucker, *Mugwumps: Public Moralists of the Gilded Age* (Columbia: University Press of Missouri, 1998), 19; *Letters,* 2:65.
4. Adams, *Great Secession Winter,* 129, 109, 161, 167.
5. *Letters,* 2:65; Simpson, *Political Education of Henry Adams,* 61.
6. Adams, *Great Secession Winter,* 131, 134.
7. B. O. Flower, *The Arena* (Boston: Arena, 1896), 1001; Adams, *Great Secession Winter,* 135, 136.
8. Adams, *Great Secession Winter,* 136.
9. *Letters,* 2:71; T. J. Stiles, *The First Tycoon: The Epic Life of Cornelius Vanderbilt* (New York: Alfred A. Knopf, 2009), 348–49;

Adams, *Great Secession Winter,* 154.

10. *Education,* 212; *Letters,* 2:66.

11. Adams, *Great Secession Winter,* 163, 162.

12. Ibid., 164, 168.

13. *Education,* 221.

14. *Letters,* 2:90, n2, 100, 95.

15. Samuels, *Young Henry Adams,* 202; *Letters,* 2:74.

16. *Education,* 224–25.

17. *Letters,* 2:72.

Chapter 16: The Professor

1. Samuels, *Young Henry Adams,* 203; Robert Mane, *Henry Adams on the Road to Chartres* (Cambridge, MA: Belknap Press of Harvard University Press, 1971), 35.

2. *Letters,* 2:79, 81.

3. Ibid., 2:81; E. Emerton, *The Practical Method in Higher Historical Instruction* (Boston: Ginn, Heath, 1884), 50.

4. *Education,* 231; *Letters,* 2:81, 82; Edward Chalfant, *Better in Darkness: A Biography of Henry Adams; His Second Life, 1862–1891* (Hamden, CT: Archon Books, 1994), 218.

5. Stewart Mitchell, "Henry Adams and Some of His Students," *Proceedings of the Massachusetts Historical Society,* 3rd series, vol. 66 (October 1936–May 1941), 295; *Education,* 235; Samuels, *Young Henry Adams,* 209.

6. Lindsay Swift, "A Course in History at

Harvard College in the Seventies," *Proceedings, Massachusetts Historical Society* (December, 1918), 75. The Wadsworth House was completed in 1726, built for Harvard's president Benjamin Wadsworth. The College's presidents ceased using the residence when incoming president Jared Sparks announced in 1849 that he would remain in his own Quincy Street home.

7. Edward Chalfant, ed., *Sketches for the North American Review* (Hamden, CT: Archon Books, 1986), 9.
8. Henry Cabot Lodge, *Early Memories* (New York: Charles Scribner's Sons, 1913), 187; Mitchell, "Henry Adams and Some of His Students," 308; William Dusinberre, *Henry Adams: The Myth of Failure* (Charlottesville: University Press of Virginia, 1980), 87; Davis D. Joyce, *Edward Channing and the Great Work* (The Hague: Martinus Nijhoff, 1974), 11; Donnan and Stock, *An Historian's World,* 33.
9. J. Laurence Laughlin, "Some Recollections of Henry Adams," *Scribner's Magazine,* (May 1921), 576.
10. Ibid., 579, 578.
11. Mane, *Henry Adams on the Road to Chartres,* 41; Swift, "Course in History," 75.
12. Swift, "Course in History," 72.
13. *Education,* 239.
14. *Letters,* 2:139.

Chapter 17: The Insurgent

1. *Letters,* 2:89.
2. Ibid., 2:86.
3. Between the Grant and McKinley presidencies (1868–1901) every elected chief executive, excepting Grover Cleveland, served in the Civil War. Two of them, McKinley and Rutherford B. Hayes, served together in the 23rd Regiment of Ohio Volunteer Infantry.
4. Matthew T. Downey, "Horace Greeley and the Politicians: The Liberal Republican Convention in 1872," *Journal of American History* (March 1967), 749; Duberman, *Charles Francis Adams,* 357. On the Governor's "Iceberg"-like bearing, Carl Schurz remembered of his initial encounter with Charles Francis, "I had never seen Mr. Adams before. The appearance of the little bald-headed gentleman with the clean-cut features and blue eyes, to whom I introduced myself . . . reminded me strongly of the portraits I had seen of President John Quincy Adams, his father. What I had read of the habitual frigidity of the demeanor of the father served me to interpret rightly the manner in which the son received me. He said that he was very glad to see me, in a tone which, no doubt, was intended for kindness. It was certainly courteous. But there was a lack of warmth and a stiffness

about it, which, as I afterwards told one of Mr. Adams's sons, to his great amusement, made me feel as though the temperature of the room had dropped several degrees." Carl Schurz, *The Reminiscences of Carl Schurz,* vol. 2 (London: John Murray, 1909), 245.

5. Duberman, *Charles Francis Adams,* 358.
6. Sproat, *"The Best Men,"* 81.
7. *Letters,* 2:137.
8. Ibid., 2:152.

Chapter 18: Clover

1. *Education,* 5. Clover's correspondence is peppered with gossipy and sometimes cutting asides. In separate 1870s letters to her father, the first from Antwerp and the second from Madrid, she observed, "The hour after dinner, with two stupid English-women, was rather severe, tho' as a study of character it was amusing" and "The Spanish women are very ugly, very fat after thirty, much powdered, and ill-dressed beyond words." Both can be found in Ward Thoron, ed., *The Letters of Mrs. Henry Adams, 1865–1883* (New York: Little, Brown, 1936), 21, 197. Henry James, who knew Clover well, called her "a perfect Voltaire in petticoats." Leon Edel, *Henry James Letters,* vol. 2 (Cambridge, MA: Belknap Press of Harvard University Press, 1975), 307.

2. Otto Friedrich, *Clover: The Tragic Love Story of Clover and Henry Adams and Their Brilliant Life in America's Gilded Age* (New York: Simon & Schuster, 1979), 136, 38; *Education,* 48.

3. John McCormick, *George Santayana: A Biography* (New Brunswick, NJ: Transaction, 2003), 14; Santayana, *Persons and Places,* 58–59.

4. *Letters,* 2:132.

5. Ibid., 2:133, 1:xxvii.

6. Ibid., 2:141, n2.

7. Friedrich, *Clover,* 144; Thoron, *Letters of Mrs. Henry Adams,* 14, 15.

8. Thoron, *Letters of Mrs. Henry Adams,* 61.

9. Natalie Dykstra, *Clover Adams: A Gilded and Heartbreaking Life* (New York: Houghton Mifflin Harcourt, 2012), 66; Thoron, *Letters of Mrs. Henry Adams,* 59.

10. *Letters,* 2:180, 227; Edel, *Letters of Henry James,* 246, 307.

Chapter 19: *Essays in Anglo-Saxon Law*

1. *Letters,* 2:178.

2. Chalfant, *Sketches for the* North American Review, 114.

3. For an illuminating discussion on the impact of German historical training in America, see the first chapter — "The European Legacy: Ranke, Bacon, Flaubert" — in Peter Novick's *That Noble Dream: The*

"Objectivity Question" and the American Historical Profession (New York: Cambridge University Press, 1988).

4. Samuels, *Young Henry Adams,* 252.
5. Laughlin, "Some Recollections of Henry Adams," 579.
6. William R. Taylor, "Francis Parkman," in Marcus Cunliffe and Robin W. Winks, eds., *Pastmasters: Some Essays on American Historians* (New York: Harper & Row, 1969), 4.
7. Henry Adams, ed., *Essays in Anglo-Saxon Law* (Boston: Little, Brown, 1876), 1.
8. Ibid., 6; Daniel Okrent, *The Guarded Gate: How Patricians and Eugenicists Kept Two Generations of Jews, Italians, and Other European Immigrants Out of America* (New York: Scribner, 2019), 48, 56.
9. James D. Richardson, *A Compilation of the Messages and Papers of the Presidents, 1789–1897,* vol. 9 (Washington, DC: Government Printing Office, 1898), 757.
10. Samuels, *Young Henry Adams,* 255; Michael Kraus and Davis D. Joyce, *The Writing of American History* (Norman: University of Oklahoma Press, 1985), 145.
11. *Letters,* 2:280.

Chapter 20: Political Adieu

1. Brooks Adams, "The Platform of the New Party," *North American Review* (July 1874), 41, 45, 59.
2. Adams, *Great Secession Winter,* 292.
3. *Letters,* 2:217, 226, 240.
4. Ibid., 2:249.
5. Michael Holt, *By One Vote: The Disputed Presidential Election of 1876* (Lawrence: University Press of Kansas, 2008), 78; Carl Schurz, *Speeches, Correspondence and Political Papers of Carl Schurz,* vol. 3, ed. Frederic Bancroft (New York: G. P. Putnam's Sons, 1913), 229; Hans L. Trefousse, *Carl Schurz: A Biography* (New York: Fordham University Press, 1998), 228.
6. *Letters,* 2:276.
7. Adams, *Great Secession Winter,* 296.
8. *Letters,* 2:279.
9. Ibid., 2:285, 292.
10. Adams, *Great Secession Winter,* 293.
11. Duberman, *Charles Francis Adams,* 510, n32.
12. *Letters,* 2:287.

Chapter 21: Filial Piety

1. *Letters,* 2:301. Lodge won his first state election — to serve in the Massachusetts House of Representatives — three years after Adams's curriculum proposal to Eliot.

2. Henry Cabot Lodge, ed., *Life and Letters of George Cabot* (Boston: Little, Brown, 1877), vi.

3. *Letters,* 2:308; Ormond Seavey, "Henry Adams and Henry Cabot Lodge — Teacher and Student: A Complicated Interaction," in William Merrill Decker and Earl N. Harbert, eds., *Henry Adams and the Need to Know* (Boston: Massachusetts Historical Society, 2005), 57; *The Nation,* July 5, 1877, 13.

4. Henry Adams, ed., *Documents relating to New England Federalism, 1800–1815* (Boston: Little, Brown, 1877), 339, 352, 356.

5. Ibid., 43, 46, 47.

6. Ibid., 144, v.

7. Seavey, "Henry Adams and Henry Cabot Lodge," *Henry Adams,* 68.

8. Henry Adams, *History of the United States of America during the Administrations of James Madison* (New York: Library of America, 1986), 1112, 1117.

9. James M. Banner Jr., *To the Hartford Convention: The Federalists and the Origins of Party Politics in Massachusetts, 1789–1815* (New York: Alfred A. Knopf, 1969), 373.

Chapter 22: Emancipation

1. Louisa Hooper Thoron to Ernest Samuels, June 27, 1943, b3, f4, ESP; Dykstra, *Clover*

Adams, 84.

2. Nagel, *Descent from Glory,* 268, 269.

3. Henry Adams, *The Degradation of the Democratic Dogma* (New York: Macmillan, 1919), 6.

4. *Letters,* 2:225, 235.

5. Ibid., 2:275.

6. Ibid., 2:302, 293, 313. Note that Henry disavowed all "university work." A year after quitting Harvard he received an offer to teach at Johns Hopkins University. Its president, Daniel Gilman, perhaps thought that Baltimore's proximity to Washington might clinch the deal. Adams tendered a definitively negative reply to Gilman: "I do not care to become again a Professor on any terms" (ibid., 2:327).

7. Ibid., 2:303.

8. Dykstra, *Clover Adams,* 92; Samuels, *Henry Adams,* 124.

9. J. C. Levenson, Ernest Samuels, Charles Vandersee, and Viola Hopkins Winner, "Supplement to *The Letters of Henry Adams:* Letters Omitted from the Harvard University Press Edition of *The Letters of Henry Adams,* Part I: 1861–1902" (Boston: Massachusetts Historical Society, 1989), 1882–1.

Chapter 23: Hearts Play

1. *Congressional Record: Containing the Proceedings and Debates of the Forty-Third Congress, Second Session,* vol. 3 (Washington, DC: Government Printing Office, 1875), 1566.
2. Michael O'Brien, *Henry Adams and the Southern Question* (Athens: University of Georgia Press, 2005), 46.
3. Sims was a prominent surgeon in Montgomery, Alabama, who experimented in the late 1840s on enslaved African American women. Later called the Father of Gynecology for his successful treatment of vesicovaginal fistula, he left his native South for New York and then Europe, where he treated Empress Eugénie de Montijo (wife of Napoleon III). Returning to New York in 1871, he helped establish the New York Cancer Hospital and served (1876–77) as president of the American Medical Association. In 2018 a statue of Sims in Central Park, across from the New York Academy of Medicine, was removed after several years of protests accusing Sims of medical racism.
4. *Letters,* 2:246.
5. Ibid., 2:315–16.
6. Ibid., 2:326–27.
7. Patricia O'Toole, *The Five of Hearts: An Intimate Portrait of Henry Adams and His*

Friends, 1880–1918 (NewYork: Clarkson N. Potter, 1990), 68; Edel, *Letters of Henry James,* vol. 2, 366.

8. *Letters,* 2:348. Adams refers to Yoshida Kiyonari, Japanese minister to the United States, 1874–81.

9. Ibid., 2:349.

10. Dykstra, *Clover Adams,* 198; *Letters,* 2:349.

11. Henry perhaps hinted at King's interest in dark-skinned and lower-class women when he wrote in the *Education,* "The women were jealous because, at heart, King had no faith in the American woman; he loved types more robust." At the time he wrote this, both King and Hay were dead and Ada Copeland King was receiving a monthly stipend and living in a house provided by Hay. She died in 1964 (*Education,* 245).

12. Chalfant, *Sketches for the* North American Review, 65; *Education,* 244.

13. Edel., *Letters of Henry James,* vol. 2, 373.

Chapter 24: Gallatin

1. Samuel Eliot Morison, *The Life and Letters of Harrison Gray Otis, Federalist, 1765–1848,* vol. 1 (Boston: Houghton Mifflin, 1913), ix; Samuel Eliot Morison, *Harrison Gray Otis, the Urbane Federalist: 1765–1848* (Boston: Houghton Mifflin, 1969). Re-

viewer John J. Waters described the latter work as "mirror[ing] the values of an older historical tradition. . . . It is written with wit, verve, and an occasional *apologia.*" *New England Quarterly* (September 1969), 448.

2. *Letters,* 2:138.
3. Henry Adams, *The Life of Albert Gallatin* (Philadelphia: J. B. Lippincott, 1880), iii.
4. Ibid., 635, 4–5.
5. Ibid., 677, 497.
6. Friedrich, *Clover,* 212. One modern historian, Robert Allen Rutland, insists upon the excellence of the biography, writing in 1990, "Henry Adams's affectionate portrait, *Life of Albert Gallatin,* has not been surpassed by modern scholarship." Robert Allen Rutland, *The Presidency of James Madison* (Lawrence: University Press of Kansas, 1990), 217.
7. *Nation,* August 21, 1879, 128.
8. *Letters,* 2:330.
9. Ibid., 2:376.

Chapter 25: *Democracy*

1. George Monteiro, ed., *The Correspondence of Henry James and Henry Adams, 1877–1914* (Baton Rouge: Louisiana State University Press, 1992), 47, n2.
2. *Letters,* 2:273.
3. Henry Adams, *Democracy: An American Novel* (New York: New American Library,

1983), 82; *Education,* 37.

4. Adams, *Democracy,* 13, 14.

5. Ibid., 14, 17.

6. Ibid., 47, 49.

7. Ibid., 23, 119.

8. Ibid., 85, 24, 167.

9. Monteiro, *Correspondence of Henry James and Henry Adams,* 52–53.

10. Thoron, *Letters of Mrs. Henry Adams,* 246–47; *Letters,* 2:457.

11. Stephen Gwynn, ed., *The Letters and Friendships of Sir Cecil Spring Rice,* vol. 1 (Boston: Houghton Mifflin, 1929), 59; Theodore Stanton, ed., *A Manual of American Literature* (New York: G. P. Putnam's Sons, 1909), 212–13; Ernest Samuels, *Henry Adams: The Middle Years* (Cambridge, MA: Harvard University Press, 1958), 69.

12. Adams, *Democracy,* 176; Elting E. Morison, ed., *The Letters of Theodore Roosevelt,* vol. 5 (Cambridge, MA: Harvard University Press, 1952), 10.

Chapter 26: Second Heart

1. *Education,* 260.

2. *Letters,* 1:301.

3. Adams Homans, *Education by Uncles,* 94; Arline Boucher Tehan, *Henry Adams in Love: The Pursuit of Elizabeth Sherman Cam-*

eron (New York: Universe Books, 1983), 28.

4. *Education,* 260, 261. Henry's grandfather John Quincy Adams also had a low opinion of Pennsylvanians. Their "fanatical passion for Andrew Jackson," he wrote, referencing Shakespeare's *Midsummer Night's Dream,* "can be compared to nothing but that of Titania Queen of the Fairies, for Bottom, after his Assification." David Waldstreicher, ed., *John Quincy Adams, Diaries, II: 1821–1848* (New York: Library of America, 2017), 337.

5. Adams Homans, *Education by Uncles,* 94; John Taliaferro, *All the Great Prizes: The Life of John Hay, from Lincoln to Roosevelt* (New York: Simon and Schuster, 2013), 188; Dykstra, *Clover Adams,* 129.

6. Taliaferro, *All the Great Prizes,* 188.

7. Tehan, *Henry Adams in Love,* 31, 41.

8. Dykstra, *Clover Adams,* 129; O'Toole, *Five of Hearts,* 91; Julia Stoddard Parsons, *Scattered Memories* (Boston: Bruce Humphries, 1938), 56. Two years after the marriage, Parsons attended a dinner party at the Camerons' and wrote of the senator's conventionality: "Mr. Cameron . . . is a remarkable man in some respects, set in his own will, with no imagination, his feet always solidly on the ground. . . . Much as I like Mr. Cameron I think the odds are

against Elisabeth in this marriage" (*Scattered Memories,* 66).

9. Samuels, *Henry Adams: The Middle Years,* 141.

10. Thoron, *Letters of Mrs. Henry Adams,* 256–57.

11. *Letters,* 2:487–88, emphasis added; 2:497, 505.

Chapter 27: Back to Bizarre

1. *Letters,* 2:424, 477, 476. While researching the *Gallatin* Adams had written to Hugh Blair Grigsby, then president of the Virginia Historical Society, of "hav[ing] unearthed much private correspondence of that time, including masses of John Randolph's . . . letters" (*Letters,* 2:339).

2. Adams, *Gallatin,* 329.

3. Henry Adams, *John Randolph* (Boston: Houghton, Mifflin, 1882), 9.

4. Ibid., 10; *Education,* 6.

5. Adams, *Randolph,* 192.

6. Ibid., 299; *Letters,* 2:468.

7. Samuels, *Henry Adams: The Middle Years,* 203; Adams, *Randolph,* 25.

8. *Letters,* 2:479; Samuels, *Henry Adams: The Middle Years,* 455, n5; Adams, *The Adams Family,* 328.

9. *Letters,* 2:424, 472–73.

10. Ibid., 2:514.

Chapter 28: Between Science and Salvation

1. Thomas Hardy, *Collected Poems of Thomas Hardy* (New York: Macmillan, 1925), 308.
2. The evolutionary idea was once a staple in Adams's classes at Harvard. A former student wrote that for Henry history "had to be treated as an evolution. Without training in science he was early captivated by the geologist, Sir Charles Lyell, and thereafter we heard much of the pteraspis in Siberia, and the first beginning of things. There was in his mind an a priori assumption that the actions of men follow certain laws, and if Adams could state these laws or trace the expected evolution he was happy." Laughlin, "Some Recollections of Henry Adams," 579, quoted in Arthur F. Beringause, *Brooks Adams: A Biography* (New York: Alfred A. Knopf, 1955), 124–25.
3. Nathaniel Hawthorne, *The Complete Novels and Selected Tales of Nathaniel Hawthorne,* ed. Norman Holmes Pearson (New York: Modern Library, 1937), 983, 989.
4. Henry Adams, *Esther: A Novel* (New York: Penguin Books, 1999), 159.
5. Louisa Hooper Thoron to Ernest Samuels, April 21, 1954, b15, f16, ESP; *Letters,* 2:133; Adams, *Esther,* xviii, xix; Friedrich, *Clover,* 303; Burke Wilkinson, *Uncommon Clay: The Life and Works of Augustus Saint*

Gaudens (New York: Harcourt, Brace, Jovanovich, 1985), 233.
6. Dykstra, *Clover Adams,* 153; *Letters,* 3:34. For a discussion of Clover and Esther overlaps, see David F. Musto, " 'Heart's Blood': Henry Adams's *Esther* and Wife Clover," *New England Quarterly* (June 1998), 266–81.
7. Adams, *Esther,* 113.
8. *Letters,* 3:416.
9. Ibid., 2:567, 568, 567, n1.
10. Ibid., 3:409.

Chapter 29: The New House

1. Friedrich, *Clover,* 287.
2. Ibid., 287–88.
3. *The Copper Handbook: A Manuel of the Copper Industry of the United States and Foreign Countries,* vol. 2 (Houghton, MI: Compiled and Published by Horace J. Stevens, 1902), 133–146; Samuels, *Henry Adams: The Middle Years,* 317.
4. *Letters,* 2:539; Sarah Luria, *Capital Speculations: Writing and Building Washington D.C.* (Durham: University of New Hampshire Press, 2006), 133.
5. Marc Friedlaender, "Henry Hobson Richardson, Henry Adams, and John Jay," *Journal of the Society of Architectural Historians* (October 1970), 233; Cater, *Henry Adams and His Friends,* lxiii–lxiv.

6. Adams Homans, *Education by Uncles,* 42–45.
7. Ernst Scheyer, *The Circle of Henry Adams: Art and Artists* (Detroit: Wayne State University Press, 1970), 61.
8. Thoron, *Letters of Mrs. Henry Adams,* 379; Friedlaender, "Henry Hobson Richardson," 238, 240, 237.
9. Thoron, *Letters of Mrs. Henry Adams,* 442; *Letters,* 2:533.
10. Mane, *Henry Adams on the Road to Chartres,* 66.

Chapter 30: Empty Heart

1. Cynthia Mills, *Beyond Grief: Sculpture & Wonder in the Gilded Age Cemetery* (Washington, D.C.: Smithsonian Institution Scholarly Press, 2014), 11.
2. Anderson, *Letters and Journals of General Nicholas Longworth Anderson,* 252.
3. O'Toole, *Five of Hearts,* 159; Leon Edel, ed., *Henry James Letters,* vol. 3 (Cambridge, MA: Belknap Press of Harvard University Press, 1980), 107, 111; Leon Edel, ed., *The Complete Tales of Henry James,* vol. 7, (Philadelphia: J. B. Lippincott, 1963), 84.
4. Thoron, *The Letters of Mrs. Henry Adams,* 52.
5. *Letters,* 2:579, 606, 590.
6. Ibid., 2:597, 600, 607, 5:592.

7. Friedrich, *Clover,* 333; O'Toole, *Five of Hearts,* 159.
8. Samuels to Dr. Abraham Myerson, November 27, 1953, b15, f14, ESP.
9. Musto, " 'Heart's Blood,' " 275; Nagel, *Descent from Glory,* 279.
10. Nagel, *Descent from Glory,* 276.
11. Friedrich, *Clover,* 318.
12. Samuels, *Henry Adams: The Middle Years,* 272, 273.
13. Mills, *Beyond Grief,* 201 n1, n3; Friedrich, *Clover,* 320.
14. *Letters,* 2:643.
15. Samuels, *Henry Adams: The Middle Years,* 283; *Letters,* 2:641, n3, 5:266.

PART II: PERFORMING HENRY ADAMS

Chapter 31: The Posthumous Life

1. *Letters,* 2:645.
2. Mabel La Farge, ed., *Letters to a Niece and Prayer to the Virgin of Chartres, by Henry Adams* (Boston: Houghton Mifflin, 1920), 70; Mark DeWolfe Howe, ed., *Holmes-Pollock Letters: The Correspondence of Mr. Justice Holmes and Sir Frederick Pollock, 1874–1932,* vol. 2 (Cambridge, MA: Harvard University Press, 1941), 18.
3. Adams, *Degradation of the Democratic Dogma,* 1–2; Friedrich, *Clover,* 167–68.
4. Robert Underwood Johnson, *Remembered*

Yesterdays (Boston: Little, Brown, 1923), 447.

5. Gwynn, *Letters and Friendships of Sir Cecil Spring Rice,* 68, 78, 81; Donnan and Stock, *An Historian's World,* 138.

Chapter 32: Japan

1. *Letters,* 2:44, 3:78; Thoron, *Letters of Mrs. Henry Adams,* 242; Christopher Benfey, *The Great Wave: Gilded Age Misfits, Japanese Eccentrics, and the Opening of Old Japan* (New York: Random House, 2003), 121.
2. Patricia Vigderman, "Henry Adams in Japan," *Southwest Review* (January 2004), 150.
3. Henry David Thoreau, *Walden and Civil Disobedience* (New York: Penguin Books, 1983), 346; Robert D. Richardson Jr., *Emerson: The Mind on Fire* (Berkeley: University of California Press, 1995), 393; Benfey, *The Great Wave,* xi–xviii.
4. It is uncertain if Henry and Clover had determined to try the Pacific in tandem, though a tantalizing hint is casually dropped into *Esther:* "How pleasant it would be to go off to Japan together and fill our sketchbooks with drawings" (Adams, *Esther,* 118).
5. *Letters,* 3:17; John L. Yarnall, *John La Farge, a Biographical and Critical Study* (Burlington, VT: Ashgate, 2012), 84, 119; Samuels, *Henry Adams: The Middle Years,*

298–99.

6. *Letters,* 3:10, 12, 13.
7. Jules Verne, *Around the World in Eighty Days,* trans. Geo. M. Towle (Philadelphia: Porter & Coates, 1873), 179.
8. John La Farge, *An Artist's Letters from Japan* (New York: Century, 1897), 1, 4, 25.
9. *Letters,* 3:16, 26.
10. Ibid., 3:18.
11. Ibid., 3:37; James L. Yarnall, "John La Farge and Henry Adams in Japan," *American Art Journal* 21, no. 1 (1989), 41, 48.
12. *Letters,* 3:15, 19, 30, 21, 27.
13. Ibid., 3:38.
14. La Farge, *Letters from Japan,* vii.
15. *Letters,* 3:51.

Chapter 33: The Historian's Tale

1. William T. Hutchinson, ed., *The Marcus W. Jernegan Essays in American Historiography* (Chicago: University of Chicago Press, 1937), 195; Noble E. Cunningham Jr., *The United States in 1800: Henry Adams Revisited* (Charlottesville: University Press of Virginia, 1988), vii; Garry Wills, *Henry Adams and the Making of America* (Boston: Houghton Mifflin, 2005), 1; Morgan, "Unread Masterpiece," 20.
2. Laughlin, "Some Recollections of Henry Adams," 582.
3. *Letters,* 2:394, 417. Vignaud maintained

his position in Paris until 1909.

4. Ibid., 2:469, 463, 439, 428. An expurgated and privately published copy of Rush's autobiography arrived in 1905; a new edition put out by Princeton University Press appeared in 1948: George W. Corner, ed., *The Autobiography of Benjamin Rush: His "Travels through Life" Together with His Common Place Book for 1789–1813* (Princeton, NJ: Princeton University Press, 1948).

5. *Letters,* 2:466, 491.

6. Adams, *History of the United States of America during the Administrations of James Madison,* 716; Henry Adams, *History of the United States of America during the Administrations of Thomas Jefferson* (New York: Library of America, 1986), 907, 280.

7. *The North America Review vol. CXXI* (Boston: James R. Osgood, 1875), 475.

8. *Letters,* 3:131.

9. *Letters,* 4:5; Charles Franklin Thwing, *Guides, Philosophers and Friends: Studies of College Men* (New York: Macmillan, 1927), 225; Samuel Eliot Morison, "A Letter and a Few Reminiscences of Henry Adams," *New England Quarterly* (March 1954), 97. According to Charles Scribner, Adams's royalties for the ten years 1903–13 came to $1,458 — about $40,000 in current dollars. This sales information can be found in Robert F. Sayre, *The Examined Self: Benja-*

min Franklin, Henry Adams, Henry James (Princeton, NJ: Princeton University Press, 1964), 73.

10. C. Waller Barrett, ed., *The Making of a History: Letters of Henry Adams to Henry Vignaud and Charles Scribner, 1879–1913* (Boston: Massachusetts Historical Society, 1959), 68; Kraus and Joyce, *Writing of American History,* 158; DeWolfe Howe, *Holmes-Laski Letters,* vol. 1, 145.

11. Cunningham, *United States in 1800,* 59–60.

12. Kraus and Joyce, *Writing of American History,* 100; Adams, *History of the United States of America during the Administrations of Thomas Jefferson,* 119–20.

13. Edward Gibbon, *Memoirs of the Life and Writings of Edward Gibbon,* ed. Oliver Farrar Emerson (Boston: Ginn, 1898), 180.

14. Samuels, *Henry Adams,* 225.

Chapter 34: Babes in Paradise

1. Paul Bourget, *Outre-mer: Impressions of America* (New York: Charles Scribner's Sons, 1895), 367; *Letters,* 2:551. Elisabeth Hodermarsky writes, "It was not the work of his artist-predecessors that provided the greatest allure for La Farge" to accept Henry's invitation, "but rather the lavish accounts of explorers such as Louis-Antoine de Bougainville, Captain James Cook, and

682

Samuel Wallis, and writers such as Pierre Loti, Herman Melville, Robert Louis Stevenson, and Charles Warren Stoddard, whose experiences in the South Pacific — often mixes of fact and fiction — enticed the artist with the notion of a tropical paradise only minimally touched by Western influence." Elisabeth Hodermarsky, "A Second Paradise: John La Farge's Search for the Sublime in the Twilight of the American Landscape Movement," in Elisabeth Hodermarsky, ed., *John La Farge's Second Paradise: Voyages in the South Seas, 1890–1891* (New Haven, CT: Yale University Press, 2010), 11.

2. Elizabeth C. Childs, "Exoticisms in the South Seas: John La Farge and Henry Adams Encounter the Pacific," in Hodermarsky, *John La Farge's Second Paradise,* 49.

3. *Education,* 290.

4. Childs, "Exoticisms in the South Seas," 65; *Letters,* 3:323, 500, 307, 301.

5. *Letters,* 3:322, 474, 484.

6. Ernest Samuels, *Henry Adams: The Major Phase* (Cambridge, MA: Harvard University Press, 1964), 24.

7. Letters, 3:290–91.

8. Ibid., 3:322, 317.

9. Sidney Colvin, ed., *The Letters of Robert Louis Stevenson,* vol. 3 (New York: Charles Scribner's Sons, 1911), 269; *Letters,* 3:296.

10. Samuels, *Henry Adams: The Major Phase,* 41.

11. Childs, "Exoticisms in the South Seas," 71.

12. Ibid., 73; La Farge, *Letters to a Niece,* 44. Adams may have planned a return to Tahiti. In a communication (now lost) to Tati's sister Marau, Henry, so Tati reported, indicated his interest in "coming" again to the island for another extended stay. Childs, "Exoticism in the South Seas," 85, n83.

13. *Letters,* 3:471, 4:156. In 1901 a new edition privately printed in Paris appeared under the title *Memoirs of Arii Taimai E Marama of Eimeo Teriirere of Tooraai Teriinui of Tahiti* by Tauraatua I Amo (Adams's adopted Tahitian name). Its slight circulation included a handful of scholarly libraries.

14. Derek Freeman to J. W. Davidson, May 27, 1967, Davidson Papers, Australian National University Archives, Series 57/119. Rupert Brooke (1887–1915) wrote the poem "Tiare Tahiti," whose final lines, "Well this side of Paradise! . . . There's little comfort in the wise," inspired the title of F. Scott Fitzgerald's 1920 debut novel *This Side of Paradise.* I'm most grateful to Doug Munro of the University of Queensland for alerting me to the Freeman quote. Perhaps sensing the expression of his own interests

and outlook in the *Memoirs,* Henry attempted to distance himself from the project with a glancing protest. "I am not the man to write Polynesian," he told Hay. "My methods are all intellectual, analytic and modern" (*Letters,* 3:434).

15. *Letters,* 3:513.

16. Ibid., 3:362, 374, 525. Henry, it should be noted, complained of Anglos as well. After twelve days in Sydney on the long return voyage home, he grumbled, "Australia and the Australians bore me. They are second-rate United States" (*Letters,* 3:520).

17. Ibid., 3:285.

Chapter 35: The First Law of Tame Cats

1. *Letters,* 3:135, 137, 142.
2. Ibid., 3:285.
3. Ibid., 3:294.
4. Ibid., 3:304.
5. Ibid., 3:406, 544.
6. Taliaferro, *All the Great Prizes,* 277.
7. Ibid., 321.
8. *Letters,* 5:95.
9. Ibid., 3:555.
10. Skip Moskey, "A Gilded Age Thanksgiving Dinner in London (1891)," *Gilded Age in America,* November 20, 2017, https://gildedage.us/larz-anderson-henry-adams-london-1891/.
11. *Letters,* 3:557.

12. Ibid., 3:557–58.
13. Ibid., 3:558.
14. Ibid., 3:582, 593, 594, 4:20, 22, 3:560; Taliaferro, *All the Great Prizes,* 270.
15. Edward Chalfant, *Improvement of the World: A Biography of Henry Adams, His Last Life, 1891–1918* (Hamden, CT: Archon Books, 2001), 63.

Chapter 36: What the Sphinx Said

1. Ernest Scheyer, "The Adams Memorial by Augustus Saint-Gaudens," *Art Quarterly* (Summer 1956), 180–81.
2. Wilkinson, *Uncommon Clay,* 236; *Letters,* 3:160.
3. Louise Hall Tharp, *Saint-Gaudens and the Gilded Era* (Boston: Little, Brown, 1969), 225; Homer Saint-Gaudens, ed., *The Reminiscences of Augustus Saint-Gaudens,* vol. 2 (New York: Century, 1913), 362.
4. *Letters,* 6:198; Samuels, *Henry Adams,* 280.
5. Parsons, *Scattered Memories,* 159. The quoted verse appears on the Graham Memorial, a marker for William Graham (1817–1885), a Scottish politician, merchant, shipper, and connoisseur (both collector and patron) of Pre-Raphaelites. The bronze work features doves — the bearers of glad tidings — flitting about plants and flowers and is presumably a light contrast to the "heavy" Adams shrine.

6. *Education,* 257–58.
7. *Letters,* 3:416, 482, n4, 496; Chalfant, *Better in Darkness,* 619.
8. *Letters,* 4:4; *Education,* 257.
9. *Letters,* 6:109.
10. Joseph P. Lash, *Eleanor and Franklin* (New York: W. W. Norton, 1971), 358.
11. John Galsworthy, *A Modern Comedy* (New York: Charles Scribner's Sons, 1931), 507.
12. John Galsworthy, *The Forsyte Saga* (New York: Scribner, 1996), 575.

Chapter 37: Chicago

1. *Education,* 268.
2. Bessie Louise Pierce, ed., *As Others See Chicago: Impressions of Visitors, 1673–1933* (Chicago: University of Chicago Press, 2004), 250–51, 276, 278.
3. *Letters,* 4:102; *Education,* 266.
4. *Letters,* 4:134.
5. Ibid., 4:133.
6. Adams, *History of the United States of America during the Administrations of James Madison,* 1345, 1334.

Chapter 38: The Gold-Bugs

1. Nagel, *Descent from Glory,* 297; Adams, *Charles Francis Adams, 1835–1915,* 200; Samuels, *Henry Adams,* 289.
2. *Letters,* 4:114, 117.

3. Nagel, *Descent from Glory,* 305.
4. *Letters,* 4:117, 121.
5. Ibid., 4:119, 125, 128.
6. Ibid., 4:121, n1, 138.
7. *Letters,* 6:705; H. W. Brands, *The Selected Letters of Theodore Roosevelt* (New York: Cooper Square Press, 2001), 139; Beringause, *Brooks Adams,* 255.
8. Max Nordau, *Degeneration* (New York: D. Appleton, 1895), 317. Arthur Herman's *The Idea of Decline in Western History* (New York: Free Press, 1997) offers a strong overview of its subject.
9. Brooks Adams, *The Law of Civilization and Decay* (New York: Macmillan, 1895), 81.
10. Letters, 4:322, 335–36; Adams, *Degradation of the Democratic Dogma,* 94. Charles Beard, perhaps the most important American historian of the first half of the twentieth century, maintained that *Law of Civilization and Decay* deserves "to be included among the outstanding documents of intellectual history in the United States and, in a way, the Western World." Beard thought the volume a living and critical statement of its time, a product of the Panic of 1893, the Populist movement, and the triumph of imperialism. He reserved for the book "a distinct position in the long line of American protests against plutocratic tendencies in American development." Charles Beard,

"Introduction," in Books Adams, *The Law of Civilization and Decay* (New York: Alfred A. Knopf, 1943), 3.
11. *Letters,* 4:130.

Chapter 39: "My Cuba"

1. *Letters,* 3:103, 104, 108, 101.
2. Ibid., 4:184, 156–57.
3. Ibid., 4:160.
4. Ibid., 4:167, 166, 161, 165.
5. Samuels, *Henry Adams: The Major Phase,* 160.
6. *Letters,* 4:180, 185.
7. George C. Herring, *From Colony to Superpower: U.S. Foreign Relations Since 1776* (New York: Oxford University Press, 2008), 307; *Letters,* 4:346.
8. *Letters,* 4:372.
9. Ibid., 4:368.
10. *Education,* 251. Cleveland harbored no affection for Henry Adams or his pro-Cuban independence friends. In a September 1895 communication to Secretary of State Richard Olney, the president nixed an appointment in the State Department, in part, because of the gentleman's dubious associates: "I write now to say that I do not think the young man we were talking about [William Phillips] will do at all. . . . I learn that he is a good deal of a club man, and, what is a settler with me, that his close

intimates are John Hay, Henry Adams, Cabot Lodge, and such." Allan Nevins, ed., *Letters of Grover Cleveland, 1850–1908* (Boston: Houghton Mifflin, 1933), 407. Rexford Tugwell, a member of Franklin Roosevelt's New Deal "Brain Trust," later wrote a biography of Cleveland in which he ventured that insecurity kept the president from cultivating his prominent Lafayette Square neighbors: "Hay was just finishing his biography of Lincoln, and Adams had retired from his Harvard professorship and was the center of an intellectual circle that Cleveland might have taken advantage of. He made no such attempt. . . . He might have given the country a vision of its possibilities in the new age of productivity that was obviously beginning; more conversation with the company available to him would have made him a better President." Rexford G. Tugwell, *Grover Cleveland* (New York: Macmillan, 1968), 146–47.

11. *Letters,* 4:432.

Chapter 40: The Tyranny of Science

1. *Letters,* 5:247–48.
2. Ibid., 2:553, 623, 625, 628.
3. Ibid., 4:21.
4. Ibid., 4:26, 27, n1.
5. Ibid., 4:37.
6. Ibid., 4:137, 205, 207, 208.

7. Ibid., 4:214, 228, n2.
8. Adams, *Great Secession Winter,* 417, 418, 419.
9. Ibid., 419–21.
10. Ibid., 422.

Chapter 41: The Felt Experience

1. *Education,* 276.
2. *Letters,* 4:312, 314; T. J. Jackson Lears, *No Place of Grace: Antimodernism and the Transformation of American Culture, 1880–1920* (New York: Pantheon Books, 1981), 132–33.
3. *Education,* 387.
4. Ibid., 275.
5. *Letters,* 4:319, 329.
6. Ibid., 4:311, 324, 321.
7. Ibid., 4:317, 312, 311.
8. La Farge, *Letters to a Niece,* 79.
9. *Education,* 278.

Chapter 42: Blame

1. *Letters,* 4:407.
2. Ibid., 4:551.
3. La Farge, *Letters to a Niece,* 16.
4. John Higham, "Anti-Semitism in the Gilded Age: A Reinterpretation," *Mississippi Valley Historical Review* (March 1957), 572.
5. Leonard Dinnerstein, *Antisemitism in America* (New York: Oxford University

Press, 1994), 41.
6. Carl N. Degler, *In Search of Human Nature: The Decline and Revival of Darwinism in American Social Thought* (New York: Oxford University Press, 1991), 46.
7. Okrent, *The Guarded Gate,* 142.
8. *Letters,* 1:82; J. C. Levenson, "The Etiology of Israel Adams: The Onset, Waning, and Relevance of Henry Adams's Anti-Semitism," *New Literary History* (Summer 1994), 573.
9. *Education,* 3; Adams, *History of the United States of America during the Administrations of Thomas Jefferson,* 212.
10. Adams, *Democracy,* 31, 32, 189.
11. *Letters,* 5:550, 551, n8.
12. Ibid., 4:333.
13. Adams, *Law of Civilization and Decay,* 352–53, 362.
14. *Letters,* 6:301.
15. Ibid., 4:335.
16. Ibid., 5:14.
17. Ibid., 5:26, 9, 27, 32–3, 26. Adams's disregard for Dreyfus may have influenced his inability to spell the officer's name correctly. He variously wrote "Dreifus" and "Dreifuss."
18. Albert S. Lindemann, *Esau's Tears: Modern Anti-Semitism and the Rise of the Jews* (New York: Cambridge University Press, 1997), 374; Samuels, *Henry Adams:*

The Major Phase, 184.

19. Owen Wister, *Roosevelt: The Story of a Friendship, 1880–1919* (New York: Macmillan, 1930), 149.
20. Levenson, "Etiology of Israel Adams," 570.
21. Hofstadter to Kazin, internal evidence suggests 1943, Alfred Kazin Papers, the Berg Collection, New York Public Library; Alfred Kazin, *New York Jew* (New York: Alfred A. Knopf, 1978), 14.

Chapter 43: The Jingo

1. *Letters,* 4:505, 523.
2. Ibid., 4:523.
3. Ibid., 4:530.
4. Ibid., 4:523, 539.
5. Ibid., 4:585, 598–99.
6. Adams Homans, *Education by Uncles,* 91; *Letters,* 4:607.
7. *Letters,* 5:616.
8. Wister, *Roosevelt,* 148.
9. *Letters,* 4:617, n1, 619.
10. Ibid., 4:644, 633, 515; Robert L. Beisner, *Twelve against Empire: The Anti-Imperialists, 1898–1900* (New York: McGraw-Hill, 1968), 44, 48.

Chapter 44: Silent and Infinite Force

1. Richard D. Mandell, *Paris 1900: The World's Fair* (Toronto: University of Toronto

Press, 1967), xi; *Letters,* 5:132, 145.

2. *Letters,* 5:169; *Education,* 299.

3. *Education,* 298. Historian Miriam R. Levin has observed, "By 1900 the mid-century idea of the modern city based on steam and railroad industries had played out to its logical conclusion. The advent of electricity, the electric and gasoline driven automobile, and the airplane, as well as steel, were the signifiers of a new, more exciting, and potentially dangerous era, freed from the old earthbound constraints." Miriam R. Levin, "Bringing the Future to Earth in Paris, 1851–1914," in Miriam R. Levin, Sophie Forgan, Martina Hessler, Robert H. Kargon, and Morris Low, eds., *Urban Modernity: Cultural Innovation in the Second Industrial Revolution* (Cambridge, MA: MIT Press, 2010), 56–57. Like Adams, the American painter and photographer Charles Sheeler (1883–1965) was interested in how machine aesthetics had come to replace older spiritual beliefs and practices. Known for his iconographic photographs of towering skyscrapers, elevated steel cranes, smoking production foundries, and vast open-hearth structures, Sheeler celebrated the promise of mass production. "Industry concerns the greatest number," he told a biographer in the 1930s. "It may be true, as has been said, that our factories are our substitute for religious expression." Sheeler

enshrined both sides of Western spiritual life on terms quite familiar to Henry Adams, contrasting the dynamo and the Virgin in his striking 1927 photographs of the Ford Motor Company's new River Rouge plant and 1929 prints of Chartres Cathedral. The two series come together in dramatic images featuring the crisscrossed conveyers at Ford and Chartres's majestic flying buttresses. When viewed together the shots suggest a unity of purpose and untapped power. Karen Lucic, *Charles Sheeler and the Cult of the Machine* (London: Reaktion Books, 1991), 14.

4. Henry Adams, *Mont-Saint-Michel and Chartres* (New York: Penguin Books, 1986), 328.
5. *Education,* 301.

Chapter 45: Lamb among Lions

1. *Letters,* 6:180, 3:576, 591, 5:716.
2. *Education,* 260.
3. *Letters,* 5:323, 357.
4. John Garraty, *Henry Cabot Lodge: A Biography* (New York: Alfred A. Knopf, 1953), 212. Named senior class poet at Brown University, Hay later published *Pike County Ballads and Other Poems* (1871), followed by *Poems* (1890).
5. *Letters,* 5:326.
6. Taliaferro, *All the Great Prizes,* 341.
7. *Letters,* 5:547.

8. Charles Downer Hazen, ed., *The Letters of William Roscoe Thayer* (Boston: Houghton Mifflin, 1926), 272–73.
9. *Letters,* 5:308, 637.
10. Ibid., 5:306.
11. Ibid., 5:129.

Chapter 46: In the Land of the Czars

1. *Letters,* 5:285.
2. Ibid., 5:268.
3. Ibid., 5:273.
4. Ibid., 5:194, 196, 201.
5. Ibid., 5:276.
6. *Education,* 320–21; *Letters,* 5:276, 285.
7. *Education,* 320; *Letters,* 5:278.
8. *Letters,* 5:279, 282.
9. *Education,* 321.

Chapter 47: None but the Saints

1. Approaching the Saint-Michel and Chartres shrines both racially and culturally, Adams insisted that "tourists of English blood and American training are seldom or never quite at home there." Instead, he continued, with their hard empiricism and reasoned religion, the Anglo-American sightseers parading through the French countryside felt Gothic art and architecture only imperfectly "as a stage-decoration" (Adams, *Mont-Saint-Michel and Chartres,* 187).

2. See Alan Trachtenberg, *The Incorporation of America: Culture and Society in the Gilded Age* (New York: Hill and Wang, 1982).

3. *Education,* 48, 47.

4. James Russell Lowell, *The Complete Poetical Works of James Russell Lowell* (Cambridge, MA: Riverside Press, 1925), 352, 353, 354, 356; *Education,* 304.

5. Adams, *Law of Civilization and Decay,* 378.

6. *Clarence King Memoirs: The Helmet of Mambrino* (New York: G. P. Putnam's Sons, 1904), 172.

7. Adams, *Mont-Saint-Michel and Chartres,* 5, 6.

8. *Letters,* 6:416.

9. Mark Twain, *A Connecticut Yankee in King Arthur's Court* (New York: Oxford University Press, 1996), 513, 538. Alice James, the sister of Henry's friends William and Henry James, thought Twain's "tedious" *Connecticut Yankee* offered an unfair portrait of medievalism: "Tis horror that these holy and moral quantities should be made fun of! To let the wit play lightly about what has long been taken with solemnity is a somersault for which the muscles of their minds are not limber eno." Alice James, *The Diary of Alice James,* ed. Leon Edel (New York: Penguin Books, 1982), 78.

10. *Education,* 175.

11. Samuels, *Henry Adams: The Major Phase,*

539–40.

12. *Letters,* 6:636.

Chapter 48: Stranded

1. *Letters,* 5:682, 686.
2. Ibid., 5:193, 538; Taliaferro, *All the Great Prizes,* 534.
3. *Letters,* 5:700, 690.
4. Samuels, *Henry Adams: The Major Phase,* 397; *Clarence King Memoirs,* iii, 160.
5. *Letters,* 6:50, 51.
6. *Clarence King Memoirs,* 167.
7. Royal Cortissoz, *The Life of Whitelaw Reid,* vol. 2 (New York: Charles Scribner's Sons, 1921), 385–86.
8. *Letters,* 6:240.
9. Ibid., 6:52.
10. Ibid., 6:61; John Hay, *Letters of John Hay and Extracts from Diary,* vol. 1 (Washington, DC: private printing, 1908), vii, viii, xii, xiv, xv.
11. Chalfant, *Improvement of the World,* 319.
12. John Hay, *Letters of John Hay and Extracts from Diary,* vol. 2 (Washington, DC: private printing, 1908), 147.
13. Ibid., 155; *Letters,* 6:191. Clara Hay's crude removal of names did provide Adams with one source of satisfaction. For years, as though working on an immense crossword puzzle, he filled in the names of those he knew.

698

14. Elting E. Morison, ed., *The Letters of Theodore Roosevelt,* vol. 6 (Cambridge, MA: Harvard University Press, 1952), 1490.
15. *Letters,* 6:52.

Chapter 49: Book of Illusions

1. Dinitia Smith, "Another Top 100 List: Now It's Nonfiction," *New York Times,* April 30, 1999; *Education,* 400; Samuels, *Young Henry Adams,* viii, ix.
2. *Education,* 30.
3. Adams, *Degradation of the Democratic Dogma,* 6.
4. Clive Bush, *Halfway to Revolution: Investigation and Crisis in the Work of Henry Adams, William James and Gertrude Stein* (New Haven, CT: Yale University Press, 1991), 6.
5. Hermann Hesse, *Steppenwolf* (New York: Henry Holt, 1963), 24–5.
6. *Education,* 389.
7. Sue Prideaux, *Edvard Munch: Behind the Scream* (New Haven, CT: Yale University Press, 2005), 150–51.
8. *Education,* 394.
9. *Letters,* 6:66, 68; William James, *The Selected Letters of William James,* ed. Elizabeth Hardwick (New York: Anchor Books, 1993), 243; DeWolfe Howe, *Holmes-Laski Letters,* vol. 1, 452.

10. *Letters,* 6:723.

Chapter 50: There Was a Boy

1. Daniel Corey, ed., *The Letters of George Santayana* (New York: Charles Scribner's Sons, 1955), 306.
2. Henry Adams, *Life of George Cabot Lodge* (Boston: Houghton Mifflin, 1911), 33–34.
3. *Letters,* 5:274; Edith Wharton, *A Backward Glance* (New York: D. Appleton-Century, 1934), 150.
4. Wharton, *A Backward Glance,* 151; Samuels, *Henry Adams: The Major Phase,* 429, 428. Referring to the "closely intimate" and "agreeably intelligent" Americans in Paris, Henry wrote to Gaskell in 1910 that "Edith Wharton is almost the centre of it" (*Letters,* 6:394).
5. *Letters,* 4:320, 6:266. Bay's brother John Ellerton Lodge joined the Asian art department of the Boston Museum of Fine Arts and later served as first director of the Freer Gallery in Washington, D.C.
6. Adams, *Life of George Cabot Lodge,* 6.
7. Ibid., 145.
8. *Letters,* 6:237.
9. J. C. Levenson, Ernest Samuels, Charles Vandersee, and Viola Hopkins Winner, "Supplement to *The Letters of Henry Adams:* Letters Omitted from the Harvard University Press Edition of *The Letters of*

Henry Adams, Part II: 1903–1916" (Boston: Massachusetts Historical Society, 1989), 1910–33.

10. Chalfant, *Improvement of the World,* 380; *Letters,* 6:412.

11. Monteiro, *Correspondence of Henry James and Henry Adams,* 78–79.

Chapter 51: To Finish the Game

1. *Letters,* 6:493; Levenson et al., "Supplement," Part II, 1908–30.

2. Samuels, *Henry Adams,* 378; *Letters,* 6:534, 538, 539. L. G. Walker Jr., clinical professor of surgery, emeritus, at the University of North Carolina, Chapel Hill, has written that Adams's stroke "would be classified today as a lesion in the left hemisphere of the brain secondary to thrombosis in the internal carotid arteries or in its tributaries, the middle cerebral artery, or the anterior cerebral artery." L. G. Walker Jr., "Henry Adams's 1912 Stroke: A Misunderstood Illness," *New England Quarterly* (June 1998), 284, n12.

3. Samuels, *Henry Adams: The Major Phase,* 533; Walker, "Henry Adams's 1912 Stroke," 285, 286.

4. Samuels, *Henry Adams: The Major Phase,* 534; Walker, "Henry Adams's 1912 Stroke," 287.

5. Susan Hansson, " 'Shall We Go to Rome?'

— The Last Days of Henry Adams," *New England Quarterly* (March 2013), 8.

6. Walker, "Henry Adams's 1912 Stroke," 288.

7. *Letters,* 6:547.

8. Ibid., 6:553.

9. Ibid., 6:546.

10. Ibid., 6:558.

11. Ibid., 6:565.

Chapter 52: The Rest in Silence

1. Cater, *Henry Adams and His Friends,* xciii.

2. Ibid., xcii.

3. *Letters,* 5:145, 598, 599–600, 591.

4. Morison, "A Letter and a Few Reminiscences of Henry Adams," 95.

5. Cater, *Henry Adams and His Friends,* c; *Letters,* 6:657, 658, 659, 663.

6. Lyall H. Powers, ed., *Henry James and Edith Wharton, Letters: 1900–1915* (New York: Charles Scribner's Sons, 1990), 312–13.

7. *Letters,* 6:660, 664.

8. Ibid., 6:757.

9. Ibid., 6:670; F. Scott Fitzgerald, *This Side of Paradise* (New York: Vintage Books, 2009), 26–27; John Kuehl and Jackson R. Bryer, eds., *Dear Scott/Dear Max: The Fitzgerald-Perkins Correspondence* (New York: Charles Scribner's Sons, 1971), 20.

10. Cater, *Henry Adams and His Friends,* ciii.

11. Mrs. Winthrop Chanler, *Roman Spring: Memoirs* (Boston: Little, Brown, 1934), 300–301.
12. Louis Auchincloss, " 'Never Leave Me,' " *American Heritage* (February 1970), 22.
13. *Letters,* 6:667.
14. Ibid., 6:635; Auchincloss, " 'Never Leave Me,' " 69.
15. *Letters,* 6:709.
16. Ibid., 6:758, 724. Adams borrows from the English poet Algernon Charles Swinburne's "Itylus": "Swallow, my sister, O sister swallow." The verse, drafted in Italy, appeared in Swinburne's popular first collection, *Poems and Ballads* (1866).
17. *Letters,* 6:753.
18. Ibid., 6:758. Thomas Babington Macaulay (1800–1859) was a popular British historian and politician. In his ability to succeed in both professions he may have captured the young Henry's imagination.
19. Alice Roosevelt Longworth, *Crowded Hours: Reminiscences of Alice Roosevelt Longworth* (New York: Charles Scribner's Sons, 1933), 269.
20. Samuels, *Henry Adams: The Major Phase,* 586.
21. Chalfant, *Improvement of the World,* 523; Cater, *Henry Adams and His Friends,* 779.

ABOUT THE AUTHOR

David Brown teaches history at Elizabethtown College in Pennsylvania. He is the author of several books including *Paradise Lost: A Life of F. Scott Fitzgerald* and *Richard Hofstadter: An Intellectual Biography.*

The employees of Thorndike Press hope you have enjoyed this Large Print book. All our Thorndike, Wheeler, and Kennebec Large Print titles are designed for easy reading, and all our books are made to last. Other Thorndike Press Large Print books are available at your library, through selected bookstores, or directly from us.

For information about titles, please call:
  (800) 223-1244

or visit our website at:
  gale.com/thorndike

To share your comments, please write:
  Publisher
  Thorndike Press
  10 Water St., Suite 310
  Waterville, ME 04901